Investment Manager Analysis

Founded in 1807, John Wiley & Sons is the oldest independent publishing company in the United States. With offices in North America, Europe, Australia, and Asia, Wiley is globally committed to developing and marketing print and electronic products and services for our customers' professional and personal knowledge and understanding.

The Wiley Finance series contains books written specifically for finance and investment professionals as well as sophisticated individual investors and their financial advisors. Book topics range from portfolio management to e-commerce, risk management, financial engineering, valuation, financial instrument analysis, as well as much more.

For a list of available titles, visit our web site at www.WileyFinance.com.

Investment Manager Analysis

A Comprehensive Guide to Portfolio Selection, Monitoring, and Optimization

FRANK J. TRAVERS

WILEY

John Wiley & Sons, Inc.

Published by John Wiley & Sons, Inc., Hoboken, New Jersey.
Published simultaneously in Canada.

For general information on our other products and services, or technical support, please
contact our Customer Care Department within the United States at 800-762-2974, outside
the United States at 317-572-3993 or fax 317-572-4002.

Wiley also publishes its books in a variety of electronic formats. Some content that appears
in print may not be available in electronic books.

For more information about Wiley products, visit our web site at www.wiley.com.

Library of Congress Cataloging-in-Publication Data:

Travers, Frank J.
    Investment manager analysis : a comprehensive guide to portfolio selection,
monitoring, and optimization / Frank J. Travers.
        p.   cm.—(Wiley finance series)
    Includes bibliographic references.
    ISBN 0-471-47886-5 (cloth)
    1. Investment analysis.   2. Portfolio management.   I. Title.   II. Series.
    HG4529.T735   2004
    332.6—dc22   2004005532

Printed in the United States of America.

10   9   8   7   6   5   4   3   2   1

To . . .

. . . my wife and best friend, Tara, who has offered me encouragement and support not just during the months it took to write this book, but over the course of our lives together.

. . . my children, Brendan, Sean, and Lauren, each of whom inspires me to be a better man than I thought I could ever be.

. . . my parents, who instilled in me a strong work ethic and who always told me that I could do anything that I put my mind to.

Contents

Introduction

According to statistics collected by Standard & Poor's and presented in its annual *Money Management Directory*, there were just over 13,000 investment advisers managing money in the United States at the end of 2002. Nearly a quarter of those firms managed more than $100 million in assets. Some are of these investment companies are large, well-known firms with dozens and sometimes hundreds or even thousands of employees and with client bases spread out across the globe; others are small one- or two-person shops that service a more localized clientele. The products they manage range from publicly traded mutual funds to commingled trusts to separate accounts designed for individual clients. In addition, the product mix is quite diverse, covering a myriad of asset classes that differ across capitalization ranges, geographical boundaries, risk levels, and a variety of other classifications.

The assets managed by these firms at the end of 2002 totaled an astounding $21.3 trillion, representing more than 75,000 public and private pension plans—and these statistics do not cover the mutual fund industry.

Given those rather impressive statistics, you would assume that a wide variety of books and scholarly research papers covering the subject of investment manager analysis would be available to plan sponsors, investment consultants, financial advisers, fund-of-funds managers, and individual investors. While some books currently available are dedicated to or include chapters on topics such as performance analysis, attribution analysis, and portfolio analysis, to my knowledge no book has combined all the elements needed to effectively analyze investment firms, products, and professionals. Since a large percentage of the investments made in the United States on a daily basis are made by professional investment managers on behalf of their clients, I thought a book detailing a methodical process by which people could evaluate investment managers and the products they manager was long overdue.

INDUSTRY CHANGES

Over the past 15 years, I have found that the investment industry has changed considerably. Information that was available only to professional investors in the late 1980s (at very high prices) is now available free to all via dozens if not hundreds of web sites on the Internet.

When I first entered this field in the late 1980s, the primary issue was how to go about finding the best investment managers for specific searches. The Internet existed back then, but was scarcely used outside of academia and the military. In addition, the process of conducting a search for an investment manager based on investment style, geography, or market capitalization was much more manual and time-consuming than it is today. Lastly, there were no real reporting standards in place back then, so I spent a great deal of time poring over reams of printed material and then entering the data into spreadsheet programs that I had designed to dissect the data and put it back together—all this in an effort to make data from different firms comparable.

The issue today is quite different. It is no longer how to *get* the information; it is what to *do* with all the information now available. Technology has obviously changed this business in many ways. For example, it has made it possible to conduct complicated statistical studies in a matter of seconds. Studies that would have taken days (or possibly weeks) just a few decades ago can now be accomplished with the push of a few buttons. In addition, advances in computer hardware have given rise to the investment software industry. As computers got smaller and less expensive and as processor speeds increased, the types and sophistication levels of analytical techniques increased right along with those advances.

There are software packages that will perform manager screens for you or analyze style, performance, or portfolio fundamentals at the touch of a button. In addition, the advent of the Internet as a source of information and communication has been nothing short of monumental. I could not function as efficiently without the Internet and e-mail capabilities.

However, these advances, while generally positive, can lead to an overload of information—in effect prompting many not to see the forest for the trees. In addition, as we come to rely more and more on computer programs to perform complex analytical functions, we tend to forget some of the theory and investment mathematics behind the analytical reports. However, having access to various analytical reports is one thing; the ability to understand and interpret the reports is another thing entirely.

Yet for all the changes that have occurred in this industry over the years, much has stayed the same. While it is true that we now have access to much more information than we did a decade ago, the most important element of the process has remained exactly the same: Investment products are invariably managed by investment professionals (even quantitative strategies need to be created, monitored, and tweaked by people). Understand the people, and you are more than halfway there. The analytical process described in this book combines both qualitative and quantitative measures, which effectively combine the art and science of evaluating and selecting investment products.

THE SEARCH PROCESS

To give a complete picture of the steps that go into a typical search for an investment manager, this book outlines the process from start to finish.

Step One: Set guidelines.

- Investment policy statement.
- Submanager guidelines.
- Setting responsibilities.
- Budget issues.
- Operational issues: time frame, asset size, etc.

Step Two: Source investment managers.

- Internal/external databases.
- Media: newspapers, magazines, journals.
- Internet.
- Professional contacts.

Step Three: Screen the universe.

- Setting minimum standards.
- Risk/return parameters.
- Fundamental characteristics.
- Style orientation.

Step Four: Request and organize information.

- Performance.
- Portfolio holdings.
- Professional biographies.
- Form ADV.
- Presentation books and firm literature.

Step Five: Analyze managers and products.

- Initial phone interview.
- Performance analysis.
- Style analysis.
- Risk analysis.

- Portfolio analysis.
- Factor analysis.
- Face-to-face meeting.
- Ranking model.

Step Six: Compare finalists.

- Investment professionals.
- Process used.
- Portfolio characteristics.
- Performance.
- Portfolio turnover.
- Fees.
- Asset allocation.

Step Seven: Select manager(s).

- Optimization relative to existing managers.
- Investment committee.

Step Eight: Prepare contract.

- Investment manager guidelines.
- Fees and calculations.

Step Nine: Monitor manager(s) hired.

- Monitoring manager(s) using all tools listed in step five.
- Transaction analysis.
- Continuously optimizing each manager versus rest of overall portfolio.

The book was structured to follow this general outline. Also bear in mind that the search process is actually more circular than linear—the analytical stage leads to the hiring stage, and once a manager is hired we start back at the analytical stage in order to monitor the manager's effectiveness. The steps previously listed do not have to be followed in strict order. When analyzing an investment manager, the steps can be altered and changed as a result of scheduling, information delays, and a variety of other factors.

OUTLINE AND STRUCTURE

The structure of this book is designed to take the reader through all the stages of the investment manager analysis process. Each chapter focuses on a different aspect of the process or on a different asset class. To better illustrate each of the formulas and concepts detailed throughout the book, I created a fictitious investment firm, CAM Asset Management, and use the data from CAM's underlying portfolio to illustrate how to perform each calculation and, more importantly, how to evaluate the results. Each formula and analytical technique discussed in the book is broken down and explained in great detail. CAM Asset Management is a fictitious investment firm that is based on a composite of investment firms that I have analyzed over the years. The investment team at CAM is also fictitious.

My ultimate goal in writing this book is to provide a practical, real-life method of analyzing investment managers—not to create a purely academic treatise. As a result, the style and tone that I employed when writing this book straddle the fence between academic and conversational.

Each chapter begins by defining all the relevant issues, concepts, and formulas. As the chapter progresses, each formula, concept, and analytical technique is identified and explained in detail. The organization of the book is also by design. The book's first part deals with all the preliminary (background) work that needs to be done before we can actually begin to analyze an investment manager. The second part focuses on traditional asset classes, such as equity and fixed-income investment managers. The final part focuses on an alternative investment product: hedge funds.

Part One

This part discusses the steps that typically precede the actual manager analysis. Chapter 1 focuses on the identification of investment guidelines and investment manager objectives. Chapters 2 and 3 outline the methods currently available to source investment managers and discuss how to quickly and efficiently obtain enough relevant information to cull the list of prospective managers down to a smaller, more manageable list.

While not the focus of this book, I consider these chapters to be the foundation with which any successful investment manager analysis could be conducted. Setting objectives is a critical element in the overall process because it provides a frame of reference by which we will be able to make efficient and effective decisions. It also allows investment manager analysts to effectively and efficiently manage their time. Naturally, once we set the objectives, we then need to find an appropriate universe of investment managers as well as a means of fine-tuning the list. Finally, it is important to develop an efficient means of collecting data for evaluation. This data needs to be easily obtained and consistent for all the investment managers under review.

Part Two

Now that we have formed our objectives and written the specific investment manager guidelines, the real fun begins. This part focuses exclusively on the process of analyzing equity and fixed income managers. Because the process in which we evaluate equity and fixed income managers is similar, rather than repeating the entire process, I chose to focus on equity in our case study (CAM Asset Management) in Chapters 4 through 13. At the end of the part a separate chapter (Chapter 14) discusses fixed income manager analysis. I elected to highlight equity manager analysis because it represents the majority of assets held by pension plans, foundations, and endowments as well as by individual investors. The equity manager analysis section sets the tone for the rest of the book.

Each chapter in Part Two provides further information about the investment manager across a variety of due diligence topics. I have structured the chapters to follow the order that I typically use when conducting investment manager analysis, but the order is not as important as completing each of the analytical stages before making any decisions.

Part Two takes you through each stage of the analytical process and provides specific formulas and their real-world applications where appropriate. This part focuses primarily on domestic (U.S.) analysis, but to address the growing global nature of this business, I have included examples of international (non-U.S.) equity portfolios when appropriate to highlight differences in the analytical approach used or to address issues raised when reviewing non-U.S. portfolios and/or investment companies.

As you read through the chapters in Part Two, you will see how the evaluation process unfolds. Conclusions based on data in Chapter 5 may be refuted based on newer information we find later on in the process or by the results of additional analytical tools employed. Because many of the conclusions stated in the book are interpretive, you will likely find yourself agreeing with my conclusions some of the time and disagreeing with them at other times. This is normal, healthy, and to be expected.

Investment manager analysis is not a pure science. As a result, we all bring our own unique experiences, prejudices, biases, and opinions to the table. This book will explain how to analyze a given investment manager; it will not tell you which one you should hire—that decision needs to be based on your own specific needs and objectives.

Part Three

This part highlights alternative investment managers—specifically, hedge funds. Hedge funds are receiving more and more attention from institutional investors with each passing year. As a result, a plethora of new hedge funds has flooded the marketplace.

While many of the analytical techniques that we use to evaluate equity and fixed income managers can also be used to evaluate alternative managers, this part will highlight the unique analytical problems that arise in these asset classes. For example, information transparency is a realistic issue when attempting to analyze hedge fund managers.

While not exhaustive, Part Three will highlight the issues and offer an outline to be used when evaluating investment managers in this area.

AUTHOR'S NOTE

I have worked very hard to bring you this book and have spent a great many hours sitting at my laptop working through the first and many subsequent drafts. I have found the process of writing this book to be both rewarding and frustrating. I have tried to make this book comprehensive, practical, and relevant to people experienced in this field as well as to newcomers—not an easy task, I can assure you.

I hope that you find this book helpful, and I would encourage you to contact me if you have any questions or suggestions related to the book or any topic related to investment manager analysis. My e-mail address is ftravers@pinestreetfunds.com. In addition, I would encourage readers to visit my due diligence web site.

Web Site: Due Diligence Network

I created this site to provide cutting-edge research and to discuss advancements in the field of investment manager analysis. It is a not-for-profit site and is supported by numerous academics and industry professionals. It contains a variety of papers, articles, and other materials relating to investment manager analysis across all asset classes, including:

- Performance analysis
- Risk analysis
- Attribution analysis
- Style analysis
- Portfolio analysis
- Interview techniques

Web site name:	Due Diligence Network
URL:	www.neckerscube.com
E-mail:	ftravers@neckerscube.com

Before the Analysis

## CHAPTER 1

Setting Investment Guidelines

Before jumping headfirst into a pool, first check to see that it is filled with water.

It might sound a bit simplistic, but before we attempt to find and analyze any investment managers, we should first have a very clear idea of what we are trying to achieve by hiring the manager. This way we will be able to put each investment product in its proper perspective. A value manager can be reviewed in the context of the value style and can be properly compared to a universe of other value managers. Likewise, a short-term domestic fixed-income portfolio can be compared to the appropriate benchmark and peer group. This practice will save time and make the process much more efficient.

Investment guidelines come in two primary stages: (1) the investment policy statement (IPS) and (2) the investment portfolio guidelines. The former concerns the overall portfolio or fund (such as a pension plan), while the latter is targeted toward each manager hired to fulfill specific objectives within the overall portfolio/fund (see Chapter 13). As common sense dictates, all investment guidelines should be well thought out and should cover every aspect of the investment process, from risk/return expectations to manager selection to portfolio monitoring. In addition, manager guidelines should leave nothing open to interpretation. Fiduciaries charged with hiring investment managers as well as the investment managers themselves should understand the guidelines and willingly agree to them. This avoids potential headaches down the road.

INVESTMENT POLICY STATEMENT

An investment policy statement sets the framework for all of the investment decisions that follow. When well written, the IPS helps to ensure that the decision-making process with respect to the management of the total portfolio will be consistent and will serve as a beacon to aid navigation through unexpected market fluctuations and sometimes tumultuous economic conditions, enabling all parties to concentrate on what they were hired to do (or what they do best). A well-written investment policy statement typically addresses, but is not limited to, the following issues:

- Philosophy or purpose.
- Return/risk objectives, including thresholds.
- Time horizon.
- Type of plan or portfolio.
- Status of plan funding.
- Actuarial assumptions, including clearly stated reasoning behind the return/risk objectives.
- Cash flow needs or liquidity.
- Strategy being employed to meet the investment objectives.
- Permissible investments (financial instruments and asset classes).
- Restricted investments (instruments and asset classes).
- Asset allocation ranges.
- Benchmark(s) for total portfolio.
- Benchmarks for each individual component of the total portfolio (asset classes, individual managers, styles, etc.).
- Plan/portfolio responsibilities (board, investment committee, consultants, etc.).
- Policies regarding external hires, such as consultants and investment managers (including language on fees, use of competitive bidding process, due diligence process, hiring/firing policies, placement of external hires on the watch list).
- Portfolio and performance evaluations (standards and procedures).
- Benchmarks and rebalancing policies.
- Diversification (by manager, portfolio size, geography, investment characteristics, asset classes, etc.).
- Portfolio execution and trading strategy.
- Operational issues (custodial, administrative, spending policy).

However, the investment policy statement should not be written in a vacuum. Economic and market conditions evolve. As they do, it is imperative that the investment policy statement be reviewed at least yearly on a strategic level and perhaps more often on a tactical level so that the portfolio has a chance to evolve along with the market.

Many pension plans currently conducting searches for alternative investment managers, such as hedge funds, only recently changed their investment policy statements to allow investments in this segment of the market. These adjustments reflect the ever-changing nature of the investment industry. Just keep in mind that all change is not necessarily good. What might be a beneficial change for some might be detrimental to others.

Because the focus of this book is investment manager analysis (not overall investment policy), this chapter should serve as a general guide or outline for the development of a new or the evaluation of an existing investment policy statement. The remainder of this chapter will highlight each of the significant sections that good investment policy statements typically contain.

Investment Objectives

This section is a critical element in the IPS document because it sets the tone for everything that follows. It is here where the portfolio's return and risk expectations are listed. Whenever the investment policy statement is reviewed, the ultimate goal is to ensure that the return and risk objectives have been achieved. As you can imagine, the objectives should be realistic and based on long-term assumptions. Many corporate pension plans got caught up in the bull market of the late 1990s and increased their pension plans' return expectations far beyond what they could reasonably expect to achieve. This resulted in faulty pension assumptions that have had a detrimental impact on many companies' financial statements and, in the case of some publicly traded companies, the prices of their underlying stocks.

For pension plans, return and risk objectives may be stated in absolute terms (example: the portfolio should return a minimum of 8% annually with a standard deviation no greater than 10% annually) or relative terms (example: the portfolio should have an annual return in excess of 200 basis points above the S&P 500 index with a standard deviation no greater than the S&P 500 index). A basis point represents $^1/_{100}$th of a percent.

Funds of funds may also state their return and risk objectives in absolute or relative terms. However, because funds of funds are, in effect, individual investment products themselves, they tend to have a much more narrow investment focus (example: small-cap, large-cap, etc.). A fund of funds' investment policy statement is typically called a "prospectus" or "offering memorandum." Because there are legal requirements, investment policy statements and prospectuses tend to have different formats, but still contain all of the points listed earlier in this chapter.

Example of Investment Objective

The financial objectives of the plan are based on a comprehensive evaluation of the capital markets in the context of modern portfolio theory and have been measured against the plan's current and projected financial needs. Based on this evaluation, the plan will be measured against a customized benchmark consisting of the following indexes in the proportions listed:

- *50% S&P 500 index*
- *10% Russell 2000 index*
- *10% MSCI EAFE index*
- *30% Lehman Aggregate index*

The investment objectives for the plan are:

- *To achieve a nominal rate of return for the total portfolio equal to or greater than the return of the customized benchmark.*
- *To achieve a real rate of return in excess of 550 basis points above inflation, measured by the consumer price index (CPI).*
- *To keep the total portfolio's level of risk, defined as annualized standard deviation, equal to or less than that of the customized benchmark.*

Responsibilities

Once the objectives have been decided upon, it is important to clearly state who will be responsible for making sure that all the goals are accomplished. This is an important section because it specifies who is responsible for every aspect of the portfolio's management. This includes boards, trustees, internal employees, external investment managers, consultants, legal advisers, and others.

This section offers guidance not only to outsiders looking to establish contact, but also among co-workers who share portfolio analysis and management responsibilities. It is basically a detailed organizational chart that sets the pecking order within an organization.

Asset Allocation

Asset allocation is the subject of entire books, so I will simply state here that it comes in several levels. First, there is strategic asset allocation. This form of asset allocation is long-term in nature and is seldom changed or altered. Changes to asset allocation that occur due to short-term shifts in economic or market conditions are most often referred to as tactical asset allocation. For a pension plan, the strategic asset allocation decision is most often arrived at by conducting an asset/liability study, where the fund's liability characteristics are considered when developing the fund's asset allocation policy.

This typically leads to a list of what asset classes and financial instruments are permitted for purchase. In addition, the list typically states the minimum and maximum weights according to asset class, market capitalization, investment style, and so on. Exhibit 1.1 depicts sample asset allocation guidelines that are broad, while the asset allocation guidelines depicted in Exhibit 1.2 break the main asset classes down into a variety of

EXHIBIT 1.1 Sample of Broad Asset Allocation Guidelines

Asset Allocation	Average %
Equity	50
Fixed income	40
Alternative asset classes	5
Cash and equivalents	5

EXHIBIT 1.2 Sample of Detailed Asset Allocation Guidelines

Asset Allocation	Minimum %	Average %	Maximum %
Traditional Asset Classes	80	90	100
Equity	40	47	60
U.S.	32	35	44
Small-cap	6	7	9
Mid-cap	7	8	10
Large-cap	19	20	25
Non-U.S.	8	12	16
EAFE	6	9	12
Emerging markets	2	3	4
Fixed Income	20	30	40
U.S.	16	25	33
Investment grade	12	20	26
Non–investment grade	4	5	7
Non-U.S.	4	5	7
Developed markets	2	3	4
Emerging markets	2	2	3
Alternative Asset Classes	0	10	20
Hedge Funds	0	5	10
Private Equity	0	5	10
Cash and Equivalents	1	3	5

subcategories. The more detailed the asset allocation, the more efficient the overall process will be. For example, it would be easier to perform attribution analysis when the asset classes have been defined in greater detail. Also, to create detailed asset allocation guidelines, you need to really think through the entire process and, ultimately, hold the investment committee or lead investment professionals responsible for the portfolio's outperformance or underperformance.

In addition to breaking out the underlying asset classes further, the detailed asset allocation guidelines set minimum, maximum, and average weights for each asset class. When setting the guidelines it is critically important to set asset allocation guidelines that parallel the return/risk parameters set in the investment objectives section of the investment policy statement. For example, it would be nearly impossible to achieve a long-term return in excess of 8 percent if the asset allocation guidelines emphasized short-term fixed income securities and prohibited equity investments and other asset classes that appear on the higher end of standard return/risk profile charts. An example of a standard risk/return profile based on long-term historical performance for various asset classes is depicted in Exhibit 1.3.

Short-term bonds appear in the low risk/low return quadrant. In order to achieve a long-term return of roughly 8%, it would be necessary to invest in some of the asset classes that appear higher up on the risk/return

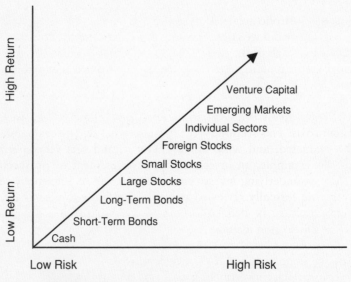

EXHIBIT 1.3   Risk/Return Profiles by Asset Class

line. A well-thought-out and well-written IPS will contain risk and return objectives that match the asset allocation ranges set within the document.

Investment Restrictions

This list is a compilation of any financial instruments (e.g., options) or investment strategies (e.g., currency hedging) that are not allowed. Restrictions can cover entire asset classes, specific transactions, countries, or exchanges, or can be taken to the individual company or organization level. Other examples include restrictions based on social, political, or religious reasons. A Catholic foundation, for example, may wish to avoid investing in "sin" stocks (typically defined as companies that are involved in the manufacture, sale, or distribution of alcohol, tobacco, and firearms). Once a process done largely by hand, the ability to flag any restricted purchases can now be achieved relatively easily at the custodial level or through various software packages. These restrictions should carry over verbatim to the investment manager guidelines (see Chapter 13) as well.

Portfolio/Performance Evaluation

Assuming you have a portfolio or fund that is up and running, it is imperative that periodic evaluations take place. As mentioned previously, the investment policy statement should be evaluated at least yearly. Questions to answer include the following:

- Has the portfolio achieved its goals?
- If not, where did we go wrong and, more importantly, how do we fix it?
- How have each of the underlying managers performed?
- Have all the underlying managers stayed within their stated investment guidelines?

These and many other questions should be asked and answered on a consistent basis. This section typically states what will be evaluated, how it will be evaluated, and who will evaluate it, and sets very specific time frames. For example, an investment policy statement or prospectus may state that the underlying investment managers will be informally reviewed quarterly and formally reviewed annually (naturally the terms *informally* and *formally* must be defined). Some of the issues that are typically addressed in this section include:

- Timing, frequency, and format of evaluations.
- Format to place investment managers on warning.
- Absolute performance.

■ Relative performance (benchmark and peer group).
■ Fundamental characteristics.
■ Attribution analysis.
■ Style analysis.
■ Risk analysis.
■ Minimum portfolio standards.
■ Fees.
■ Reporting standards and issues.

Operational Issues

Any number of things can be placed in this section, such as legal, accounting, custodial, administrative, and other issues. In addition, this section can also contain language that addresses the issue of proxy voting. Some organizations place that decision entirely with the underlying investment managers, while others place specific restrictions on particular issues that may arise. For example, a pension plan may specify that all proxy votes are to be voted as the company management sees fit, with the exception of issues relating to movement of labor from the United States to countries overseas.

CONCLUSION

The investment policy statement is a critical element in the ongoing management of any pension plan or investment fund. The guidelines set the tone for all the underlying investment manager searches and play a key role in the actual due diligence performed on any investment managers under review. The more explicit the investment policy statement, the easier it will be to actually manage the underlying pension plan or investment fund. In addition, because the risk/return objectives should be clearly stated in the investment policy statement, it is easier to evaluate the success or failure of the underlying pension plan or investment fund. As we learn in Chapter 9 ("Attribution Analysis"), we can conduct relative attribution analysis only when we have something concrete (a single index or a combination of indexes) to which to compare allocations and performance.

As we work our way through the investment manager analysis process, we will create a detailed set of risk and return objectives for the sample manager we select for the case study and build the underlying analysis one step at a time. This chapter has laid out a brief outline for developing an effective investment policy statement; Chapter 2 introduces a means of finding a broad list of potential investment managers and then demonstrates how to cull the broad list down to a few highly attractive candidates.

Investment Manager Sourcing

Sourcing investment managers is much easier today than it was just a decade and a half ago. In the late 1980s, when I started in this business, the main question was *how* to find investment managers and to figure out the most efficient way of obtaining information about them and the investment products they managed. The search process was very time-consuming because much of the work that needed to be done was done manually. It was not uncommon to fax and/or mail out requests for information (RFIs) and then wait until the managers filled in all the information and mailed back the completed forms. Then the real work began. Often we would have to manually enter the data into our own systems and check its accuracy. Only after this manual process had been completed for all (or most) of the managers in a particular search could the analytical process begin.

INDUSTRY CHANGES

The question today is not how to find information, but *what* to do with the tons of information that we now have access to. Three factors have played a key role in this development:

1. Computer industry
2. Internet
3. Financial media

Developments in the Computer Industry

First and foremost, the geometric increase in semiconductor chip speed and the decrease in computer size and prices gave rise to the financial software industry. Although a handful of software packages existed in the 1980s, they tended to be cumbersome and rather expensive. The technology revolution changed all this. New software companies invigorated the industry,

11

improving on existing technologies and methodologies while at the same time creating competitive pressure on prices. In other words, better technology became available faster and cheaper. As you will see later in the chapter, there are actually online databases that provide for free what would have cost thousands of dollars just a decade ago.

The Internet

The rise in popularity of the Internet has increased investor know-how and provided information to the average investor that previously had been available only to large investment firms and consultants. Investment management firms, consultants, funds of funds, and pension plans have all taken advantage of this medium by creating and maintaining web sites. (How to effectively mine these web sites for useful information is discussed in later chapters). In addition, more financial web sites have popped up in the past five years than I care to count. These include online versions of print newspapers, magazines, and journals, not to mention online financial sites that were created specifically for this medium. While some web sites are better and more informative than others, the bar regarding the dissemination of information has unquestionably been raised to new heights. And what discussion of Internet-based information would be complete without mention of the impact that e-mail has had on our jobs and, in some cases, our lives? The days when we had to stand by the fax machine or call down to the mail office to check whether the mail had been delivered are a distant memory. E-mail allows us to instantaneously exchange data, including marketing brochures, performance sheets, biographies, and investment portfolios, at the push of a button. Investment manager analysts can now request specific data in a specific format and simply download the file once it has been received via e-mail.

The Financial Media

The last major event that increased and improved the quantity and quality of information now available to us was the rise in popularity of television media dedicated to business and financial news, such as CNBC. In addition to business/finance-oriented networks, a number of network and cable stations have adopted specialized programming to cover the business and investing field. These programs bring the investment industry into our offices and homes 24 hours a day and seven days a week. And it is not just a U.S. phenomenon—many countries around the world feature U.S. investment–oriented programming as well as programming unique to their own countries or regions. The average homemaker now has almost as much access to the global financial markets as the seasoned investment professional. In addition, these programs often feature interviews with portfolio managers, analysts, traders, investment strategists, investment commentators, and CEOs of publicly traded corporations.

It astounds me that the information I receive for free from general-interest web sites such as Yahoo.com and MSN.com and business/investment-focused web sites such as MarketWatch.com and Bloomberg .com, is often greater than the amount of information that I had available to me a decade ago, which was available to me at no small expense.

NONLINEAR PROCESS

I have often heard and seen the investment manager analysis process described as linear in nature, meaning step one leads to step two, which leads to step three and so on. I, on the contrary, have found that the process is nonlinear most of the time. Exhibit 2.1 illustrates the typical work flow involved in the investment manager analysis process.

Many things can influence the order in which a search is carried out. For example, it might be necessary to modify the sequence because certain members of the investment committee will be unavailable for a while or because

EXHIBIT 2.1 Typical Work Flow

Step One	Setting Guidelines	Before the Analysis
Step Two	Screening Database	
Step Three	Selection of Finalists	
Step Four	Performance Analysis	
Step Five	Risk Analysis	
Step Six	Portfolio Analysis	
Step Seven	Questionnaire Review	
Step Eight	Form ADV Review	
Step Nine	Initial Interview	Analytical Process
Step Ten	Meeting Memo	
Step Eleven	Historical Portfolio Analysis	
Step Twelve	On-site Visit	
Step Thirteen	Meeting Memo	
Step Fourteen	Manager Ranking Model	
Step Fifteen	Summary of Analysis	Conclusion/Decision
Step Sixteen	Hire/Fire Decision	

new information has emerged that will likely change the final candidate list. As a fund of funds manager responsible for hiring managers/funds, all with different investment objectives, I often find myself shifting back and forth between steps depending on the fund and depending on the information I have received from investment managers.

I am always searching for new investment managers. Even when I am perfectly happy with the investment managers I have selected and hired, I am always on the lookout for managers I can place on the "bench." The bench consists of managers that I could quickly and easily use as potential replacements for managers currently managing assets for me. If for any reason I should find it necessary to fire an investment manager or look to reduce a manager's allocation, I always try to make sure that I have two or more replacements that I can use immediately. This means that I have to know the bench managers as well as I know the managers I have actually hired. Exhibit 2.2 depicts the preferred investment manager setup.

Notice that for each investment manager (or style), we have several possible replacements all lined up. This is critical to the continuous management of the overall portfolio. If, for example, we had to fire one of our managers and did not have any alternatives to choose from when that time came, we could find ourselves in a great deal of trouble. Depending on where we were in our search process at the time we fired the manager, we would have to take the time to complete the search and find one or more alternatives. As

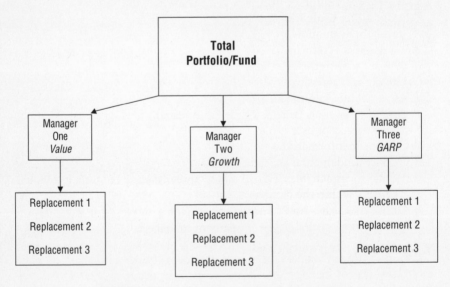

EXHIBIT 2.2   Preferred Investment Manager Setup

you will see in this book, the search process can take quite some time to complete effectively.

So where do investment manager names come from? The answer ranges from internal databases and third party databases to various media outlets and each investment manager analyst's personal Rolodex of industry contacts. The sections that follow describe each source.

THIRD PARTY DATABASES

These databases usually come in one or more of the following formats: CD-based, hard copy books, and Web-based. Some basic databases are available for free, while others can be quite expensive. The companies providing these databases are a mix of new entrants to the field as well as old favorites. These manager databases have experienced circular growth over the years, as advances in technology led to increases in competition, which, in turn, led to further advances in the underlying software.

CD and Web-based databases offer a wide range of services, including:

- Firm information.
- Product information.
- Contact person/phone number/fax number/e-mail address.
- Web site address.
- Biographical information.
- Textual description of firm/product philosophy and process.
- Performance evaluations.
- Statistical evaluations.
- Style analysis (returns-based).
- Risk analysis (returns-based).
- Attribution analysis (returns-based).
- Index and peer group data.
- Comparative tools (versus indexes and peers).
- Ability to accept user input.
- Composite information.
- Product fundamental characteristics.
- Ability to attach files (Word docs, spreadsheets, etc.) to individual managers within the database.
- Ability to create cover letters and e-mail a request for information (RFI) to any selected list of investment managers.

Some of the online databases even include real-time news updates relating to investment management firms, investment products, and specific investment professionals. To provide an idea of the many fields (or investment criteria) that are available in the typical third party database, here is a list of the fields that I use most often in various investment manager searches.

Firm Information

- Assets under management (AUM).
- Growth of AUM.
- AUM broken out by asset class/product.
- Assets gained by calendar year.
- Assets lost by calendar year.
- Assets gained by asset class and product type.
- Assets lost by asset class and product type.
- Total employees, portfolio managers, analysts, traders.
- Legal/regulatory judgments against firm.

Product Information

- General

  - Bottom up, top down.
  - Quantitative versus fundamental.
  - Active versus passive.
  - Turnover.
  - Fees.
  - Separate account, commingled fund, mutual fund.
  - Number of securities in portfolio.
  - Average weight in top 10 securities.
  - Number of investment professionals working on product.
  - Portfolio manager tenure.
  - Recent additions or losses to investment team.
  - Product assets (current and historical asset growth/loss).
  - Number of accounts (historical account growth/loss).
  - Association for Investment Management and Research (AIMR) compliance.

- Equity-Specific

  - Market capitalization (average, smallest, largest).
  - Fundamental characteristics (price-earnings ratio, dividend ratio, growth rates, etc.).

- Fixed-Income-Specific

  - Duration.
  - Quality (average and breakout).
  - Maturity.
  - Sector allocations.

Performance Information

- Calendar year versus benchmark and peer group average.
- Cumulative periods versus benchmark and peer group average.
- Annualized periods versus benchmark and peer group average.
- Drawdown.

Risk Information

- Sharpe ratio versus benchmark and peer group.
- Risk/return charts versus benchmark and peer group.
- Tracking error.
- Downside deviation.
- Sortino ratio.

Style Information

- Style regression.
- Style grid.
- Rolling style scores.

My experience with manager databases has been very positive, but not without issues. Here are some of the major pros and cons of using third party databases.

Pros

- *Ready-made, self-contained database.* No muss, no fuss. The databases have been preprogrammed and tested by professionals.
- *Depth of information.* They typically contain information on thousands and even tens of thousands of investment managers and products covering a variety of asset classes and geographical locations. As indicated previously, these databases provide manager/product data and typically have dozens of dynamic (searchable, sortable) fields.
- *Quick results.* A screen can often be started and finished in a short period of time. Users can often build a screen (or series of screens) and create scores of reports and other analytical output in a matter of minutes.
- *Flexibility.* These databases have become very flexible over the years. Many systems allow users to input their own manager information, update performance manually, link files to specific manager records, produce personalized reports, and create user-specific fields for additional tracking. Many systems offer the option of allowing the user to add the firm's logo to reports—making the system useful for client reporting and marketing purposes.

Cons

- *Cost.* The expansive databases and increased functionality can be expensive. Many systems are available with price tags under $10,000 per annum, but some have price tags significantly higher.
- *Accuracy.* While most data contained in these databases is accurate, I have often found that information I get from the databases differs from information sent to me by the underlying investment managers. To put this comment in perspective, let's explore how information typically gets into a database. The typical database provider asks the managers listed in its database to provide specific information to it by a specific date and in a specific format. This could be via e-mail or through direct entry on the database firm's web site. The manager—not the database firm—is responsible for the accuracy of the information. The database firm is responsible for taking the reams of information that it receives and accurately transfering it to its database. Some investment managers may unknowingly provide incorrect information about their firms/products to the database provider. Some might intentionally provide misleading information.
- *Timing.* Database providers do a commendable job of getting, compiling, and updating their databases on a monthly and quarterly basis, but the fact is that it does take some time to do all of this and some investment managers are not able to get their updated information included in the database. To remedy this, database providers often update their databases in several traunches.

SAMPLE SCREENING CRITERIA AND TECHNIQUES

This section highlights an actual example of the screening phase of an investment manager search. The results from this search will provide a starting point for the examples used to illustrate the formulas and concepts discussed throughout the book. When the screen is completed, we will select one of the products and use it to illustrate each and every formula, analytical technique, and methodology in this book.

Screening Process

Background Information The U.S. Equity Market Leaders Fund ("the Fund") recently discovered that Deep Value Advisors (DVA), one of two small-cap value managers currently managing assets for the Fund, lost several of their investment professionals in the past week (they left to start up their own hedge fund). After meeting with the remaining team members at DVA, the Fund's investment team decided to fire DVA and find a replacement immediately. The Fund would normally look at its small-cap value bench, but found out that each of the bench managers had recently closed their small-cap value products to new assets (this is a common occurrence in the small-cap asset class).

As a result, the Fund's investment team needs to conduct a search from scratch. They decide to run screens using a third party database to aid the search process. However, before any screen can be run, a discussion of the Fund's objective is necessary. The Fund's broad objective is to hire equity managers that are well established in their particular asset classes ("leaders," as the Fund's name clearly states). The Fund is benchmarked against the Wilshire 5000 Equity Index, an index that represents the total U.S. equity market. As a result, the Fund is permitted to invest in equities that range from small-cap to mid-cap to large-cap.

Screen Objective

Find a short list of U.S. small-cap value products for possible inclusion in the Fund. The manager is a replacement for DVA. The size of the allocation will be approximately $20 million (based on the current market value of DVA's portfolio).

There are five minimum manager requirements for inclusion in the search:

1. Three-year track record.
2. Three-year Sharpe ratio in the top quartile among peer group.
3. Portfolio that will complement the fund's small-cap growth component.
4. Maximum fee of 100 basis points per annum.
5. To qualify as a market *leader*, the head portfolio manager needs to have at least 10 years' experience managing small-cap portfolios.

Based on these objectives and requirements, the search will be pretty wide open. The Fund's investment team has, however, made some very specific requests with respect to manager tenure and product life. Using the information on the Fund's overall objective and the specific manager requirements, we can create a screen that fulfills our requirements.

Screening Criteria

Asset Class/Style Criteria

1. Include only U.S. equity products—this will eliminate all fixed income, cash, and other asset classes from consideration in this screen.
2. Include only small-cap equity products—this refines the screen by eliminating all products that are not small-cap.
3. Include only value style—this further refines the screen by excluding all nonvalue products.

At this point, the screen lists a universe of all U.S. small-cap value products. It is important to remember that a number of products that make it through the screen may not actually fit the small-cap value criteria because the data is provided by each investment manager. Because different people define "small cap" and "value" differently, the results will need to be more closely analyzed.

Performance Criteria

4. Include only products with track records greater than or equal to three years—per the stated requirements.
5. Include only products with three-year Sharpe ratios greater than or equal to 25th percentile within the total small-cap value universe; the 25th percentile represents the cutoff from the top 25% of the products in this universe (which is the top quartile) and the remaining 75% of the products.

Fee Criteria

6. Include only products with management fees less than or equal to 1%—per the requirements.
7. Include only products with no performance fees; while most (99%) of the traditional small-cap products do not charge any kind of performance fee, this restriction will eliminate the few that do.

Portfolio Criteria   The restrictions state that the chosen manager must complement the Fund's small-cap growth managers. This part of the search cannot be carried out at the screening stage. Instead, the Fund's investment team will have to wait until the portfolio analytics stage to effectively consider this requirement. The word *complement* needs to be defined further before any realistic assessment can be made and the results properly analyzed. The analytical stage is covered in Chapters 4 through 12.

Manager's Tenure Criteria   Most third party databases include fields that list the portfolio manager's and analyst's tenure on the product they are currently managing. However, the restriction states that the lead portfolio manager needs to have a minimum of 10 years managing small-cap portfolios in general, not necessarily the portfolio he or she is managing currently. We could screen based on tenure managing the current product, but it would likely eliminate most of the managers in this universe. It would be better to exclude this requirement at this stage of the search process. However, it will be revisited when we receive the professionals' biographies from the investment firms in the next stage of the process.

Product's Status Criteria

8. Product is "open" for new investments, meaning that the investment management firm is still accepting assets. Experienced investment manager analysts may include "closed" products or run the screen a second time and review the list of closed products. I always look at closed products because there is a good chance that I know someone at that firm who might be able to fit in an allocation for me. In addition, database information is not updated on a real-time basis and, as a result, sometimes the information contained in a database is stale—or just incorrect. Also, many managers reopen certain products for a variety of reasons: (1) steep market decline decreases the product's assets to the point where it can receive additional funds, (2) manager has change of mind and sets the maximum asset size higher, (3) manager recently lost some client assets. It doesn't hurt to send a quick e-mail or make a phone call to verify that the product in question is still closed or to inquire if there are any plans to open it in the future.

9. Product assets are greater than or equal to $50 million—this is an arbitrary number. Many organizations set the minimum asset size for a given product much higher than this. However, given the fact that small-cap products in general, and value-oriented small-cap products in particular, tend to close to new assets at lower levels than products in other asset classes, I thought it would be prudent to keep this number on the low side.

Based on the various search criteria set, we have six main categories of screens that combine to make a total of nine different screening criteria. After entering all nine factors into our database and running the screen, we are left with a list of investment managers that might be appropriate candidates for our search. Exhibit 2.3 depicts how the size of the manager universe was impacted by each of the criteria we used in the screening process.

Exhibit 2.4 is a report that compares various characteristics of the managers that made it all the way through the initial screen.

This report gives us a good starting point for discussions about the

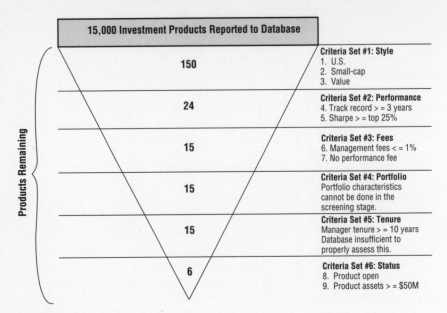

EXHIBIT 2.3   How Size of Manager Universe Is Impacted by Screening Criteria

search and about the individual managers. But this is merely the first step in the sourcing process. Before we move on to the other methods of sourcing managers, let's review a list of popular third party databases that exist in the marketplace today. This list represents databases that I have used at one time or another as well as other popular databases that I am aware of. While the list contains many of the most popular databases currently in use, it is not all-inclusive.

Database Provider	Web Site
Effron/PSN	www.effron-psn.com
Checkfree Mobius	www.checkfreeinvsvcs.com
Pertrac	www.pertrac2000.com
InvestWorks	www.investworks.com
Nelson Marketplace	www.nelsoninformation.com
Money Management Directory	www.mmdaccess.com
Morningstar	www.morningstar.com
Lipper Analytics	www.lipperweb.com
Investor Force	www.investorforce.com
Big Dough	www.bigdough.com

EXHIBIT 2.4 Comparison of Manager Characteristics

Manager	Firm/Product Data*				Returns-Based Data* (Annualized)			
	Inception Date	Firm Assets	Product Assets	Manager Tenure[†]	3-Year Performance	5-Year Performance	3-Year Standard Deviation	5-Year Standard Deviation
CAM Asset Management	1/1/98	$410M	$350M	5.5	7.9	8.6	24.2	23.1
Zenith Capital	1/1/93	$13.6B	$1.3B	6.5	6.4	4.4	22.2	23.1
Revco Partners	1/1/00	$150M	$150M	3.5	7.2	n/a	24.7	n/a
Alders Asset Management	3/1/97	$1.2B	$800M	6.4	6.6	5.0	25.8	26.1
Eagle Capital Management	2/1/00	$210M	$90M	3.4	8.2	n/a	25.1	n/a
Cross Capital Management	4/1/97	$1B	$400M	6.3	7.9	7.5	25.1	23.6
S&P 600 SmallCap Index					2.4	3.7	21.5	22.2
S&P 600 SmallCap Value Index					8.0	3.8	23.3	21.2

* All data through June 2003.
[†]Manager tenure is stated in years and represents period managing current product.

INTERNAL DATABASES

Internal investment manager databases are collections of information investment manager analysts receive directly from investment managers as well as the analytics and meeting memos that they prepare during the due diligence process. An internal database can simply be a well-organized directory of relevant information broken out by manager name and/or asset class or it can be a special program designed for proprietary use by the investment manager analyst's firm. An internal manager database typically includes data from managers currently under contract, bench managers, and managers that have been rejected for whatever reason in the past. Regardless of the type or sophistication of an internal database, the following data should be considered for inclusion:

- *Meeting memos.* These memos include the reviewer's assessment of the product, portfolio manager, analysts, traders, and any other information that the reviewer feels is relevant to evaluate the product. Ultimately, the memo includes conclusions based on all the data available at that time.
- *Performance analysis.* This includes both the performance figures provided by the investment manager as well as the analytics that the analyst has performed based on those figures.
- *Portfolio evaluations.* Fundamental evaluation of a given investment product at a point in time and over a defined period of time offers invaluable clues regarding the investment manager's philosophy, style, and methodology.
- *Risk analysis.* Performance analysis is like a two-sided coin. One side deals with reward and the other side deals with risk. A good internal database will have as much (if not more) analytics on risk attributes as it does on reward.
- *Presentations.* Investment firms spend a great deal of time creating and maintaining presentation books for marketing purposes. While I do not rely on the information contained in these presentations, they often help me with my evaluation of the investment manager under review.
- *Form ADVs.* This form is a regulatory requirement for all registered investment firms. It will be covered in detail in Chapter 7, but for summary purposes, the ADV lists information about a firm's organization, ownership structure, funds and assets under management, and the investment professionals working at the firm.
- *Monthly/quarterly reports.* Investment firms often create brief monthly and more detailed quarterly reports that cover the general market/economic environment as well as the portfolio/fund under re-

view. I always try to get these reports going back as far as possible because they offer insight into the portfolio for a time when I had no real involvement.

While I have used several *fancy* databases over the years, more than anything else I have found myself referring back to the bound notebooks that I have used to record the events of each and every meeting I conduct. I use my handwritten notebooks as references whenever I write a formal meeting memo. As I have conducted well over a thousand meetings in my career, I have several dozen notebooks all sitting nicely on my bookshelf (I'm currently in the process of scanning them so they are available to me electronically).

Whenever I conduct a search, I refer back to my internal database to supplement the list created by the third party database. I also use it to eliminate managers that made it through the initial screens. For example, I might take the list of six candidates (refer to Exhibit 2.4) and add some names to the search even if they had been eliminated based on the criteria set in the screening process.

For example, I might know of an investment manager who left his firm a year ago to start up a small-cap value product for a large, foreign-owned investment company. The individual in question may have previously managed a small-cap value product for a different firm for 15 years and may have put together one of the best and most consistent track records in that asset class over the period. Because this manager's "new" small-cap value product does not have a three-year track record (as specified by the screening criteria), this product would have been eliminated. Based on this data, it might be a good idea to include this manager in the search and see how his product compares to the six products identified in the screening process. Our internal database might also force us to eliminate products.

MEDIA/INTERNET

Never discount the power and reach of the media. This includes television, newspapers, financial magazines, and professional journals. In recent years, the Internet has provided access to dozens of informative resources regarding investment managers, from online versions of financial publications to information available only via the Internet. In addition, the Internet has provided a great resource for finding news on specific managers and on the investment industry in general. Search engines, like Google, allow investment manager analysts to search for news on specific investment managers, asset classes, and other areas of the investment industry and obtain scores of useful facts in seconds.

EXHIBIT 2.5 Partial Media List

Print (Main-Stream)	Journals	Web Sites	Television
Wall Street Journal	*Financial Analysts Review*	Yahoo.com	CNBC
Financial Times	*CFA Digest*	MSN.com	CNN
BusinessWeek	*Journal of Alternative Investments*	MarketWatch.com	PBS
Fortune	*Journal of Investing*	FundAlert.com	National stations
Forbes	*Journal of Portfolio Management*	Morningstar.com	Local stations
Mutual Fund magazine	*Journal of Private Equity*	Bloomberg.com	
Bloomberg magazine	*Journal of Fixed Income*	TheStreet.com	

However, as I mentioned earlier in the chapter, this can sometimes lead to information overload. Exhibit 2.5 is a partial list of the media sources that I frequently consult.

INVESTMENT CONSULTANTS

Investment consultants can be utilized at any stage in the due diligence process. Many pension plans hire consulting firms to do all the background work for a search and to present their top selections for each search they conduct. The pension plan's investment committee or plan sponsor then makes the final decision on whom to hire (and fire). Organizations with small investment staffs tend to hire consultants because they might not have the time, personnel, or know-how to conduct a search on their own. Large organizations often utilize consultants (despite the fact that they have ample resources) as a means of providing a safety net and a sounding board for ideas.

In a recent survey, *Plan Sponsor* magazine found that roughly 40% of the survey's respondents stated that they use investment consultants in one or more ways (see Exhibit 2.6).

The survey results indicate that at least half of the pension plans that utilize consultants' services look for advice and help regarding investment manager analysis. Exhibit 2.7 is a list of selected major U.S. and global pension consultants that were included in the *Plan Sponsor* magazine survey.

INDUSTRY CONTACTS

The more investment managers you meet, the more contacts you make and the fatter your Rolodex becomes. Networking is essential in this business. I

EXHIBIT 2.6 *Plan Sponsor* Consultant Service Usage Survey Results

	2003	2002
1. Performance measurement/attribution	62%	69%
2. Investment policy	55%	65%
3. Manager search/selection/RFPs*	50%	66%
4. Plan design	47%	—
5. Asset allocation	40%	69%
6. Risk management	29%	29%
7. Manager/provider transitions	22%	32%
8. Plan terminations/mergers	18%	26%
9. Other	15%	19%

*RFP = request for proposal.
Source: Plansponsor.com: "Survey: The Anatomy of Consulting Relationships."

EXHIBIT 2.7 Pension Consultant List—*Plan Sponsor* Survey

Investment Consultants in *Plan Sponsor* Survey

A. G. Edwards	Ennis Knupp & Associates	Raymond James
Aon Consulting	Evaluation Associates	RBC Dain Hauscher
Arnerich Massena	Frank Russell	Resources for Retirement
Buck Consultants	Hewitt Investment Group	Rocaton Investment
Callan Associates	KPMG	Advisors
Cambridge Associates	Legg Mason	R. V. Kuhns
Clark Consulting	Marco Consulting Group	R. W. Baird
CRA RogersCasey	Marsh	Segal Advisors
C. W. Cammack	McDonald Investments	Smith Barney
Defined Contribution	Mercer Investment	Summit Strategies
Advisors	Consulting	Towers Perrin
Deloitte Consulting	Merrill Lynch	UBS
DeMarche	Milliman USA	Wachovia
Dimeo Schneider	Morgan Stanley	Watson Wyatt
Edward Jones	New England Pension	Wilshire Associates
	Consultants	

Source: Plansponsor.com: "Survey: The Anatomy of Consulting Relationships."

have many contacts in the pension, consulting, and fund of funds industry, and I can assure you that a great deal of scuttlebutt on investment firms and specific investment professionals has worked its way through this network. However, I have often found that new ideas can come from just about any contact.

I have been given good leads from software vendors (always a good source of information because vendors that supply software to investment managers can often provide unique insights into which firms seem to have their act together and, more importantly, which firms do not). I make it a habit to build rapport with software vendors and other service providers in the investment industry and often ask them if they have any clients (managers) that they are impressed with and, conversely, that they are not too impressed with.

The investment business is responsible for many trillions of dollars, yet remains a pretty tight-knit community. I can usually find someone who has access to information that I am looking for (or who knows someone who has the information). Because it is such a small community, portfolio managers, analysts, and traders often have many friends among their peer groups. It is not uncommon for a portfolio manager to suggest that I call a buddy of his if I'm looking to make a specific allocation. And, as I highlight later in the book, I often ask investment managers during the interview stage who they feel is their greatest competition.

MODIFYING THE SEARCH

Now that we have created a screened list of investment managers through networking and using the third party databases and our own internal databases, it is time modify the list based on the other sources of information we have discussed. At this stage it is usually best to distribute the search guidelines and the initial screen's results to the members of your investment committee and set a date and time for review and discussion. While this meeting is technically not necessary, I have found that a group of investment manager analysts can offer unique insights and apply their personal knowledge base to the search in a way that a single analyst cannot.

Using the initial screened list of small-cap value managers in Exhibit 2.4 as a starting point, a number of changes can be made. A sample of a modified list is shown in Exhibit 2.8. This report is the same one used previously, but has been modified to include the insights of the investment committee members. For example, Cross Capital Management has been crossed out because the investment committee knew from experience that this firm has recently experienced significant personnel turnover. Kiuley Capital Advisors has been added, despite having a short product history.

EXHIBIT 2.8 Revised Search List

Manager	Firm/Product Data*				Returns-Based Data* (Annualized)			
	Inception Date	Firm Assets	Product Assets	Manager Tenure†	3-Year Performance	5-Year Performance	3-Year Standard Deviation	5-Year Standard Deviation
CAM Asset Management	1/1/98	$410M	$350M	5.5	7.9	8.6	24.2	23.1
Zenith Capital	1/1/93	$13.6B	$1.3B	6.5	6.4	4.4	22.2	23.1
Revco Partners	1/1/00	$150M	$150M	3.5	7.2	n/a	24.7	n/a
Alders Asset Management	3/1/97	$1.2B	$800M	6.4	6.6	5.0	25.8	26.1
Eagle Capital Management	2/1/00	$210M	$90M	3.4	8.2	n/a	25.1	n/a
~~Cross Capital Management~~	~~4/1/97~~	~~$1B~~	~~$400M~~	~~6.2~~	~~7.9~~	~~7.5~~	~~25.1~~	~~23.6~~
Kinley Capital Advisors	12/03	$100M	$100M	0.5	n/a	n/a	n/a	n/a
S&P 600 SmallCap Index					2.4	3.7	21.5	22.2
S&P 600 SmallCap Value Index					8.0	3.8	23.3	21.2

*All data through June 2003.
†Manager tenure stated in years and represents period managing current product.

The investment committee learned from reading industry news that the portfolio management team from Beasley Investments that left that firm last year had done so to start up Kiuley Capital Advisors. The investment committee decided to include this firm pending further analysis.

Kiuley is highlighted in italics because its very short history will need to be evaluated before we can realistically consider the firm for this search. Cross Capital was eliminated due to employee turnover. While one of the original portfolio managers is still at the firm and managing the small-cap value product, his two key partners decided to leave the firm just a few months prior to running the screen. It is an example of how screened data can be misleading. Cross was able to keep its manager tenure at 6.3 years because one of the three founding partners still works on the product. As you can see from the returns-based data, Cross appears to be an attractive candidate, but knowing that two-thirds of the team that was responsible for achieving those excellent results is no longer with the firm, we can effectively toss those results out the window.

CONCLUSION

Good investment managers can be found in a multitude of places, including third party databases, internal or external contacts, newspapers, magazines, journals, television, and so on. However, along with the good investment managers, you will likely find many more that are not all that good or are just not a good fit with your specific investment objectives or goals.

Most databases include information on thousands of different investment firms, so the investment manager analyst must reduce the list of *possible* candidates to a list of *probable* candidates. This is done by applying both quantitative and qualitative restrictions to the universe of appropriate investment products. The results of these largely mechanized screens must then be overlaid with some good old-fashioned common sense. The result is a short list of investment products that better enable the investment manager analyst to focus the search efforts on investment products that are appropriate candidates and have a realistic possibility of being hired or being included in the manager bench.

Now that we have stated our investment objectives and screened for a short list of investment products that meet our needs, we can almost start the analytical process. But first, we need to contact the managers in the short list and request basic information about their individual firms and the underlying products we are looking to review. Chapter 3 introduces a means of requesting this information in an efficient way.

Request for Information

Now that we have set our internal investment guidelines and created an initial list of investment managers that we need to look into, it is time to start the data collection stage—formally known as the request for information (RFI).

So far, we have a lot of information that we have combined from a number of different sources. This information has allowed us to make some quick qualitative and quantitative assessments of the managers from the initial universe (the initial universe in the small-cap value screen highlighted in Chapter 2 initially included 150 small-cap value products). As a result, some managers were eliminated and others were added. While this information is very helpful, it is only the tip of the iceberg. In order to properly perform a comparative analysis and ultimately select a manager for hire, we will need information directly from the investment managers.

FORMAL QUESTIONNAIRE

Many firms elect to send out a lengthy questionnaire at this stage. These questionnaires tend to be massive, often in excess of 40 pages—particularly those sent out by consulting firms. However, I do not believe that this is appropriate or efficient at this stage because many of the managers that we have identified will be quickly eliminated after we have performed a preliminary review based on responses to the initial RFI. It is a bit unfair to ask all the managers to fill out a massive questionnaire, when just a few data items will suffice. We will send out our own version of the formal questionnaire later in the process—once we have narrowed the list down further. This way we can avoid wasting managers' time and ours as well. It is a simple matter of efficiency—formal questionnaires take a long time to fill out, and they take a long time to review as well.

SIMPLE QUESTIONNAIRE

In order to optimize our time and streamline the overall search process, we will need only enough information at this level to eliminate managers as well as to pass others on to the next level. I have found that the following information usually provides everything I need:

- *Historical performance.* Even though we have the performance from our databases, it is important to get the historical performance information directly from the investment manager to ensure that the numbers are correct. In addition, you should request the full performance disclosures as well as composite information.
- *Current portfolio.* As you will see in later chapters, portfolio evaluation is a critical element in the overall investment manager analysis process. The portfolio will tell you many things about the management team and the product in question. Alternatively, you may request that each manager provide specific portfolio information, such as portfolio characteristics (price-earnings ratio, price/sales, earnings growth, etc.), sector weights, industry weights, percentage of product in top 10 holdings, and so on. I prefer to receive the portfolio so I can run the analytics myself.
- *Professional bios.* Because the people who manage a given product are the most important factor in its past successes and its potential success in the future, it is important to get an understanding of who the investment professionals are and where they have been.
- *Marketing book or presentation.* Most firms have ready-made presentations that they can send to you. While the quality and quantity of information differs from manager to manager, most provide information on the firm, the investment product, the investment team, and the investment process. While I do not place any major emphasis on these presentations, they do provide some very useful preliminary information and often provide me with a list of questions to ask the managers if/when I interview them later on in the process.
- *Form ADV.* Investment management firms are required to file this form with the Securities and Exchange Commission (SEC) if they manage more than $25 million of client assets. The form provides a wealth of firm and investment professional information. The form is also available via the SEC's web site. See Chapter 7 for more detail on the ADV.

SAMPLE REQUEST FOR INFORMATION

Using the information from the sample small-cap value manager search from Chapter 2, I have created a generic RFI that can be used in letter format for direct mailing/fax or for e-mail format (which I generally prefer). I also generally post an RFI to a web site and invite investment firms that feel they meet the criteria to contact me. This is another way to find new investment products that are not listed in the databases.

To: Manager Contact
From: Frank J. Travers, CFA
Re: Small-cap value search—request for information

Greetings,

The Investment Committee of the U.S. Equity Market Leaders Fund is currently gathering information on U.S. small-cap value managers for a search we are working on. An initial screen has identified your organization as a potential candidate for this search. For your information, I have included important information relating to this search:

Reason for Search:

■ Investment professional turnover at one of the Fund's existing small-cap value managers led to their termination and subsequent search for a replacement.

Mandate/Timing:

■ The manager selected will take over the existing manager's portfolio, which has a current market value of approximately $20 million. Responses to this RFI are expected no later than December 15th. The Fund's investment committee will review all responses and contact you within two weeks of receiving your responses.

Search Criteria:

■ U.S. small-cap equity manager with value orientation.
■ Minimum of $50 million assets in product.
■ Minimum three-year track record.
■ Because the Fund's theme is to provide its clients access to leaders in the field of investment management, your lead portfolio manager must have greater than 10 years' experience managing small cap portfolios (over career, not just product in question)

Information Requested:

1. Historical performance—Provide monthly performance history net of fees. In addition, please include performance disclosures. The disclosures must include composite information.
2. Current portfolio—Provide the following information on the portfolio for the most recent month end in Microsoft Excel format:

stock tickers, stock names, number of shares held for each stock. Please include the amount of cash and cash equivalents.

3. Professional biographies—Provide bios for all firm members who have responsibilities for this product. This includes portfolio managers, analysts, traders, strategists, marketers, and client service professionals. Separately, please include the names of any professionals who worked on this product but left the firm within the past three years.

4. Marketing presentation—Please include a copy of your off-the-shelf marketing presentation.

5. Form ADV—If you are an investment advisory firm registered in the United States, provide a copy of the latest Form ADV submitted to the SEC.

Contact Information:

Frank J. Travers, CFA, is leading this search, so please address all responses to him and contact him directly if you have any questions. Information will be accepted via e-mail, which is preferred, or standard mail at the following addresses (faxed information will not be accepted):

E-mail:	scvsearch@temlf.com
Address:	111 Bridge Street, 1st Floor
	New York, NY 10022

If you have any questions or require any additional information, feel free to contact me anytime. Thank you for your time and effort.

Sincerely,

Frank J. Travers, CFA
Investment Committee Member

The letter's format is important because it represents your organization's first impression with the investment management community and with the managers in the distribution list. A poorly written letter or one where the objectives are confusing does not reflect well on you or your organization. Additionally, a confusing letter will prolong the information-gathering process, as some of the investment firms will need to contact you to clarify information, while others will misinterpret the request and send the wrong information. In the latter case, you will need to contact the manager and ask for the information a second time. The bottom line is that the process will not be an efficient one.

The sample letter was designed to be informative and to the point. I have seen RFIs that are up to 10 pages in length, containing pages of unnecessary text. While some searches do require more explanation, I have found that most can be effectively communicated on one or two pages. The sample letter defines the search parameters, clearly indicates what is required of the investment managers, and states the formats that will be accepted. The last, and quite important, section states who is in charge of the search and provides detail on how to communicate with that person. Too many firms conducting searches are intentionally vague about this, leading to some degree of confusion. Despite how well written the letter is, some managers will require clarification and others will want to call just to set up a dialogue.

CONCLUSION

Let's review the process thus far. We have identified our investment objectives and used those objectives to develop a series of criteria to perform an efficient screen of our databases. We culled the initial universe of 150 products down to a mere 6 products. Once we identified the products in our mostly quantitative screening process, we reviewed the results and added a manager and deleted a manager based on some qualitative information and assessments.

The final list of candidates was then contacted to request some basic information for our review. When the responses start to come back to us, then the real fun begins. Once that information is received, we can start the actual investment manager analysis process. Chapter 4 will review the basics of performance analysis and explain each formula and concept with examples based on the information that we receive from the RFIs we sent out.

Equity and Fixed Income Manager Analysis

Performance Analysis

A t the end of the preceding chapter, we e-mailed out a request for information to a list of fictitious investment managers. CAM Asset Management was the first of these to e-mail back to us all of the information we requested, so we start the due diligence process by evaluating this manager. We use the information from CAM's RFI as a case study throughout the equity manager analysis part of this book. Each chapter highlights the formulas, methods, and concepts behind the due diligence process and uses CAM's small-cap value product as an example. In addition, the book evaluates, explains, and interprets each example given. The goal is to be both academic and practical.

As part of the package of information that CAM sent to us, we received a spreadsheet with the monthly returns and some annualized numbers for comparative purposes. Exhibit 4.1 shows the feedback from CAM regarding their historical performance as requested in the RFI.

INTRODUCTION

The concept of investment performance is simple: how well (or poorly) a given investment product did over a discrete period of time. Performance can be thought of in absolute terms (how much money was made or lost) or in relative terms. The relative comparison can be made against a benchmark index or the average return for similar investment products, also know as a peer group or universe comparison. It is also common to combine several different benchmarks to create a single benchmark that is more indicative of the underlying investment manager's product.

However, in reality, performance statistics have been responsible for more bad hiring decisions than any other statistics. In this chapter, we discuss the various methods in which performance can be calculated and demonstrate each calculation by using real-world examples. This chapter is

EXHIBIT 4.1 Feedback from CAM

CAM Asset Management
Performance Summary
June 30, 2003

Annualized Performance (Periods Ended June 2003)

	YTD	1 Year	3 Years	5 Years	Inception
CAM	15.9%	−2.7%	7.9%	8.6%	9.7%
S&P 600 SmallCap Index	12.9%	−3.6%	2.4%	3.7%	4.5%

Monthly Performance

	1998	1999	2000	2001	2002	2003
January	−1.23%	−0.70%	−2.30%	6.79%	2.32%	−3.45%
February	8.34%	−7.21%	15.34%	−4.56%	−1.34%	−3.21%
March	5.67%	−0.20%	−6.54%	−3.21%	10.89%	0.23%
April	1.21%	7.21%	−1.76%	7.54%	5.11%	9.17%
May	−5.21%	4.51%	−2.11%	3.45%	−5.21%	8.76%
June	1.89%	5.82%	4.54%	1.24%	−3.43%	4.21%
July	−8.34%	0.20%	−2.17%	−1.45%	−15.87%	
August	−19.45%	−5.12%	8.26%	−0.65%	0.02%	
September	6.45%	1.90%	−1.16%	−9.45%	−6.50%	
October	4.89%	1.10%	1.17%	5.21%	3.45%	
November	5.42%	5.20%	−7.23%	9.94%	6.54%	
December	4.99%	10.45%	10.34%	8.32%	−3.21%	

broken out into four sections, each dealing with a different aspect of investment manager performance:

1. *Conceptual aspects of performance measurement.* In order to effectively analyze an investment manager's performance, we must first understand how performance is calculated. This section, which highlights the many formulas used to calculate and evaluate performance, lays the foundation for the rest of the chapter.
2. *Practical application of formulas.* In this section, we analyze CAM's performance utilizing a variety of performance measures and tools, including performance comparisons, data tables, and graphical illustrations.
3. *AIMR guidelines.* The Association for Investment Management and Research (AIMR) has developed a series of performance guidelines that are voluntary, but widely employed by investment management firms as well as by the people who are charged with analyzing them.

4. *Composite analysis.* Because performance streams are often represented by a composite of many separate accounts and/or funds, we analyze the composite methodology and work through several analytical tools that will help us to better understand and evaluate a given composite.

CONCEPTUAL ASPECTS OF PERFORMANCE MEASUREMENT

Dollar Weighted Returns

The simplest form of performance measurement is the dollar weighted return (DWR), which measures the amount of money gained or lost from the beginning of a review period to the end of a review period, as a percentage of the original dollars invested.

Formula 4.1 (Dollar Weighted Return)

$$DWR = \left(\frac{EMV - BMV}{BMV} \right)$$

where EMV = Ending market value.
       BMV = Beginning market value.

Note: All market values should include corporate actions that have an impact on the value of the portfolio, such as dividends and interest.

Example Let's assume that on December 31, we invested $1,000,000 in CAM's small-cap value product and that the value of that investment increased during the month, finishing at $1,100,000 on January 31. Let's assume that we did not make any contributions or distributions during that period (cash flows are important and will be discussed later in the chapter). Using formula 4.1, we calculate the following return for the month of January:

$$DWR = \left(\frac{\$1,100,000 - \$1,000,000}{\$1,000,000} \right) = \left(\frac{\$100,000}{\$1,000,000} \right) = 0.10$$

The answer, 0.10, is in decimal format. To convert it to percentage format, simply multiply it by 100.

Formula 4.2 (Conversion of Decimal Return to Percentage Format)

$$(\text{Decimal Return} \times 100) = \text{Percentage Return}$$

Using the information from our example, we use formula 4.2 to calculate the percentage return: $(0.10 \times 100) = 10.0\%$.

So, our initial $1,000,000 investment grew by $100,000 in absolute dollar terms or by 10% in percentage terms.

Chain-Linking Returns

In the previous example, we calculated the dollar weighted return for our $1 million investment in CAM for the month of January. Let's extend the example to include performance for the following month. To calculate the February return, we use the market value at the end of January as the beginning market value ($1,100,000). The value of the portfolio at the end of February was $1,200,000. Using the formula for dollar weighted return, we calculate the following:

February Return

$$\left(\frac{\$1,200,000 - \$1,100,000}{\$1,100,000} \right) = \left(\frac{\$100,000}{\$1,100,000} \right) = 0.091 \text{ (in decimal format)}$$

In percentage terms, the February return was: $0.091 \times 100 = 9.10\%$.

Total Period Return (January and February)

$$\left(\frac{\$1,200,000 - \$1,000,000}{\$1,000,000} \right) = \left(\frac{\$200,000}{\$1,000,000} \right) = 0.20$$

In percentage terms, the total period return was: $0.2 \times 100 = 20.0\%$. Let's summarize:

Initial market value (12/31): $1,000,000
Ending market value (2/28): $1,200,000

	% Return	Gain/Loss
January return:	10.00%	$100,000
February return:	9.10%	$100,000
Total period return:	20.00%	$200,000

What we immediately notice is that the returns from January and February do not equal the total period return when added together (19.10% versus 20.00%). This is due to compounding—while the dollar gain was the same in each month ($100,000), the percentage required to achieve that return in February was lower than it was in January because we started the month with a higher beginning market value. The same is true when the portfolio decreases in value.

To properly combine the returns for January and February to match the total period return, we must chain-link the returns using the following formula:

Formula 4.3 (Chain-Linked Return)

$$CLR = [(1 + PDR^1) \times (1 + PDR^2) \times \ldots \times (1 + PDR^n)] - 1$$

where PDR^1 = Period decimal return for period 1.
PDR^2 = Period decimal return for period 2.
PDR^n = Period decimal return for final period.

Note: The periods in question can be monthly, quarterly, or annually, or can cover any period you specify. In addition, the periods can measure different time intervals. For example, PDR^1 can measure a single month, while PDR^2 can measure a six-month period. In the aforementioned example, the total chain-linked return would cover a seven-month period.

Example Using the summary data from the previous example for January and February, we calculate the chain-linked return as follows:

CLR = [(1 + January Decimal Return) × (1 + February Decimal Return)] – 1
CLR = [(1 + 0.10) × (1 + 0.091)] – 1
CLR = [(1.10) × (1.091)] = 1.20
CLR = 1.20 – 1 = 0.20 (in decimal format)
CLR = 0.20 × 100 = 20.0% (in percentage format)

So we can arrive at the correct total period return by using the dollar weighted average for the entire period or by chain-linking the individual period (in this case monthly) returns. Using the chain-linking formula, we can calculate what the total period return would have been if the return for both January and February was 10%.

(1.10) × (1.10) = 1.21
1.21 – 1 = 0.21
0.21 × 100 = 21.0%

Due to compounding the total period return would have been 21.0% and the absolute dollar gain would have been $210,000. Using these formulas, we can start with the returns and work our way back to the dollar amounts or start with the dollar amounts and work our way to the returns.

Cumulative Returns

Now that we can calculate dollar weighted returns and have discussed the formula for chain-linking the individual period returns, we can put together a cumulative return table and graph. This is a basic, often-used method of displaying an investment manager's performance over a period of time. There are two ways of showing this information: (1) using actual dollar growth or (2) using the returns to illustrate the theoretical growth of a dollar (in other words, how an initial investment of $1 has grown over the review period).

The actual calculation for cumulative return is a continuous application of the chain-linking formula already outlined, where the initial return is the first period return and each subsequent cumulative return chain-links the previous cumulative return figure to the current return period. The formula is broken out to better illustrate its application:

Formula 4.4 (Cumulative Return)

Period	Formula	Notes
Period 1	PDR^1	Measures period 1
Period 2	$(1 + PDR^1) \times (1 + PDR^2) = PDR^{1\cdots2}$	Measures periods 1–2
Period 3	$(1 + PDR^{1\cdots2}) \times (1 + PDR^3) = PDR^{1\cdots3}$	Measures periods 1–3
Period 4	$(1 + PDR^{1\cdots3}) \times (1 + PDR^4) = PDR^{1\cdots4}$	Measures periods 1–4
Final period	$(1 + PDR^{1\cdots n-1}) \times (1 + PDR^n)$	Measures periods 1–n

where $PDR^{1\cdots n-1}$ = Next-to-last period.
$\qquad\quad PDR^n$ = Last period.

Each progressive cumulative return is calculated by simply chain-linking the previous total period return to the next period return. This calculation can continue over the entire performance period of for some subset of the period. However, it is critical that the performance be linked in calendar order (from first period to last) to get an accurate picture of the actual growth.

We have thus far calculated the dollar weighted return for CAM's small-cap value portfolio for January and February. We will now extend this example to include returns for an entire calendar year. The data listed in Exhibit 4.2 is dollar weighted and assumes that no cash flows into or out of the portfolio took place during the year.

EXHIBIT 4.2   Returns for an Entire Calendar Year

Period	Month	Return (Decimal)	Return (%)	Formula	Cumulative Return
PDR^1	January	0.100	10.0%	PDF^1	10.0%
PDR^2	February	0.091	9.1%	$(1 + PDF^1) \times (1 + PDF^2) = PDF^{1...2}$	20.0%
PDR^3	March	0.034	3.4%	$(1 + PDR^{1...2}) \times (1 + PDR^3) = PDR^{1...3}$	24.1%
PDR^4	April	0.012	1.2%	$(1 + PDR^{1...3}) \times (1 + PDR^4) = PDR^{1...4}$	25.6%
PDR^5	May	0.037	3.7%	$(1 + PDR^{1...4}) \times (1 + PDR^5) = PDR^{1...5}$	30.2%
PDR^6	June	0.023	2.3%	$(1 + PDR^{1...5}) \times (1 + PDR^6) = PDR^{1...6}$	33.2%
PDR^7	July	0.004	0.4%	$(1 + PDR^{1...6}) \times (1 + PDR^7) = PDR^{1...7}$	33.8%
PDR^8	August	0.006	0.6%	$(1 + PDR^{1...7}) \times (1 + PDR^8) = PDR^{1...8}$	34.6%
PDR^9	September	0.042	4.2%	$(1 + PDR^{1...8}) \times (1 + PDR^9) = PDR^{1...9}$	40.2%
PDR^{10}	October	0.081	8.1%	$(1 + PDR^{1...9}) \times (1 + PDR^{10}) = PDR^{1...10}$	51.6%
PDR^{11}	November	0.029	2.9%	$(1 + PDR^{1...10}) \times (1 + PDR^{11}) = PDR^{1...11}$	56.0%
PDR^{12}	December	0.002	0.2%	$(1 + PDR^{1...11}) \times (1 + PDR^{12}) = PDR^{1...12}$	56.3%

The formula column in Exhibit 4.2 clearly shows how the cumulative return calculation works by displaying the formula's incremental adjustments throughout the calendar-year period examined in the example.

Exhibit 4.3 takes the resulting cumulative returns and displays them in graphical format. The cumulative graph could also be displayed by applying the period returns to a theoretical dollar value. For example, if we set the beginning value at $1, we would have ended the 12-month period with $1.56 (because the cumulative return for the period was 56.3%). The growth of a dollar is depicted in Exhibit 4.4.

Exhibit 4.5 reviews CAM's historical cumulative performance since its inception (as a growth of a dollar chart) and compares it to the broad

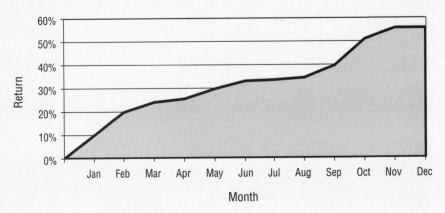

EXHIBIT 4.3   Cumulative Performance Chart

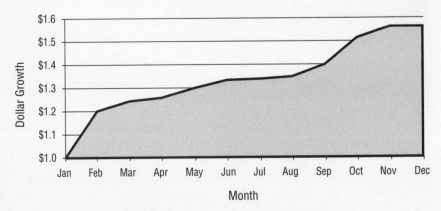

EXHIBIT 4.4   Cumulative Growth of $1

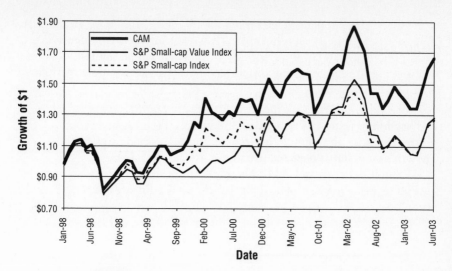

EXHIBIT 4.5   Cumulative Performance Comparison

small-cap and small-cap value indexes. The results should not be surprising given the performance figures stated in Exhibit 4.1.

Annualized Returns

What if I told you that over the past 10 years a portfolio had gained 100% (doubling in value over the period). While this information is useful in determining an absolute dollar gain, it does not tell us anything about the typical portfolio's annual returns, which is generally a better-understood measure. To solve this we could simply divide the total return (100%) by the number of years (10) to come up with an average return of 10% per year; but, due to compounding, this would be inaccurate. The proper way to determine a given product's annual return (taking the effects of compounding in consideration) is to apply the following formula:

Formula 4.5 (Annualized Return)

$$[(1 + DWR) \wedge (1 \div YRS)] - 1$$

where DWR = Dollar weighted return (in decimal format).
         YRS = Total number of years of period under review.
         $\wedge$ = Raised to the ( ) power. For example, 3 $\wedge$ (2) is translated
             as 3 raised to the 2nd power, the result of which is equal to
             3 times 3, or 9.

Note: The exponent can be stated to reflect differences in the frequency of the underlying return periods. For example: If the underlying return periods are stated in a monthly format, we can apply the following: $(12 \div \#$ of months$)$; if stated in quarterly format, we can apply the following: $(4 \div \#$ of quarters$)$.

Applying formula 4.5 to our example, we calculate the following annualized return (100% in decimal format is 1.00):

$$\text{Annualized Return} = [(1 + 1.00) \wedge (1 \div 10)] - 1$$
$$= [(2.00) \wedge (0.10)] - 1$$
$$= 1.07177 - 1 = 0.07177$$

In percent format:

$$\text{Annualized Return} = 0.07177 \times 100 = 7.17\%$$

The impact of compounding is clearly evident when you compare the average return (10%) to the annualized return (7.17%). An investment firm can, therefore, state its product's historical returns in cumulative and/or annualized terms. When analyzing performance figures, make sure you are aware of the performance methodology. By simply annualizing returns for products with different time periods, we can standardize each product's return and make any comparisons more meaningful.

Adjusting for Cash Flows

So far, we have calculated returns based on the assumption that there were no contributions or distributions of assets during the measurement periods. However, in the real world, cash flows are a part of everyday business. Cash flows into or out of an investment manager's portfolio can be the result of many different investment decisions. For example, an investor might contribute assets to or redeem assets from a specific investment product based on asset allocation changes, funding requirements, or concerns regarding the underlying investment professionals. Whatever the reason, cash flows can have a big impact on return calculations.

To illustrate how cash flows can impact portfolio returns let's review the following example:

BMV (Jan. 1): $1,000,000
EMV (Jan. 31): $2,000,000

Using the formula for dollar weighted return (4.1), we calculate the following return:

$$\left(\frac{\$2,000,000 - \$1,000,000}{\$1,000,000}\right) = \left(\frac{\$1,000,000}{\$1,000,000}\right) = 1.00 \times 100 = 100\%$$

A one-month return of 100%—that is amazing . . . or is it?

What I left out from this example was the fact that there was a $900,000 contribution to this portfolio at the end of business on January 30. Given this information, it is clearly unfair to use the dollar weighted return formula to determine the portfolio's return for January.

At this point, you might be inclined to simply adjust the dollar weighted return by the amount of the cash flow. This can be done in the following way:

Formula 4.6 (Cash Flow Adjusted Dollar Weighted Return—CFADWR)

$$\text{CFADWR} = \left(\frac{\text{EMV} - \text{BMV} - \text{Net Cash Flows}}{\text{BMV} + \text{Net Cash Flows}}\right) - 1$$

$$\text{CFADWR} = \left(\frac{\$2,000,000 - \$1,000,000 - \$900,000}{\$1,000,000}\right) - 1$$

$$\text{CFADWR} = \left(\frac{\$100,000}{\$1,900,000}\right) - 1$$

$$\text{CFADWR} = 1.0526 - 1 = 0.0526 = 5.26\%$$

where Net cash flows = Inflows – Outflows

After all, the portfolio gained $1,000,000 in value over the month, but $900,000 was due to an additional contribution—not the investment manager's investment acumen. Investment managers should be credited only for the value that *they* add to the portfolio—not what is given to them. However, the cash flow adjustment does not take into account the timing of any cash flows. In our example, if the portfolio was given the $900,000 on the first business day of the measurement period, then the 5.26% return would be fair because the portfolio manager or team would have had the money to invest over the entire measurement period as opposed to one day (January 31) in our example. But what if the money was added to the portfolio toward the end of the measurement period? In this instance, it would be unfair (and inaccurate) to calculate the return based on the assumption that the manager had the assets for the entire period.

So we need to apply a formula that takes contributions and distributions into account and adjusts them based on their timing. In this chapter, we discuss two variations of the return calculation that take cash flows and their timing within a period into account: (1) the modified Dietz formula and (2) the time weighted formula. The former represents a very close approximation of cash flow adjusted returns, while the latter provides for a more exact result.

Modified Dietz

The modified Dietz formula is named for its creator and is best described as a quick and relatively accurate approximation of the return for a portfolio over a discrete period of time. It adjusts for cash flows coming into and going out of a portfolio by adjusting the cash flow amounts based on the actual amount of time that the assets were invested in the portfolio. In addition, it can incorporate as many cash flows as needed.

Formula 4.7 (Modified Dietz Return)

$$MDR = \left(\frac{EMV - BMV - Cont + Dist}{BMV + \sum (NTWCF)} \right)$$

where   EMV = Ending market value.
          BMV = Beginning market value.
          Cont = Sum of all contributions.
          Dist = Sum of all distribution.
          NTWCF = Net time weighted cash flows.

$$NTWCF = \sum_{CF^n}^{CF^1} \left[\left(\frac{\# \text{ of Days Invested}}{\text{Total } \# \text{ of Days in Period}} \right) \times \text{Cash Flow} \right]$$

where CF^1 = Cash flow #1.
          CF^n = Cash flow #n.

Note: Contributions are positive numbers; distributions are negative numbers.

The numerator of this formula simply calculates the dollar gain in the portfolio (EMV − BMV) and then adjusts that figure for the net cash flows (by subtracting all contributions and adding all distributions). The denominator is where the actual time adjustments take place (NTWCF).

The time weighted cash flow (TWCF) adjusts each cash flow to reflect only the amount of time the assets were actually invested in the portfolio (or available for investment in the portfolio). The net TWCF (NTWCF) would be the sum of the results of each individual TWCF. Using the previous example, we would apply formula 4.6 to calculate the return using the modified Dietz methodology:

BMV:	$1,000,000
EMV:	$2,000,000
Contribution:	$900,000
Contribution date:	January 30
Distribution:	None
Distribution date:	N/a

Let's calculate the modified Dietz return using the following steps:

Step 1: Calculate the TWCF for each cash flow that took place during the measurement period.

$$TWCF = \sum_{CF^n}^{CF^1}\left[\left(\frac{\text{\# of Days Invested}}{\text{Total \# of Days in Period}}\right) \times \text{Cash Flow}\right]$$

$$TWCF = \left[\left(\frac{1}{31}\right) \times \$900,000\right] = \$29,032.26$$

The number of days the contributed assets were available for investment was 1 because the contribution took place on January 30—leaving only the 31st for any portfolio investments. The total number of days in the period (January) was 31, so the fraction of days available for investment relative to the total number of days in the period was 1/31. We simply multiply this fraction by the actual dollar amount of the cash flow ($900,000) to calculate the TWCF. The $29,032.26 represents the portion of the $900,000 contribution that we are actually going to apply toward the portfolio's return for the month. Now, let's calculate the modified Dietz return.

$$MDR = \left(\frac{MVE - MVB - Cont + Dist}{MVB + \sum(NTWCF)}\right)$$

$$MDR = \left(\frac{\$2,000,000 - \$1,000,000 - \$900,000 + \$0}{\$1,000,000 + \$29,032.26}\right)$$

$$MDR = \left(\frac{\$100,000}{\$1,029,032.26}\right) = 0.0972 \times 100 = 9.72\%$$

We can now compare these results to the results that we achieved using the cash flow adjusted dollar weighted return (formula 4.6), which we calculated to be 5.26%. This is in stark contrast to the return we calculated using the modified Dietz formula, which was 9.72%. The difference in returns clearly highlights the impact that cash flow timing has on performance.

Time Weighted Returns

Time weighted returns utilize many of the formulas already discussed in this chapter to create a very accurate way of calculating returns that account for cash flows during the review period. The only caveat is that it is necessary to value the portfolio every time there is a cash flow into or out of the portfolio, and this is not always possible. Single-manager portfolios can be valued relatively easily (depending on the underlying assets), but multiple-manager portfolios can be a bit of a challenge. For a pension plan, it would be nearly impossible to value every manager across every asset class each time monies are added, subtracted, or reallocated. Liquidity also plays a part, as some portfolio holdings might not trade on a daily basis and, as a result, may not have daily pricing available. Lastly, there is a cost factor involved in valuing a portfolio (or series of portfolios) each time a cash flow takes place. As a result, most pension plans calculate performance only at regular intervals (most often on a monthly basis).

In this case, the modified Dietz formula is a better choice because it represents a close approximation based on the amount and timing of the cash flows. The modified Dietz formula does not require that the portfolio be revalued on the date of each cash flow.

Formula 4.8 (Time Weighted Return)

$$TWR = [(1 + PDR^1) \times (1 + PDR^2) \times \ldots \times (1 + PDR^n)] - 1$$

where PDR^1 = Period decimal return from start date to end of business on the date previous to the initial cash flow.

PDR^2 = Period decimal return from the end of business on the date previous to the initial cash flow to end of business on the date previous to the second cash flow.

PDR^n = Period decimal return from the end of business on the date previous to the last cash flow to the end of the measurement period.

This formula is the same as the one used to calculate chain-linked returns (formula 4.3). The only difference is that we are adjusting each period return based on cash flows into and out of the portfolio. Whenever a cash flow occurs, we must value the portfolio as of the instant prior to the cash flow. To keep things simple, we will value the portfolio as of the end of the previous business day. So if a cash flow takes place on the 15th of a given month, we will value the portfolio as of the end of the previous business day. If the 15th falls on a Wednesday, then we will value the portfolio as of the end of business on Tuesday; if the 15th falls on a Monday, we will use the previous Friday as the valuation date. The same holds true for holidays.

From a total performance perspective, valuing the portfolio on the prior business day makes sense; however, it might be unfair to value the underlying investment manager's portfolio under any of these three conditions:

1. *Very large cash flow.* The time weighted return formula as stated previously assumes that the assets contributed to a portfolio are invested instantly on the date of the cash flow. In the real world, this is often not practical. Liquidity and market conditions may force an investment manager to invest newly contributed cash over a period of days, weeks, and sometimes months.
2. *Liquidity of both the market and the underlying investments slated for purchase.* An example of problems due to market liquidity would include periods of time when investors are holding back from the market or when investors are panic selling. In either case, it might be difficult or unwise to rush and purchase securities. An example of problems due to individual security liquidity would include the purchase of small-cap or micro-cap stocks that typically trade less frequently than large-cap stocks. In this case, a rush to purchase less liquid small-cap or micro-cap stocks might cause an artificial run-up in their prices, resulting in a negative impact on the underlying portfolio.
3. *Contribution dates.* Some investment managers specify certain dates in which they will accept new assets or make portfolio distributions. We see this more often in traditional commingled funds, hedge funds, and private equity funds. The cash flow dates can be stated as monthly, quarterly, semiannually, or at any interval the investment manager and underlying clients contractually agree to.

To better understand the time weighted return calculation, we calculate the return for the following portfolio based on the market values and cash flows indicated.

Example We made a $1,000,000 investment in the CAM portfolio on December 31. The portfolio's value at the end of January was $2,000,000.

During the month we made a contribution of $450,000 on January 15 and another contribution of $350,000 on January 30. Because we are required to value the portfolio as of the end of business on the dates previous to the cash flows, we valued the portfolio on January 14 at $1,050,000 and on January 29 at $1,575,000 (see Exhibits 4.6 and 4.7).

EXHIBIT 4.6 Data Table for Time Weighted Return Example

Date	Market Value	Cash Flow	Notes
1-Jan	$1,000,000		1st return period
14-Jan	$1,050,000		PDR[1]
15-Jan		$450,000	2nd return period
29-Jan	$1,575,000		PDR[2]
30-Jan		$350,000	3rd return period
31-Jan	$2,000,000		PDR[3]

EXHIBIT 4.7 Summary Table

Date	Market Value	Cash Flow	Notes	Time Weighted Return
1-Jan	$1,000,000		1st return period	
14-Jan	$1,050,000		PDR[1]	5.00%
15-Jan		$450,000	2nd return period	
29-Jan	$1,575,000		PDR[2]	5.00%
30-Jan		$350,000	3rd return period	
31-Jan	$2,000,000		PDR[3]	3.90%

Step 1: Calculate the individual period returns.

$$PDR^1 = \left(\frac{EMV - BMV - CF}{BMV + CF} \right)$$

$$PDR^1 = \left(\frac{\$1,050,000 - \$1,000,000 - \$0}{\$1,000,000 + \$0} \right)$$

$$PDR^1 = \left(\frac{\$50,000}{\$1,000,000} \right)$$

$$PDR^1 = 0.05$$

$$PDR^1 = 5.00\%$$

$$PDR^2 = \left(\frac{EMV - BMV - CF}{BMV + CF} \right)$$

$$PDR^2 = \left(\frac{\$1,575,000 - \$1,050,000 - \$450,000}{\$1,050,000 + \$450,000} \right)$$

$$PDR^2 = \left(\frac{\$75,000}{\$1,500,000} \right)$$

$$PDR^2 = 0.05$$

$$PDR^2 = 5.00\%$$

$$PDR^3 = \left(\frac{EMV - BMV - CF}{BMV + CF} \right)$$

$$PDR^3 = \left(\frac{\$2,000,000 - \$1,575,000 - \$350,000}{\$1,575,000 + \$350,000} \right)$$

$$PDR^3 = \left(\frac{\$75,000}{\$1,925,000} \right)$$

$$PDR^3 = 0.039$$

$$PDR^3 = 3.90\%$$

Using the returns calculated for each individual return period, we can now apply formula 4.8 to calculate the time weighted return for the period (the month of January in this case).

$$TWR = [(1 + PDR^1) \times (1 + PDR^2) \times (1 + PDR^3)] - 1$$
$$TWR = (1.05 \times 1.05 \times 1.039) - 1$$
$$TWR = 1.1455 - 1$$
$$TWR = 0.1455 \text{ (in decimal format)}$$
$$TWR = 14.55\% \text{ (in percent format)}$$

PRACTICAL APPLICATION OF PERFORMANCE FORMULAS

Now that we can effectively calculate performance on an absolute basis, we can begin to analyze the performance compared to relevant benchmarks. A benchmark is a group of financial instruments that are pooled together to represent a particular element within an asset class, an entire asset class, or the entire market. For example, the Frank Russell 2000 Index (Russell 2000) is designed to represent the returns of the U.S. small cap market. The Russell 2000 is further subdivided into growth and value indexes for accurate style comparisons.

Equity Benchmarks

Benchmark selection is a critical element of the analytical process because it effectively allows us to compare apples to apples. Exhibit 4.8 provides a list of some of the more popular U.S. equity benchmarks along with descriptions and some factual data. This exhibit breaks the range of benchmarks into categories based on market capitalization and investment style. Exhibit 4.9 is similar to the previous exhibit, only it illustrates the range of non-U.S. equity benchmarks and breaks the list out by geographical region and investment style.

EXHIBIT 4.8   U.S. Equity Benchmarks

Market Capitalization	Investment Style		
	Value	Core	Growth
All-Cap	Russell 3000 Value	Wilshire 5000 Russell 3000	Russell 3000 Growth
Large-Cap	Barra/S&P 500 Value Russell 1000 Value Wilshire Large Value	S&P 500 Dow Jones Russell 1000 Wilshire 5000	Barra/S&P 500 Growth Russell 1000 Growth Wilshire Large Growth
Mid-Cap	Barra/S&P Mid Value Russell 2500 Value Wilshire Midcap Value	S&P MidCap Russell 2500 Wilshire MidCap	Barra/S&P Mid Growth Russell 2500 Growth Wilshire MidCap Growth
Small-Cap	Barra/S&P Small Value Russell 2000 Value Wilshire Small Value	S&P SmallCap Russell 2000 Wilshire Smallcap	Barra/S&P Small Growth Russell 2000 Growth Wilshire Small Growth
Micro-Cap		DFA 9-10 Wilshire Microcap Callan Microcap	

EXHIBIT 4.9 Non-U.S. Equity Benchmarks

Geographical Region	Investment Style		
	Value	Core	Growth
World	MSCI World	MSCI World FT World	MSCI World
EAFE	MSCI EAFE	MSCI EAFE FT EAFE	MSCI EAFE
Developing Markets	MSCI Individual Country	MSCI Individual Country FT Individual Country	MSCI Individual Country
Emerging Markets	MSCI Individual Country	MSCI Emerging Markets	MSCI Individual Country

Now that we have discussed how to calculate performance and have identified a wide variety of potential benchmarks, we can start to apply them to the case study. Using the data from the CAM Investment Manager report shown in Exhibit 4.1, we can target some of the U.S. small-cap benchmarks identified in Exhibit 4.8.

You may remember from the RFI that we did not ask the manager to provide annualized returns or to make any benchmark comparisons, but CAM did this anyway. Note that CAM uses the S&P 600 SmallCap Index for comparative purposes. However, our discussion on investment benchmarks identified several small-cap "value" benchmarks that might be a more appropriate comparison than the broad or "core" S&P 600 index.

In any case, we will take the historical monthly returns that CAM provided and calculate the product's performance utilizing the performance formulas covered earlier in this chapter. Using the chain-linking and annualizing formulas, we calculate returns for CAM and compare those returns to the S&P 600 SmallCap Value Index as well as the style neutral S&P 600 SmallCap Index (see Exhibit 4.10).

The highlighted rows represent the value added, or the rate of return for the CAM portfolio in excess of the benchmark return over the same period of time. This exhibit clearly indicates that CAM has performed very well relative to both the small-cap index and the small-cap value index. In fact, the only period in which the CAM portfolio underperformed either benchmark was in the three-year annualized return versus the small-cap value benchmark—and it was only by a modest 0.1%. Since the portfolio's inception, January 1998, it had outperformed the small-cap benchmark by 5.2% (520 basis points) and the small-cap value benchmark by 5.00%

EXHIBIT 4.10 Relative Annualized Performance (Periods Ended June 2003)

	YTD	1 Year	3 Years	5 Years	Inception
CAM	15.9%	–2.7%	7.9%	8.6%	9.7%
S&P SmallCap Value Index	13.0%	–8.4%	8.0%	3.8%	4.8%
Value added	*2.9%*	*5.7%*	*–0.1%*	*4.7%*	*5.0%*
S&P SmallCap Index	12.9%	–3.6%	2.4%	3.7%	4.5%
Value added	*3.0%*	*0.8%*	*5.5%*	*4.8%*	*5.2%*

(500 basis points) on an annualized basis. For future reference, make note that a "basis point" represents a 0.01% return and can be stated as either positive or negative. This exhibit clearly shows that CAM has performed well in the recent past (year-to-date, one-year periods) and over the longer term (five-year and inception periods).

However, the three-year comparative return is more subdued. We can deduce that something had a negative impact on relative performance roughly two to three years ago. To gain a better understanding of when this occurred, we review the calendar year performance in Exhibit 4.11.

The relative performance table in Exhibit 4.11 indicates what we had expected—that the CAM portfolio had experienced some performance problems in the middle of its track record relative to the small-cap value benchmark. Specifically, the CAM portfolio underperformed the small-cap value index in years 2000 and 2001.

Exhibit 4.12 breaks down the performance of the CAM portfolio and contrasts it to the performance of the benchmarks on a monthly basis. The table lists the monthly returns and calculates the value added in the columns to the right. The value added is simply the difference of the return of the CAM portfolio minus that of the benchmark. The highlighted numbers represent negative relative performance. This table is simple in design, but tells plenty about the portfolio's performance history and specifically about its performance consistency.

EXHIBIT 4.11 Calendar Year Performance

	1998	1999	2000	2001	2002	2003 (YTD)
CAM	0.9%	24.1%	14.8%	10.7%	–9.6%	15.9%
S&P SmallCap Value Index	–5.1%	3.0%	20.9%	13.1%	–14.5%	13.0%
Value added	*5.9%*	*21.0%*	*–6.1%*	*–2.4%*	*4.9%*	*2.9%*
S&P SmallCap Index	–1.3%	12.4%	11.8%	6.5%	–14.6%	12.9%
Value added	*2.2%*	*11.7%*	*3.0%*	*4.2%*	*5.0%*	*3.0%*

EXHIBIT 4.12 Monthly Performance Comparison

	Monthly Performance History			Value Added CAM Portfolio Versus	
	CAM Portfolio	Small Cap Index	Small Cap Value Index	Small Cap Index	Small Cap Value Index
Jan-98	-1.23%	-2.0%	-2.1%	0.72%	0.84%
Feb-98	8.34%	9.1%	8.4%	-0.77%	-0.03%
Mar-98	5.67%	3.8%	5.0%	1.85%	0.71%
Apr-98	1.21%	0.6%	0.7%	0.62%	0.56%
May-98	-5.21%	-5.3%	-4.4%	0.08%	-0.84%
Jun-98	1.89%	0.3%	-0.1%	1.60%	1.94%
Jul-98	-8.34%	-7.7%	-9.2%	-0.69%	0.91%
Aug-98	-19.45%	-19.3%	-18.0%	-0.15%	-1.41%
Sep-98	6.45%	6.1%	5.3%	0.33%	1.15%
Oct-98	4.89%	4.6%	4.4%	0.25%	0.52%
Nov-98	5.42%	5.6%	4.3%	-0.21%	1.15%
Dec-98	4.99%	6.4%	3.9%	-1.40%	1.06%
Jan-99	-0.70%	-1.3%	-1.1%	0.56%	0.45%
Feb-99	-7.21%	-9.0%	-8.1%	1.80%	0.93%
Mar-99	-0.20%	1.3%	-0.4%	-1.49%	0.19%
Apr-99	7.21%	6.6%	8.7%	0.60%	-1.50%
May-99	4.51%	2.4%	4.0%	2.08%	0.52%

(Continued)

EXHIBIT 4.12 (*Continued*)

	Monthly Performance History			Value Added CAM Portfolio Versus	
	CAM Portfolio	Small Cap Index	Small Cap Value Index	Small Cap Index	Small Cap Value Index
Jun-99	5.82%	5.7%	6.1%	0.13%	-0.25%
Jul-99	0.20%	-0.9%	-1.6%	1.08%	1.76%
Aug-99	-5.12%	-4.4%	-4.2%	-0.72%	-0.93%
Sep-99	1.90%	0.4%	-1.8%	1.48%	3.74%
Oct-99	1.10%	-0.3%	-2.3%	1.35%	3.41%
Nov-99	5.20%	4.2%	2.2%	1.02%	2.96%
Dec-99	10.45%	8.2%	2.7%	2.23%	7.71%
Jan-00	-2.30%	-3.1%	-5.1%	0.80%	2.82%
Feb-00	15.34%	13.4%	4.5%	1.95%	10.82%
Mar-00	-6.54%	-3.7%	3.7%	-2.84%	-10.23%
Apr-00	-1.76%	-1.7%	0.7%	-0.05%	-2.46%
May-00	-2.11%	-3.0%	-1.6%	0.85%	-0.48%
Jun-00	4.54%	5.9%	2.9%	-1.37%	1.67%
Jul-00	-2.17%	-2.5%	2.0%	0.29%	-4.14%
Aug-00	8.26%	8.9%	5.8%	-0.60%	2.42%
Sep-00	-1.16%	-2.7%	-0.2%	1.56%	-0.96%
Oct-00	1.17%	0.6%	0.5%	0.54%	0.68%
Nov-00	-7.23%	-10.4%	-6.6%	3.18%	-0.62%
Dec-00	10.34%	12.3%	14.1%	-1.98%	-3.78%
Jan-01	6.79%	4.3%	7.9%	2.50%	-1.13%
Feb-01	-4.56%	-6.1%	-4.2%	1.54%	-0.34%

Outperformance Period

Underperformance Period

Mar-01	-3.21%	-4.6%	-4.2%	1.38%	0.94%
Apr-01	7.54%	7.6%	6.0%	-0.08%	1.52%
May-01	3.45%	1.9%	2.5%	1.54%	0.90%
Jun-01	1.24%	3.7%	3.8%	-2.43%	-2.58%
Jul-01	-1.45%	-1.7%	-0.9%	0.22%	-0.51%
Aug-01	-0.65%	-2.3%	-1.6%	1.63%	0.96%
Sep-01	-15.55%	-13.5%	-14.3%	-2.03%	-1.24%
Oct-01	5.21%	5.3%	4.6%	-0.12%	0.64%
Nov-01	7.54%	7.3%	8.0%	0.22%	-0.46%
Dec-01	6.54%	6.8%	7.2%	-0.23%	-0.68%
Jan-02	2.32%	0.9%	1.9%	1.45%	0.45%
Feb-02	-1.34%	-1.7%	-0.4%	0.38%	-0.91%
Mar-02	10.89%	7.9%	8.7%	2.99%	2.20%
Apr-02	5.11%	2.8%	4.1%	2.28%	1.02%
May-02	-5.21%	-4.1%	-3.8%	-1.07%	-1.42%
Jun-02	-3.43%	-5.2%	-4.5%	1.74%	1.04%
Jul-02	-15.87%	-14.1%	-16.3%	-1.75%	0.39%
Aug-02	0.02%	1.0%	-0.1%	-0.93%	0.15%
Sep-02	-6.50%	-6.1%	-7.4%	-0.38%	0.86%
Oct-02	3.45%	3.2%	2.0%	0.25%	1.44%
Nov-02	6.54%	5.2%	5.4%	1.34%	1.14%
Dec-02	-3.21%	-3.4%	-2.6%	0.16%	-0.57%
Jan-03	-3.45%	-3.4%	-4.1%	-0.01%	0.68%
Feb-03	-3.21%	-3.2%	-3.7%	-0.01%	0.49%
Mar-03	0.23%	0.8%	-0.3%	-0.56%	0.54%
Apr-03	9.17%	8.1%	9.0%	1.05%	0.13%
May-03	8.76%	8.1%	9.3%	0.70%	-0.56%
Jun-03	4.21%	2.6%	3.0%	1.61%	1.24%

The CAM portfolio significantly outperformed the small-cap value benchmark in the period beginning July 1999 and ending February 2000. This is significant because it coincides with the end of the bull run in the equity market, particularly the final stages of the technology bubble. This information is contrary to what we would normally expect a value manager to show for this period, as value was generally out of favor. Investment managers and products that had a *growth* philosophy or style largely dominated over this period. Over that eight-month period, the CAM portfolio returned 28.2% versus a –5.8% return for the small-cap value benchmark and a 17.6% return for the broad small-cap benchmark. These comparisons are extraordinary and very unusual for a value manager over that period of time.

This period of extreme outperformance was followed immediately by a longer period of underperformance that began the following month, March 2000, and ended a year later in February 2001. Over this period of relative underperformance, the CAM portfolio gained a modest 3.8% versus a gain of 26.0% for the small-cap value benchmark and a loss of –0.4% for the broad small-cap benchmark. In addition, the CAM portfolio experienced some choppy performance in the period beginning June 2001 and ending in February 2002. The examination of the performance numbers relative to the benchmarks on a monthly basis has graphically illustrated that the CAM portfolio needs to be examined more closely over specific periods if we are going to gain a thorough understanding of the portfolio and, ultimately, make an accurate assessment of the portfolio manager's skill.

Because the CAM portfolio returns have several performance periods that seem out of line with the small-cap value benchmark and possibly more in line with the small-cap growth benchmark, Exhibit 4.13 takes the monthly comparison table and adds the small-cap growth benchmark for comparative purposes. The exhibit also focuses exclusively on the two periods of out/underperformance previously identified.

The highlighted numbers in the "value added versus" columns represent months of negative relative performance. A quick glance at this table indicates that the CAM portfolio acted more like the growth index during the first period under review (7/99–2/00), as the relative performance numbers are smaller when compared to the growth index versus the value index. The table further indicates that the CAM portfolio achieved returns somewhere in between the value and growth benchmarks over the subsequent period (3/00–2/01). In summary, the table shows that the CAM portfolio performed in exactly the opposite manner in each period, as it outperformed the value index and underperformed the growth index in period one, which reversed in the following period. The summary performance statistics can be found in Exhibit 4.14.

EXHIBIT 4.13 Monthly Performance Comparison versus Small-Cap Value and Growth Indexes for Outlier Periods

| | Monthly Performance History | | | Value Added Versus | |
	CAM Portfolio	Small Cap Value Index	Small Cap Growth Index	Small Cap Value Index	Small Cap Growth Index
Jul-99	0.20%	−1.6%	−0.2%	1.76%	0.44%
Aug-99	−5.12%	−4.2%	−4.6%	−0.93%	−0.53%
Sep-99	1.90%	−1.8%	2.4%	3.74%	−0.47%
Oct-99	1.10%	−2.3%	1.5%	3.41%	−0.41%
Nov-99	5.20%	2.2%	5.8%	2.96%	−0.57%
Dec-99	10.45%	2.7%	12.4%	7.71%	−1.97%
Jan-00	−2.30%	−5.1%	−1.4%	2.82%	−0.92%
Feb-00	15.34%	4.5%	20.9%	10.82%	−5.52%
Mar-00	−6.54%	3.7%	−9.1%	−10.23%	2.58%
Apr-00	−1.76%	0.7%	−3.8%	−2.46%	2.05%
May-00	−2.11%	−1.6%	−4.3%	−0.48%	2.17%
Jun-00	4.54%	2.9%	9.1%	1.67%	−4.55%
Jul-00	−2.17%	2.0%	−6.8%	−4.14%	4.67%
Aug-00	8.26%	5.8%	12.1%	2.42%	−3.79%
Sep-00	−1.16%	−0.2%	−5.3%	−0.96%	4.16%
Oct-00	1.17%	0.5%	0.8%	0.68%	0.39%
Nov-00	−7.23%	−6.6%	−15.0%	−0.62%	7.77%
Dec-00	10.34%	14.1%	9.2%	−3.78%	1.15%
Jan-01	6.79%	7.9%	0.1%	−1.13%	6.71%
Feb-01	−4.56%	−4.2%	−8.5%	−0.34%	3.93%

EXHIBIT 4.14 Cumulative Performance in Outlier Periods

| | | | Benchmarks | |
Out/Underperformance Periods	CAM Portfolio	Small Cap	Small Cap Value	Small Cap Growth
July 1999 to February 2000	28.2%	17.6%	−5.8%	40.2%
Value added		10.6%	34.0%	−12.0%
March 2000 to February 2001	3.8%	−0.4%	26.0%	−22.7%
Value added		4.2%	−22.2%	26.5%

Up/Down Market Analysis

Another very effective type of performance analysis takes into account the movement in the overall market. The up/down chart uses a benchmark's returns as a starting point and compares the returns of the benchmark for each negative period (in our case, months) to the corresponding return for the portfolio under review (the *down* part of the analysis). The same is done for months where the benchmark experiences positive returns (the *up* part of the analysis). We then simply calculate a cumulative return for all the negative and positive months respectively for the benchmark and the portfolio under review.

Exhibits 4.15 and 4.16 are examples of CAM's up/down chart versus both the small-cap value index and the broad small-cap index.

Focusing on the down market aspect of each of these illustrations (the two bars on the left side of the charts), we note that the CAM portfolio managed to preserve some capital when the market moved into negative territory. In Exhibit 4.15, we can see that the CAM portfolio had declined a cumulative –72.6% versus –75.9% for the small-cap value index. This means that on a cumulative basis, the portfolio has proven to be a bit more defensive than the index. The numbers are similar when compared to the broad small-cap index in Exhibit 4.16 (at –76.3% versus –78.5% for the index). What the numbers do not tell is how the portfolio manager was able to achieve that relative performance or how much additional risk, if any, the manager took on to outperform the benchmark in down markets.

When we look at the performance of the CAM portfolio relative to either benchmark during positive periods (months), we see that the portfo-

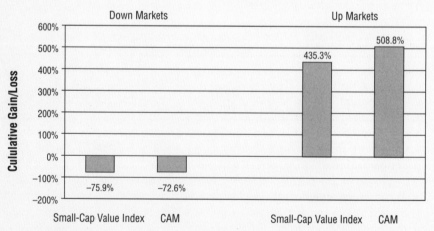

EXHIBIT 4.15 Up/Down Chart: CAM versus Small-Cap Value Index

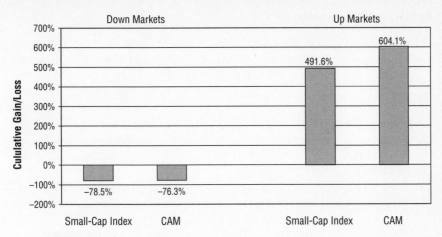

EXHIBIT 4.16   Up/Down Chart: CAM versus Broad Small-Cap Index

lio had been a star when the market was moving up. On a cumulative basis, the CAM portfolio outperformed the small-cap value index by 74% (509% versus 435% for the index) and the broad small-cap index by 112% (604% versus 492% for the index) in positive periods. However, we have already discovered that the CAM portfolio experienced the largest component of its relative outperformance during a single eight-month period (7/99–2/00). Because we have already flagged this period as an outlier (as the returns appear to be more indicative of the growth style than the value style) and have agreed to perform more analytics to get to the bottom of things, we will exclude those months from this particular analysis and see what the CAM portfolio was able to do once the flagged period was removed.

Exhibits 4.17 and 4.18 represent the same up/down charts as before; however, we have excluded the outlier period (July 1999 to February 2000) from review.

What a difference. The exclusion of the eight-month outlier period had a profound impact on the up market comparisons, particularly when we look at the performance of the CAM portfolio relative to the small-cap value index (Exhibit 4.17). The cumulative performance comparison in up months went from an outperformance in excess of 70% (including the outlier period) to an underperformance of –34% (excluding the outlier period). However, the CAM portfolio still managed to outperform the broad small-cap index significantly (55%) in the up (positive) months. When we review the down market comparisons in Exhibits 4.17 and 4.18, we can see that the CAM portfolio still managed to outperform each index during down (negative) months.

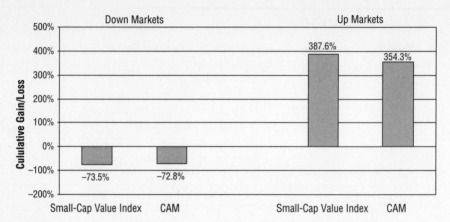

EXHIBIT 4.17 Up/Down Chart versus Small-Cap Value Index—Excluding Outlier Period

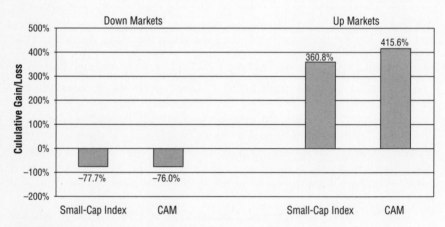

EXHIBIT 4.18 Up/Down Chart versus Broad Small-Cap Index—Excluding Outlier Period

When I review a manager whose portfolio experiences a period of extreme outperformance or underperformance, I like to remove the period in question to see how the portfolio performs in *normal* circumstances. It is essential to gain a full understanding of what happened during the outlier period before we can make an informed decision regarding the product. These types of questions usually spark some interesting discussions during the interview phase of the investment manager analysis process.

Peer Group Comparison

In addition to analyzing an investment product against appropriate benchmarks, peer group comparisons are also a popular method of assessing relative performance. A peer group is simply a group (also referred to as a universe) of investment products with similar investment objectives. Several consulting firms calculate peer group universes on a regular basis. In addition, most (if not all) of the third party databases discussed in Chapter 2 have peer universes built right into the software. Many of the third party databases available for purchase also give users the ability to create peer universes based on their own unique sets of criteria. However, a peer group analysis is simple to create in a spreadsheet if you have the underlying return data.

Exhibit 4.19 contains information about various breakpoints in the

EXHIBIT 4.19   Peer Group Comparison—Small-Cap Value Universe

Peer Group Breakpoints

	Performance Breakpoints (%)			
Percentile	YTD	1 Year	3 Years	5 Years
5th	19.7	−0.2	13.7	9.1
25th	16.3	−3.5	10.4	7.6
50th	14.2	−8.0	8.1	5.6
75th	12.7	−10.2	7.7	3.8
95th	9.3	−13.5	3.1	1.0

CAM and Small-Cap Indexes Performance

	Performance (%)			
	YTD	1 Year	3 Years	5 Years
CAM	15.9	−2.7	7.9	8.6
Small-cap	12.9	−3.6	2.4	3.7
Small-cap value	13.0	−8.4	8.0	3.8
Small-cap growth	12.7	1.2	−4.5	2.0

Ranking within Peer Universe

	Percentile Rankings			
	YTD	1 Year	3 Years	5 Years
CAM	30th	20th	61st	14th
Small-cap	70th	27th	98th	77th
Small-cap value	61st	55th	54th	75th
Small-cap growth	75th	1st	100th	89th

small-cap value peer universe in the top part of the table and then lists CAM's portfolio returns as well as the benchmark returns in both absolute format (under the heading "performance") and in relation to the peer universe (under the heading "percentile rankings").

The data for the peer universe listed under the heading "performance breakpoints" is determined by calculating the percentile ranking of each product's return in the peer universe for each period under review. A product that has a return in the first percentile of returns in the peer universe has performed in the top 1 percent of the group—or another way of stating this is to say that a product that has first percentile performance has beaten 99 percent of the products in the peer universe. Conversely, a product that performs in the 100th percentile has performed worse than all the other products in the peer universe. A product that has returned in the 50th percentile has performed right in the middle of the peer group. Note that in Exhibit 4.19 we do not show the 1st and 100th percentiles. Instead, we start with the 5th percentile and end with the 95th percentile. This is done to eliminate any outliers that may stretch the performance range beyond what is reasonable and to help avoid errors in percentile rankings due to the inclusion of products that don't fit perfectly in the peer category (more on this later on). Looking at the YTD column as a point of reference, we see that the CAM portfolio's 15.9% return places it at the 30th percentile in the peer universe. The percentile ranking improves to 20th over the one-year period, falls dramatically to 61st over three years, and increases, just as dramatically, to the 14th percentile over the five-year period. Exhibit 4.20 is a very popular way of graphically showing the data in Exhibit 4.19.

This graph is commonly referred to as a quartile chart because the breakpoints separate into four return ranges. The first quartile ranges from the 5th to 25th percentile, the second quartile ranges from the 25th to 50th percentile, the third quartile ranges from the 50th to the 75th quartile, and the fourth quartile ranges from the 75th to the 95th percentile. As the chart indicates, the top box represents the first quartile and the bottom box represents the fourth quartile. The CAM portfolio, which is represented in this chart by a bold "**c**," had been a consistent second-quartile performer over the YTD, one-year, and three-year periods. However, the portfolio moved firmly into the first quartile over the five-year period.

The five-year quartile distribution also indicates that more than half of the small-cap manager universe outperformed the small-cap benchmarks over that period of time. We can graphically see this in Exhibit 4.20 by looking at where the three benchmarks rank over the five-year period. The chart illustrates that all three benchmarks ranked in the 3rd or 4th quartiles. We should keep this in mind when making any assessment of CAM's relative outperformance over historical periods.

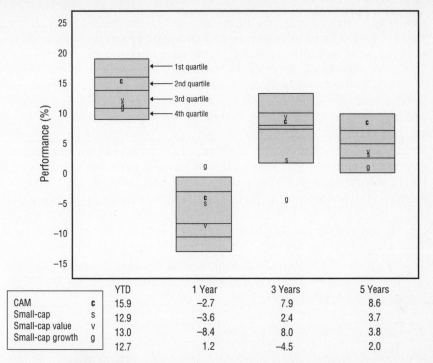

EXHIBIT 4.20   Quartile Chart—Small-Cap Value Universe

		YTD	1 Year	3 Years	5 Years
CAM	c	15.9	−2.7	7.9	8.6
Small-cap	s	12.9	−3.6	2.4	3.7
Small-cap value	v	13.0	−8.4	8.0	3.8
Small-cap growth	g	12.7	1.2	−4.5	2.0

AIMR'S PERFORMANCE PRESENTATION STANDARDS (PPS)

Prior to the performance presentation standards discussed in this section, investment managers were free to report performance in any manner that they saw fit. As you can imagine, that was problematic. Issues such as inconsistency, inaccuracy, and deceptive reporting made it hard to efficiently analyze a group of potential investment managers. Thankfully, AIMR's Performance Presentation Standards (PPS) changed all that in the 1990s. Exhibit 4.21 highlights AIMR's time line.

In this section of the chapter, we will briefly cover the provisions and requirements established in the April 2001 AIMR PPS guidebook. The complete guidebook can be downloaded free of charge from AIMR's web site at www.aimr.com. In addition, the web site includes a great deal of data relating to performance issues reviewed in this book, such as attribution standards.

The AIMR PPS consists of five main provisions that cover the traditional

EXHIBIT 4.21　AIMR's Performance Presentation Standards Time Line

1987	The Financial Analyst Federation's committee for PPS publishes the first version of PPS in the *Financial Analysts Journal*
1995	AIMR sponsors the Global Investment Performance Standards (GIPS) committee to develop global performance standards
1999	AIMR officially endorses the GIPS
2000	AIMR establishes the Investment Performance Council (IPC) to help implement the GIPS on a worldwide basis
April 2001	GIPS is adopted or in the process of being adopted by 25 countries

asset classes and an additional four provisions that cover various alternative asset classes. Each of the nine provisions contains a number of requirements that need to be met before an investment management firm can claim AIMP PPS compliance. In addition, each provision contains some recommendations that do not need to be followed, but are strongly suggested. Here are some of the specific requirements under each provision. A full list can be obtained via AIMR's web site.

Provisions for Traditional Asset Classes

1. *Input data.* Rules for the inclusion and exclusion of performance data to ensure fair and comparable investment performance presentations.

   ■ All data necessary to calculate AIMR compliant performance records must be available.
   ■ Portfolio valuations must be based on market value.
   ■ Portfolio valuation must be done at a minimum on a quarterly basis.

2. *Calculation methodology.* Rules to ensure all investment returns are calculated using the same calculation methodologies.

   ■ Total return, which includes all realized and unrealized gains, must be used.
   ■ Returns must be time weighted.
   ■ Composites must be asset weighted.
   ■ Trading costs must be deducted from performance.

3. *Composite construction.* When investment firms report performance for a given product, it is in the form of a composite. An investment management firm calculates a composite by aggregating all the portfolios they manage with similar investment objectives.

■ All fee-paying, discretionary accounts must be included in at least one composite.

■ New portfolio accounts must be added on a timely basis.

■ Composites must include terminated accounts in the historical record.

■ Carve-outs cannot be treated as separate composites.

4. *Disclosures.* While the PPS affords greater consistency in performance reporting by specifying rules that must be adhered to in creating performance presentations, exceptions do exist. The performance disclosures provide the investment management firms a chance to comment on the data underlying the performance presentations so that we can put the performance in its proper context.

■ Definition of firm used to determine total assets under management.

■ Availability of complete list and description of all the firm's composites.

■ Minimum asset level (if any) below which portfolio are not included in a composite.

■ Use of derivatives.

■ Statement on whether fees are reported net or gross of management fees and other fees paid by the firm's clients.

■ Currency used in performance calculation and presentation.

5. *Presentation and Reporting.* The PPS provides a format for reporting the results of the previous four provisions. Once again, the goal is to make performance comparisons relevant by making the actual presentation of results as consistent as possible.

Provisions for Nontraditional Asset Classes

6. *Real estate.* Due to the illiquid nature and the general lack of readily available secondary pricing in real estate, a separate set of performance presentation guidelines was created to directly address this asset class.

7. *Venture and private placements.* AIMR developed another set of criteria for this asset class in recognition of the issues that present themselves regarding performance calculation methodologies and timing.

8. *Wrap-fee accounts.* AIMR defines a wrap account in the same way as the SEC. Based on its unique characteristics, separate standards were created.

9. *After-tax performance.* A set of restrictions was created to allow for the effective and efficient evaluation of tax implications as they relate to the performance presentations.

COMPOSITE ANALYSIS

A composite is used by investment managers to consolidate all of the port-folios that they manage into a single return stream for marketing purposes. As highlighted in the preceding AIMR PPS section, there are rules with re-gard to how a manager can construct these composites. However, there is still plenty of room for ambiguity.

As an investment manager analyst, it is incumbent upon you not only to understand how an investment manager has constructed their compos-ite, but to look into the statistics to see if any abnormalities exist. While AIMR does not require a specific format in which managers are to report their composite information, investment firms have largely adopted their strongly worded suggestions.

Exhibit 4.22 displays the composite performance disclosures for CAM Asset Management.

We have already examined the performance for the CAM small-cap value product, but the information regarding the composite is very helpful in evaluating and understanding the product's performance. The standard deviation figure, a common measure of portfolio risk, will be discussed in detail in the next chapter.

Number of Portfolios

This column tells us that CAM ended its first year of operation with just one portfolio under management, but the number of portfolios increased considerably over the subsequent periods, with the greatest expansion oc-curring in 1999 and 2000. Given that the small cap product experienced excellent absolute and relative performance (versus the broad small-cap in-dex), the growth in client accounts is not surprising. Account growth slowed down in 2002 and in the first six months of 2003.

The disclosures do not, however, mention if CAM has lost any ac-counts. Despite the fact that CAM's total number of clients grew, it is pos-sible that clients left as well. This can be helpful information to see when trying to determine how consistent a manager's client base is.

Composite Dispersion

This is a lot of information that relates directly to how consistently the investment manager manages different accounts within a composite. The figure is derived simply from subtracting the return of the account with the lowest return over the period (annually in this case) from the return of the account with the highest return for the same period. In other words, the composite dispersion number calculates the range of returns

EXHIBIT 4.22 CAM's Composite Performance Disclosures

CAM Asset Management
Small Capitalization Equity Composite

Year	Gross Return	Net Return	Index Return	Number of Portfolios	Composite Dispersion	Year-End Composite Assets (US$Mil)	Year-End Firm Assets (US$Mil)	% of Firm Assets
6/30/2003	16.89%	15.89%	12.97%	40	2%	$375.6	$467.1	80%
2002	-8.60%	-9.60%	-14.47%	37	4%	$311.1	$377.3	82%
2001	11.74%	10.74%	13.10%	35	4%	$338.1	$383.2	88%
2000	15.78%	14.78%	20.86%	27	5%	$275.9	$299.5	92%
1999	25.08%	24.08%	3.03%	16	3%	$124.2	$124.2	100%
1998	1.85%	0.85%	-5.06%	1	0%	$ 18.0	$ 18.0	100%
Standard deviation	22.65%		21.83%					

Notes: CAM is an SEC-registered investment adviser that specializes in small-capitalization equity management. The results presented herein have been prepared and presented in compliance with the AIMR PPS and GIPS for the entire period shown. Monthly composite results have been linked geometrically and are asset weighted by beginning-of-month asset values of included portfolios. Monthly results of included portfolios are time weighted. The composite is managed using a value-oriented, bottom-up investment strategy. The benchmark used in this report is the S&P 600 SmallCap Index. The index returns include dividends. The composite is composed of all small cap accounts managed against the aforementioned index whose investment guidelines do not differ materially from the guidelines established by CAM for its small cap accounts. Net product performance reflects the payment of management fees and trading costs. CAM charges a flat 1.00% management fee for accounts with assets less than $25 million and 0.80% for accounts with assets over $25 million. The fee schedule is described in full in CAM's Form ADV, which is available on request. The composite was created on January 31, 1998, and all numbers and figures were calculated using and reported in U.S. dollars. The composite contains only fee-paying accounts. Leverage was not used in the management of any of the accounts included in this composite. There is no minimum size criterion for composite membership.

from high to low. This number is meaningful because we calculate most, if not all, performance-related statistics from the reported composite average. As a result, our expectations are then based on the average weighted return in the composite. It is important to know that it is possible to invest in a specific product and receive a return that is higher or lower than the reported average.

However, dispersion is not necessarily a bad thing. Investment managers that invest accounts from a model portfolio and rebalance all accounts when the model changes tend to have tighter dispersion numbers. In contrast, a manager that lets a portfolio "age" can experience wider swings in account dispersion—especially during volatile periods of time.

While the high-low dispersion figure is useful, it can lead us to some questionable conclusions. A composite with a great number of accounts may have a few outlier portfolios that stretch the dispersion figure, leading the analyst to infer that dispersion is generally high. To resolve this issue, the analyst can request the underlying portfolio returns for each account and can calculate the percentage of accounts with returns within one standard deviation of the mean and, if necessary, within two standard deviations of the mean.

Step 1: Calculate the average return for the period (yearly in this case)

$$\text{Average Account Return} = \frac{\sum \text{AAR}^{1\cdots}}{\text{\# Accounts}}$$

where AAR^1 = Annual account return for year 1 for each account in the composite.

Note: This formula includes only accounts that were fully invested for the entire year. Accounts that were invested for a portion of a given year are not included in that year, but would be included in the following year (assuming they stayed in the composite for the full year). Accounts with large cash inflows and/or large cash outflows during a given year might experience additional dispersion compared to accounts that did not experience large inflows/outflows because the timing of the asset inflow/outflow might impact returns. In this case, the analyst might elect to exclude these accounts from the calculation.

Step 2: Calculate the standard deviation of accounts for the period. The formula for this statistic will be covered in detail in the next chapter.

Step 3: Determine how many of the composite accounts have returns within +/– one standard deviation of the average account return and take that number as a percentage of the total number of accounts. This gives you the percentage based on number of accounts. It is also helpful to calculate this statistic in relation to assets as opposed to number of accounts. To do this, add the assets from each of the accounts that fall within one standard deviation of the average account and take that sum as a percentage of the total assets in the composite.

Year-End Composite/Firm Assets

The "composite assets" column goes hand in hand with the number of accounts column. When reviewed together, they give the analyst a very clear indication of the product's development over time. By focusing on either column in isolation, you run the risk of not seeing the big picture. For example, it is possible to lose accounts but see a substantial increase in assets under management. This could be due to market appreciation on the remaining accounts or to the addition of a single large account or a combination of both.

To remedy this, I typically request the following additional information:

- Number of accounts gained each year.
- Number of accounts lost each year.
- Amount of assets redeemed each year.
- Amount of assets gained each year.

Armed with this additional information, the analyst can quickly determine what influenced the composite's asset growth—inflow of new accounts, inclusion of new accounts with large asset base, or market appreciation. The math also works when assets decline rather than increase.

The total firm assets column tells us how big the total firm is and gives us a good indication as to a given product's importance to the firm. The last column in the performance disclosures ("% of firm assets") is simply the ratio of the product's assets taken as a percentage of the total firm assets. The higher the percentage, the more important the product is likely to be to the firm's revenue base. However, percentage of assets as an indicator of contribution to overall firm revenues can be misleading when the firm in question also manages products with incentive (performance) fees, such as hedge funds, private equity funds, and other "alternative" asset classes. It is not uncommon for incentive fees to represent between 20% and 30% of the absolute profit generated by the product. As a result, it is possible for a firm to generate more revenue from alternative asset classes despite a lower asset base.

Comparing the composite and firm assets stated in CAM's composite disclosures, we can also see that the amounts differ from the figures we got from the third-party database after running the screen (Exhibit 2.4). This could be a simple error or something more. In any case, it gives us something to follow up with when we speak to the manager.

Fine Print

What would disclosures be without the fine print? The performance disclosures shown in Exhibit 4.22 appear at the bottom of the report. While no one enjoys reading the fine print, it is an essential part of the analysis. A great deal of information can be obtained simply by reading through the notes section of the performance disclosures.

The notes in CAM's performance disclosures tell us that the performance figures were "prepared and presented in compliance with the AIMR PPS and GIPS for the entire period shown." As a result, we now know that CAM claims to have adhered to all of the regulations covered in the previous section. The notes do not, however, state that the results have been verified through an official "AIMR audit." This audit is not performed by AIMR; rather it is typically performed by an accounting firm with expertise in AIMR procedures and regulations. It would be a good idea to follow up with CAM to see if they have or plan on having an audit to verify AIMR compliance. If they have had an audit done, request a copy of the letter prepared by the audit firm. If not, it might be a good idea to find out why and to possibly do a spot check of the composite to test how complete CAM was when they put the composite figures together.

## CHAPTER 5

Risk Analysis

s last year's best-performing manager the best choice to hire today? Not necessarily. To make that assessment, we need to understand what risks that manager took to achieve those stellar results.

Just as there are two sides to a coin, there are two sides to returns-based analysis. Performance is usually the most prevalent, but in many ways risk is just as important (if not more important). Investment manager analysts who make the decision to hire or fire an investment manager based solely on that manager's historical performance are effectively flipping a coin to make their investment decisions. It is this "heads you win, tails you lose" mentality that is responsible for more investment losses and heartache than anything else I have seen in this industry.

DEFINING RISK

Before we delve into the formulas and concepts behind the various risk tools at our disposal, we must first define risk. While this sounds easy, it is actually pretty difficult because risk means different things to different people. While there are many risks inherent in the hiring of an investment manager and/or fund, this chapter will focus on the risks that are exclusively performance based.

Loss of Capital

If the recent market decline has taught us anything, it is that it is possible to lose a significant amount of money in a very short period of time. The bull market that the United States experienced in the latter half of the 1990s seemed to lull many investors into forgetting that loss of capital is a distinct possibility—especially over short time periods. An entire series of statistical measures will be introduced later in the chapter that have been created to address the issue of downside risk—or risk of loss.

Opportunity Risk

Unlike the loss of capital, which is an absolute measure, opportunity risk is relative in nature. Opportunity risk is defined as the possibility of under-performing a benchmark. The benchmark can be a generally accepted se-curities index, the underlying investment's peer group, or some unique benchmark created by the investor. The bottom line, however, is the same in any case: Investors hate to see other similar investments perform better than their own.

Shortfall Risk

This risk is often measured against some future liability. A pension fund, for example, might need to plan for an increase in pension liabilities based on actuarial projections. An individual investor may plan a series of invest-ments to represent the future funding of his or her children's college tu-ition. The risk we are talking about here is the risk of coming up short over a specified period of time.

All of the performance-based risks just mentioned and described in de-tail throughout the chapter are backward looking. They are based on his-torical performance as opposed to future projections. As a result, it is important to understand that they are meant to convey probabilities of fu-ture behavior based on past behavior. And as we all know, probability does not equal certainty.

> *Performance Disclaimer:*
> "Past performance may not be indicative of future results."

Most investment firms include a passage similar to this quotation in their marketing materials. While the exact wording may change from firm to firm, the message is the same.

When we make an investment in a particular fund or with a particular investment manager/team, we also make assumptions as to the return we might expect over the life of the investment. Risk is the uncertainty that goes along with our return expectations or assumptions. Different asset classes have different return and risk expectations. For example, it has been demonstrated that over the long term small-cap stocks exhibit greater risk (based on the volatility of returns) than do large-cap stocks. As a result, we would demand a greater return from our small-cap invest-ments than our large-cap investments based on the higher level of risk as-sumed. As a general rule, the higher the expected risk, the higher the expected return should be. Given the choice between two investments with exactly the same return expectations but with different risk assumptions, prudence would dictate that we should select the product with the lower level of risk.

MEASURES OF RISK

To create a numerical representation of risk, we often use variability of returns as a proxy for measuring uncertainty. By using the variability in an investment product's historical return stream, we can create a variety of simple statistical measures that will allow us to put performance in perspective.

Return Histogram

A simple way to measure the variance of returns is to create what is known as a histogram. When using this method, you select a series of return ranges, such as the ones set in Exhibit 5.1, and then count the number of returns that fall within each range.

Both the table and graph in Exhibit 5.1, which represent CAM's historical performance, illustrate that 49% of the portfolio's monthly returns have been greater than +5% or less than –5% on a monthly basis. The portfolio's excellent long-term performance record can be attributed largely to the fact that its monthly return has exceeded 5% on 21 occasions (32% of the time).

Standard Deviation

Standard deviation is the most popular method of measuring an investment's variability in performance. This statistical measure is designed to first calculate the average return of an investment product over a period of time and then to calculate the typical (standard) difference (deviation) from the average. As a result, we can think of standard deviation as a measure of an investment product's historical return dispersion.

Formula 5.1 (Cumulative Standard Deviation)

$$\text{Standard Deviation} = \sqrt{\frac{\sum (\text{IR} - \text{PA})^2}{N}}$$

EXHIBIT 5.1 Return Histogram

Ranges	Count	% of Total
>5%	21	32%
4% to 5%	5	8%
3% to 4%	2	3%
2% to 3%	1	2%
1% to 2%	6	9%
0 to 1%	3	5%
–1% to 0	3	5%
–2% to –1%	5	8%
–3% to –2%	3	5%
–4% to –3%	5	8%
–5% to –4%	1	2%
<–5%	11	17%

where IR = Portfolio's individual monthly return. The returns can be
based on daily, monthly, or quarterly performance periods or
on any period you can consistently apply. It is important that
the measurement period be consistently applied.

PA = Portfolio's average return, based on the following formula:

$$PA = \frac{\sum IR_{1\,to\,N}}{N}$$

N = the total number of return observations.

Formula 5.1 represents the formula for standard deviation based on
what is known as a "population" as opposed to a "sample." The only difference between the two types of standard deviation is that the calculation
based on the population uses the product's entire performance history,
whereas the sample calculation is based on some subset of the product's
history. The only technical adjustment in the formula is that the denominator changes from "N" to "N – 1."

As with many statistical measures, the longer the data set the more statistically significant the result. If, for example, we were to calculate the
standard deviation for a particular investment product that has a history of
just one year (12 months), we would be much less confident about the results. This is because over shorter time periods, one or more outlier returns
might have a larger impact on the overall calculation than is appropriate.

As a general rule, a data set that consists of a minimum of 20 data
points (period returns) is a good starting point. Anything less and you
should take the results with a grain of salt. Once an investment product's
performance history goes past three years (36 months), the results become
more meaningful.

In Exhibit 5.2, we have used the historical performance record of
CAM's small-cap value product and calculated its standard deviation. The
actual monthly performance numbers are shown on the left of the table,
while the calculation for standard deviation is broken out in to steps on the
right side of the table. As the exhibit illustrates, the cumulative standard
deviation for this product is 6.49. But what does this figure actually mean
and how do we interpret it?

Before we can analyze the results we need to make sure that our results
are comparable to the performance figures calculated in the previous chapter. As you recall, the most efficient and effective way to measure the return
of an investment product with a history greater than one year is to annualize the performance. The same holds true when we look at the risk side of
the equation. To properly assess the variability of historical returns, we
first need to annualize the standard deviation figure. The formula used to
annualize standard deviation is highlighted in formula 5.2.

EXHIBIT 5.2 Example of Standard Deviation Using CAM's Performance

CAM's Small-Cap Value Portfolio

Date	Monthly Returns (MR)	Deviation from Average (DFA)	Absolute Value of DFA Squared (SDFA)
Jan-98	−1.23%	−2.22%	4.94
Feb-98	8.34%	7.35%	53.98
Mar-98	5.67%	4.68%	21.87
Apr-98	1.21%	0.22%	0.05
May-98	−5.21%	−6.20%	38.48
Jun-98	1.89%	0.90%	0.80
Jul-98	−8.34%	−9.33%	87.11
Aug-98	−19.45%	−20.44%	417.92
Sep-98	6.45%	5.46%	29.78
Oct-98	4.89%	3.90%	15.19
Nov-98	5.42%	4.43%	19.60
Dec-98	4.99%	4.00%	15.98
Jan-99	−0.70%	−1.69%	2.87
Feb-99	−7.21%	−8.20%	67.29
Mar-99	−0.20%	−1.19%	1.42
Apr-99	7.21%	6.22%	38.65
May-99	4.51%	3.52%	12.37
Jun-99	5.82%	4.83%	23.30
Apr-03	9.17%	8.18%	66.86
May-03	8.76%	7.77%	60.33
Jun-03	4.21%	3.22%	10.35
Average	0.99%	Sum	2,779.64

To calculate the cumulative standard deviation

Step One:	Determine average return	=	0.99
Step Two:	Calculate DFA for each month		See table
Step Three:	Calculate SDFA for each month		See table
Step Four:	Sum all the SDFAs	=	2,779.64
Step Five:	Divide figure in step four by total number of observations (66) (Jan. 1998 to June 2003)	=	42.12
Step Six:	Take the square root of 42.12	=	6.49

To annualize the standard deviation

Multiply 6.49 by the square root of the return frequency used (in this case, the frequency is monthly). $\sqrt{12} = 3.46$

$= 6.49 \times 3.46$

$= 22.48$

Formula 5.2 (Annualized Standard Deviation ASD)

$$ASD = CSD \times \sqrt{RFP}$$

where CSD = Cumulative standard deviation.
       RPF = Return period frequency (monthly = 12, quarterly = 4, etc.).

The result of the annualized standard deviation calculation for CAM's small-cap value portfolio is 22.48.

The graph in Exhibit 5.3 simply shows the monthly returns (represented by the bars) in the context of the maximum/minimum standard deviation bands we calculated. The black bars in the chart represent months that fell outside of the +/–1 standard deviation band. A total of 16 monthly returns fell outside the band (8 positive and 8 negative). This downside deviation will be discussed at length later in the chapter. However, at this point in our analysis, we can quickly determine if these outlier return periods are really outliers by simply comparing the portfolio's return in each of these months to the appropriate index return.

As Exhibit 5.4 illustrates, the returns that we have labeled as outlier periods (8/98, 9/01, and 7/02) are not outlier periods when compared to the small-cap benchmarks.

This leads us to conclude that these numbers in isolation tell us little about the portfolio's level of risk. The numbers alone do not tell us if a small-cap value portfolio with a historical standard deviation of 22.48% can be considered to be high-risk or low-risk. To understand the portfolio's

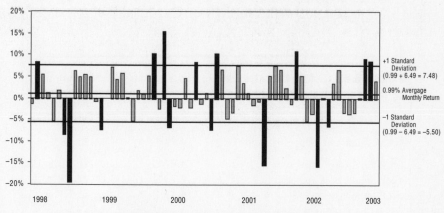

EXHIBIT 5.3 Historical Monthly Returns

EXHIBIT 5.4   Comparison of Outlier Period Returns

	Outlier Months		
	8/98	9/01	7/02
CAM small-cap value portfolio	–19.5	–15.6	–15.9
S&P SmallCap Value Index	–18.0	–14.3	–16.3
S&P SmallCap Growth Index	–20.5	–17.7	–12.0
S&P SmallCap Index	–19.3	–13.5	–14.0

true level of risk, we must compare the standard deviation to some benchmark or other representation of the asset class. If, for example, I told you that the small-cap value benchmark has a standard deviation over the same time period of 35%, only then could we conclude that the CAM portfolio has exhibited less risk, as defined by standard deviation, over time.

Exhibit 5.5 illustrates the annualized performance and standard deviation of CAM's small-cap value portfolio compared to several benchmarks over the time period from January 1998 to June 2003.

Based on the return and risk statistics presented in Exhibit 5.5, we can conclude that the CAM small-cap value portfolio had much better long-term performance than did any of the benchmarks or the return of the median small-cap value manager. Now the question is whether the portfolio manager or team in charge of the CAM product took on extra risk to achieve those wonderful returns. Since the CAM portfolio's standard deviation of 22.48% is roughly in line with the standard deviation of the three small-cap indexes and the small-cap value manager median, we can hypothesize that CAM did not take any significant risks beyond those taken by the indexes over the period. We will be able to verify the hypothesis when we conduct a thorough analysis of CAM's portfolio holdings in Chapter 6.

EXHIBIT 5.5   CAM's Annualized Performance and Standard Deviation

	Performance	Standard Deviation
CAM small-cap value portfolio	9.73%	22.48%
S&P SmallCap Value Index	4.77%	20.95%
S&P SmallCap Growth Index	2.73%	24.67%
S&P SmallCap Index	4.50%	21.83%
Median small-cap value fund	5.01%	23.55%

Return/Risk Graph

Now that we have established a form of return variance that is generally viewed as a strong measure of portfolio risk (standard deviation), we can apply the two sides of the coin in a simple, yet effective analytical measure. The return/risk graphic is one of the most popular methods of displaying the relationship between a portfolio's historical performance and the risk it assumed to achieve those returns.

Like they say: A picture speaks a thousand words. The graphic in Exhibit 5.6 clearly delineates the relationship between reward and risk for CAM's small-cap value portfolio compared to the relevant indexes. As investment manager analysts, we would like the managers we hire to appear in the upper left-hand corner of the graph because that area represents higher performance and lower risk relative to the other alternatives displayed in the graphic. The risk/return graph is very durable, as it can be used to compare a specific product to any number of benchmarks or to a subset of its appropriate peer group of investment managers or the entire peer group (although in the latter case it becomes impossible to include product labels due to the sheer volume of points that tend to be included).

The risk/return graph does not rely exclusively on annualized performance and standard deviation as the return and risk variables. For example, we can substitute any of the risk measures that follow in this chapter for standard deviation, or we can substitute upside or downside returns in place of total annualized returns. The bottom line is that this graphical format is as simple to calculate and interpret as it is flexible.

Looking at the graph in Exhibit 5.6, we can quickly see that the CAM small-cap value product achieved superior performance and did so

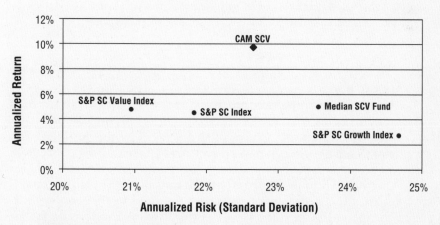

EXHIBIT 5.6 Return/Risk Graph for CAM's Small-Cap Value Portfolio

with a level of risk that was less than the median small-cap value fund and the small-cap growth index, but a shade higher than the overall small cap index and a bit more than the small-cap value index since its inception in 1998.

Sharpe Ratio

Thus far we have established that return and risk go hand in hand and can be calculated separately and displayed side by side. The Sharpe ratio, named for its creator, Nobel laureate William Sharpe, was one of the first statistical measures that factored both return and risk into a single formula, thus giving us a single statistical measure of risk-adjusted return.

Formula 5.3 (Sharpe Ratio)

$$SR = \frac{APR - RFR}{StdDevAPR}$$

where
- APR = Annualized portfolio return.
- RFR = Annualized risk-free rate (90-day T-bills are typically used as a proxy).
- StdDevAPR = Annualized standard deviation of the portfolio's returns.

We can use formula 5.3 to calculate the Sharpe ratio for the CAM small-cap value portfolio. To simplify the calculation, we will assume that risk-free rate's annualized rate of return was an even 2.00% over the time period being used (January 1998 to June 2003).

Sharpe ratio calculation for CAM's small-cap value portfolio:

$$SR(CAM\ SCV) = \frac{APR - RFR}{StdDevAPR} = \frac{9.73 - 2.00}{22.48} = \frac{7.73}{22.48} = 0.344$$

However, the Sharpe ratio for the CAM SCV portfolio in isolation does not provide us with any great insight. The 0.344 result simply states the incremental return per unit of total risk taken by the portfolio. This translates as follows: For every 1 percent of risk taken by the portfolio, it achieved a 0.34% rate of return. But it does not tell us whether this figure is good or bad. The only way of effectively gauging CAM's Sharpe ratio is to compare it to a benchmark or to a peer group. Using the same methodology for the small-cap indexes, we can calculate the Sharpe ratio for the small-cap indexes and peer group.

Sharpe Ratio Comparison (Sorted from High to Low)

CAM small-cap value portfolio	0.344
S&P SmallCap Value Index	0.132
Median small-cap value fund	0.128
S&P SmallCap index	0.115
S&P SmallCap Growth Index	0.030

The results clearly indicate that CAM's portfolio had achieved risk-adjusted returns far in excess of any of the benchmarks listed. In fact, CAM's Sharpe ratio is more than twice that of the most appropriate benchmark (S&P small-cap value benchmark) and the median small-cap value fund.

M² Ratio

Another Nobel Prize–winning economist, Franco Modigliani, and his granddaughter, Leah Modigliani, a portfolio strategist at Morgan Stanley, created the Modigliani-Modigliani ratio. It is referred to as the M-squared ratio or the M² ratio.

Like the Sharpe Ratio, the Modiglianis' statistic seeks to measure how well portfolios/funds perform after adjusting for risk. To make this adjustment, the M's delever a portfolio until its volatility (as measured by standard deviation) matches that of its benchmark. Put differently, for a portfolio whose historical volatility has been less than its benchmark's, they expand the portfolio by leveraging it at an assumed borrowing rate; and for a portfolio whose volatility has been greater than its benchmark's, they contract it and invest the hypothetical proceeds at an assumed yield. The assumed interest rate for both borrowing and lending is typically the yield on short-term Treasury bills. This adjustment produces a portfolio-specific "equity share" or a leverage ratio that equates the portfolio's risk to that of its benchmark. The portfolio's actual return is then multiplied by its equity share, and the product of this calculation is compared to the benchmark's actual return to determine whether the portfolio had outperformed or underperformed the benchmark on a risk-adjusted basis.

So what is the difference between the Sharpe and M² ratios? In my view, the M's created not a better mousetrap, but a different one. The M² ratio is, perhaps, more user-friendly in that it is stated in actual performance terms as opposed to the Sharpe ratio, which is stated in somewhat more abstract terms.

Whatever method you prefer, just keep in mind that the individual ratios are meaningless in absolute terms. These figures are meaningful only when they can be compared to ratios of similar products or benchmarks.

Information Ratio

The information ratio is used to measure a manager's performance against its appropriate benchmark. This measure explicitly relates the *degree* by which the portfolio/fund has beaten its benchmark to the *consistency* by which the portfolio/fund has beaten the benchmark. It is basically a measure of efficiency (or consistency) calculated by dividing the excess rate of return (alpha) by the standard deviation of the excess rate of return stream (tracking error).

Formula 5.4 (Information Ratio)

$$IR = \frac{Alpha}{Tracking\ Error}$$

where   Alpha = Average of the portfolio's excess monthly returns over a specific benchmark.
     Tracking Error = Standard deviation of the alpha.

We can use formula 5.4 to calculate the information ratio for the CAM small-cap value portfolio:

$$IR(CAM\ SCV) = \frac{Alpha}{Tracking\ Error} = \frac{0.42}{1.30} = 0.33$$

Like so many of these statistical measures, the 0.33 figure we calculated takes on more meaning when we compare the results to other products with similar mandates. For example, we could compare the information ratio we calculated for CAM against other managers we might have under consideration.

Treynor Ratio

Just as the Sharpe ratio was named for William Sharpe, the Treynor ratio was named after its creator, Jack Treynor. The numerators of the Sharpe and Treynor ratios are identical; it is in the denominator where the two risk measures differ. While the Sharpe ratio is concerned with total risk (standard deviation), the Treynor ratio is concerned only with systematic or market risk (as measured by beta).

Formula 5.5 (Treynor Ratio)

$$TR = \frac{APR - RFR}{Beta}$$

To fully understand the Treynor ratio and its application as a risk-adjusted performance measure, we must understand what beta is and how it is calculated. The first point that needs to be made is that beta is a comparative measure, meaning it needs to be calculated in relation to some stated benchmark. It is critically important that the benchmark being used be appropriate to the portfolio or fund under review. The beta can be interpreted as the slope of the line in a regression equation or in a capital asset pricing model (CAPM) context. The only difference is that excess portfolio and index returns are used in the CAPM calculation whereas total portfolio and index returns are used in the regression format.

Because this book is focused more on the practical application of investment methodologies and less so on formal statistical derivations, I will avoid a full discourse on beta. Beta can be easily calculated using any statistical software package or simply by using the beta function in Microsoft Excel or some other spreadsheet package.

Beta can be interpreted in the following way:

- *Beta > 1:* The portfolio or fund under review is more volatile than the index being used. For example, it can be interpreted that if the market goes up 10%, a portfolio with a beta of 1.5 would be expected to go up 15% (1.5 times the market).
- *Beta < 1:* The portfolio or fund under review is less volatile than the index being used. For example, it can be interpreted that if the market goes up 10%, a portfolio with a beta of 0.5 would be expected to go up 5% (0.5 times the market).
- *Beta = 1:* The portfolio or fund under review exhibits volatility that is equal to the index being used. For example, it can be interpreted that if the market goes up 10%, a portfolio with a beta of 1.0 would be expected to go up 10% (equal to the market return).

To calculate a portfolio's beta using Microsoft Excel, use the following format:

=SLOPE (A1:A30,B1:B30)

Statistically, beta is the slope of the regression equation. The Excel formula can be interpreted as follows: The term "A1:A30" represents the historical portfolio returns in column format. The term "B1:B30" represents the historical index returns in column format.

So the Treynor ratio can best be described as a measure of a given portfolio's historical returns in excess of those that could have been returned on a riskless investment per unit of market risk assumed. Because the denominator of this ratio is wholly dependent on the benchmark chosen for the regression analysis, the overall validity of the Treynor ratio is dependent on the validity of the selected index as it relates to the underlying portfolio or fund. This is in direct opposition to the Sharpe ratio, which is self-contained, as it is based only on the historical returns of the portfolio or fund under review.

Using the data previously calculated, we can calculate the Treynor ratio for the CAM small-cap value portfolio and the median small-cap value fund:

$$TR(\text{CAM SCV}) = \frac{APR - RFR}{Beta^*} = \frac{9.73 - 2.00}{0.9977} = \frac{7.73}{0.9977} = 7.75$$

$$TR(\text{Medium SC Fund}) = \frac{APR - RFR}{Beta^*} = \frac{5.01 - 2.00}{0.9912} = \frac{3.01}{0.9912} = 3.04$$

Note: The beta was calculated using the S&P small-cap value index in the regression. The small-cap value index was used in this example because it best represents the portfolio's stated style. As was the case with the Sharpe ratio comparison, the CAM portfolio once again came out on top, beating the median small-cap fund by a multiple of more than two times.

Jensen's Alpha

This risk-adjusted performance measure is similar to the Treynor ratio in that it is derived from the regression of historical portfolio return data against of some stated benchmark. Jensen's alpha can best be described as the difference between a portfolio's actual return and a return that could have been attained on a benchmark portfolio that employed the same risk (market risk measured by our friend beta). Another way of stating it is that the Jensen ratio is the portfolio's actual return minus its statistically derived expected return. It is basically a measurement of the ability of an actively managed portfolio to achieve returns above those that are purely a reward for bearing market risk. Or put in more simplistic terms: Does the active management of a specific product add or detract value from some benchmark? If the answer is yes, then you have benefited from making an active allocation to this investment product. If the answer if no, then you would have been better off either hiring a different (and presumably better) investment manager or investing in a passively managed account (an index fund, for example).

Formula 5.6 (Jensen's Alpha)

$$JA = APR - EPR$$

where APR = Actual portfolio return.
        EPR = Expected portfolio return = RFR + [Beta(MR − RFR)].

where RFR = Risk-free rate.
        MR = Market return.

To calculate the Jensen's alpha statistic for the CAM small-cap portfolio and the median small-cap fund, we must complete two steps: calculate the expected return and subtract that figure from the actual return.

Step 1: Calculate the expected portfolio return.

$$
\begin{aligned}
\text{EPR (CAM SCV)} &= \text{RFR} + [\text{Beta (MR} - \text{RFR)}] \\
&= 2.0 + [.9977(4.77 - 2.00)] \\
&= 2.0 + 2.76 \\
&= 4.76
\end{aligned}
$$

$$
\begin{aligned}
\text{EPR (Median SC Fund)} &= \text{RFR} + [\text{Beta(MR} - \text{RFR)}] \\
&= 2.0 + [.9912(4.77 - 2.00)] \\
&= 2.0 + 2.75 \\
&= 4.75
\end{aligned}
$$

Note: The S&P small-cap value index was used to calculate the beta and to represent the market return.

Step 2: Subtract the expected return from the actual return.

$$
\begin{aligned}
\text{JA (CAM SCV)} &= \text{APR} - \text{EPR} \\
&= 9.73 - 4.76 \\
&= 4.97
\end{aligned}
$$

$$
\begin{aligned}
\text{JA (Median SC Fund)} &= \text{APR} - \text{EPR} \\
&= 5.01 - 4.75 \\
&= 0.26
\end{aligned}
$$

When interpreting Jensen's alpha, any positive number represents a value added over the reference index and can best be thought of as a measure of an investment manager's skill as opposed to performance based on market movements. The CAM small-cap value portfolio experienced positive Jensen's alpha, so it was, in theory, a better selection than the reference index. Its calculated alpha was also considerably higher than the one calculated for the median small-cap value manager (4.97 versus 0.26). However, an investment in the median small-cap value fund would still have provided some value added over the reference index.

Downside Deviation

Standard deviation is a measure of volatility that takes all returns into account, both negative and positive. However, to many investors, the fear of losing money in absolute terms is more indicative of investment risk. Downside deviation addresses this concern and takes it one step further by defining downside risk as the risk of not achieving some predefined target return. The target return can be based on long-term historical returns for a specific asset class or on any other measures you might see fit.

Formula 5.7 (Downside Deviation)

$$DD = \sqrt{\frac{\sum (PR - TR)^2}{N}}$$

where PR = Portfolio return.
     TR = Target return. Important note: PR − TR must be less than zero. This ensures that we are looking only at return shortfalls.
     N = Total number of return observations (including returns for months where PR − TR ≥ 0).

Formula 5.8 (Annualized Downside Deviation)

$$\text{Annualized } DD = DD \times \sqrt{RPF}$$

where RPF = Return period frequency (i.e., monthly = 12, quarterly = 4, etc.).

Using these formulas to calculate the downside deviation and then annualizing the figures, we can compare the CAM small-cap value product to the indexes. I assumed an annual target rate for the benchmark of 5%, which translates to 0.42% on a monthly basis (5 ÷ 12 = 0.42).

	Downside Deviation	Annualized Downside Deviation
CAM small-cap value portfolio	4.66	16.14
S&P SmallCap Index	4.63	16.05
S&P SmallCap Growth Index	5.11	17.71
S&P SmallCap Value Index	4.53	15.71

The results from the table can be interpreted by saying that the CAM small-cap portfolio has a higher propensity for downside returns based on the monthly target return of 0.42% than do all but one of the small-cap indexes. The small-cap growth index, however, has a higher propensity for downside return based on the same monthly target return than does CAM or any of the other small-cap benchmarks.

Sortino Ratio

Another risk-adjusted performance measure, named after its creator Frank Sortino, adopts the concept of downside deviation as a more realistic measure of portfolio risk than standard deviation (Sharpe) or beta (Jensen). This statistic also differs from the Sharpe and Jensen ratios, by substituting a target or hurdle rate in place of the risk-free rate used in the numerator of the Sharpe and Jensen measures.

Formula 5.9 (Sortino Ratio)

$$SR = \frac{APR - TR}{ADD}$$

where   APR = Annualized portfolio return.
        TR = Annualized target rate.
     ADD = Annualized downside deviation.

By using the same downside deviation figures previously calculated and keeping the target rate of return constant at 5% annually (0.42% monthly), we can calculate the Sortino ratio for the CAM portfolio and the small-cap benchmarks.

	Annualized Downside Deviation	Sortino Ratio
CAM small-cap value portfolio	16.14	0.29
S&P SmallCap Index	16.05	−0.03
S&P SmallCap Growth Index	17.71	−0.13
S&P SmallCap Value Index	15.71	−0.01

As expected, the CAM portfolio (0.29) has the highest (best) Sortino ratio. The Sortino ratio for each index is negative because none of them had an annualizd return greater than the target rate (5.00%). As such, the numerator for each index's Sortino ratio was negative.

The way to interpret the Sortino ratio using our example is to state that the CAM portfolio's risk-adjusted performance is superior to the benchmark selections provided, but focusing just on the downside risk, the CAM portfolio carries higher downside risk than the broad and value indexes.

Regression-Based Risk Statistics

The formulas for the following regression-based statistics are well beyond the scope of this book, but can be found in any basic statistics textbook or in a number of web sites. Instead of including the technical formulas for each statistic, this book will illustrate how to calculate each using the formulas available in Microsoft Excel, which most people have access to.

Correlation   Correlation measures the degree of association between two investments. In our case, it measures the degree of association between two or more return streams. It measures how strongly the variables are related, or change, with each other. If two variables tend to move up or down together, they are said to be positively correlated. If they tend to move in opposite directions, they are said to be negatively correlated. The return streams can include both manager/fund returns and index returns. The quantitative measure of the degree of correlation between two return streams is called the correlation coefficient. Two return streams are considered perfectly correlated when their correlation coefficient is equal to 1 and perfectly negatively correlated when their correlation coefficient is equal to –1. As with all statistical measures, the more data points (the longer the performance history), the more significant the results. As a rule of thumb, I tend to consider two years' worth of monthly data (24 data points) to be the absolute minimum when calculating correlation and the other regression-based statistics that follow.

Single Correlation Coefficient in Excel

$$=\text{correl(RS1,RS2)}$$

where   RS1 = Return stream one.
      RS2 = Return stream two.

Notes: In Excel, all functions (formulas) need to be preceded by an "=" symbol. If you do not start off with the "=" symbol, Excel will assume that you have entered text and will not treat it as a function.

The return streams are known as ranges in Excel and are expressed in the following format: A1:A25. In this example, the range starts in cell A1 and includes all the cells from A1 to A25 and the proper Excel Syntax is = correl (A1:A25,B1:B25). In this example, we use two return ranges: A1:A25 and B1:B25.

Correlation Matrix   Microsoft has a very useful add-in that comes with all versions of Excel called the "Analysis ToolPack." It is available under the "Tools" button under "Data Analysis". If you do not see it, go to the "Tools" button and click "Add-Ins," select "Analysis ToolPack," and click "OK" (the program will prompt you to insert your Microsoft Office disks). To create a correlation coefficient matrix, simply select correlation from the Data Analysis menu and select the return streams under review. In the following example, I used the Analysis ToolPack to calculate the correlation coefficients of the CAM small-cap portfolio, broad small-cap index, the small-cap growth index, and the small-cap value index (see Exhibit 5.7).

Using the information from the matrix, we can quickly see that the CAM small-cap value portfolio is highly correlated to each of the three small-cap indexes. Of particular interest is the fact that the CAM portfolio has a higher correlation to the broad small-cap index (0.98) and the small-cap growth index (0.93) than it does to the small-cap value index (0.92). However, when we consider the analysis we have performed thus far, it falls in line with results achieved elsewhere. We have determined that CAM's portfolio seems to exhibit both value and growth characteristics and because the broad small-cap index includes both value and growth

EXHIBIT 5.7   Sample of Correlation Coefficient Matrix Using Analysis ToolPack

	CAM SC	SmallCap	SmallCapG	SmallCapV
CAM SC	1.00			
SmallCap	0.98	1.00		
SmallCapG	0.93	0.96	1.00	
SmallCapV	0.92	0.94	0.80	1.00

stocks, it is not surprising to see that it has the highest correlation with CAM's portfolio.

The correlation coefficient can (and should) be used to find out the degree of association between CAM's returns and those of its peer group as well as the other managers in the Emerging Leaders Fund.

Covariance   Covariance measures the degree to which two variables move together over time relative to their individual mean returns. It is calculated by multiplying the correlation between two variables by the standard deviation for each of the variables. The covariance is similar to the correlation coefficient in that it measures the relationship between a pair of variables. However, unlike the correlation coefficient it is not standardized (in a correlation coefficient the covariance is divided by the standard deviations of x and y).

Calculating Covariance in Excel

$$=covar(RS1, RS2)$$

where   RS1 = Return stream one.
        RS2 = Return stream two.

Notes: See notes in the correlation section for comments on Excel Syntax.

R^2 (R-squared) R^2 is the square of the correlation coefficient. When calculating this statistic, you compare the return stream of the product/fund under review (known as the dependent variable) to an appropriate benchmark or other measures, such as median manager returns or the returns of another investment manager (known as the independent variables). The R^2 statistic can be interpreted as the proportion of variance in the dependent variable attributable to the variation in the independent variable.

Calculating R-squared in Excel

$$=rsq(RS1, RS2)$$

where   RS1 = Return stream one (dependent variable).
        RS2 = Return stream two (independent variable).

Value at Risk (VaR)

VaR answers the following question: What is the maximum amount of money that one could expect to lose with a given probability over a specific period of time? The calculated answer can be summed up in a single number and, as a result, is intuitive and easily understood. The concept of VaR was developed in the 1980s by U.S. banks and was created to address the growing use and complexity of the derivates market.

VaR has grown into one of the most significant forms of risk analysis utilized in the marketplace today because it can be calculated for a single investment and can be aggregated at the portfolio level. In addition, it can work just as effectively across asset classes. For example, it is possible to create a VaR statistic for your equity portfolio as well as your fixed income portfolio. When combined, you will have the worst-case scenario for actual dollar loss at the specified probability.

VaR Example 1: VaR Calculation for Single Equity Holding

Question: What is the maximum loss over a 10-day period for a $10 million investment in IBM with a 99% level of confidence?

Step 1: Determine the level of volatility of IBM stock.

- Calculate IBM's average daily volatility for the past 12 months by taking the average standard deviation of the daily prices over the past 12 months. Assume that the daily standard deviation of IBM stock for the past 12 months was 2%.

Step 2: Determine the daily dollar standard deviation (DDSD).

DDSD = Dollar Amount of Investment × Daily Standard Deviation
$$= \$10,000,000 \times 2\%$$
$$= \$200,000$$

Step 3: Determine the time horizon adjustment and multiply it by the daily dollar standard deviation.

- Because we have calculated the daily standard deviation and the question asks what the VaR is over a 10-day period, we need to "scale" the daily VaR statistic.
- This scaling factor is simply the square root of the number of trading days in question. In our example, we are looking for the 10-day VaR, so we take the square root of 10.

$$\text{Time Horizon Adjustment} = \sqrt{\text{\# of Trading Days}}$$
$$= \sqrt{10}$$
$$= 3.16$$

$$3.16 \times \$200,000 = \$632,000$$

Step 4: Multiply by confidence level.

■ Basic statistics give us the following multipliers based on level of confidence:

90% confidence: 1.28
95% confidence: 1.65
99% confidence: 2.33

■ Because we are looking to determine VaR with a 99% level of confidence, we will use 2.33 as our multiplier.

$$VaR = \$632,000 \times 2.33$$
$$= \$1,472,560$$

Based on this VaR calculation we can now state the following: we are 99% certain that the maximum loss that our $10 million investment in IBM could incur over any given 10-day period is $1,472,650.

The VaR calculation for a single investment is pretty simple and straightforward; however, once we start to create portfolios of investments, the calculation becomes geometrically more difficult and far beyond the scope of this book. The following example illustrates how we can calculate a VaR statistic for a portfolio of two stocks.

VaR Example 2: VaR Calculation for Portfolio of Equity Holdings

Question: What is the maximum loss over a 10-day period for a portfolio that consists of a $10 million investment in IBM and a $5 million investment in Cisco with a 99% level of confidence?

Step 1: Determine the daily dollar standard deviation (DDSD) for each individual holding.

DDSD = $ Investment × Daily Standard Deviation × Time Adjustment
DDSD (IBM) = $10,000,000 × 2% × 3.16 = $632,000
DDSD (Cisco) = $5,000,000 × 3% × 3.16 = $474,000

As you can see, I have condensed steps 1 and 2 from the previous example into a single step.

Step 2: Determine the DDSD for the portfolio. In this example, we assume that the level of correlation between IBM and Cisco is 0.70.

■ This is where it starts to get a bit more statistically and mathematically complicated. Using the following formula, we determine the DDSD for the two-stock portfolio.

DDSD (Portfolio) =

$$\sqrt{\left[DSD(IBM)^2 + DSD(Cisco)^2 \right] + \left[\# Inv \times Corr \times DSD(IBM) \times DSD(Cisco) \right]}$$

where   # Inv = Number of investments in the portfolio (two in our example).

Corr = Correlation of returns between IBM and Cisco. As the number of investments in the portfolio rises beyond two investments, a correlation (or covariance) matrix must be calculated and factored in appropriately. Plugging in the numbers from our example, we come up with this calculation:

$$\sqrt{(632,000^2 + 474,000^2) + (2 \times 0.70 \times 632,000 \times 474,000)}$$
$$= \$1,021,664.23$$

Step 3: Multiply by confidence level.

■ Because we are looking to determine VaR with a 99% level of confidence, we will use 2.33 as our multiplier.

$$VaR = \$1,021,664.23 \times 2.33$$
$$VaR = \$2,380,477.66$$

Based on this VaR calculation we can now state that we are 99% certain that the maximum loss that our portfolio (which consists of a $10 million investment in IBM and a $5 million investment in Cisco) could experience over any given 10-day period is $2,380,477.66.

It should be highlighted that the level of correlation between these two investments has a profound impact on the final VaR number—the higher the level of correlation, the higher the final VaR number, and vice versa. For example, let's assume that the level of correlation between IBM and Cisco was 0.90 instead of the 0.70 used in the example. This would change our calculated VaR for the portfolio:

Correlation (IBM and Cisco)	VaR
−0.50	$1,326,905.07
0.20	$2,009,770.07
0.70	$2,380,477.66
0.90	$2,513,898.19

As the table above demonstrates, the level of correlation between the two investments can have a big impact on the estimated VaR. In our example, there is virtually no chance that the correlation between the two technology stocks used (IBM and Cisco) would be negative, as both are bellwether technology stocks that move more or less in tandem. I included the VaR calculation with a negative correlation (−0.50) for illustrative purposes only. The drop in the calculated VaR is quite large in this case, because the negative correlation means that the two investments move in opposite directions (i.e., when IBM moves up, Cisco moves down).

VaR Calculation Methodology   VaR can be calculated using any one or combination of the following methodologies: parametric, Monte Carlo simulation, and historical simulation.

Parametric Methodology   The parametric method applies a specific equation estimate VaR using predefined parameters. In the two preceding VaR examples, we employed the parametric methodology by utilizing an equation based on volatility (standard deviation) and correlation. The main advantages of this method are its simplicity and minimal data requirements. However, because the parametric equation utilizes statistics that work best in portfolios that are linear or normally distributed, it tends to be less accurate for nonlinear or skewed portfolios (as is often the case in alternative investments, such as hedge funds).

Monte Carlo Simulation Method   The Monte Carlo simulation method is more involved than the parametric method. This method estimates VaR by simulating numerous scenarios and revaluing the portfolio based on each scenario. The advantages of using this method are that it is more accurate than the parametric method across a wide range of investment types (including nonlinear and nonnormally distributed portfolio) and that it provides a full range of potential portfolio values. The main disadvantage to using this method is that it requires a very high level of computational resources.

Historical Method   The historical method estimates VaR by taking actual historical data and revaluing the portfolio for each change in the market. The advantages to this method are very similar to those in the Monte Carlo simulation method. The key disadvantage is that a massive amount of historical data is required. In addition, historical data that is not relevant to the current environment may create problems with the estimated VaR, as it will factor in irrelevant or meaningless data.

## CHAPTER 6

Portfolio Analysis

One of the best ways of getting to understand the people behind a given investment product is to analyze the results of their collective efforts—the underlying investment portfolio. After all, what better way of researching what an individual investment manager or investment team does than by studying the actual portfolio holdings? The portfolio holdings will be the driving force behind the portfolio's future success or may be a harbinger of bad things to come.

In the initial RFI, we asked the investment manager for a sample portfolio. We requested a simple list of the portfolio holdings as of the most recent month-end. In addition, we asked for security identifiers (stock tickers in our example) and the actual names of the stocks held in the portfolio. The last request is not necessary, but is often helpful when attempting to verify that a particular stock holding is correct.

The investment manager analyst has a number of viable options to choose from when conducting portfolio analysis. On the commercial side, there are dozens of third party packages available. Some of these packages work off of a main software package that is installed on your computer and updated either daily, weekly, monthly, or quarterly. Other third party packages are available 24/7 via the Internet. Some of the more popular third party portfolio analysis packages are Barra, Wilshire, FactSet, Baseline, Reuters, Northfield, Zephyr, and Bloomberg.

Another option would be to use whatever data source you have (FactSet, Bloomberg, Baseline, MSN, etc.) and create your own portfolio analysis. While I have always had third party software and databases available to me throughout my career, I have consistently used a combination of the third party software and portfolio analysis reports of my own creation.

One potential issue that might arise when conducting a search to fill a specific asset class and style revolves around the nonstandardization of basic classifications, definitions, and formulas for basic portfolio characteristics. There are basically two reasons why an investment manager analyst would want to do the portfolio analysis in-house: more control or consistency. The latter is a big problem when data comes from different sources. For example, most of the major index providers have their own (unique) sector and industry classifications for each stock. As long as you get all of your information from the same source (assuming that that source uses the same data provider throughout the analysis), you should be fine; but in the real world, data comes from multiple sources and, as a result, becomes very difficult to analyze on a comparative basis. By simply requesting the underlying data, inputting the data into our own system, and printing the reports ourselves, we can avoid this issue completely.

Regardless of what methodology you choose to employ, the information should be treated the same. Just one word of caution: Because so much information is available, it is possible to experience information overload or information crossover. Information crossover occurs when an analyst produces so many reports based on the same data that much of the information reviewed in later reports has already been covered completely or in part in previous reports. The result is an inefficient use of time.

Using the portfolio information provided to us by CAM Asset Management, we can input the data into our portfolio analysis system and produce the portfolio summary report in Exhibit 6.1.

The report in this exhibit contains a wealth of information on each stock included in the CAM portfolio at the end of last month. This chapter will illustrate a systematic method of evaluating both the summary-level data as well as the detail on each specific stock in the portfolio.

SUMMARY-LEVEL DATA

Once we prepare a portfolio analysis, we start from the top down and look at various types of summary-level data. This will give us a relatively quick overview of a portfolio's exposures and biases. Then we look at the portfolio from the bottom up or at the stock level.

Sector Weights

We can first look at the sector weightings for the CAM portfolio in absolute terms (see Exhibit 6.2). What is striking is that more than 70% of the portfolio is represented by just three sectors: consumer cyclical, health care, and financial services. While this analysis represents the portfolio at single point in time, we must note for future reference that CAM's small-cap value product might contain a high level of sector concentration risk. While this is not necessarily a bad thing, it might expose our overall portfolio to undue or unexpected risks. If we decide to take this product further along in the due diligence process, we must inquire about the current sector concentration,

EXHIBIT 6.1 CAM Small-Cap Value Portfolio Summary Report

	Descriptive Data					Performance Data				Valuation Data						Earnings Data					Liquidity	
Name	Sector	Industry	%Port	Mkt Cap		Mtd	Qtd	6Mo	12Mo	FP/E	P/E LTM	P/B	P/S	P/CF	Ern% LTM	Rev% LTM	ROE	30 day ERUp	30 day ERDn	Quick	LtD/Cap
CSK ADR	Information Tech	IT Consulting & Svc.	3.4%	$2,677		7.4	27.4	108.2	59.1	–	29.4	3.4	0.9	–	–15.0	–5.1	–	–	–	0.8	24.0
Interpore Int'l	Health Care	HC–Supplies	3.2%	$ 291		1.0	21.1	92.0	140.0	40.8	52.6	3.9	4.5	41.7	55.0	16.5	7.8	0.0	0.0	2.7	0.0
Multimedia Games	Consumer Services	Casinos & Gaming	2.8%	$ 470		34.2	43.3	89.2	32.5	15.4	16.8	5.6	1.4	11.1	38.0	32.9	36.9	0.0	1.0	2.0	6.0
Navigators Group	Financials	Insurance–Prop./Cas.	2.7%	$ 256		–7.4	9.0	26.4	41.6	10.8	14.3	1.4	0.9	13.5	188.0	47.2	10.4	0.0	0.0	–	6.0
Columbia Sportswear	Consumer Cyclical	Apparel & Accessory	2.7%	$2,196		3.4	2.6	41.9	18.8	18.8	20.1	4.4	2.5	17.0	21.0	10.5	24.4	0.0	0.0	2.9	4.0
Acambis ADR	Health Care	Biotechnology	2.6%	$ 514		–8.7	–14.9	36.3	17.9	–	–	5.1	–	–	–	–	–	0.0	1.0	0.7	23.0
Pediatrix Med'l Grp.	Health Care	HC–Services	2.5%	$1,122		3.0	29.2	83.2	15.0	13.1	16.5	2.2	2.2	15.1	50.0	16.4	12.6	0.0	0.0	1.4	4.0
Amer. Eagle Outfitter	Consumer Cyclical	Retail–Apparel	2.5%	$1,087		–13.1	–19.3	2.7	8.2	14.4	13.8	1.8	0.7	8.4	–17.0	4.9	14.1	24.0	0.0	1.5	2.0
BP Prudhoe Bay Rlty.	Energy	Oil & Gas–Expl./Prod.	2.4%	$ 428		–1.1	4.6	32.1	33.8	–	8.1	26.9	8.0	8.4	50.0	49.5	–	0.0	0.0	–	0.0
HCC Insurance Hldgs.	Financials	Insurance–Multiline	2.3%	$1,891		–0.7	–1.7	13.8	18.2	12.5	15.5	2.0	2.3	14.3	62.0	40.9	13.6	0.0	0.0	–	24.0
Decoma Int'l	Consumer Cyclical	Auto Parts & Equip.	2.3%	$ 525		–1.8	17.8	52.3	28.6	10.6	9.2	1.6	0.2	3.7	26.0	10.1	14.6	1.0	2.0	0.7	16.0
Ralcorp Hldgs.	Consumer Noncyclical	Packaged Foods/Meats	2.2%	$ 807		–2.5	11.0	6.4	10.2	14.1	14.4	1.8	0.6	8.8	10.0	2.7	12.5	0.0	0.0	0.6	25.0
Greater Bay Bancorp.	Financials	Regional Banks	2.2%	$1,105		1.2	3.9	45.1	20.4	14.2	10.5	1.8	2.2	8.2	–4.0	18.2	18.0	2.0	0.0	–	38.0
Sky Fin'l Group	Financials	Diversified Banks	2.2%	$2,096		–3.9	3.5	14.4	13.1	12.6	13.9	2.4	3.7	11.8	9.0	19.3	18.7	0.0	1.0	–	68.0
Renal Care Group	Health Care	HC–Services	2.2%	$1,673		–5.9	–3.0	9.5	7.9	15.2	17.1	2.9	1.7	12.1	21.0	16.7	16.9	0.0	0.0	1.8	0.0
Option Care	Health Care	HC–Services	2.2%	$ 251		2.9	4.3	41.5	50.8	13.8	16.1	2.0	0.7	12.6	16.0	29.7	13.1	0.0	0.0	3.1	5.0
Cherokee	Consumer Cyclical	Apparel & Accessory	2.2%	$ 170		–3.6	5.9	41.3	45.2	–	12.7	6.5	4.8	11.0	7.0	10.5	91.7	–	–	1.4	0.0

(Continued)

103

EXHIBIT 6.1 *(Continued)*

	Descriptive Data					Performance Data				Valuation Data					Earnings Data					Liquidity	
Name	Sector	Industry	%Port	Mkt Cap	Mtd	Qtd	6Mo	12Mo	FP/E	P/E LTM	P/B	P/S	P/CF	Ern% LTM	Rev% LTM	ROE	30 day ERUp	30 day ERDn	Quick	LtD/ Cap
Pogo Producing	Energy	Oil & Gas-Expl./Prod.	2.2%	$2,924	-1.5	5.9	13.9	21.6	15.1	12.1	2.4	2.8	5.5	295.0	72.6	21.1	3.0	3.0	1.8	31.0
Linens 'n Things	Consumer Cyclical	Specialty Stores	2.1%	$1,074	-17.7	0.7	17.0	5.2	14.1	16.0	1.6	0.5	9.5	9.0	14.9	10.4	1.0	0.0	0.1	0.0
Curtiss-Wright	Information Tech	Aerospace/Defense	2.1%	$ 724	3.9	11.7	16.7	10.7	–	15.1	1.7	1.1	10.9	16.0	65.7	11.7	0.0	0.0	1.2	24.0
Prosperity Banc	Financials	Regional Banks	2.1%	$ 424	1.5	10.9	28.5	12.2	15.7	16.9	2.6	5.5	13.5	29.0	38.7	19.0	0.0	0.0	–	15.0
St. Mary Land & Expl.	Energy	Oil & Gas-Expl./Prod.	2.1%	$ 753	-10.5	-7.3	1.1	1.3	13.9	12.6	2.3	2.5	6.6	253.0	73.4	18.5	5.0	0.0	0.8	29.0
Heritage Fin'l	Financials	Regional Banks	2.1%	$ 141	0.1	-0.1	-1.0	22.3	16.7	16.8	2.1	3.9	13.8	14.0	3.4	11.9	0.0	0.0	–	0.0
Glacier Bancorp	Financials	Regional Banks	2.1%	$ 559	1.6	11.4	12.8	28.1	–	15.5	2.3	4.3	11.8	28.0	22.3	16.9	0.0	0.0	–	5.0
First South Bancorp	Financials	Regional Banks	2.0%	$ 141	-14.4	-3.8	-1.9	-9.6	–	14.3	2.9	3.9	13.4	36.0	22.1	19.1	–	–	–	0.0
America's Car-Mart	Consumer Cyclical	Specialty Stores	2.0%	$ 239	52.5	64.1	144.2	134.0	15.2	17.2	3.3	1.5	16.8	28.0	21.4	21.7	0.0	3.0	9.5	26.0
Berry Petroleum	Energy	Oil & Gas-Expl./Prod.	2.0%	$ 407	-2.5	1.8	21.9	7.2	16.1	13.4	2.3	2.6	8.7	39.0	31.5	17.6	0.0	0.0	0.8	8.0
ICU Medical	Health Care	HC-Supplies	2.0%	$ 357	-7.6	-12.7	-1.3	-27.2	16.2	19.1	2.5	3.7	14.9	18.0	19.4	13.5	0.0	0.0	8.9	0.0
Jakks Pacific	Consumer Cyclical	Leisure Products	1.9%	$ 306	2.4	-7.4	18.6	-8.8	8.7	9.7	0.8	1.0	7.5	-26.0	6.5	9.0	0.0	0.0	4.4	21.0
Invision Technology	Information Tech	Aerospace/Defense	1.9%	$ 441	-3.3	-1.0	8.3	-7.7	15.6	4.2	1.6	0.8	4.1	666.0	319.7	46.8	0.0	0.0	2.3	1.0
Sterling Bancshares	Financials	Regional Banks	1.9%	$ 530	-4.5	-8.2	0.3	-2.4	18.8	12.8	2.0	2.1	7.9	21.0	21.3	16.8	0.0	1.0	–	64.0
Remington Oil & Gas	Energy	Oil & Gas-Expl./Prod.	1.8%	$ 495	-2.4	-1.3	6.6	10.6	12.5	15.5	2.4	3.5	7.0	1,090.0	52.6	15.6	4.0	2.0	1.1	14.0
Nat'l Med. Hlth. Card	Health Care	HC-Services	1.7%	$ 103	10.3	39.9	48.7	47.6	–	16.4	3.5	0.2	9.7	43.0	24.7	25.2	0.0	0.0	0.7	1.0
MB Fin'l	Financials	Regional Banks	1.7%	$ 792	3.3	10.6	24.0	27.6	14.1	16.1	2.2	4.2	10.6	24.0	20.6	14.5	0.0	0.0	–	25.0
Cantel Medical	Health Care	HC-Equipment	1.5%	$ 128	5.0	-0.6	4.5	5.4	15.1	17.2	2.0	1.0	11.2	8.0	7.7	12.4	2.0	0.0	1.9	22.0
Rehabcare Group	Health Care	HC-Facility	1.5%	$ 283	7.9	16.4	-4.5	-10.6	13.8	12.8	1.4	0.5	9.3	17.0	0.8	10.8	1.0	0.0	3.0	0.0

Company	Sector	Subsector	%	$																
Cole (Kenneth) Prod.	Consumer Cyclical	Apparel & Accessory	1.5%	$ 521	-3.3	34.0	19.2	28.6	—	18.2	3.1	1.2	14.5	57.0	15.4	17.5	0.0	0.0	2.0	0.0
Allegiant Bancorp	Financials	Diversified Banks	1.5%	$ 348	-3.4	0.0	19.5	10.8	14.5	15.7	2.1	3.7	13.1	9.0	28.4	12.8	0.0	0.0	—	64.0
Churchill Downs	Consumer Services	Casinos & Gaming	1.4%	$ 510	4.4	-2.1	10.7	-1.4	22.1	17.8	2.3	1.1	10.6	31.0	3.3	11.9	0.0	0.0	0.6	32.0
RLI	Financials	Insurance–Prop./Cas.	1.3%	$ 842	-0.1	0.1	22.5	18.0	13.8	15.8	1.8	1.9	14.8	36.0	32.1	12.5	0.0	1.0	—	0.0
Amer. Woodmark	Consumer Cyclical	Building Products	1.3%	$ 356	-11.9	-4.7	1.5	-5.8	10.5	11.9	2.1	0.6	6.2	-8.0	11.9	19.0	1.0	0.0	1.0	10.0
U.S. Physical Therapy	Health Care	HC–Facility	1.2%	$ 150	-18.9	-6.6	9.8	9.5	19.5	18.9	3.9	1.5	13.8	5.0	13.6	21.0	2.0	0.0	5.3	0.0
Possis Medical	Health Care	HC–Equipment	1.2%	$ 285	-15.8	14.7	-3.7	-13.6	29.1	32.0	6.1	5.0	25.8	47.0	35.4	24.1	3.0	0.0	6.4	0.0
New Century Fin'l	Financials	Thrifts & Mortgage Fin.	1.2%	$1,050	16.2	-2.0	36.5	67.6	5.0	5.4	2.6	1.4	5.2	82.0	72.8	48.9	0.0	5.0	1.6	71.0
Amer Real Estate Ptr.	Financials	Diverse Fin'l Svc.	1.2%	$ 557	4.8	-3.3	15.0	29.5	—	12.8	0.5	1.9	8.6	-28.0	-11.5	4.0	—	—	17.9	13.0
Catalina Marketing	Commercial Services	Advertising	1.1%	$ 817	9.2	-13.9	-21.0	-17.9	15.0	14.9	2.7	1.7	8.4	-6.0	6.2	23.6	1.0	0.0	0.8	17.0
Bisys Group	Information Tech	Services–Data Proc.	1.1%	$1,618	-28.3	-28.4	-19.4	-17.3	17.1	13.6	2.1	1.7	9.6	2.0	10.7	16.2	17.0	0.0	0.9	28.0
Blue Rhino	Consumer Cyclical	Retail–Home Improve.	1.0%	$ 197	-15.4	-7.7	8.5	-36.3	14.6	11.6	1.6	0.8	7.9	43.0	25.2	17.5	2.0	1.0	0.8	31.0
Polymedica	Health Care	HC–Supplies	1.0%	$ 675	17.5	15.6	74.1	71.9	—	15.8	3.3	1.8	7.9	12.0	25.2	22.0	1.0	0.0	3.8	1.0
Gildan Activewear	Consumer Cyclical	Apparel & Accessory	0.9%	$ 660	-5.6	6.8	13.1	20.1	—	15.4	4.1	1.5	12.3	59.0	22.0	20.8	1.0	0.0	1.5	18.0
Orthodontic Centers	Health Care	HC–Services	0.9%	$ 400	12.9	-1.6	51.2	-27.8	6.9	6.5	0.9	1.0	4.7	-12.0	-0.1	13.7	1.0	0.0	2.8	18.0
Pxre Group	Financials	Reinsurance	0.6%	$ 218	-1.0	-9.3	-16.4	-26.7	—	5.6	0.7	0.6	—	811.0	77.6	12.9	0.0	0.0	—	0.0
PRG-Schultz Int'l	Industrials	Services–Div./Comm'l	0.5%	$ 369	-9.8	-3.9	-21.2	-36.2	17.1	11.7	1.1	0.9	7.2	42.0	16.5	9.2	0.0	0.0	1.1	32.0
Atlantic Coast Airlin.	Industrials	Airlines	0.5%	$ 402	6.5	-36.1	37.0	-29.3	8.7	9.0	1.4	0.5	6.3	-6.0	24.9	15.3	0.0	1.0	1.9	25.0

(Continued)

EXHIBIT 6.1 (Continued)

	Descriptive Data				Performance Data				Valuation Data					Earnings Data					Liquidity	
Name	Sector	Industry	%Port	Mkt Cap	Mtd	Qtd	6Mo	12Mo	FP/E	P/E LTM	P/B	P/S	P/CF	Ern% LTM	Rev% LTM	ROE	30 day ERUp	30 day ERDn	Quick	LtD/ Cap
Nordic Amer. Tanker	Industrials	Marine	0.5%	$ 119	-0.4	-2.8	-1.8	1.9	-	5.2	1.1	3.7	4.0	199.0	91.5	-	-	-	16.4	22.0
Coinstar	Industrials	Services–Div./Comm'l	0.4%	$ 297	-12.3	-28.9	-19.8	-40.6	16.3	13.2	2.8	1.8	6.1	150.0	17.4	30.0	0.0	0.0	1.1	12.0
Total Entertainment Services	Consumer Services	Restaurants	0.3%	$ 108	-1.1	18.4	33.2	29.0	12.8	14.9	2.4	0.9	8.6	23.0	29.0	19.3	0.0	2.0	0.1	9.0
Charles & Colvard	Consumer Cyclical	Apparel & Accessory	0.2%	$ 63	-3.2	15.0	5.7	-14.5	-	29.8	1.4	3.7	28.0	23.0	18.2	5.3	-	-	8.6	0.0
Total Portfolio				$ 777	0.1	6.3	29.6	21.6	11.8	15.8	3.2	2.2	11.0	74.1	29.1	17.4	0.4	1.3	1.9	15.6

Legend:

% Port = Dollars invested in a given stock as a % of total market value.

Mkt Cap = Company's # shares outstanding × current price. A measure of the total mkt value for a given company.

Mtd = Month-to-date return

Qtd = Quarter-to-date return

6Mo = Return over last 6 months

12Mo = Return over last 6 months

FP/E = Price/earnings ratio using analyst's forward earnings estimates

P/E LTM = Price/earnings ratio using actual company earnings over the last 12 months.

P/B = Price/book ratio

P/S = Price/sales ratio

P/CF = Price/cash flow ratio

Ern% LTM = Percentage change in earnings over the last 12 months

Rev% LTM = Percentage change in revenue over the last 12 months

ROE = Return on Equity

30 day ERUp = # of analyst's estimates that have increased in the past 30 days

30 day ERDn = # of analyst's earnings estimates that have decreased in the past 30 days

Quick = Quick ratio

LtD/Cap = Ratio of long-term debt/market capitalization

EXHIBIT 6.2   Sector Weight Comparison

	CAM SCV	SCV Index	SC Index	SCG Index
Basic Materials	0.0%	8.8%	5.9%	3.2%
Energy	10.4%	4.9%	4.9%	4.9%
Consumer Noncyclicals	2.2%	3.3%	3.0%	2.7%
Consumer Cyclicals	20.6%	15.9%	16.1%	16.3%
Consumer Services	4.6%	6.9%	7.2%	7.4%
Industrials	1.8%	8.0%	6.1%	4.2%
Utilities	0.0%	5.2%	3.5%	1.9%
Transportation	0.0%	3.6%	3.0%	2.4%
Health Care	23.8%	5.5%	11.1%	16.6%
Technology	8.4%	15.8%	17.6%	19.5%
Telecommunications	0.0%	0.2%	0.2%	0.1%
Commercial Services	1.1%	6.2%	7.3%	8.4%
Financial Services	27.0%	15.8%	14.1%	12.4%

ask about historical sector concentration, and, if we conclude that we should expect this type of concentration in the portfolio in the future, ask what impact it would have on our overall portfolio's small-cap exposure and the overall portfolio as a whole.

Based on the sector concentration we just discovered combined with the portfolio's historical tendency to significantly outperform the three comparative indexes, it is not surprising to find that the CAM portfolio is weighted very differently than any of the three small-cap indexes listed in Exhibit 6.2. In fact, with the lone exception of the consumer noncyclical sector, the CAM portfolio differs significantly than the indexes in every single sector.

Exhibit 6.3 lists CAM's general sector exposures relative to the indexes. The portfolio was overweight in four sectors and underweight in seven. While the sector orientation of value versus growth portfolios can move along wide ranges over time (due to the nature of the marketplace, business cycle, and economy), several sectors are generally considered to be favored more by value managers, while other sectors have been generally favored by growth managers. Among the sectors typically favored by value managers are: basic materials, industrials, utilities, and financials. However, the current CAM small-cap value portfolio is weighted in what can be termed a very unique way. The following section discusses the portfolio's sector weights:

■ *Basic materials.* The portfolio had a zero weight in this sector, which has historically been considered a value sector (as evidenced by the

EXHIBIT 6.3 CAM's Sector Weights Relative to the Indexes

Overweight	Neutral	Underweight
Energy	Consumer Noncyclical	Basic Materials
Consumer Cyclical		Consumer Services
Health Care		Industrial
Financial		Transportation
		Technology
		Telecommications
		Commercial Services

small-cap value index's 8.8% weighting). According to the Barra/S&P indexes, this sector includes the following industries: metals and mining, gold, forest products, paper, and chemicals.

■ *Energy.* The portfolio, which has a 10.4% weight in this sector, was more than twice the size of the three small-cap indexes' weight in this sector. This sector includes the following industries: energy reserves and production, oil refining and oil services.

■ *Consumer noncyclical.* This is the only sector in which the portfolio is weighted closely to the indexes. The noncyclical sector includes: food and beverage, alcohol, tobacco, home products, and grocery stores.

■ *Consumer cyclical.* The portfolio's weighting, at 20.6%, is high, but only 4% to 5% above the range of the small cap indexes. This sector includes: consumer durables, motor vehicles and parts, apparel, textiles, clothing stores, specialty retail, department stores, construction, and real property.

■ *Consumer services.* The portfolio is slightly underweight relative to the indexes. This sector includes: publishing, media, hotels, restaurants, entertainment, and leisure.

■ *Industrial.* The portfolio has a very small weight in this sector, at just 1.8%, compared to a range of 4.2% to 8.0% for the small-cap indexes. This sector includes: environmental services, heavy electrical equipment, heavy machinery, and industrial parts.

■ *Utilities.* The portfolio does not hold any securities that fall into this category. This sector includes: gas and electric utility companies.

■ *Transportation.* The portfolio does not hold any securities that fall into this category. This sector includes: railroads, airlines, trucking, sea, and freight.

■ *Health care.* At just under a 24% weight, this is the portfolio's single largest "positive" bet versus the indexes, which hold weights in the 5% to 17% range. This sector includes: medical services, medical products and supplies, drugs, and biotechnology.

■ *Technology.* The portfolio is significantly underweight in this sector. The portfolio's 8.4% weighting is less than half of the small-cap value index and even less than the broad and growth indexes. This represents the portfolio's largest negative sector bet. Due to the high correlation of stocks in the technology sector, the portfolio would take a hit relative to the small-cap indexes if technology stocks take off. This sector includes: electronic equipment, semiconductors, computer hardware, business machines, computer software, defense and aerospace, and Internet.

■ *Telecommunication.* The portfolio does not hold any securities that fall into this category. This sector includes: telephone and wireless communications companies.

■ *Commercial services.* The portfolio weight in this sector is small, at just 1.1% versus a range of 6% to 8% for the small-cap indexes.

■ *Financial services.* This sector represents the portfolio's single largest exposure, at 27% of the portfolio. While the small-cap value index has a considerable weight in this area (15.8%), the portfolio eclipses it by over 10%. This sector includes: life and health insurance, property and casualty insurance, banks, thrifts, securities and asset management, financial services, and equity real estate investment trusts (REITs).

Another interesting fact is that the CAM SCV portfolio does not hold any securities in four of the 13 sectors listed in this chapter. The total weight of these four sectors was 17.8% in the small-cap value index, 12.6% for the broad small-cap index, and 7.6% for the small-cap growth index. So the CAM portfolio is different not just because it has overweighted several sectors, but baecause it has avoided other sectors completely.

Industry Weights

Now that we have looked at the allocation from a broad (sector) view, we can start to drill down into the portfolio and go into more detail. Another way to break down a portfolio's allocation is to look at its underlying industry classifications. Just as with the sector breakdown, industry classification differs from index to index and, subsequently, from firm to firm. Again, the solution is to perform all of the analysis working from our own system.

The data in Exhibit 6.1 displays each stock in the CAM small-cap portfolio as well as its respective industry classification. Using the data from this exhibit, we can determine if the portfolio has diversified its allocations within each sector and ascertain the level of industry concentration, just as we did in the preceding section on sector weights.

Not surprisingly, the top five industries are part of the sectors in which the portfolio is overweight relative to the small-cap indexes. Portfolio concentration rears it head again, as the industry table in Exhibit 6.4 illustrates. The sum of the top five industries in the portfolio is just under half of the total portfolio.

The entire energy sector weight is focused in one single industry: oil and gas exploration; and more than half of the portfolio's 27% weight in financials is in regional banks (14%). Once we look beyond the top 10 industries in the portfolio, we find that the industry with the next highest

EXHIBIT 6.4   CAM's Industry Weights

Regional Banks	14.0%	
Oil & Gas—Expl./Prod.	10.4%	
HC Services	9.5%	Sum of top 5 industries = 47.6%
Apparel & Accessory	7.5%	
HC Supplies	6.2%	
Casinos & Gaming	4.3%	
Specialty Stores	4.1%	
Insurance—Prop./Cas.	4.0%	
Aerospace/Defense	4.0%	
Diversified Banks	3.7%	
IT Consulting & Svc.	3.4%	
HC Facility	2.7%	
HC Equipment	2.7%	
Biotechnology	2.6%	
Retail—Apparel	2.5%	
Insurance—Multiline	2.3%	
Auto Parts & Equip.	2.3%	
Packaged Foods/Meats	2.2%	
Leisure Products	1.9%	
Building Products	1.3%	
Thrifts & Mortgage Fin.	1.2%	
Diverse Fin'l Svc.	1.2%	
Advertising	1.1%	
Services—Data Proc.	1.1%	
Retail—Home Improve.	1.0%	
Services—Div./Comm'l	0.9%	
Reinsurance	0.6%	
Airlines	0.5%	
Marine	0.5%	
Restaurants	0.3%	
Total	100.0%	

weight (technology consulting and services) is a mere 3.4% of the total portfolio. In fact, the top 10 industries comprise 68% of the total portfolio. Now we can state that the portfolio is concentrated not just on a sector basis, but on an industry basis as well. The bottom line is that the portfolio might experience some of the added volatility that concentration has a tendency of providing. You can take this analysis further by researching the top industries to see where they are in their performance cycles as well as comparing this portfolio's sector/industry weights to some other top investment managers in the same asset class.

Market Capitalization Analysis

According to the portfolio summary statistics at the bottom of the report in Exhibit 6.1, the CAM small-cap portfolio has a weighted average market capitalization of $777 million. We can use this information to ascertain where this portfolio fits in relative to the small-cap indexes.

According to the data in Exhibit 6.5, the CAM small-cap value portfolio clearly falls into the market cap range of the small-cap indexes. However, a weighted average can contain outliers. Exhibit 6.6 breaks the CAM portfolio into market capitalization ranges, totals the portfolio's exposure to each range, and counts the number of stocks that fall into each range.

Looking at data in this table, we can see that the CAM portfolio has more than 10% of the portfolio in stocks with market caps above $2 billion.

EXHIBIT 6.5 Weighted Market Capitalization Comparison

CAM Small-cap value portfolio	**$777 million**
S&P SmallCap Index	$875 million
S&P SmallCap Value Index	$684 million
S&P SmallCap Growth Index	$1.07 billion

EXHIBIT 6.6 Market Capitalization Ranges

	% in Portfolio	# Stocks
$0 to $250M	15.3%	12
$251M to $500M	32.8%	19
$501M to $1B	25.3%	15
$1B to $2B	16.1%	8
$2B to $3B	10.4%	4

But before we can make any assessments as to whether this is appropriate, we need to discuss the market cap ranges. If you were to ask five investment professionals what the cutoff level would be for a small-cap stock, you might get five different answers. To make matters simple, I define the market cap spectrum in the following way:

Market Capitalization	Range
Micro-cap	Less than $500 million
Small-cap	$500 million to $2 billion
Mid-cap	$2 billion to $10 billion
Large-cap	Greater than $10 billion

However, how you decide to define the market cap breakpoints is not as important as applying them consistently. With these cap ranges in mind, we can look at Exhibit 6.6 and make some quick assessments:

Nearly half (48.1%) of the portfolio falls into the "micro-cap" range (31 out of 58 stocks). Of those stocks, roughly 15% of them have market caps under $250 million (12 stocks). A look at the portfolio report in Exhibit 6.1 tells us that only one stock had a market cap under $100 million (the apparel company—Charles & Colvard). While the micro-cap universe has the largest number of stocks in the overall marketplace, it seems to have a large percentage of the smaller-weighted names in the portfolio. This should prompt questions relating to the historical market cap breakdown because investment history dictates that smaller market capitalization ranges experience greater long-term performance, but do so at a higher level of risk. Because this portfolio represents a single point in time, it does not give us any indication as to historical tendencies (or the future).

Just over 10% of the portfolio is in stocks with market caps above $2 billion (four stocks). Again, looking at the portfolio report in Exhibit 6.1, we can see that two of the four stocks with market caps over $2 billion are just barely over that mark (SkyFinancial Group at $2.1 billion and Columbia Sportswear $2.2 billion). However, based on the performance data we can guestimate that these two stocks crossed over the small-cap threshold into mid-cap territory due to price appreciation, as they increased in price 14% and 42%, respectively, over the previous year. Furthermore, we can make the same assumption about CSK, which more than doubled in price over the year. The one stock that seems to defy the small cap range is Pogo Producing, at more than $2.9 billion; its 21.6% appreciation in price over the year indicates it did not begin the year with a market cap below the $2 billion level. This leads us to the conclusion that the stock has been in the portfolio for more than a year. The alternative would be that CAM recently purchased the stock in clear violation of its internal policies and investment mandate. If we take this product to the next step in the evaluation and conduct an interview with the portfolio manager, we should inquire about the firm's market cap breaks.

In addition, both Interpore and Multimedia Games (the second and third largest holdings in the portfolio) experienced massive price appreciation over the prior six months, at 92.0% and 89.2%, respectively. If CAM purchased these microcap securities before they rose in price, then it would seem that this portfolio might have gotten some of its value added performance in the current year from the micro-cap names.

Portfolio Weights

We have discussed how the portfolio can be broken out by sector, industry, and market cap. We can also extrapolate some good data simply from the way in which a portfolio manager/team weights individual stocks in a portfolio.

Exhibit 6.7 indicates that the portfolio is concentrated mostly in the 1% to 3% range in terms of individual stock weights (88% of the portfolio). Only 9 stocks out of 58 have a portfolio weighting less than 1%, and the portfolio does not have any stocks with a portfolio weight that exceeds 4% (the top-weighted stock, CSK ADR, represents 3.4% of the portfolio). Again, due to the static nature of this type of analysis, we should wait until we perform some type of historical analysis before we make any definitive judgments. With respect to the CAM portfolio, I would state at this point that it is reasonably tight and that there appears to be some kind of portfolio weighting guidelines in place. One interesting piece of information that comes from Exhibit 6.1 is that after the top-weighted stock (CSK ADR), the next three names (Interpore, Multimedia Games, and Navigators Group) all fall into the micro-cap range.

EXHIBIT 6.7 Individual Stock Weighting Ranges

Portfolio Weight (%)	% in Portfolio	# in Portfolio
0–1	4.8%	9
1–2	29.9%	21
2–3	58.7%	26
3–4	6.6%	2
4–5	0.0%	0
> 5%	0.0%	0

Number of Holdings

A very quick measure of portfolio diversification is to count the number of holdings in a given portfolio. A portfolio, for example, with fewer that 25 holdings is generally considered to be "concentrated." However, there is no consensus as to what constitutes a well-diversified portfolio versus an "overdiversified" portfolio. An overdiversified portfolio is one with so many holdings that it mimics an index and, therefore, provides no value added through active management. Experience has taught me to take this figure into consideration with all of the others discussed in this chapter (and other chapters as well).

It is important to note that a concentrated portfolio is not necessarily a bad one. In fact, a concentrated portfolio in concert with other portfolio allocations might better optimize the overall portfolio. Just keep in mind that a concentrated portfolio might experience more volatility (defined as distribution of returns or standard deviation) than portfolios that are well diversified or when measured against various indexes.

Percent in Top Ten

Another gauge of concentration is the sum of the weights of the top 10 stocks in the portfolio. Exhibit 6.8 provides a simple summary of the top 10 positions in CAM's small-cap value portfolio.

Alone, this number doesn't tell us too much, but when compared to other products in the same asset class, it takes on more meaning. An analysis of the universe of small-cap value mutual funds indicates that the average small-cap value fund has 29.2% of its assets in the top 10 holdings.

EXHIBIT 6.8   Percent in Top Ten

Stock Name	Weight
CSK ADR	3.4%
Interpore Int'l	3.2%
Multimedia Games	2.8%
Navigators Group	2.7%
Columbia Sportswear	2.7%
Acambis ADR	2.6%
Pediatrix Med'l Grp.	2.5%
Amer. Eagle Outfitter	2.5%
BP Prudhoe Bay Rlty.	2.4%
HCC Insurance Hldgs.	2.3%
Percent in Top Ten	27.1%

Based on this information (and the information we gather on the other small-cap value finalists), we can feel comfortable that CAM is operating within industry norms and not taking any undue risks relative to its peers based on position size.

FUNDAMENTAL ANALYSIS

Performing fundamental analysis is analogous to looking under the hood before buying a car. With the exception of index funds, which emulate specific indexes, and certain hedge funds designed to neutralize the effects of investment style, a portfolio can be identified by its fundamentals just like our fingerprints can identify us.

Value managers tend to exhibit certain fundamental characteristics that are widely indicative of the value style. The same holds true for growth managers and growth at a reasonable price (GARP) managers. As such, we can look at summary level fundamental characteristics and make certain assumptions about a given investment manager and/or product.

Exhibit 6.9 generalizes the tendencies that growth and value managers exhibit for individual stocks as well as overall portfolio characteristics. The typical value manager exhibits lower valuation ratios and growth figures, whereas the typical growth manager has higher valuation ratios, but correspondingly higher growth figures. In essence, the growth manager pays extra for that growth. As investment manager analysts, we can select from hundreds of fundamental characteristics. At this stage of the

EXHIBIT 6.9   Style Matrix

	Value Style	Growth Style
Price-earnings (P/E)	Lower	Higher
Price/book value	Lower	Higher
Price/cash flow	Lower	Higher
Price/sales	Lower	Higher
Debt/equity	Lower	Higher
Earnings growth	Lower	Higher
Revenue growth	Lower	Higher
Sales growth	Lower	Higher
Return on equity (ROE)	Lower	Higher
Return on assets (ROA)	Lower	Higher

process, I generally focus on a dozen or so standard fundamental measures that cover the following areas:

- *Valuation-based characteristics.* Typically measured with a ratio that has the stock's price in the numerator and some measure of portfolio value in the denominator (e.g., price-earnings ratio).
- *Growth-based characteristics.* These are historical growth measures. They can include a number of factors, such as earnings growth, revenue growth, sales growth, and so on.
- *Liquidity characteristics.* These measures focus on the company's financial position and can include such factors as total debt/equity, interest coverage ratios, and so on.

To keep matters simple, I tend to select a few fundamental characteristics from each group and review the portfolio from the top down and bottom up. The remainder of the chapter describes a number of fundamental characteristics for each section and then uses the CAM small-cap value portfolio to illustrate how to interpret the data.

Valuation-Based Fundamental Characteristics

Price-Earnings (P/E)

$$P/E = \frac{\text{Current Price}}{\text{EPS}}$$

$$\text{where EPS} = \frac{\text{Net Income} - \text{Dividends on Preferred Stock}}{\text{Average Outstanding Shares}}$$

This is a valuation ratio that measures a company's share price relative to its earnings per share (EPS). The numerator (price) is usually depicted as the current price of the stock, but when calculating historical P/E, the price at the time of the earnings is appropriate. The denominator of this ratio, however, can be open to interpretation because earnings can be defined in a number of ways:

- *GAAP EPS.* This EPS figure is earnings per share that are reported in SEC filings and are based on generally accepted accounting principles (GAAP). Despite the fact that specific accounting principles are used, company management can still manipulate the data to meet their own needs.

- *Normalized EPS.* The earnings figure includes only items that are ongoing, and excludes any events that are unusual or one-time occurrences.
- *Pro forma EPS.* This form of EPS can be manipulated to include and/or exclude specific items based on the whims of company management.
- *Headline EPS.* This EPS figure is the one that appears in a company's earnings press release. It can be a GAAP or pro forma EPS figure—the only way to know would be to read the entire press release (which few people tend to do).

As long as you know which form of EPS you are reviewing and as long as you use the same form of EPS for all stocks within a portfolio and for each manager and index used in your analysis, you should be fine.

Price/Book

$$P/B = \frac{\text{Current Price}}{\text{Book Value per Share}}$$

$$\text{where } BVPS = \frac{\text{Assets} - \text{Liabilities}}{\text{Average Outstanding Shares}}$$

The P/B ratio provides a measure of how expensive (higher P/B) or inexpensive (lower P/B) a company might be. Another way of interpreting the P/B ratio would be to look at it as a measure of how much a company might be worth in case of bankruptcy. However, it is important to note that a company's book value should be used relative to its peer group, as book value tends to differ significantly from sector to sector and from industry to industry.

Price/Cash Flow

$$\text{Price/Cash Flow} = \frac{\text{Current Price}}{\text{Cash Flow per Share}}$$

$$\text{where } CFPS = \frac{\text{Noncash Charges} + \text{Net Income after Taxes}}{\text{Average Outstanding Shares}}$$

Cash flow is the amount of cash that a company generates and uses over a specific period and can be used as a measure of a company's financial strength. Cash flow represents the net of the incoming and out-going cash to a given company. The cash inflow comes from customers, lenders, and investors, while the cash outflows go to salaries, suppliers, and creditors. A company that has an adequate amount of cash on hand to meet its future liabilities is generally considered to be in a better financial condition than a company that does not have the ability to generate enough cash to meet its future expenses or needs. Just like the other price-based ratios, a company with a lower P/CF ratio is likely to be viewed as undervalued and vice versa.

Many analysts prefer this ratio to the P/E ratio because it is harder to manipulate a company's cash figure than it is to manipulate the earnings figure (as explained earlier).

Price/Free Cash Flow

$$\text{Price/Free Cash Flow} = \frac{\text{Current Price}}{\text{Free Cash Flow per Share}}$$

$$\text{where } \text{FCFPS} = \frac{\text{FCF}}{\text{Average Outstanding Shares}}$$

where FCF = Net income + Depreciation and Amortization – Changes in working capital – Capital expenditures

Free cash flow is meant to measure cash that a company is spending right now. That is why we add back depreciation and amortization to the figure (as both represent future cash outlays). A high relative FCF can be interpreted as an indicator of how high or low a company's up-front costs are—or, stated differently, how much cash a company has left over after paying its bills for ongoing activities and growth. FCF is a "show me the money" figure. A growing FCF figure is typically interpreted as a harbinger of good things to come, such as increases in earnings. A company with a rising FCF and a low share price might be perceived by investors as a strong value.

Price/Sales

$$\text{Price/Sales} = \frac{\text{Current Price}}{\text{Sales per Share}}$$

where $SPS = \dfrac{\text{Revenue}}{\text{Average Outstanding Shares}}$

The revenue figure typically covers the past 12 months or the prior fiscal year. This ratio is used as a measure of a firm's sales growth relative to its current share price. A lower P/S ratio relative to other stocks can be interpreted as more of a value because in simple terms the lower ratio represents higher sales compared to the share price. Just like the other price-related ratios previously covered, the P/S ratio can differ from sector to sector and from industry to industry. Also, an increase in the denominator (sales per share) would need further review to ascertain whether the growth in sales is real or manufactured by creative accounting methods.

Portfolio Analysis—Valuation Data   Now that we have discussed just some of the valuation ratios available to the investment manager analyst, we can apply them to the CAM small-cap value portfolio. To better focus on the valuation ratios, Exhibit 6.10 takes the information from Exhibit 6.1 and recreates it with only the information relevant to this section.

Starting from the top down, we can compare the portfolio's overall statistics to those of the small-cap indexes.

Exhibit 6.11 indicates that CAM's P/E is right in line with the small-cap value index and below those of the broad and growth-oriented indexes. Given CAM's value style, this is a good sign. However, CAM's other portfolio valuation statistics are considerably higher than the small-cap value index. In fact, they look more like the small-cap growth index's numbers. It is also fairly obvious that the P/E ratios fall into a reasonably tight range around the portfolio's average. I have highlighted four portfolio companies (CSK, Interpore, Possis Medical, and Charles & Colvard) with P/Es significantly higher than the portfolio average and the small-cap indexes. Conversely, it appears that only one portfolio company (Acambis ADR) does not have positive earnings for the prior 12-month period (this company's P/E ratio is listed as "–", which in this case denotes a negative number). Given that CAM considers itself a value-driven firm, I would inquire about these stocks.

At this point, we can start to include aspects of the other portfolio analysis we have already performed. We had previously determined that the CAM small-cap value portfolio is concentrated mainly in three broad sectors (cyclical, financials, and health care). The health care sector is traditionally considered to be more growth oriented than value oriented because the companies tend to have higher valuation ratios associated with their higher growth rates. Because the CAM portfolio has about a quarter

EXHIBIT 6.10 Valuation Analysis of CAM's Portfolio

	Descriptive Data				Valuation Data			
Name	Sector	Industry	%Port	Mkt Cap	P/E LTM	P/B	P/S	P/CF
CSK ADR	Information Tech	IT Consulting & Svc.	3.4%	$2,677	29.4	3.4	0.9	—
Interpore Int'l	Health Care	HC—Supplies	3.2%	$ 291	52.6	3.9	4.5	41.7
Multimedia Games	Consumer Services	Casinos & Gaming	2.8%	$ 470	16.8	5.6	1.4	11.1
Navigators Group	Financials	Insurance—Prop./Cas.	2.7%	$ 256	14.3	1.4	0.9	13.5
Columbia Sportswear	Consumer Cyclical	Apparel & Accessory	2.7%	$2,196	20.1	4.4	2.5	17.0
Acambis ADR	Health Care	Biotechnology	2.6%	$ 514	—	5.1	Na	—
Pediatrix Med'l Grp.	Health Care	HC—Services	2.5%	$1,122	16.5	2.2	2.2	15.1
Amer Eagle Outfitter	Consumer Cyclical	Retail—Apparel	2.5%	$1,087	13.8	1.8	0.7	8.4
BP Prudhoe Bay Rlty.	Energy	Oil & Gas—Expl./Prod.	2.4%	$ 428	8.1	26.9	8.0	8.4
HCC Insurance Hldgs.	Financials	Insurance—Multiline	2.3%	$1,891	15.5	2.0	2.3	14.3
Decoma Int'l	Consumer Cyclical	Auto Parts & Equip.	2.3%	$ 525	9.2	1.6	0.2	3.7
Ralcorp Hldgs.	Consumer Noncyclical	Packaged Foods/Meats	2.2%	$ 807	14.4	1.8	0.6	8.8
Greater Bay Bancorp	Financials	Regional Banks	2.2%	$1,105	10.5	1.8	2.2	8.2
Sky Fin'l Group	Financials	Diversified Banks	2.2%	$2,096	13.9	2.4	3.7	11.8
Renal Care Group	Health Care	HC—Services	2.2%	$1,673	17.1	2.9	1.7	12.1
Option Care	Health Care	HC—Services	2.2%	$ 251	16.1	2.0	0.7	12.6
Cherokee	Consumer Cyclical	Apparel & Accessory	2.2%	$ 170	12.7	6.5	4.8	11.0
Pogo Producing	Energy	Oil & Gas—Expl./Prod.	2.2%	$2,924	12.1	2.4	2.8	5.5
Linens 'n Things	Consumer Cyclical	Specialty Stores	2.1%	$1,074	16.0	1.6	0.5	9.5
Curtiss-Wright	Information Tech	Aerospace/Defense	2.1%	$ 724	15.1	1.7	1.1	10.9
Prosperity Banc	Financials	Regional Banks	2.1%	$ 424	16.9	2.6	5.5	13.5
St. Mary Land & Expl.	Energy	Oil & Gas—Expl./Prod.	2.1%	$ 753	12.6	2.3	2.5	6.6
Heritage Fin'l	Financials	Regional Banks	2.1%	$ 141	16.8	2.1	3.9	13.8

Glacier Bancorp	Financials	Regional Banks	2.1%	$ 559	15.5	2.3	4.3	11.8
First South Bancorp	Financials	Regional Banks	2.0%	$ 141	14.3	2.9	3.9	13.4
America's Car-Mart	Consumer Cyclical	Specialty Stores	2.0%	$ 239	17.2	3.3	1.5	16.8
Berry Petroleum	Energy	Oil & Gas—Expl./Prod.	2.0%	$ 407	13.4	2.3	2.6	8.7
ICU Medical	Health Care	HC—Supplies	2.0%	$ 357	19.1	2.5	3.7	14.9
Jakks Pacific	Consumer Cyclical	Leisure Products	1.9%	$ 306	9.7	0.8	1.0	7.5
Invision Technology	Information Tech	Aerospace/Defense	1.9%	$ 441	4.2	1.6	0.8	4.1
Sterling Bancshares	Financials	Regional Banks	1.9%	$ 530	12.8	2.0	2.1	7.9
Remington Oil & Gas	Energy	Oil & Gas—Expl./Prod.	1.8%	$ 495	15.5	2.4	3.5	7.0
Nat'l Med. Hlth. Card	Health Care	HC—Services	1.7%	$ 103	16.4	3.5	0.2	9.7
MB Fin'l	Financials	Regional Banks	1.7%	$ 792	16.1	2.2	4.2	10.6
Cantel Medical	Health Care	HC—Equipment	1.5%	$ 128	17.2	2.0	1.0	11.2
Rehabcare Group	Health Care	HC—Facility	1.5%	$ 283	12.8	1.4	0.5	9.3
Cole (Kenneth) Prod.	Consumer Cyclical	Apparel & Accessory	1.5%	$ 521	18.2	3.1	1.2	14.5
Allegiant Bancorp	Financials	Diversified Banks	1.5%	$ 348	15.7	2.1	3.7	13.1
Churchill Downs	Consumer Services	Casinos & Gaming	1.4%	$ 510	17.8	2.3	1.1	10.6
RLI	Financials	Insurance—Prop./Cas.	1.3%	$ 842	15.8	1.8	1.9	14.8
Amer Woodmark	Consumer Cyclical	Building Products	1.3%	$ 356	11.9	2.1	0.6	6.2
U.S. Physical Therapy	Health Care	HC—Facility	1.2%	$ 150	18.9	3.9	1.5	13.8
Possis Medical	Health Care	HC—Equipment	1.2%	$ 285	32.0	6.1	5.0	25.8
New Century Fin'l	Financials	Thrifts & Mortgage Fin.	1.2%	$1,050	5.4	2.6	1.4	5.2
Amer Real Estate Ptr.	Financials	Diverse Fin'l Svc.	1.2%	$ 557	12.8	0.5	1.9	8.6
Catalina Marketing	Commercial Services	Advertising	1.1%	$ 817	14.9	2.7	1.7	8.4
Bisys Group	Information Tech	Services—Data Proc.	1.1%	$1,618	13.6	2.1	1.7	9.6
Blue Rhino	Consumer Cyclical	Retail—Home Improve.	1.0%	$ 197	11.6	1.6	0.8	7.9
Polymedica	Health Care	HC—Supplies	1.0%	$ 675	15.8	3.3	1.8	7.9
Gildan Activewear	Consumer Cyclical	Apparel & Accessory	0.9%	$ 660	15.4	4.1	1.5	12.3
Orthodontic Centers	Health Care	HC—Services	0.9%	$ 400	6.5	0.9	1.0	4.7

(Continued)

121

EXHIBIT 6.10 (Continued)

	Descriptive Data				Valuation Data			
Name	Sector	Industry	%Port	Mkt Cap	P/E LTM	P/B	P/S	P/CF
Pxre Group	Financials	Reinsurance	0.6%	$ 218	5.6	0.7	0.6	–
PRG-Schultz Int'l	Industrials	Services—Div./Comm'l	0.5%	$ 369	11.7	1.1	0.9	7.2
Atlantic Coast Airln.	Industrials	Airlines	0.5%	$ 402	9.0	1.4	0.5	6.3
Nordic Amer. Tanker	Industrials	Marine	0.5%	$ 119	5.2	1.1	3.7	4.0
Coinstar	Industrials	Services—Div./Comm'l	0.4%	$ 297	13.2	2.8	1.8	6.1
Total Entertainment	Consumer Services	Restaurants	0.3%	$ 108	14.9	2.4	0.9	8.6
Charles & Colvard	Consumer Cyclical	Apparel & Accessory	0.2%	$ 63	29.8	1.4	3.7	28.0
Total Portfolio				$ 777	15.8	3.2	2.2	11.0

Legend:
% Port = Dollars invested in a given stock as a % of total market value.
Mkt Cap = Company's # shares outstanding × current price. A measure of the total mkt value for a given company.
P/E LTM = Price/earnings ratio using actual company earnings over the last 12 months.
P/B = Price/book ratio
P/S = Price/sales ratio
P/CF = Price/cash flow ratio

EXHIBIT 6.11   Summary Level Valuation Characteristics

	P/E	P/B	P/S	P/CF
CAM Small-cap value portfolio	15.8	3.2	2.2	11.0
S&P SmallCap Value Index	15.5	1.4	0.6	7.6
S&P SmallCap Index	17.4	1.9	0.8	9.7
S&P SmallCap Growth Index	19.5	3.2	1.4	13.2

of its assets in this sector versus just 5.5% for the small cap-value index, we should not be surprised to see that some valuation ratios are higher than that index.

We can also drill down to the individual stock level by highlighting stocks that have valuation ratios significantly below or above the portfolio average. In Exhibit 6.10, the valuation ratios of several stocks that appear to be outliers have been highlighted. At this point, we as an investment manager analyst can elect to wait until we speak directly with the portfolio manager to ask about these outliers or we can look into the issues on our own. I always research outlier stocks myself so I can discuss the issues and challenge the portfolio manager during subsequent interviews.

Growth-Based Fundamental Characteristics

Return on Equity (ROE)

$$ROE(1) = \frac{\text{Net Income}}{\text{Shareholders' Equity}}$$

ROE is a means of comparing the profitability of a company to other companies in the same industry. The simple form of the formula is shown as ROE(1), but the ROE figure can also be decomposed into three categories, as illustrated in ROE(2).

$$ROE(2) = \text{Profit Margin} \times \text{Asset Turnover} \times \text{Financial Leverage}$$

where   Profit Margin = Net Income ÷ Sales
        Asset Turnover = Sales ÷ Assets
     Financial Leverage = Assets ÷ Shareholders' Equity

By using the methodology depicted in ROE(2), the investor can delve deeper into the underlying ROE number and see what is driving the growth in ROE over a period of time. By looking at these three critical areas, an investor can gauge how effective the underlying company management is and make an assessment of management's ability to get the job done.

Return on Assets (ROA)

$$ROA(1) = \frac{Net\ Income + Interest\ Expense}{Total\ Assets}$$

The ROA calculation indicates what return a company is generating based on the firm's assets (or investments). Because ROA is used as a measure of analyzing a company's return on investments, it is sometimes referred to as ROI (or return on investments).

ROA can also be calculated by disaggregating the underlying parts. The resulting formula, ROA(2), gives the investor the ability to dig deeper into the ROA number and make certain informed assumptions as to the underlying cause and effect.

$$ROA(2) = Profit\ Margin \times Asset\ Turnover$$

As is the case with all the measures discussed in this chapter, the ROA numbers only take on meaning when compared to companies in the same industry. For example, a capital-intensive company (such as an automaker) will have different ROA than a less capital-intensive company (such as a software firm). As a result, it would be unfair to compare the two companies' ROA numbers against each other.

Price/Growth (PEG)

$$PEG\ Ratio = \frac{P/E}{Annual\ EPS\ Growth}$$

The PEG ratio is a means of combining a measure of a company's value (P/E) and its growth (EPS growth) and is widely considered to be an indicator of a stock's potential value. However, as the P/E section explained, the earnings figures can be manipulated and stated in a number of different ways. As always, it is important to consistently apply the earnings measures in both the numerator and the denominator. Because the PEG ratio in simplest terms is just a ratio of value to growth, the lower the resulting ratio the better the value (or the more bang you get for the buck).

Earnings Estimates

Earnings estimates are computed by analysts that sell their research (known as sell-side research) through brokerage firms. These estimates of earnings are tabulated by several companies and packaged in many different ways.

- *Estimate consensus.* This is the average earnings estimate based on all available sell-side research.
- *High/low estimate.* As the consensus represents the average, the high and low estimates are often presented to show the range of estimates.
- *Earnings revisions.* Analysts update their models when new information makes itself available. After adjusting their valuation models, analysts will then adjust (revise) their earnings estimates. Some investors interpret upward earnings revisions as positive news because upward revisions imply that the analysts that cover a given stock have new information that caused them to increase the underlying value of the firm or the firm's future growth potential. Revisions are tracked based on different time periods (5-day, 30-day, 60-day, etc.).
- *Price/forward earnings.* This is the P/E ratio using forward EPS estimates based on the earnings consensus. By using this ratio, the investor can make assumptions on a company's current valuation (price) based on the estimated earnings of the company. A company with a price/forward earnings less than its P/E based on historical earnings can be interpreted as undervalued relative to future growth potential, as the denominator in the forward P/E ratio (forward earnings estimates) would be higher than in the past 12 months.

Revenue/Sales Growth

Both revenue and sales are stated plainly in a company's income statements. As a result, it is easy to extract these figures from the current and historical financial statements and compare their rate of growth through time. A simple way to measure revenue or sales growth is to calculate the growth in the underlying numbers over the past year, three years, or five years, or for any other period that the data will allow.

Portfolio Analysis—Growth Data Once again, starting with overall portfolio statistics we can see in Exhibit 6.12 that the CAM small-cap portfolio has overall portfolio statistics that are very different from what one would expect from a value manager. The CAM portfolio's ROE, for example, was 17.4% (compared to 11.7% for the broad small-cap index, 16.8% for the small-cap growth index, and 6.8% for the small-cap value index). In addition, the portfolio's earnings and revenue growth over the past 12 months was 74.1% and 29.1%, respectively. However, these numbers should likely

EXHIBIT 6.12 Growth Analysis of CAM's Portfolio

| | Descriptive Data | | | | Earnings Data | | | | |
Name	Sector	Industry	%Port	Mkt Cap	Ern% LTM	Rev% LTM	ROE	30 Day ERUp	30 Day ERDn
CSK ADR	Information Tech	IT Consulting & Svc.	3.4%	$2,677	-15.0	-5.1	—	—	—
Interpore Int'l	Health Care	HC—Supplies	3.2%	$ 291	55.0	16.5	7.8	0.0	0.0
Multimedia Games	Consumer Services	Casinos & Gaming	2.8%	$ 470	38.0	32.9	36.9	0.0	1.0
Navigators Group	Financials	Insurance—Prop./Cas.	2.7%	$ 256	188.0	47.2	10.4	0.0	0.0
Columbia Sportswear	Consumer Cyclical	Apparel & Accessory	2.7%	$2,196	21.0	10.5	24.4	0.0	0.0
Acambis ADR	Health Care	Biotechnology	2.6%	$ 514	—	—	—	0.0	1.0
Pediatrix Med'l Grp.	Health Care	HC—Services	2.5%	$1,122	50.0	16.4	12.6	0.0	0.0
Amer Eagle Outfitter	Consumer Cyclical	Retail—Apparel	2.5%	$1,087	-17.0	4.9	14.1	24.0	0.0
BP Prudhoe Bay Rlty.	Energy	Oil & Gas—Expl./Prod.	2.4%	$ 428	50.0	49.5	13.6	0.0	0.0
HCC Insurance Hldgs.	Financials	Insurance—Multiline	2.3%	$1,891	62.0	40.9	14.6	0.0	0.0
Decoma Int'l	Consumer Cyclical	Auto Parts & Equip.	2.3%	$ 525	26.0	10.1	12.5	1.0	2.0
Ralcorp Hldgs.	Consumer Noncyclical	Packaged Foods/Meats	2.3%	$ 807	10.0	2.7	18.0	0.0	0.0
Greater Bay Bancorp	Financials	Regional Banks	2.2%	$1,105	-4.0	18.2	18.7	2.0	0.0
Sky Fin'l Group	Financials	Diversified Banks	2.2%	$2,096	9.0	19.3	16.9	0.0	1.0
Renal Care Group	Health Care	HC—Services	2.2%	$1,673	21.0	16.7	13.1	0.0	0.0
Option Care	Health Care	HC—Services	2.2%	$ 251	16.0	29.7	13.1	0.0	0.0
Cherokee	Consumer Cyclical	Apparel & Accessory	2.2%	$ 170	7.0	10.5	91.7	—	—
Pogo Producing	Energy	Oil & Gas—Expl./Prod.	2.2%	$2,924	295.0	72.6	21.1	3.0	3.0
Linens 'n Things	Consumer Cyclical	Specialty Stores	2.1%	$1,074	9.0	14.9	10.4	1.0	0.0
Curtiss-Wright	Information Tech	Aerospace/Defense	2.1%	$ 724	16.0	65.7	11.7	0.0	0.0
Prosperity Banc	Financials	Regional Banks	2.1%	$ 424	29.0	38.7	19.0	0.0	0.0
St. Mary Land & Expl.	Energy	Oil & Gas—Expl./Prod.	2.1%	$ 753	253.0	73.4	18.5	5.0	0.0
Heritage Fin'l	Financials	Regional Banks	2.1%	$ 141	14.0	3.4	11.9	0.0	0.0
Glacier Bancorp	Financials	Regional Banks	2.1%	$ 559	28.0	22.3	16.9	0.0	0.0
First South Bancorp	Financials	Regional Banks	2.0%	$ 141	36.0	22.1	19.1	0.0	0.0
America's Car-Mart	Consumer Cyclical	Specialty Stores	2.0%	$ 239	28.0	21.4	21.7	—	3.0
Berry Petroleum	Energy	Oil & Gas—Expl./Prod.	2.0%	$ 407	39.0	31.5	17.6	0.0	0.0
ICU Medical	Health Care	HC—Supplies	2.0%	$ 357	18.0	19.4	13.5	0.0	0.0
Jakks Pacific	Consumer Cyclical	Leisure Products	1.9%	$ 306	-26.0	6.5	9.0	0.0	0.0
Invision Technology	Information Tech	Aerospace/Defense	1.9%	$ 441	666.0	319.7	46.8	0.0	0.0
Sterling Bancshares	Financials	Regional Banks	1.9%	$ 530	21.0	21.3	16.8	0.0	1.0
Remington Oil & Gas	Energy	Oil & Gas—Expl./Prod.	1.8%	$ 495	1,090.0	52.6	15.6	4.0	2.0

Company	Sector	Industry	% Port	Mkt Cap	Ern% LTM	Rev% LTM	ROE	30 day ERUp	30 day ERDn
Nat'l Med. Hlth. Card	Health Care	HC—Services	1.7%	$ 103	43.0	24.7	25.2	0.0	0.0
MB Fin'l	Financials	Regional Banks	1.7%	$ 792	24.0	20.6	14.5	0.0	0.0
Cantel Medical	Health Care	HC—Equipment	1.5%	$ 128	8.0	7.7	12.4	2.0	0.0
Rehabcare Group	Health Care	HC—Facility	1.5%	$ 283	17.0	0.8	10.8	1.0	0.0
Cole (Kenneth) Prod.	Consumer Cyclical	Apparel & Accessory	1.5%	$ 521	57.0	15.4	17.5	0.0	0.0
Allegiant Bancorp	Financials	Diversified Banks	1.5%	$ 348	9.0	28.4	12.8	0.0	0.0
Churchill Downs	Consumer Services	Casinos & Gaming	1.4%	$ 510	31.0	3.3	11.9	0.0	0.0
RLI	Financials	Insurance—Prop./Cas.	1.3%	$ 842	36.0	32.1	12.5	0.0	1.0
Amer Woodmark	Consumer Cyclical	Building Products	1.3%	$ 356	-8.0	11.9	19.0	1.0	0.0
U.S. Physical Therapy	Health Care	HC—Facility	1.2%	$ 150	5.0	13.6	21.0	2.0	0.0
Possis Medical	Health Care	HC—Equipment	1.2%	$ 285	47.0	35.4	24.1	3.0	0.0
New Century Fin'l	Financials	Thrifts & Mortgage Fin.	1.2%	$1,050	82.0	72.8	48.9	0.0	5.0
Amer Real Estate Ptr.	Financials	Diverse Fin'l Svc.	1.2%	$ 557	-28.0	-11.5	4.0	—	—
Catalina Marketing	Commercial Services	Advertising	1.1%	$ 817	-6.0	6.2	23.6	1.0	0.0
Bisys Group	Information Tech	Services—Data Proc.	1.1%	$1,618	2.0	10.7	16.2	17.0	0.0
Blue Rhino	Consumer Cyclical	Retail-Home Improve.	1.0%	$ 197	43.0	25.2	17.5	2.0	1.0
Polymedica	Health Care	HC—Supplies	1.0%	$ 675	12.0	25.2	22.0	1.0	0.0
Gildan Activewear	Consumer Cyclical	Apparel & Accessory	0.9%	$ 660	59.0	22.0	20.8	1.0	0.0
Orthodontic Centers	Health Care	HC—Services	0.9%	$ 400	-12.0	-0.1	13.7	1.0	0.0
Pxre Group	Financials	Reinsurance	0.6%	$ 218	811.0	77.6	12.9	0.0	0.0
PRG-Schultz Int'l	Industrials	Services—Div/Comm'l	0.5%	$ 369	42.0	16.5	9.2	0.0	0.0
Atlantic Coast Airln.	Industrials	Airlines	0.5%	$ 402	-6.0	24.9	15.3	0.0	1.0
Nordic Amer.Tanker	Industrials	Marine	0.5%	$ 119	199.0	91.5	—	—	—
Coinstar	Industrials	Services—Div/Comm'l	0.4%	$ 297	150.0	17.4	30.0	0.0	0.0
Total Entertainment	Consumer Services	Restaurants	0.3%	$ 108	23.0	29.0	19.3	0.0	2.0
Charles & Colvard	Consumer Cyclical	Apparel & Accessory	0.2%	$ 63	23.0	18.2	5.3	—	—
Total Portfolio				$ 777	74.1	29.1	17.4	0.4	1.3

Legend:

% Port = Dollars invested in a given stock as a % of total market value.

Mkt Cap = Company's # shares outstanding × current price. A measure of the total mkt value for a given company.

Ern% LTM = Percentage change in earnings over the last 12 months

Rev% LTM = Percentage change in revenue over the last 12 months

ROE = Return on Equity

30 day ERUp = # of analyst's estimates that have increased in the past 30 days

30 day ERDn = # of analyst's earnings estimates that have decreased in the past 30 days

be adjusted downward because several individual outlier stocks in the portfolio (which are highlighted in Exhibit 6.12) pulled these figures higher. For example, Remington Oil and Gas is listed as having 12-month earnings growth in excess of 1,000% (10 times).

The last two columns of data in Exhibit 6.12 represent the sell-side analyst's revisions over the last 30-day period. I like to review this data because it gives me a very quick overview of how analysts are currently reviewing a given stock. For example, we can see that American Eagle Outfitters, a retail clothing store, has had 24 analysts revise their earnings estimates upward for this company in the past 30 days and has not had any analysts revise their estimates downward over the same period. Bisys Group had similar numbers, with 17 upward revisions and 0 downward revisions. These figures will give me some things to discuss with the investment manager during the interview stage of the process.

Liquidity-Based Fundamental Characteristics

Debt/Equity

$$\text{Debt/Equity} = \frac{\text{Total Liabilities}}{\text{Shareholders' Equity}}$$

This ratio states the relationship of a company's total debt to its underlying equity value or, stated differently, what proportion of equity and debt a company is using to finance its assets. A ratio with a value greater than 1 means that assets were financed mainly with debt. A ratio of less than 1 indicates that a company has financed its assets more through equity. While debt is not inherently bad, as a general rule a company with a high D/E ratio is considered more risky than a company with a lower D/E ratio. As stated previously, it is important to compare individual stocks to their appropriate peer group, as some sectors/industries generally use more debt than others.

Current Ratio

$$\text{Current Ratio} = \frac{\text{Current Assets}}{\text{Current Liabilities}}$$

The current ratio represents a fast and easy way of assessing a company's ability to pay its short-term obligations (liabilities)—the higher the ratio, the more liquid the company. This ratio is also known as the liquidity ratio and the cash ratio.

Quick Ratio

$$\text{Quick Ratio} = \frac{\text{Current Assets} - \text{Inventory}}{\text{Current Liabilities}}$$

This ratio simply measures how quickly a company can convert its assets to cash. While inventory has a value, it would take longer to liquidate; thus it is excluded from the calculation. This ratio, which is also known as the acid test ratio, is a stricter version of the current ratio.

Portfolio Analysis—Liquidity Data On a total portfolio basis, the average stock in the CAM small-cap portfolio has enough cash to meet its obligations, as the overall quick ratio is 1.9 (see Exhibit 6.13). Yet, a number of companies show up with negative results—meaning that they have an insufficient amount of cash on hand—while several others seem to have too much cash on hand (e.g., Nordic American Tanker). The report also illustrated that the overall level of company debt as a percentage of capital is high. Several of the portfolio companies appear to have no long-term debt, while others seem to have significant long-term debt.

Another good way of checking on the liquidity of the portfolio is to look into the volume of each holding in the portfolio. This allows us to question specific company holdings and to compile a weighted average volume for the total portfolio to compare against other managers we are reviewing. Most investment databases (and Web-based investment sites) offer a number of statistics related to stock volume. I tend to focus on average daily stock volume (such as 30-day, 90-day, 12-month) instead of just a single day's worth because the average tends to smooth out the number and helps to quickly eliminate any outliers. Using the volume information at the stock level, we can calculate how many days it would take to fully liquidate the position using the following formula:

$$\text{\# Days to Exit} = \frac{\text{\# of Shares}}{\text{Average Shares Traded}}$$

This can be calculated for each stock in the portfolio and then weighted to determine a figure for the total portfolio. Since CAM invests in a number of micro-cap stocks (stocks with market caps less than \$500 million), a determination of portfolio liquidity based on daily volume is critical.

EXHIBIT 6.13 Liquidity Analysis of CAM's Portfolio

	Descriptive Data				Liquidity	
Name	Sector	Industry	%Port	Mkt Cap	Quick	LtD/Cap
CSK ADR	Information Tech	IT Consulting & Svc.	3.4%	$2,677	0.8	24.0
Interpore Int'l	Health Care	HC—Supplies	3.2%	$ 291	2.7	0.0
Multimedia Games	Consumer Services	Casinos & Gaming	2.8%	$ 470	2.0	6.0
Navigators Group	Financials	Insurance—Prop./Cas.	2.7%	$ 256	—	6.0
Columbia Sportswear	Consumer Cyclical	Apparel & Accessory	2.7%	$2,196	2.9	4.0
Acambis ADR	Health Care	Biotechnology	2.6%	$ 514	0.7	23.0
Pediatrix Med'l Grp.	Health Care	HC—Services	2.5%	$1,122	1.4	4.0
Amer Eagle Outfitter	Consumer Cyclical	Retail—Apparel	2.5%	$1,087	1.5	2.0
BP Prudhoe Bay Rlty.	Energy	Oil & Gas—Expl./Prod.	2.4%	$ 428	—	0.0
HCC Insurance Hldgs.	Financials	Insurance—Multiline	2.3%	$1,891	—	24.0
Decoma Int'l	Consumer Cyclical	Auto Parts & Equip	2.3%	$ 525	0.7	16.0
Ralcorp Hldgs.	Consumer Noncyclical	Packaged Foods/Meats	2.2%	$ 807	0.6	25.0
Greater Bay Bancorp	Financials	Regional Banks	2.2%	$1,105	—	38.0
Sky Fin'l Group	Financials	Diversified Banks	2.2%	$2,096	—	68.0
Renal Care Group	Health Care	HC—Services	2.2%	$1,673	1.8	0.0
Option Care	Health Care	HC—Services	2.2%	$ 251	3.1	5.0
Cherokee	Consumer Cyclical	Apparel & Accessory	2.2%	$ 170	1.4	0.0
Pogo Producing	Energy	Oil & Gas—Expl./Prod.	2.2%	$2,924	1.8	31.0
Linens 'n Things	Consumer Cyclical	Specialty Stores	2.1%	$1,074	0.1	0.0
Curtiss-Wright	Information Tech	Aerospace/Defense	2.1%	$ 724	1.2	24.0

Company	Sector	Industry				
Prosperity Banc	Financials	Regional Banks	2.1%	$ 424	—	15.0
St. Mary Land & Expl.	Energy	Oil & Gas—Expl./Prod.	2.1%	$ 753	0.8	29.0
Heritage Fin'l	Financials	Regional Banks	2.1%	$ 141	—	0.0
Glacier Bancorp	Financials	Regional Banks	2.1%	$ 559	—	5.0
First South Bancorp	Financials	Regional Banks	2.0%	$ 141	—	0.0
America's Car-Mart	Consumer Cyclical	Specialty Stores	2.0%	$ 239	9.5	26.0
Berry Petroleum	Energy	Oil & Gas—Expl./Prod.	2.0%	$ 407	0.8	8.0
ICU Medical	Health Care	HC—Supplies	2.0%	$ 357	8.9	0.0
Jakks Pacific	Consumer Cyclical	Leisure Products	1.9%	$ 306	4.4	21.0
Invision Technology	Information Tech	Aerospace/Defense	1.9%	$ 441	2.3	1.0
Sterling Bancshares	Financials	Regional Banks	1.9%	$ 530	—	64.0
Remington Oil & Gas	Energy	Oil & Gas—Expl./Prod.	1.8%	$ 495	1.1	14.0
Nat'l Med. Hlth. Card	Health Care	HC—Services	1.7%	$ 103	0.7	1.0
MB Fin'l	Financials	Regional Banks	1.7%	$ 792	—	25.0
Cantel Medical	Health Care	HC—Equipment	1.5%	$ 128	1.9	22.0
Rehabcare Group	Health Care	HC—Facility	1.5%	$ 283	3.0	0.0
Cole (Kenneth) Prod.	Consumer Cyclical	Apparel & Accessory	1.5%	$ 521	2.0	0.0
Allegiant Bancorp	Financials	Diversified Banks	1.5%	$ 348	—	64.0
Churchill Downs	Consumer Services	Casinos & Gaming	1.4%	$ 510	0.6	32.0
RLI	Financials	Insurance—Prop./Cas.	1.3%	$ 842	—	0.0
Amer Woodmark	Consumer Cyclical	Building Products	1.3%	$ 356	1.0	10.0
U.S. Physical Therapy	Health Care	HC—Facility	1.2%	$ 150	5.3	0.0
Possis Medical	Health Care	HC—Equipment	1.2%	$ 285	6.4	0.0
New Century Fin'l	Financials	Thrifts&Mortgage Fin.	1.2%	$1,050	1.6	71.0
Amer Real Estate Ptr.	Financials	Diverse Fin'l Svc.	1.2%	$ 557	17.9	13.0
Catalina Marketing	Commercial Services	Advertising	1.1%	$ 817	0.8	17.0

(Continued)

131

EXHIBIT 6.13 *(Continued)*

| Name | Descriptive Data | | | | Liquidity | |
	Sector	Industry	%Port	Mkt Cap	Quick	Ltd/Cap
Bisys Group	Information Tech	Services-Data Proc.	1.1%	$1,618	0.9	28.0
Blue Rhino	Consumer Cyclical	Retail-Home Improve.	1.0%	$ 197	0.8	31.0
Polymedica	Health Care	HC—Supplies	1.0%	$ 675	3.8	1.0
Gildan Activewear	Consumer Cyclical	Apparel & Accessory	0.9%	$ 660	1.5	18.0
Orthodontic Centers	Health Care	HC—Services	0.9%	$ 400	2.8	18.0
Pxre Group	Financials	Reinsurance	0.6%	$ 218	–	0.0
PRG-Schultz Int'l	Industrials	Services—Div./Comm'l	0.5%	$ 369	1.1	32.0
Atlantic Coast Airln.	Industrials	Airlines	0.5%	$ 402	1.9	25.0
Nordic Amer. Tanker	Industrials	Marine	0.5%	$ 119	16.4	22.0
Coinstar	Industrials	Services—Div./Comm'l	0.4%	$ 297	1.1	12.0
Total Entertainment	Consumer Services	Restaurants	0.3%	$ 108	0.1	9.0
Charles & Colvard	Consumer Cyclical	Apparel & Accessory	0.2%	$ 63	8.6	0.0
Total Portfolio				$ 777	1.9	15.6

## CHAPTER 7

Information Gathering

At each stage of the investment manager analysis process thus far, we stopped to make the decision as to whether the investment firm and product under review should make it to the next step in the process. We can often quickly make the decision not to analyze an investment manager further by reviewing some or all of the data initially provided by the investment manager during the risk analysis stage of the due diligence process. For example, if the investment managers under review have a history of taking on too much risk or recently experienced employee turnover, we may elect to eliminate them from further consideration in only a few minutes.

The investment firms that make it past the performance analysis, risk analysis, and portfolio analysis stages are then sent a detailed questionnaire to fill out and send back to me. Along with the questionnaire, I also request a copy of the firm's Form ADV. This chapter includes a sample questionnaire and discusses the attributes of a typical Form ADV.

QUESTIONNAIRE

Many firms send out a copy of their questionnaire at the beginning of the due diligence process. While I understand that it would be nice to start off the due diligence process with a nicely filled out questionnaire, I recognize that it requires a great deal of effort to complete this. As a result, I try to send questionnaires only to firms that have a realistic chance of making it through the analytical process and possibly getting hired in the end. It has been my experience that more than half of the managers that I start taking through the process are dismissed pretty early on. If I can identify these managers without asking them to complete a lengthy questionnaire (remember, it might take an investment management firm weeks to fill out a lengthy questionnaire), it would be efficient to do so. By doing this, I am not just being kind to the investment management firm, I am also helping to keep my investment manager due diligence process as efficient as possible. A number of factors can dictate the time it takes to complete one of these questionnaires:

- *Manager in demand.* An investment manager that has a "hot" product or has a product in a "hot" asset class might become overwhelmed with requests for information (RFIs), which often include questionnaires.
- *Staffing issues.* An investment firm might be understaffed in this department or might have inefficient people in charge of the process.
- *Size/visibility of search.* Investment firm, like most others, must prioritize their time and energy. Often, this means that questionnaires and RFIs are filled out in an order that reflects the potential contribution size (i.e., an RFI that might translate into $100 million will get preferential treatment over an RFI that represents a possible $5 million contribution). Sometimes it is not the size of the possible contribution, but the visibility of the search (e.g., impressing a top consulting firm might provide great visibility and heighten the potential for assets in the future). Moreover, a small contribution from a well-respected firm or organization could also help push your RFI or questionnaire further down the list.

I have included a sample questionnaire in this chapter to serve as a guideline for readers. The questionnaire consists of four sections:

1. Organization
2. Firmwide Professional Staff
3. Operations
4. Product Information

The questionnaire's first three sections ask questions that are relevant to all investment firms, regardless of the asset class under review. The fourth section is the only one that needs to be tweaked when considering other asset classes. In this chapter, that section is written to address equity products. When we discuss other asset classes (fixed income and hedge funds) in later chapters, we will need to make adjustments only to the fourth section.

DUE DILIGENCE QUESTIONNAIRE
U.S. Equity

Please read these instructions before completing this questionnaire.

Should any questions not be applicable, please indicate as such by responding with "n/a" or "not applicable." All market value information should be stated in millions unless indicated otherwise. Please note the difference between individual and organizational accounts. Please enter responses to the questions in the spaces provided and/or in an attached document.

If you are responding with information on more than one product, please copy section four (Product Information) and answer it separately for each additional product. The first three sections (which deal with firm and broad organizational questions) remain the same regardless of the number of products included.

In the case of multiple product submission, clearly label each product at the beginning of its respective section four.

Any supporting materials must be clearly referenced to the appropriate question and appropriately labeled.

Information and supplemental attachments that are strictly promotional in nature should not be used.

Questionnaire Return Address:

Frank J. Travers, CFA
Investment Manager Analyst
Emerging Leaders Fund
New York, NY 11111
Phone: 212-XXX-XXXX
Fax: 212-XXX-XXXX
svcsearch@emlf.com

Section One: Organization

1. Provide the following organizational information:
   a. Firm name.
   b. Address (list the addresses of each office and describe each office's function).
   c. Main contact person (include telephone/fax numbers and e-mail address).
2. Firm's ownership structure, including:
   a. Ownership broken out by each individual and entity.
   b. Any affiliated companies or joint ventures, including any deals currently in the works and any planned deals.
   c. Recent changes or planned changes to the ownership structure.
   d. If another company owns your firm, what percentage of the parent company's revenue does your firm contribute? Please indicate how the percentage of revenue has changed over the life of the arrangement.
   e. An organizational chart, including any affiliated companies, joint ventures, and other entities that contribute in some way to your firm's investment and operational management.

3. Please include a copy of your most recent audited financial report. In addition, provide the name of your contact at the accounting firm that completed the firm's last audit. Include the contact's phone number.
4. Has your firm changed auditors in the past five years? If so, please explain why.
5. Has your organization, affiliates, parent company, officers, or principals been involved in litigation, legal proceedings, or investigations by any regulatory authority related to your firm's investment activities? If so, please provide a brief explanation, including the current status and/or the resolution of this action.
6. Describe the details of your firm's office space, including:

   a. Approximate size in square feet.
   b. Number of offices.
   c. Location of investment, trading, administration, and operations functions.

7. Does your firm have errors and omissions insurance or any other relevant insurance?

   a. If yes, please list the names of the insurance companies, the dollar amount of the coverage, and the coverage period.
   b. If no, please explain why not.

8. Please include your firm's web site address.

SECTION TWO: FIRMWIDE PROFESSIONAL STAFF

1. List the total number of employees in your organization by department:

	12/02	12/01	12/00	12/99
Portfolio managers				
Research analysts				
Economists				
Trading				
Compliance				
Marketing				
Administration				
Client service				
Other (specify)				
Total*				

*The total number of professional staff must match with the actual number of investment staff employed by the firm.

2. Provide biographies of all key investment professionals at your firm. Include biographies for personnel responsible for the product(s) under review as well as any investment professionals who may work on other products.
3. Describe the compensation structure for your firm's portfolio managers and research analysts, including incentives, bonuses, performance-based compensation, and equity ownership.
4. Provide the names of all investment professionals who have resigned, been terminated, or transferred/rotated to another department within the past five years. Provide a brief explanation for each departure. List any replacements for these vacancies.

Employee Name/Title	Resignation/Termination/Rotation	Reason

SECTION THREE: OPERATIONS

Reporting

1. Provide copies of any monthly and quarterly portfolio/market/economic reports that your firm has prepared. Include copies of all relevant monthly and quarterly reports for the past 12 months.
2. What is the timing of the monthly and quarterly reports? Please state the answer as number of days following the month/quarter end.

Regulatory

3. Please provide a copy of your firm's current SEC Form ADV (Parts I and II).
4. Discuss your firm's compliance procedures. Provide a copy of your firm's written compliance procedures if applicable.
5. What measures does you firm take to ensure compliance?
6. Who is responsible for checking that compliance procedures are met?
7. What is the frequency of the compliance checks?
8. What systems are in place for ensuring that portfolio managers are within client guidelines?
9. Has your firm ever found any violations of internal compliance procedures? If so, what were they and what steps were taken to remedy the situation?

Reconciliation/Administration

10. What pricing source(s) do you use?
11. Which custodian bank does your firm employ?
12. How often do you reconcile with the custodian bank?
13. When you find pricing differences, what is your procedure for reconciliation?

Systems/Backup/Disaster Recovery

14. What is your firm's plan regarding the backup of computer files and systems? Please provide a copy of your firm's written backup plan if available. Include the following information in your answer:

    a. How often do you perform a complete backup of all files?
    b. Who is responsible for the process?
    c. In the event of a disaster, how long would it take to become fully functional?
    d. What is your procedure for archiving paper files?

15. Please describe your firm's computer database and systems environment for securities research, fund accounting, risk management, performance measurement, and client reporting.
16. Describe any electronic interfaces with clients, brokers, and custodians.

SECTION FOUR: PRODUCT INFORMATION (EQUITY)

Clients/Assets

1. Provide the following data for the firm and product-specific assets (in millions). Insert additional rows if you have more than four products. Include the status of each product (open to new clients/assets or closed).

	Open/Closed	12/03	12/02	12/01	12/00	12/99
Product #1						
Product #2						
Product #3						
Product #4						
Total firm assets						

2. Please list any products that your firm has completely liquidated or merged with existing products. Include the reason(s) why the product was liquidated and/or merged with another product.

3. Complete the following client-related information:

	12/03	12/02	12/01	12/00	12/99
Total Firm					
# Clients					
# Clients gained (year)					
# Clients lost (year)					
Assets					
Assets gained (year)					
Assets lost (year)					
% Firm assets with top five clients					
Product-Specific					
# Clients					
# Clients gained (year)					
# Clients lost (year)					
Assets					
Assets gained (year)					
Assets lost (year)					
% Firm assets with top five clients					

Performance Data

4. Provide monthly historical performance figures (net of all fees) in the following table. Add rows to the table if the track record goes back further than five years.

	Jan	Feb	Mar	Apr	May	Jun	Jul	Aug	Sep	Oct	Nov	Dec
2003												
2002												
2001												
2000												
1999												

5. Is the performance history submitted AIMR compliant? If yes, has this performance history been certified by an independent auditor? Please provide a copy of the audit results. If no, please explain.
6. Please describe the data and methodology used to calculate the performance record stated in the previous question.

Description	Y/N	Explanation
Composite of separate accounts		
Equal weighted		
Size weighted		
Record linked from prior affiliation		
Representative account		
Commingled/mutual fund		
Simulated performance		

7. Please provide a copy of the full performance disclosures for the product under review. The disclosure should include the following for each year-end:

   a. Number of accounts included in the composite.
   b. Assets of those accounts.
   c. Number of accounts managed in a similar style, but not included in the composite.
   d. Assets of those accounts.
   e. Reasons why those accounts were not included in the composite.
   f. Number of accounts added to/subtracted from the composite in each year.

8. Please state the most appropriate benchmark for the product under review and include its performance history for the same time period listed previously for the product.

	Jan	Feb	Mar	Apr	May	Jun	Jul	Aug	Sep	Oct	Nov	Dec
2003												
2002												
2001												
2000												
1999												

9. Please provide performance attribution in the following format:

Year	Product Return	Index Return	+/–	Reasons for Out/Underperformance (please be as thorough as possible)
2003				
2002				
2001				

10. Do you utilize any internal or third party performance and/or attribution software/systems? If yes, please provide a list of the systems used and their purposes. In addition, please include with this questionnaire a sample of the attribution report for the latest month or quarter end.
11. What is the product's capacity? At what point would you close to new clients? At what point would you close to new assets from existing clients?

Portfolio Data

12. Please provide a representative portfolio for each of the last four quarter-end dates. The portfolios should be provided in Microsoft Excel format and should include the following information: security identifier (ticker), number of shares held, and each security's name. Include the following information regarding the selected representative account:

    a. Type of account.
    b. Account's inception date.
    c. Account size.
    d. Monthly historical performance for the account (to determine how closely it tracks the composite).

13. Provide the following geographical allocation data for the product in percentage of total assets (add rows for countries not included in the table, but are part of the portfolio):

Country	12/03	12/02	12/01	12/00	12/99
North America					
United States					
Canada					
Europe					
Austria					
Belgium					
Denmark					
Finland					
France					
Germany					
Ireland					
Italy					
Netherlands					
Norway					
Spain					
Sweden					
Switzerland					
United Kingdom					
Other					
Pacific Basin					
Australia					
New Zealand					
Hong Kong					
Japan					
Other					
Cash and Equivalents					

14. Provide the following sector allocation data for the portfolio in percentage of total assets (please use the sector descriptions provided in the table):

Sector	12/03	12/02	12/01	12/00	12/99
Basic Materials					
Commercial Services					
Consumer Cyclicals					
Consumer Noncyclicals					
Consumer Services					
Energy					
Financial Services					
Health Care					
Industrials					
Technology					
Telecommunications					
Transportation					
Utilities					

15. Provide industry allocation data for the portfolio in percentage of total assets for the top 20 industries:

12/03			12/02			12/01		
#	Industry	Weight	#	Industry	Weight	#	Industry	Weight
1			1			1		
2			2			2		
3			3			3		
4			4			4		
5			5			5		
6			6			6		
7			7			7		

(Continued)

12/03			12/02			12/01		
#	Industry	Weight	#	Industry	Weight	#	Industry	Weight
8			8			8		
9			9			9		
10			10			10		
11			11			11		
12			12			12		
13			13			13		
14			14			14		
15			15			15		
16			16			16		
17			17			17		
18			18			18		
19			19			19		
20			20			20		

16. Provide the following summary data for the portfolio in percentage of total assets:

	12/03	12/02	12/01	12/00	12/99
Fundamental Characteristics					
P/E (historical—last 12 months)					
P/E (forward 12 months)					
Earnings growth (1 year)					
Earnings growth (3 years)					
ROE					
Dividend yield					
Portfolio turnover					

	12/03	12/02	12/01	12/00	12/99
Market Capitalization					
Weighted market cap					
Average market cap					
% market cap < $100M					
% market cap from $100M to $500M					
% market cap from $500M to $1B					
% market cap from $1B to $2B					
% market cap from $2B to $3B					
% market cap from $3B to $5B					
% market cap from $5B to $10B					
% market cap > $10B					

Dedicated Product Investment Professionals

17. Include the names of all investment professionals (portfolio managers, analysts, traders, etc.) who work directly on the product under review.

Name	Product Responsibility	Years Working at Firm	Years Working on Product	Other Products Individual Works On	Other Responsibilities

18. Provide the names of all investment professionals who have worked on the product and have resigned, been terminated, or transferred/rotated to another department within the past five years. Provide a brief explanation for each departure. List any replacements for these vacancies.

Employee Name/Title	Resignation/ Termination/ Rotation	Reason(s)	Name of Replacement

19. Describe the structure of the investment management team. Include the following information:

    a. Name(s) of key decision maker(s). Be specific—identify the individual(s) who actually make(s) buy and sell decisions.
    b. Lead portfolio manager.
    c. Portfolio manager's backup.

Investment Philosophy and Process

20. Define your investment philosophy.
21. Define your investment style.
22. Describe in detail the investment process employed by the investment team in the management of the product. Include a description of how individual research and ideas make it (or don't make it) into the portfolio.
23. Buy/sell discipline:

    a. Market-cap restrictions.
    b. Geographical restrictions.
    c. Percent ownership of underlying companies.
    d. Fundamental characteristics.
    e. Liquidity constraints.

24. Do you have stop-loss procedures in place? If yes, describe the details. If no, explain your methodology regarding stocks that drop significantly in price. Please list the three largest percentage losers currently in the portfolio and explain the investment thesis for each.

25. Do you set price targets for all purchases? If yes, do you ever hold a security beyond the initial price target? Explain.
26. Describe your portfolio construction procedures. Include detail on each of the following:

    a. What types of securities are considered for purchase?
    b. What is the universe of possible investments?
    c. Do you have a minimum number of holdings?
    d. What were the fewest and most holdings ever held in the portfolio? Indicate the appropriate dates.
    e. How are individual position weights determined?
    f. What is the maximum position size at cost and at market value for any individual position? Have you ever violated this constraint?
    g. List any portfolio constraints regarding geography, sector, industry, market cap, and liquidity.

27. What is your investment edge? What differentiates you from your competition? Include a list of the firms/products that you consider to be your biggest competitors.
28. Is there a sector or industry in which you believe your firm has a particular edge? If yes, please elaborate.

Risk Controls

29. Describe your firm's risk management controls and procedures.
30. Who is responsible for the product's risk management?
31. With what frequency are risk management reports created and evaluated by the appropriate personnel?
32. What (if any) systems do you have in place to help manage risk?
33. Do you employ any third parties to conduct regular or periodic risk analysis or generate risk reports? If yes, please provide a list of the firms' names and their specific functions.
34. What is the 1-day, 10-day, and 30-day VaR for the current portfolio?
35. Do you perform scenario analysis or stress testing of the portfolio? If yes, provide the most recent results. If no, please explain why not.

Fees/Minimum

36. What is the product's fee schedule?
37. Do you currently offer the same product to any entity based on a reduced fee scale? If yes, explain.
38. Has the fee schedule changed in the past three years?
39. What is the product's minimum account size?

FORM ADV

This form is a requirement for any investment adviser that registers with the SEC and/or the individual states. It contains a great deal of data and must be periodically updated by the underlying investment management firms.

The ADV filing consists of three main sections:

1. Part IA: This part of the ADV provides a wealth of information regarding the underlying investment firm, the people who own and control the firm, and the people or entities that work for or are affiliated with the firm. Part IA also has additional "Schedules" that supplement the data in the main body of text.
2. Part IB: This part of the ADV asks questions that are required by state securities authorities.
3. Part II: This is basically the underlying investment firm's brochure. This section must be continuously amended and offered to all of the firm's current clients annually.

The filings require the investment management firm to complete a set of fixed questions under the following headings:

Item 1:	Identifying Information
Item 2:	SEC Registration
Item 3:	Form of Organization
Item 4:	Successions
Item 5:	Information about the Advisory Business
Item 6:	Other Business Activities
Item 7:	Financial Industry Affiliations
Item 8:	Participation or Interest in Client Transactions
Item 9:	Custody
Item 10:	Control Persons
Item 11:	Disciplinary Information
Item 12:	Small Business Determination
Schedule A:	Owners and Officers
Schedule B:	Indirect Owners
Schedule D:	Detailed explanation of answers to questions asked in Part IA

You can request a copy of the Form ADV from the investment management company that you are analyzing or you can simply log on to the SEC's web site and download the information yourself. These forms have been available via the SEC's web site (for no charge) since 2001.

According to the SEC's web site, there are currently (December 2003) more than 7,500 investment management firms that have registered their ADVs electronically, and thus these ADVs are available via the SEC's web site (www.sec.gov).

As you can see from the screenshot in Exhibit 7.1, the SEC has made it very easy to find an investment management firm. You can search for the investment firm even if you do not know its full name simply by selecting that search option and typing in part of the firm's name.

DATA FROM THE MANAGER

In addition to the volumes of data that are available in the completed questionnaire and the Form ADV, we can also get some very useful information from the materials that we requested from the manager in our initial RFI.

Marketing Presentation/Brochure

Investment management firms often spend a great deal of time (and money) creating marketing presentations. While these presentations differ in form and style from one firm to the next, they more than likely cover much of the same ground. These brochures often include sections

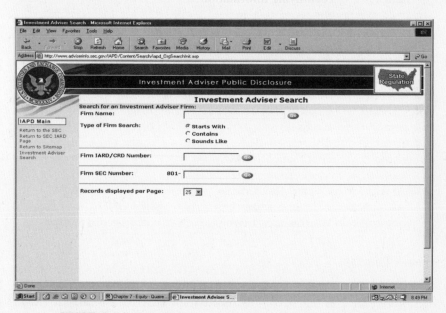

EXHIBIT 7.1   SEC's Web Site—Investment Manager Search Page

that cover the firm's history, professional bios, product statistics, investment process, and investment philosophy. Some of them even include examples of stock purchases and sales complete with explanations behind the transactions.

Just keep in mind that these marketing presentations were designed to entice readers. Take in the information with a healthy dose of skepticism.

Portfolio/Fund Fact Sheets

The portfolio/fund fact sheet is often a stripped-down version of the marketing presentation that has been reengineered to fit on a single sheet of paper (one side or both front and back). If given both a marketing book and a fact sheet, I will often check the two for any discrepancies. Sometimes the fact sheet contains some morsel of information that did not make it into the full marketing presentation or vice versa.

Monthly/Quarterly Portfolio Reports/Updates

Portfolio managers often write monthly and/or quarterly investment reports or updates that delve into the inner workings of the portfolio in detail. These reports are a fantastic way of peeking inside the inner workings of the portfolio manager or portfolio team. I always ask to receive copies of these kinds of reports going back at least a full year. If historical reports are available beyond a one-year period, I will often ask for them as well. I have found that many of the portfolio and performance-related questions that I come up with over the course of the due diligence process can be either fully or partially answered in these reports.

In addition, because the reports are usually written by the portfolio manager or a member of the investment team (and sometimes by a marketing or client service professional), I have an opportunity to compare what the portfolio manager tells me about historical portfolio events today and what was said in the reports back at the time in question. Using CAM as an example, the monthly/quarterly reports would serve two purposes:

1. As a check on what Mark (and/or Jim) tell me in our meetings.
2. As a means of finding good information that may lead to intelligent questions during the interview phase of the due diligence process.

Press Clippings

Investment firms usually track their media exposure and will often include reprints of articles that favorably reflect their firm, their products, and/or their staff. Again, keep in mind that the investment firm will not likely send you reprints of articles that are unfavorable.

NEWS SEARCH

Another great source of information regarding an investment firm, its products, and its staff can be found in what I term the "news search." Today there are literally hundreds of outlets for news, stories, articles, papers, and interviews. As a professional due diligence analyst, I conduct a news search every single working day so that I do not miss any important stories. And with the growth in the Internet as a resource, the amount of information that is available is staggering. Here are the primary news sources.

Newspapers—Print and Online

Good old-fashioned print newspapers are a wonderful source of topical news on broad topics such as the markets and the economy, but they also contain loads of information on investment firms, products, and investment professionals. Some of the big-name financial papers, such as the *Wall Street Journal, Financial Times,* and *Investor's Business Daily,* provide information on investment firms and investment products and funds on a daily basis. In addition to providing information on investment products you might be reviewing at any given time, they often provide fresh new leads. As mentioned in Chapter 2 "Investment Manager Sourcing," the daily newspapers often provide interviews with investment professionals and product/fund reviews that could be of interest to you when conducting a search now or in the future.

In addition to the print newspapers that are available, many newspapers are also updated regularly on the Internet. Each of the newspapers listed previously has a web site that is updated daily. Some papers charge an annual fee for viewing content and some charge only for certain articles you might want to have access to, but most are available on the Web free of charge. This is especially the case for smaller, local newspapers. One of the great advantages that the Internet provides us in our research is the ability to access literally thousands of local newspapers via the Web. Whenever I search news sources for information on a specific investment manager or investment professional, I start by looking at the major papers and sources *Wall Street Journal,* etc.); however, I also make a point of looking through the online versions of local newspapers. For example, if I am researching a firm that is located in St. Louis, Missouri, I will search through all the newspapers that are specific to that geographical area. A listing of local newspapers can be found by searching for the term "local newspaper links" in any of the popular search engines (such as Google) or by going to one of the following sites:

■ The Internet Public Library (www.ipl.org/div/news/)—The IPL is a wonderful resource that provides thousands of links to local newspapers from around the world. The web site is organized according to region, country, and state/province.
■ News Voyager (www.newspaperlinks.com/voyager.cfm)—Click on a state and get a list of newspapers that are available online.
■ NewsLink (http://newslink.org/)—This site offers a long list of U.S.-based newspapers broken into a variety of categories. Links to non-U.S. papers are also provided.

You will be surprised how often a local newspaper will include information on a local firm that adds value to your investment manager research. In addition, it is often possible to obtain information on specific investment professionals, both in a professional and in a personal capacity, by combing through these local resources. To save time, I skip the current news offered on these sites and go right to the archived information to perform a variety of searches. As in any Internet-based information search, I use a specific methodology to gain the most possible hits.

Tips for Internet-Based Information Searches

■ Start by searching from the top down or in the broadest manner possible, and then focus the search as results come in. I usually search for information in this order: (1) company, (2) product, (3) people.
■ Use quotation marks to isolate search phrases. By putting quotes around phrases (not single-word searches), you ensure that the search engine looks for the exact phrase you entered. This means the search engine will search for only the entire phrase (i.e., each word you entered in the same exact order in which you entered them). However, if you enter a phrase without the quotation marks around it, the search engine will search for any document that has all the words you entered anywhere in the World Wide Web. What's the difference? Using CAM Asset Management as the search phrase with and then without quotation marks can yield very different results. The search with quotes will be more focused and may return just a few results but they will likely be relevant, whereas the search without quotes will be more general in nature and may come up with thousands and, sometimes, millions of hits (depending on the search engine) that are not what you are looking for.

As a side note, the use of quoted phrases in conjunction with single search terms or nonquoted phrases can help to cull a long list to one that is more manageable. For example, if you were searching for a portfolio manager named John Smith, it would be inefficient to search for the name "John Smith" or the title "portfolio manager" with or without quotes because you would likely get millions of hits. However, if you search for "John Smith" and "portfolio manager" together, you might be able to come up with a more focused list.

■ When using search engines, be mindful of your spelling. When you ask a search engine to search for the term "portfolio manager," that is the exact spelling it will use in the search. However, many publications use abbreviations and/or other words entirely in their stories. So in addition to the search term "portfolio manager," you might want to search for: "portfolio mgr," "asset manager," "asset mgr," "investment manager," "investment mgr," "fund manager," "fund mgr," and so on.

■ Follow threads of information. When you conduct a search and come up with a series of hits, click into each hit and be mindful that any one of them might have links to more information.

■ Use the "find" option (which is under "edit" on the toolbar) to quickly locate where your specific search term appears in a web page or Web-based document. This comes in handy when you are looking at expansive web sites and/or very long Web-based documents. The find function allows you to zero in on exactly what you are looking for in seconds.

Magazines

While published less frequently than newspapers, magazines are another good source of potential information. Industry-specific magazines, such as *Fortune, Forbes, Money,* and *Kiplinger's Personal Finance,* often provide in-depth interviews with investment professionals as well as insightful analysis of specific investment firms and their products. As with newspapers, most of the print magazines are also available in some form via the Internet. Some offer all content for free, others charge a fee, while others offer some middle ground. In addition, it should be noted that most local libraries carry a wide assortment of these magazines for your review. The local branch library near my home, for example, receives hundreds of magazines, many of which are business or investment oriented. You can visit or call your local library or check to see if it has a web site to see what magazines it receives.

Newsletters

Another great source of information can be found in industry-specific newsletters. In the investment industry, there are dozens of newsletters available that cover a variety of topics. Institutional Investor Publications alone currently produces 20 weekly/monthly newsletters that range in scope from broad marketing news to news on that focuses exclusively on the hedge fund arena.

Dedicated Investment Sites

In addition to all the news sites and magazine sites, there are many dedicated investment web sites, such as MarketWatch.com, Bloomberg.com, and Morningstar.com. And don't discount sites like Yahoo!, MSN, and Lycos, because they often have great financial subsections as well.

CHAPTER 8

Initial Interview

Let's step back and review what we have accomplished thus far and determine what the next steps in the process should be (see Exhibit 8.1). After collecting data from several different small-cap value managers, we selected CAM Asset Management's small-cap value product to review (among others). Once we received a package of information from CAM, we started the analytical process by conducting returns-based analysis (performance and risk analysis). Then we took the underlying portfolio into consideration by performing detailed portfolio analysis. Next, we sent CAM a detailed questionnaire to fill out and we went on to the SEC's web site and downloaded CAM's Form ADV. In addition to this information, we have a copy of

EXHIBIT 8.1 The Next Step: Set Up an Initial Interview

Step 1	Setting Guidelines	Done	Background Work
Step 2	Screening Database	Done	
Step 3	Selection of Finalists	Done	
Step 4	Performance Analysis	Done	Manager Specific
Step 5	Risk Analysis	Done	
Step 6	Portfolio Analysis	Done	
Step 7	Questionnaire/ADV Review	Done	
Step 8	Initial Interview	←	If we decide to take CAM to the next level, then we need to set up a meeting
Step 9	Attribution/style analysis		
Step 10	On-site Visit		
Step 11	Manager Ranking Model		
Step 12	Decision		

CAM's marketing presentation (we requested this as part of the initial packet of information (Chapter 3).

If we decide that CAM's small-cap value portfolio is worth taking to the next step, we will need to set up some kind of meeting with the investment manager or one of the other decision makers for the portfolio under review. I rarely hold meetings just with marketing or client service professionals because at this stage in the process, I have done a fair amount of due diligence and have put together a list of targeted investment-related questions that I feel can be answered only by the investment professionals. In addition, because the people involved in the management of the underlying portfolio are the most important piece of the puzzle, I'm looking to gain an initial understanding of what makes the investment manager or team tick. No marketer or client service professional can relay this information to me—it has to come from the proverbial horse's mouth.

As Exhibit 8.1 illustrates, the next logical step in the process is to set up an initial investment meeting. However, before we do so we need to determine if a given manager is worth the time and effort. Thus far, we have limited the level of work we have done and kept it at a minimum. We have analyzed performance data, quickly reviewed a sample portfolio, and read through some basic information about the firm and the underlying product. However, it is at this stage in the process when we start to put in some time and effort. Meetings take time to prepare for, set up, and actually sit through. In addition, we have more detailed analytical work to perform in the next few stages as well as an on-site visit. On-site visits are lengthy meetings where the investment manager analyst travels to visit the investment management firm. They are time-consuming and often take some time to set up.

So that we can keep using CAM Asset Management as a case study, we will take them on to the next level and set up a meeting.

INITIAL MEETING

Experience has taught me that the initial meeting does not have to be face-to-face, but that is not a hard-and-fast rule. I conduct initial meetings via conference call roughly 90 percent of the time. This way, I do not waste the portfolio manager's or my time. In addition, I often set up rules for initial meetings. The first rule is that it should be no longer than 45 minutes. If I can't gain a solid understanding of an investment manager's process in that amount of time then there is a problem. A typical initial phone conference takes less than half an hour.

The reason why I can keep these meetings so short is because I have already done a lot of homework on the investment firm and the product under review. I do not have to ask basic questions because I have likely found the answers in the data already provided to me or through the internal analytics that I would have performed thus far in the process.

To better illustrate the format for an initial interview, I have created a fictional phone conference between the portfolio manager at CAM Asset Management, Mark Innes, and myself. The following transcript does not include every word that would be spoken during one of these meetings. I have eliminated the introductions, niceties, and any other information that is not relevant to this chapter. In addition, I have included some commentary in specific places to explain my reasoning behind certain questions or my interpretation of Mark's answers. The commentary appears in italics after each relevant question or response from Mark.

Transcript of conference call between Frank J. Travers, CFA, and Mark Innes, portfolio manager of the CAM small-cap value product.

[Conversation picks up after introductions.]

FT: Tell me about yourself.

MI: Do you have a copy of my bio?

FT: Yes, but as you know it just lists where you previously worked and the dates you were there. I'm looking to get a feel for what you did previously and how you ended up at CAM.

Remember, the three P's: people, process, and performance. Because the people involved in the investment process are the key element in making a decision to hire a particular investment firm, it is important to delve into each professional's background. However, due to the fact that this is a short initial phone conference, I tend to keep this line of questioning short. I will follow up in more detail if I conduct an onsite visit, during which I will try to get to know each investment professional who works on the product.

MI: Sure, just tell me when I start to bore you.

FT: Okay.

MI: I started out in this industry back in 1982 when I graduated from Penn State University. I had received my undergraduate in finance. I took a position as an equity analyst covering consumer cyclicals with a small asset management firm out of Los Angeles called Mackey Capital Partners. I recognized pretty early on that their investment style and mine did not mesh, so I left in 1985 and started my own firm, IAM, short for Innes Asset Management.

FT: Let's back up. What was so different about your styles?

It seems interesting to me that Mark took the job in the first place. If it was so obvious that their styles didn't mesh in his first few weeks of employment, why didn't this come up when he was interviewing? It could be that he was just out of school and didn't have the experience to recognize the incompatibility at that time, or it could be something else. In any case, this line of questioning will help me to get to know him better and will tell me something about his decision-making skills.

MI: They were a quantitative shop. They de-emphasized fundamental analysis and focused exclusively on statistical measures of mean reversion. You know . . . look for stocks trading below their mean, then find the ones with some catalyst that will push them back to that mean level.

FT: I'm surprised that you had a sector specialty at a quantitative shop. They tend to be generalists.

MI: Good point. I got a bit ahead of myself. When I had started there, I worked on a product that had a fundamental orientation, but the firm decided shortly after I joined that they preferred to focus exclusively on the quant product. I was essentially reassigned at that point.

FT: How long had you been there?

MI: Not long. A month maybe.

FT: So, within a month you had gone from performing fundamental analysis on consumer stocks to working on a quant-oriented product.

MI: Yes.

FT: What were your specific job responsibilities after the change?

MI: Jack-of-all-trades. I did portfolio reconciliation, trading, reporting, and some client service.

FT: You stayed with the firm for another three years before finally leaving.

MI: Yes.

FT: What took so long?

MI: At that time I didn't know what I wanted to do. Fortunately, the firm made the decision for me when they went out of business. I had made some good contacts in those three years, so I decided to branch out on my own.

His answers have me a bit confused. He knew three years earlier that he didn't fit in, but never did anything about it. It was only when he had no choice that he made a move—and what a move. Additionally, his decision to start his own firm at that stage in his career seems a bit premature.

FT: Seems pretty adventurous for a guy in his mid-twenties with just three years' experience under his belt.

MI: Chalk it up to inexperience and, to some extent, cockiness. I shut down the business less than a year later. I had a few clients, but not nearly enough to make a living. Suffice it to say that I lost my shirt. Should I go on?

FT: Yes.

MI: I took a position as the co–portfolio manager of a small-cap equity mutual fund at Atlantis Capital and basically stayed there until I started CAM with my two partners.

FT: So you stayed there for just over 10 years.

MI: Yes. Good firm, strong product mix. I was the co-manager of their small-cap mutual fund along with another guy for a few years and then took over full control of the fund when he retired back in the early 1990s.

FT: Tell me how you progressed at Atlantis. You know . . . how had your portfolio management skills developed and changed in the 10 plus years you were there? How many people did you have working with you and what were their roles?

MI: [*Joking*] I feel like I'm on the witness stand here. Most people just want me to explain what I do now.

FT: [*Not joking*] Then I'm doing my job well.

In order to understand how someone invests today, I have always found that it is important to chart their progress over time. After all, investment firms often tout their investment staff's level of industry experience (as does CAM in their marketing presentation), so it is only fair to inquire about that experience.

MI: At Atlantis, I managed the product in what the consultants might call a GARP process—growth at a reasonable price. I have always been a value investor at heart, but I refuse to buy a stock simply because it's cheap. Once I took over the fund full tilt, I made some slight modifications over the ensuing years. Rather than screening just for value-oriented factors, like most other value managers, I started to include growth factors. I look for companies with strong profitability, defined by ROE, as well as both top- and bottom-line revenue growth.

Bells should be going off at this point. The fact that Mark spent a decade investing using a GARP methodology is not surprising based on the returns-based analysis and portfolio analysis that we have performed. The CAM portfolio has consistently exhibited growth characteristics, from its excessive outperformance in the growth-oriented market of 1999 to the extremely high weight in the health care sector, usually favored by growth managers. His comment about changing the investment criteria at Atlantis piqued my interest.

FT: Who was your co-manager and what was the difference between the portfolio when he was there versus when you took over?

MI: His name is Chris Ahearn. I would best describe his style as deep value. He was "old school" value and, as you can imagine, we had some pretty interesting discussions in our years together.

FT: Chris was the lead portfolio manager?

MI: Yes. He was one of the original founding partners of the firm back in the 1970s. The changes that I incorporated can best be described when we discuss CAM's philosophy and process. The process that we utilize at CAM is an extension of the one that my team and I utilized at Atlantis for many years.

FT: Let's talk about CAM. Why did you branch out a second time and start your own firm?

MI: The fund at Atlantis had gotten too big to effectively manage. I thought it should close at $750 million, but because its performance was so good, it was always an easy sell. As you know, Atlantis is a huge firm with billions in assets under management across a dozen or so asset classes. As a result, at the time when I left to form CAM the fund had over $1.2 billion in assets. I couldn't manage the fund the way I wanted to because of the size.

FT: So what did you do while you managed the fund at Atlantis . . . buy more issues?

MI: That's right. I like a portfolio with between 40 and 60 names. When I left, the fund had about 100 names.

FT: But performance was still good?

MI: Yes and no. The fund's long-term performance numbers were still at the top of the list, but the more recent numbers were about average. It was at this time that Jim and Andy, my two current partners, approached me about starting CAM. I thought it was a good idea. I had put away enough money over the years, so that wasn't an issue.

As a double check, I will load the historical performance information for the small-cap fund that Mark managed while he was at Atlantis. I will focus on three time frames: (1) when Chris was the lead portfolio manager, (2) when Mark was the lead portfolio manager, and (3) the last two years of performance (to see the impact of the fund's size on returns).

FT: Tell me about Jim and Andy. How did you meet? What do they do at CAM? What are their strengths and weaknesses? Actually, I'd like to know what your strengths and weaknesses are, too.

MI: I think I'd rather have them address that question. My strength is my ability to find strong value stocks. I'm a stock picker—pure and simple. My weakness is worrying about operational business issues. That's what Andy does so well. He is the CEO and COO of the firm. As far as how we all met, I have known Andy since my university days. Jim and Andy had met and worked together at a firm called Victory Asset Management. VAM is a firm that caters to the high net worth crowd. Jim managed clients' assets and Andy was in charge of marketing and client service.

I am not familiar with VAM. I will make a point of researching this company so I can form a more complete picture of Andy's and Jim's investment backgrounds and overall levels of experience.

FT: Does Andy have any investment responsibilities?

According to their marketing presentation, Andy does have investment responsibilities. However, the presentation is not specific as to what those responsibilities are. Since his background is not investment related and because Mark stated that Andy is the CEO and COO, I wanted to clarify this issue.

MI: He markets the product and is also part of our investment committee. He, Jim, and I sit on that committee. We also have a young analyst, Tara, who does a lot of the grunt work at this time. We hope to train her and move her directly into stock analysis.

FT: How many people did you have working with you at Atlantis versus CAM?

MI: At Atlantis, I had four analysts working for me. They each worked on different sectors, but they did not have any decision-making authority. If they had a stock they thought should be in the portfolio, they pitched the idea to me. I flat out rejected it, accepted it, or told them to go back and answer some additional questions. At Atlantis, I was a generalist. Here at CAM, I work on the portfolio with three others: Jim, Andy, and Tara.

FT: But Andy is more operations and Tara seems a bit junior at this time. Is it fair to say that you and Jim co-manage the portfolio?

I ask this question so that I can determine exactly who does what. It is important to understand who the decision maker is. I'm looking to see if it is Mark alone, Mark and Jim, or some other combination. The answers to this line of questions will help me to focus my questions if I conduct a second meeting or an on-site meeting later on in the process.

MI: Andy and Tara contribute plenty, but you are right—it's basically Jim and I calling the shots.

FT: Tell me about that. How do you and Jim split the job? Are you generalists or do you have specific sector responsibilities?

MI: We are all generalists. I can go into the investment process if you like.

FT: Okay.

MI: As you know, we are a small-cap shop. We specialize in stocks with market caps below $1 billion. We start off by screening our database for stocks with caps less than $1 billion—so we have room for them to grow. And we also eliminate stocks with caps below $100 million, penny stocks, and illiquid stocks.

We already know from our analysis that the portfolio has a few stocks with market caps below $100 million.

FT: Define "illiquid" for me.

MI: We don't have any hard and fast rules here—just that we will not purchase a stock in which we wouldn't be able to close out our position within a week without materially impacting the price of that stock. Naturally, things can happen after we purchase a stock that make it less liquid. But we tackle those issues on a case-by-case basis.

FT: Who trades the portfolio?

MI: Jim and I rotate that responsibility. Andy also kicks in from time to time. Just remember that our turnover is pretty low—about 30% per year. We are more of a buy-and-hold firm.

FT: What value factors do you screen for?

MI: The initial screen looks to isolate companies with low relative P/E, P/B, and P/CF and high or growing revenues and earnings.

FT: Give me the cutoff for the price-related factors and tell me what growth and earnings factors you focus on at this initial screening stage.

MI: Each of the factors we screen for is relative to our small cap universe. We use the Baseline database to rank each small-cap stock based on our criteria, such as P/E, P/S, and so on; then we focus only on the top quartile of names. This is just using the value criteria. After this is done, we overlay the results with the growth and earnings criteria—we use earnings growth, revenue growth, and ROE. We rank the remaining stocks according to these criteria and take only the top quartile of stocks from this list. So the net result is that we start off with about 2,000 small-cap companies. We eliminate the illiquid names and the penny stocks and are left with something like half of that figure. The valuation criteria narrow that list to about 250 names, which is the top quartile or top 25%.

Then the growth overlay reduces that list again to about 75 names. At this stage, the computer has done all the work. We then take the list of 75 names and start to perform detailed fundamental analysis on the list.

Mark's answer confirms our previous conclusions regarding the portfolio's growth element. But here we can finally start to understand exactly why the stocks in the CAM portfolio have such strong growth tendencies—they actually screen for companies that exhibit strong relative growth.

FT: Who does the screening?

Again, I am just trying to get a complete picture of who does what. This information is certainly helpful when making a decision to hire a given investment firm, but it is pure gold years later when a company has experienced employee turnover. When I reevaluate a company in the years that follow, I can refer back to my notes to see how current employees have progressed and can also check to see what responsibilities some of the departed employees had previously.

MI: Tara. It's pretty automated. The database can be manipulated to do just about anything in a flash.

FT: So you have a list of 75 or so names to evaluate. What happens at this point?

MI: Tara e-mails the list to each of us first thing every Monday morning. We each look it over on our own for a while, then have a meeting at some point in the morning. We are a small shop, so we don't set formal meeting times. The four of us convene in our conference room and discuss the list for an hour or so. We divide up the stocks among ourselves and go back to our offices to start the analytical process.

FT: How is the list divided, and when do you discuss the results?

MI: We don't have any formal methodology in place—we simply check off the names that we are each going to follow. I may, for example, know a company reasonably well. So if that company were in the list, I would offer to take it based on my previous experiences. Only when one of us feels that they have found a stock that is worthy of making it into the portfolio do we spend any time discussing it among ourselves. Keep in mind that this is an ongoing process. We always have a list of stocks that we are evaluating. But again, our turnover is not too high. Buying a new stock is a big deal for us. On average, we buy only about 15 to 20 new stocks in a given year. So we analyze hundreds of stocks in detail and act on only a small fraction of those—not to mention the names that make it to our list but are eliminated before we do a full workup on them.

FT: Talk to me about portfolio construction. Do you have set rules?

MI: For the most part, we do have set rules. But we have made some exceptions over the years. For starters, we feel that a portfolio of 50 to 60 stocks is ideal for us. Based on those numbers, we typically establish a new stock in the portfolio with a weight between 1% and 2%, with the average weight coming in right in the middle.

FT: You had said earlier that at Atlantis you thought an optimal portfolio would have between 40 and 60 names. Now the numbers are between 50 and 60 names. Why the change?

MI: The range hasn't really changed; it's been tightened a bit.

FT: What about maximum and minimum weights for individual stocks?

MI: We don't have any minimum weighting rule per se, but the portfolio might have some stocks with small weights simply due to buying or selling activity. For example, we might take a week or so to fully liquidate a position for fear that we might move the price down. In a case like that we will sell off that stock in pieces. Obviously toward the end of the sale period, the stock's weight in the portfolio will be very low compared to the rest of the portfolio. Vice versa with stocks that we take our time buying into.

I would like a firmer answer regarding position constraints and will make note that it should be addressed during the on-site visit.

FT: I understand that you have no set maximum position size, but give me a realistic idea of how high you would let a stock's weight rise in the portfolio. Would you let it rise to 6%, 8%, 10%, or more?

MI: Good point. I would say that 5% would be an informal maximum size, but we have made some exceptions.

I will require a list of these exceptions to properly gauge how much position risk CAM is willing to take.

FT: According to the portfolio you gave me, you currently have six stocks with a weight of 0.6% or less, with the smallest, Charles & Colvard, being just 0.2% of the portfolio. It looks like several of them took a hit over the year. Pxre, Atlantic Coast, and Coinstar are all down big this year. But your two smallest portfolio positions, Charles & Colvard and Total Entertainment, are actually up this year.

MI: You're right about the three down stocks. They are down at the bottom because they lost most of their value this year. The other two are examples of stocks that we started to buy at the end of last month. Today, those two stocks are fully weighted.

FT: Tell me about the three dogs. What was your initial investment premise, why have they fallen so far this year, and what actions, if any, are you going to take?

Everything we have discussed so far is theoretical as far as I'm concerned. I feel the best way to understand what makes an investment manager tick is to dig into the portfolio itself. I'm looking to get a better understanding of how Mark researches companies and makes investment decisions, and also how his investment experience and process cause him to reevaluate portfolio stocks that have performed poorly. It's easy for managers to discuss winners, but I have found it more telling to talk about stocks that have lost value as well. Managers' answers tell me about their convictions and how strictly they adhere to their investment process. Unfortunately, to keep the conference call within the prescribed time frame, we will not have the time to discuss more than a few stocks. We can do this in greater detail during later meetings.

[Mark and I spend a few minutes discussing Pxre, Atlantic Coast, and Coinstar.]

FT: Let's take a step back. Could you describe how you analyze a stock from beginning to end?

MI: Sure. You should already have an idea of how I operate based on our discussions so far, so I will speak in broad terms and you can jump in with questions as you like. Again, after we have had our Monday meeting, we each have a list of stocks to review. Some of the names are pretty easy. I have been doing this for quite a few years and have gotten familiar with many companies over that period. So I can sometimes reduce the list by half just by looking at it. Also keep in mind that the list does not change significantly from week to week because we are applying the same criteria to the same universe of stocks weekly. As a result, many of the stocks on the current list were on the previous list as well. However, during earnings reporting periods, the list does tend to change more.

FT: Because the newly reported figures change the reported valuation and growth factors?

MI: Exactly. When I start to evaluate a stock, I begin by looking at the company with something akin to a Porter framework. What is the product? Are there any barriers to entry? Who is the competition? And so on. We have created a series of reports that focus on the fundamental data and stock history. This comes right off the database. I will look at the company's annual reports and its web site and will read through company press releases going back a few years. Tara helps out with all of this. If I want to take a stock deeper into our process, I will ask Tara to put together a detailed package for me. This package contains several valuation models that we have created internally as well as various searches for news on the company via the Internet.

FT: Who provides the inputs to the valuation models? You or Tara?

MI: Good question. The inputs basically come from me, but Tara and I will sit down and go through the logic and the factors that led to the inputs. This is basic training as far as I'm concerned.

Sounds like Tara does quite a lot of work. When I had requested the initial information package from CAM, it was sent to me by Tara, so it looks like she does a little of everything. I need to get a better understanding of what her duties are and will definitely plan on talking to her during the on-site visit.

FT: Is Tara ready to take on more analytical responsibility?

MI: Yes. In fact, we have started to give her some individual stock responsibility. Jim and I will obviously oversee what she does, and all portfolio decisions are made by Jim and me.

FT: Tell me about that. Who is the final decision maker—you or Jim? Or is it both of you?

MI: Jim and I need to agree on a stock before we will purchase it.

FT: What about stock sales?

MI: The same. But we can make sale decisions on our own if the situation warrants it. I learned this the hard way early on in my career at Atlantis. I basically watched a stock lose an additional 20% of its value because I could not reach my partner for a few hours.

FT: Chris?

MI: Yes.

FT: Where was he?

MI: Off-site doing a company visit.

FT: Speaking of company visits, do you do them?

MI: We will meet with company management when they are in town or presenting at a conference. We don't see any reason to go out and visit the actual company offices.

FT: Does that mean you speak to the company's management before making an investment?

MI: Most of the time. Sometimes we get what we need from their investor relations person.

FT: Let's talk about the portfolio for a bit. I would like to ask some specific questions about some of the holdings. You currently have a few stocks with market caps above $2 billion. How long will you hold a stock before you sell it?

Now I'm starting to ask some of the questions that we raised during the initial phases of the due diligence process.

MI: As I mentioned before, we only buy stocks with market caps below $1 billion, but we will hold a stock until it reaches $2.5 billion. We have a few stocks in the $2 billion to $2.5 billion range and we will likely begin to sell them shortly. Just keep in mind that each of these larger names rose to the levels they are at because of price appreciation. They are winners and our clients have made a lot of money from these investments. CSK, for example, has more than doubled this year.

FT: Tell me about CSK. It is a foreign company trading in the U.S. as an ADR [American depositary receipt]. Do you have a policy about foreign-based stocks?

MI: No. ADRs are fair game, just like any other stocks—as long as they meet all the criteria.

[At this point, Mark discusses CSK in some detail.]

FT: As you know, I have already done a fair amount of due diligence on your firm and the small-cap value product. I would like to spend the remainder of this call going through those questions if that is okay with you.

MI: Fire away.

FT: Let's start with your track record. You have amassed some very good numbers.

MI: Thanks.

FT: However, your returns seem to be more indicative of growth than value during specific times in CAM's history—specifically, the period from mid-1999 right to the end of the bull market in early 2000. Your numbers seem unusually high compared to the value indexes and your value peers. Then your numbers fall off a cliff for the next year or so. What's the deal?

MI: Our bottom-up stock selection led us to some huge winners. We were different from the benchmark and most of the other small-cap value managers because of our stock selection and our asset allocation.

FT: I assume you are referring to sector and industry weights?

MI: Yes.

FT: The only thing I can come up with that explains the level of out-performance during the growth-oriented bull market would be somewhat large allocations to the hot areas of that time: technology, Internet, and biotechnology. Or perhaps some large allocations to a few hot stocks.

MI: Right on all counts. We had exposure to tech and health care. As you know, both of those areas surged in that period. Some of the names we had in the portfolio surged so far so fast that we had some individual portfolio weights rise to uncomfortable levels. We had to sell off many shares just to keep the portfolio balanced at times. But it is important to reiterate that the stocks came into the portfolio based solely on bottom-up selection, not sector calls or bets.

Once again, I will need to see the list of stocks that rose above the informal 5% maximum limit.

FT: What sector exposures did you have at that time. Give me some examples of how far out of whack some of the individual portfolio weights had become.

MI: Technology peaked at about 30%. Health care was about the same.

FT: At the same time?

MI: Yes.

FT: Wow, 60% of a value portfolio in tech and health care. That is highly unusual.

MI: Two things: First, we are not a normal value firm—we factor growth into the equation; second, we recognize that we carried things a little too far. But we weren't alone. It was a crazy time in financial market history.

FT: Be that as it may, I would have found it hard to consider your product a value product back then. It also poses problems for me when selecting a benchmark to evaluate your product's history. Do other investment manager analysts ask you about this?

MI: Not really. Our numbers are first-rate, our team is experienced and motivated, and we plan on closing the product soon—when its assets reach $500 million. Most of our recent clients and potential clients look at those things.

FT: According to your performance disclosures, your small-cap product has about $375 million in assets at midyear. How much do you manage today?

MI: That number has risen considerably. I think we have roughly $450 million now. We got two big accounts just last month—one for $25 million, the other for $20 million.

FT: So you have about another $50 million to go before you close?

MI: Yes and no. We will close to new clients at $500 million, but will accept another $100 million from existing clients.

FT: At Atlantis, you thought you could manage $750 million. What is different now?

MI: Nothing. My partners and I would rather play it safe than potentially hurt the product and, as a result, our clients. We still feel we could effectively manage $750 million, but we have to account for appreciation as well. If we formally close at $600 million, we would expect the assets to rise as a result of underlying price appreciation. We want to be in a position not to get caught with our pants down.

I like this answer because it takes into account future growth. Too many firms close when the level of assets reaches their absolute maximum, leaving little to no room for future expansion in assets. This is usually when products with good long-term performance start to become average or below-average performers.

FT: Is it fair to say that the very same factors that drove the massive outperformance in the latter half of 1999 were also responsible for the underperformance in 2000–2001?

MI: Once again, you are right on with your analysis. We took a hit just like everyone else did at that time. When the market turned, no one was safe.

FT: But didn't your positions in tech and health care put you in a worse position than most of your value brethren?

MI: I don't know about other managers, but in theory I would agree.

FT: My analysis indicates that if you were to exclude the period at the end of 1999, which we have already established is not typical for you, then your product's performance goes from top of the pack to middle of the list.

MI: That's a theoretical exercise that I leave to the consultants. The fact is that we invested in those stocks and subsequently those sectors because of rigorous bottom-up, fundamentally driven stock selection. We didn't make any sector bets. We stand behind every investment we made.

FT: Due to time constraints, we can't dig into this any deeper, but would you mind e-mailing me a list of the technology and health care stocks that you held back then? I can look through the list and come back to you with specific questions.

The 1999 period is a critical component of CAM's outperformance, and, as a result, it is critical to fully understand what they did and why they did it. Remember that those who forget the past are doomed to repeat it. While I will reserve judgment on the "value" issue at this time, I will need additional information to reach an informed, intelligent conclusion when the time comes.

MI: Sure, I can have Tara send that to you today.

FT: Great. Let's move to the present time. I ran your portfolio through my analytical program and was surprised to see that more than 70% of the portfolio is focused in just three sectors, one of which is health care. Can you comment on your current sector allocation?

MI: We simply go where the value and opportunity to make money is. We don't have any formalized sector rules. It is our belief that to constrain pure bottom-up stock selection of to nullify a big reason why you would hire us in the first place. That said, we would be hard-pressed to allocate more than a third of the portfolio to any single sector. We didn't do it back in 1999–2000 and we would not do it today.

FT: Could you have your assistant copy and send me all of the research you have done on a single portfolio holding? I would like to get an idea of the level of detail that you go into. Looking at your research notes will give me more insight into your investment process than talking about it on the phone.

MI: I think that can be arranged. I would have to ask that you not share this information with anyone, though. And keep in mind that the notes were not intended to be seen by anyone other than us, so it might look like a mess to you.

FT: Understood. I'm just trying to make an informed decision. I ask most portfolio managers for examples of their research, so I have seen just about everything. Don't worry about the mess; I would prefer to see your notes just as you see them.

MI: Any stock in particular?

FT: How about Columbia Sportswear?

MI: Done. Any particular reason why you selected that stock?

FT: No reason other than I know it pretty well. I have had the pleasure of discussing it with several other managers. I have another question. Again, looking at your performance disclosures, it looks like CAM started a different product back in 2000. I say this because the small-cap product's assets as a percentage of total firm assets dropped from 100% in 1998 and 1999 to less than 100% thereafter.

This information was also disclosed to us in the Form ADV.

MI: We started a small-cap hedge fund in 1999 and incubated it with the partners' money. It had done so well that we started to offer it to a select group of our clients in 2000. It has exceeded our expectations, performing even better than the long-only product.

This information could be very important. Mark has never managed a hedge fund before, and I would be interested in discussing his "short" methodology as well as going into detail about how the hedge fund is constructed and how he finds time to manage both products. Lastly, based on our brief discussion I sense that Mark likes to be in charge— if this hedge fund is successful, he might decide to branch off on his own again just to focus on it (the higher fees and looser investment guidelines often attract entrepreneurial investment managers—managers just like Mark).

FT: How much are you managing in the hedge fund? Would you describe its objective and style?

MI: We now have more than $100 million in assets and have already decided to close it to new investors. It is a continuation of our small-cap value philosophy, but we can short stocks as well. The objective is positive absolute return in any market environment.

FT: This fund is outside the objectives of this phone conference, but answer a few simple questions for me. First, who manages the product? Second, what is the fee schedule on the hedge fund? Third, could you e-mail me some information on the hedge fund— performance, exposures, offering memorandum?

MI: I take the lead on the hedged product. I'm responsible for the short positions, and the long positions come directly from our dedicated long-only portfolio. The long side of the portfolio does not precisely mirror the small-cap product, but it is reasonably close.

FT: Who calls the shots?

MI: I do. I guess you can say that the hedge fund is my baby. The fee schedule is standard: 1% base fee and 20% performance fee. I can send you the information you requested along with the research package for Columbia Sportswear.

[Phone conference ends after some small talk.]

The initial interview transcribed here would have lasted a little over half of an hour, but the information we obtained in that brief time is crucial. Now that I have had a chance to learn more about Mark, the portfolio, the firm, and the hedge fund, I can start to collate all of the information that we have gathered thus far and begin to form an opinion of CAM Asset Management and its small-cap value product.

One of the things that I enjoy about this business is that each meeting that I do is different. While most meetings follow a loose format, I never really know where they will end up. There were dozens of questions that I could have asked Mark but didn't due to time constraints. I chose a plan of attack that would focus more on two areas: (1) Mark himself and (2) the portfolio. Based on the phone conversation, I would say that Mark is definitely not a strict value manager; however, that is not a bad thing. This portfolio might not fit nicely into the preset style categories that consultants are so fond of, but that does not mean that it would not be a good fit with the other managers in the Market Leaders Fund, which employs specialist managers across the style and market cap spectrum.

While I am a little uneasy about the sector concentration, I have to admit that the portfolio's risk statistics are not outlandish and that the return/risk measures, such as Sharpe and Sortino ratio, all point toward the CAM portfolio as adding significant value relative to its underlying risk.

MEETING MEMO

An investment manager analyst by definition meets with investment managers throughout the year. This means dozens and even hundreds of phone conferences, face-to-face meetings, and on-site visits. In order to keep all of the data gleaned from these meetings organized and consistent, I make a point to write a memo that contains the relevant details from any such meeting. These memos address the following subject matter:

- Background
- Firm Information
- Investment Professional Information
- Support Staff Information
- Performance/Risk Discussion
- Portfolio Discussion
- Issues/Concerns/Questions
- Follow-up Required
- Conclusion

Most of the information contained in the memo comes from the conversations that we have had with the investment professionals at CAM. The rest comes directly from the analytical work that we have performed ourselves during the initial phases of the due diligence process. In addition to making the due diligence process more organized, the memo forces us to put the meeting in perspective because a conclusion (or decision) is required at the end of every memo.

I have included a sample memo based on the phone interview with CAM.

To: Investment Committee
From: Frank J. Travers, CFA
Re: CAM Asset Management Small-Cap Value Product

BACKGROUND

The Market Leaders Fund is currently searching for a small-cap value manager as a replacement for XYZ Asset Management. XYZ was terminated following the departure of several key investment personnel (see XYZ memo dated September 15, 2003). Frank J. Travers, CFA, is in charge of this search, and the deadline for final review is in three weeks.

FIRM INFORMATION

CAM Asset Management was formed in 1997 and is owned by Mark Innes (40%), Andrew Wares (30%), and Jim Bradshaw (30%). The firm specializes in small cap investing and currently has two product offerings: a small-cap value (which we have determined is really more indicative of GARP) product and a small-cap long/short hedge fund. The hedge fund's long exposure closely mirrors the holdings in the small-cap value portfolio. The three partners are supported by Tara Fitzpatrick, who migrated from being a general assistant to her current position as a junior analyst. In addition, CAM has a receptionist who doubles as an executive assistant to the group. The firm's Form ADV is included in the attachments for a more detailed review.

INVESTMENT PROFESSIONAL INFORMATION

Mark Innes

1982 to 1985	Analyst, Mackey Capital Partners
1986 to 1991	Co–portfolio manager, Atlantis Capital's small-cap mutual fund
1991 to 1997	Lead portfolio manager of Atlantis Capital's small-cap fund
1997 to Present	Partner, co–portfolio manager of CAM's small-cap product, lead manager of firm's hedge fund

Andrew Wares

1983 to 1997	Director of client service at Victory Asset Management
1997 to Present	Partner, CEO/CFO/COO at CAM

James Bradshaw

1983 to 1997	Portfolio manager, balanced accounts (high net worth) at Victory Asset Management
1983 to 1997	Director of research/portfolio manager at Victory Asset Management
1997 to Present	Partner, co–portfolio manager of CAM's small-cap product

SUPPORT STAFF INFORMATION

Tara Fitzpatrick

1994 to 1995	Video store clerk
1995 to 1996	Administrative assistant at the Carlyle Company, a real estate management firm
1996 to 1997	Office manager at Hendricks Consulting, a management consulting firm
1997 to 1999	Portfolio assistant at CAM
1999 to Present	Junior portfolio analyst at CAM

PERFORMANCE/RISK DISCUSSION

The small-cap value portfolio has experienced very good performance relative to the small-cap value peer group; however, portfolio data provided by the manager seems to indicate that CAM is not a "pure" value shop (see Exhibit 8.2). The table illustrates the small-cap value product's performance relative to the small-cap benchmarks as well as the peer group of small-cap value managers.

While the overall track record is strong, the portfolio has experienced some choppy returns. In particular, the portfolio experienced very strong performance in the 1998 to 1999 period, which has been established as a growth-oriented market. In our conversation with Mark Innes, the portfolio manager, we confirmed that the portfolio was weighted in sectors not typically favored by value managers, such as technology and health care (at their peak in the 1998–1999 period, these two sectors held a combined weight of more than 60% in the portfolio). The CAM portfolio also exhibited good performance relative to its peer group (refer to the peer group chart in the attachments). Over the past five years, the CAM portfolio achieved returns that placed it in the first quartile of products with similar investment objectives. In more recent periods, the portfolio's performance placed it in the second quartile. This is based on the poor relative performance in the 2000–2001 period.

Up/down market analysis (Exhibit 8.2) versus the small-cap value index clearly indicates that CAM had significantly outperformed the

EXHIBIT 8.2 CAM versus Benchmarks—Annualized and Calendar
Year Performance

Annualized Performance (Periods Ended June 2003)

	YTD	1 Year	3 Years	5 Years	Inception
CAM	15.9%	−2.7%	7.9%	8.6%	9.7%
S&P SmallCap Value Index	13.0%	−8.4%	8.0%	3.8%	4.8%
Value added	*2.9%*	*5.7%*	*−0.1%*	*4.7%*	*5.0%*
S&P SmallCap Index	12.9%	−3.6%	2.4%	3.7%	4.5%
Value added	*3.0%*	*0.8%*	*5.5%*	*4.8%*	*5.2%*

Calendar Year Performance

	1998	1999	2000	2001	2002	2003 (YTD)
CAM	0.9%	24.1%	14.8%	10.7%	−9.6%	15.9%
S&P SmallCap Value Index	−5.1%	3.0%	20.9%	13.1%	−14.5%	13.0%
Value added	*5.9%*	*21.0%*	*−6.1%*	*−2.4%*	*4.9%*	*2.9%*
S&P SmallCap Index	−1.3%	12.4%	11.8%	6.5%	−14.6%	12.9%
Value added	*2.2%*	*11.7%*	*3.0%*	*4.2%*	*5.0%*	*3.0%*

index during months in which the index return was positive, while
only moderately underperforming the index during months in which
the index return was negative. However, when we excluded the strong
1999 performance period (which was based largely on the portfolio's
extreme weighting on growth-oriented stocks), the portfolio's relative
performance in up markets goes from a large value added to a large
value subtracted.

CAM's small-cap portfolio exhibited slightly more variation in returns than did the small-cap value index, with an annualized standard
deviation since inception of 22.7% versus 21.0% for the index. However, the CAM portfolio did experience slightly lower standard deviation than the median small-cap value fund over the same period. The
CAM portfolio's Sharpe ratio since its inception, at 0.34, is nearly
three times that of the small-cap value index and the median small-cap
value mutual fund. Likewise, the CAM portfolio exhibited better
Sortino, Treynor, and Jensen ratios than did the small-cap indexes and
the median small-cap value mutual fund. As a result, we can conclude
that, based on absolute and risk-adjusted historical performance, the
CAM portfolio looks attractive.

PORTFOLIO DISCUSSION

CAM employs a bottom-up, fundamental approach toward individual stock selection as well as portfolio construction. Mark Innes informed me during the call that they are driven almost exclusively by bottom-up stock selection. When asked about risk controls, Mark indicated that they place some restrictions on maximum individual stock weights (5%) and broad sector weightings (maximum of one-third of the total portfolio). Based on the current portfolio provided to us and the discussion that I had with Mark, it is clear that CAM takes a fair amount of sector concentration risk. Of particular interest are the actual sectors in which they have historically held high weights: technology and health care—both of which are widely considered to be more growth oriented than value oriented. Currently, the CAM portfolio has roughly 70% of its holdings concentrated in just three broad sectors (consumer cyclicals, health care, and financials).

Back in the 1999–2000 period, the portfolio had more than 60% concentrated in technology and health care stocks. The portfolio is highly concentrated based on industry weights as well, with nearly 50% of the portfolio concentrated in the top five industries.

An analysis of the current portfolio indicates that the weighted average market capitalization is $777 million versus $684 million for the small-cap value index. In addition, roughly half of the portfolio (31 stocks) fall into the micro-cap range (stocks with market caps under $500 million).

Individual portfolio positions seem to be concentrated in the 1% to 3% range (based on the current portfolio), but we need to check on this historically, as Mark indicated in our conversation that some stock weightings had gotten out of hand during the run-up in the market in 1999–2000.

Fundamentally, the portfolio does not look like either value or growth; rather it exhibits characteristics of each. The portfolio's price-earnings ratio is in line with the small-cap value index, but is substantially higher in other price-based areas (price/sales, price/book, price/cash flow). However, the portfolio is definitely geared more toward the growth style when looking at the earnings and revenue growth figures. Lastly, the portfolio's individual holdings also seem to have strong cash positions (liquidity) and, thus, the ability to pay off debts and fund internal growth.

Based on the fundamental portfolio analysis, I would initially conclude that the current portfolio is more indicative of the GARP (growth at a reasonable price) style than either value or growth. However, the portfolio does offer an attractive P/E as well as strong growth rates.

ISSUES/CONCERNS/QUESTIONS

1. I am concerned with the portfolio's sector bets, despite the fact that they are coming from the bottom up.
2. The portfolio has a tendency toward investing in sectors that are traditionally more growth oriented. In isolation, this is not an issue; however, if we were to include this manager in our Market Leaders Fund, I would be concerned that its weighting in technology and health care might rise to uncomfortable levels based on the CAM portfolio in combination with our other growth-oriented managers.
3. Another issue involves the current level of product assets in relation to the capacity limit that CAM has set. Currently, the CAM small-cap portfolio has roughly $450 million in assets. Mark stated that they would close the product to new assets at $500 million (leaving room for an additional $100 million in contributions from existing clients). In addition, CAM manages about $100 million in its hedge fund product. I do not know what portion is long, but will assume for now that the fund has another $50 to $60 million in long assets. This would bring the firm's level of small-cap assets over the $500 million mark. It seems that CAM is in the process of receiving some pretty large contributions. I have to wonder if that is due to the very good track record. If so, I would be concerned that these new assets might be the first ones to leave should the portfolio experience any performance hiccups (i.e.: relative underperformance in a widely value-driven market).
4. I am also concerned that the firm is actively managing a small-cap long/short hedge fund. Mark seems to be in complete control of this product. Based on the differing fee structures, it is likely more profitable at this stage to focus just on the hedge fund. I need to get a better sense that Mark has strong ties to the firm and that he won't branch off to start his own firm to focus on the hedge fund product.

FOLLOW-UP REQUIRED

1. Need to contact list of references.
2. Need to conduct background check on all three partners (pending positive on-site visit).
3. Once Mark sends the additional information regarding positions in 1999–2000, need to analyze the holdings in relation to concentration risk.

4. Need to conduct a historical portfolio analysis.
5. Need to analyze CAM's portfolio relative to our other small-cap manager to determine if CAM's growth element is repetitive and/or to highly correlated to the growth manager.

CONCLUSION

CAM's small-cap value product is stylistically somewhere between growth and value product. I feel that is safe to consider it GARP or value with a growth bias. I am concerned by the portfolio's historical tendency toward taking certain concentration risks (e.g., individual stock weights ran up in the growth market of 1999/early 2000, and both sector and industry weights have been and still are pretty concentrated) and need to probe a bit deeper into the hedge fund product. However, the firm has achieved solid results without taking risks that are too far removed from the small-cap value universe. The on-site visit will help to determine if this firm/product should be considered for inclusion in the Market Leaders Fund.

## CHAPTER 9

Attribution Analysis

Portfolio attribution allows the analyst to slice and dice a portfolio in a variety of different ways, providing a means of numerically assessing what a portfolio manager has done well and not so well—in effect, creating a quantitative, results-oriented assessment of a manager's skill set. It is the only truly quantitative means we have of making a determination of skill. Attribution can be done in isolation, which is often referred to as absolute attribution or contribution to total return, or it can be done relative to some benchmark. In either case, the methodology is pretty straightforward, but requires a fair amount of underlying portfolio data, particularly when performing the analysis over multiple periods. Attribution results can often shed light on an investment manager's perceived skills and aid the due diligence analyst in making a more informed decision when it comes to hiring or firing an investment manager.

Attribution analysis can be simplified and calculated based on static portfolios or it can include transactional data for the period in question.

- *Static portfolios.* This method does not take into account any transactions that may have occurred between the start and end dates of the analysis. It can be considered to be an estimate as opposed to true attribution analysis. Two factors play a critical role in the analysis when using static portfolios: (1) time period under evaluation and (2) portfolio turnover. I have found monthly and even quarterly time periods to be acceptable when portfolio turnover (amount and number of transactions) is low. However, when evaluating a portfolio in which the manager trades frequently, it is more efficient to perform attribution based on static portfolios for shorter time periods. For example, if using a static portfolio for a three-month time frame, the analysis would not take into account any stocks that were bought and sold during the period. The more transactions that were made during the period, the less accurate the results may be.
- *Complete portfolios including all transactions.* This method takes into account each and every transaction that is made by the portfolio

manager for a specific portfolio over a defined time period. As a result, it yields the most accurate results, but is obviously more data (and labor) intensive.

Lastly, the decision to hold cash and cash equivalents is every bit as much an investment decision as sector allocations and individual purchases and sales. A portfolio manager's decision to hold cash in lieu of stocks (or bonds or whatever financial instruments are outlined in the portfolio's investment objectives) will have one of three potential effects on the underlying portfolio: positive, negative, or neutral (none). I typically treat cash as a separate asset class, separate and distinct from any sector or industry classifications. To keep things simple, the examples outlined in this chapter do not include cash or cash equivalents.

ABSOLUTE ATTRIBUTION ANALYSIS

As the name implies, this method of portfolio attribution looks at the portfolio in isolation. It can also be referred to as contribution to portfolio return. Because portfolio-based attribution analysis is built from the bottom up, the analysis can be dynamic and take many different shapes. An equity portfolio can be broken down into the following categories: individual positions, industries, sectors, market caps, regions, countries, and fundamental characteristics (such as price/earnings, price/book, etc.).

Attribution analysis can be performed for a single month or can be bootstrapped to create a historical analysis. The historical analysis is data intensive, but the results are well worth the time and effort.

Attribution by Individual Positions

This analysis simply measures each stock's contribution to the portfolio's total return.

Formula 9.1 (Individual Position's Contribution to Portfolio Return)

$$\text{IPA} = \text{Weight}_{bp} \times \text{Return}_{fp}$$

where   IPA = Individual position attribution.

        Weight_{bp} = Stock's weight at the beginning of the period, which translates to the last business day of the preceding month. For example, if calculating the IPA for the month of January, the beginning period weight would be December 31 (or the last business day of December).

Return$_{fp}$ = Stock's return for the full period. Using the previous example, the full period return would be for the month of January.

We use the weight at the beginning of the period rather than the weight at the end of the period because the weight at the end of the period reflects the performance of the underlying stock. For example, if a single stock in a portfolio had a 5% weight at the beginning of the period and the stock increased in price by 20% over the period, the stock's weight at the end of the period would increase to 6% (assuming all other stocks remained the same over the period). Using the end-of-period weight would overstate that stock's contribution to the total portfolio's return. Now that we can calculate the IPA, we can build any level of absolute attribution analysis desired.

Sector-Level Attribution Analysis

To build the attribution analysis by sector, simply combine the underlying stocks by sector and add the IPAs.

Formula 9.2 (Sector-Level Portfolio Attribution)

$$SLA_s = \sum IPA_{s1} \dots IPA_{sn}$$

where SLA_s = Attribution for a particular sector within a portfolio.
IPA_{s1} = Individual position attribution for stock 1 in a particular sector.
IPA_{sn} = Individual position attribution for stock n in a particular sector, where stock n is the final stock in that sector. For example, if a portfolio has 10 technology stocks, n would equal 10.

Exhibit 9.1 is an example of sector-level attribution analysis based on the most recent portfolio given to us by CAM for their small-cap product. The returns stated in the example are for the last quarter and, as a result, the beginning-of-period weights are for the last business day before the quarter began.

As highlighted in formula 9.1, the IPA for each individual position is the product of the beginning period weight and the return for the period. The total SLA for the consumer cyclical sector is simply the sum of the IPAs of 12 consumer cyclical stocks held in the CAM small-cap portfolio.

EXHIBIT 9.1   Sector-Level Attribution for CAM Small-Cap Value Portfolio Consumer Cyclicals

Stock Name	Weight$_{bp}$	Return$_{fp}$	IPA
Columbia Sportswear	2.60%	2.6	0.07
Amer. Eagle Outfitter	3.05%	–19.3	–0.59
Decoma Int'l	1.92%	17.8	0.34
Cherokee	2.04%	5.9	0.12
Linens 'n Things	2.10%	0.7	0.02
America's Car-Mart	1.65%	64.1	1.06
Jakks Pacific	2.09%	–7.4	–0.15
Cole (Kenneth) Prod.	1.12%	34.0	0.38
Amer. Woodmark	1.34%	–4.7	–0.06
Blue Rhino	1.12%	–7.7	–0.09
Gildan Activewear	1.56%	6.8	0.11
Charles & Colvard	0.17%	15.0	0.03
SLA for Consumer Cyclical Sector			1.23

When we use this methodology for each of the sectors in CAM's portfolio, we come up with the table in Exhibit 9.2.

Exhibits 9.2 and 9.3 break out CAM's sector attribution for the period under review, clearly illustrating that the SLA was positive in seven out of the nine sectors that the portfolio was invested in, with health care contributing more than any other sector (1.31% out of the portfolio's 3.94% total return for the period). The sector-level attribution analysis is

EXHIBIT 9.2   Sector-Level Attribution for CAM Small-Cap Portolio

Sector	SLA
Commercial Services	–0.23
Consumer Cyclical	1.23
Consumer Noncyclical	0.27
Consumer Services	0.87
Energy	0.08
Financials	0.58
Health Care	1.31
Industrials	–0.53
Information Technology	0.36
Total for CAM Small-Cap Portfolio	3.94

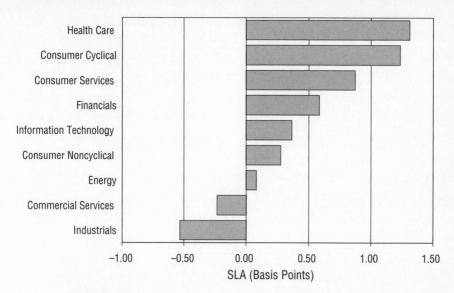

EXHIBIT 9.3   CAM's Sector-Level Attribution Summary Graph

made more powerful when we consider the IPA for the positions within each sector. For example, the SLA for the consumer services sector was 0.87 basis points; however, a quick look at the IPAs for each stock in this sector indicate that the entire SLA for the sector was due to a single stock, Multimedia Games, which surged more than 43% over the period. An analysis of the IPAs across all of the sectors, however, indicates that CAM's performance for this period is spread out nicely among dozens of stocks. The results of this analysis will allow us to question the portfolio manager more intelligently when we conduct the on-site visit. Rather than asking the portfolio manager to summarize the product's performance in a general way, we can focus directly on the portfolio's strong and weak points.

Industry-Level Attribution Analysis

To calculate industry-level attribution analysis, we would use the same exact methodology and formulas we used to calculate the sector-level attribution, only we would sum the IPAs by industry instead of by sector (see Exhibits 9.4 and 9.5).

EXHIBIT 9.4   Industry-Level Attribution for CAM
Small-Cap Portolio

Industry	ILA
Advertising	−0.23
Aerospace/Defense	0.20
Airlines	−0.27
Apparel & Accessory	0.70
Auto Parts & Equip.	0.34
Biotechnology	−0.46
Building Products	−0.06
Casinos & Gaming	0.82
Diverse Fin'l Svc.	−0.04
Diversified Banks	0.07
HC—Equipment	0.14
HC—Facility	0.15
HC—Services	1.07
HC—Supplies	0.41
Insurance—Multiline	−0.04
Insurance—Prop./Cas.	0.23
IT Consulting & Svc.	0.73
Leisure Products	−0.15
Marine	−0.02
Oil & Gas—Expl./Prod.	0.08
Packaged Foods/Meats	0.27
Regional Banks	0.45
Reinsurance	−0.06
Restaurants	0.05
Retail—Apparel	−0.59
Retail—Home Improve.	−0.09
Services—Data Proc.	−0.56
Services—Div./Comm'l	−0.24
Specialty Stores	1.07
Thrifts & Mortgage Fin.	−0.02
Total for CAM Small-Cap Portfolio	3.94

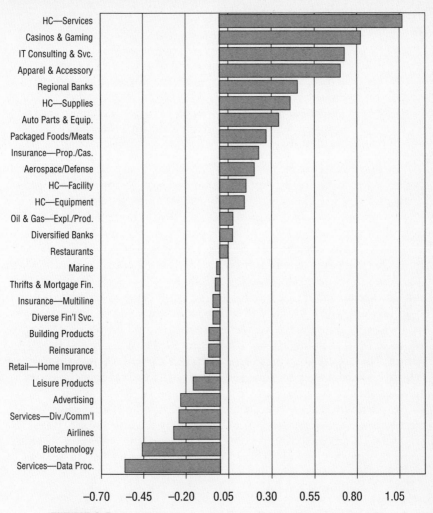

EXHIBIT 9.5   CAM's Industry-Level Attribution Summary Graph

Formula 9.3 (Industry-Level Portfolio Attribution)

$$ILA_I = (IPA_{i1} \ldots IPA_{in})$$

where ILA_I = Attribution for a particular industry within a portfolio.

IPA_{i1} = Individual position attribution for stock 1 in a particular industry.

IPA_{in} = Individual position attribution for stock n in a particular industry, where the nth stock is the final portfolio stock in that industry.

By digging deeper into the portfolio, we can gain a better understanding of what is really driving portfolio returns. Sector-level attribution analysis is very useful, but when combined with industry-level analysis, it is even more powerful. Exhibit 9.6 takes the attribution analysis of CAM's portfolio to a new level by combining sector, industry, and position attribution analysis in a single report. To keep the example simple, I have selected the sector that contributed the most to CAM's total portfolio return, which according to the sector-level analysis (Exhibit 9.2) was the health care sector. Just keep in mind that Exhibit 9.6 is a small component of the full analytical report, which includes all sectors, industries, and positions.

When we drill down from the top to the bottom (from sector to industry to individual holdings), we can put all of the pieces of the puzzle together. The largest contributor to the health care sector was the services industry. When we dig into the services industry, we see that the entire return was due to two stocks, National Med and Pediatrix. When we speak to the portfolio manager and analysts during the on-site meeting, we can elect to focus on these names or to review why the other stocks were relatively flat. When analyzing a portfolio manager, it is important to understand the impetus behind their successful choices, as well as an analysis of the other, less successful holdings.

EXHIBIT 9.6   Combination Attribution Analysis

Sector/Industry Attribution

Health Care Sector	ILA		HC—Services Industry	Weight$_{bp}$	Return$_{fp}$	IPA
HC—Equipment Industry	0.14		Nat'l Med. Hlth. Card	1.2%	39.9	0.49
HC—Facility Industry	0.15		Option Care	2.1%	4.3	0.09
HC—Services Industry	1.07		Orthodontic Centers	0.9%	−1.6	−0.02
HC—Supplies Industry	0.41		Pediatrix Med'l Grp.	2.0%	29.2	0.57
Biotechnology Industry	−0.46		Renal Care Group	2.3%	−3.0	−0.07
Total for Health Care Sector	1.31		Total for Health Care Services Industry			1.07

Other Absolute Attribution Measures

As you can see from the two preceding sections in this chapter, the formulas used to calculate sector-level and industry-level attribution are identical. The same is true when calculating attribution by market capitalization and by various fundamental characteristics. So rather than repeating the formulas again, I will simply discuss each form of the analysis.

Market Cap–Level Attribution Analysis You can also perform absolute attribution for a portfolio according to some preset market cap breaks. For example, you can select micro-cap (less than $500 million), small-cap (from $500 million to $2 billion), mid-cap (from $2 billion to $10 billion), and large-cap (greater than $10 billion) ranges. When a portfolio specializes in a single market capitalization range, you can select your own breakpoints within that range. For example, when analyzing the CAM small-cap portfolio, we can break out the portfolio's market capitalization exposures in increments of $250 million or any other increment that is meaningful to the portfolio evaluation (see Exhibit 9.7). Once the ranges or increments are set, the attribution formula is the sum of the beginning period weights for each stock times the returns of each stock for the period in a particular cap range.

It is clear from the results of the market-cap range attribution analysis that a large portion of the portfolio's return came from micro-cap stocks (stocks with caps below $500 million). A total of 2.60% out of the 3.94% return (or roughly two-thirds) came from micro-cap stocks. If the portfolio has a history of allocating a significant portion of its assets to micro-cap stocks, we might have to consider including a micro-cap index for comparative performance and portfolio analytics. In addition, the allocation to micro-cap stocks may have implications with respect to overall portfolio liquidity and risk.

Fundamental Characteristics–Level Attribution Analysis In addition to setting market-cap ranges or increments, we also have the ability to create

EXHIBIT 9.7 Sector-Level Attribution for CAM Small-Cap Portolio

Market-Cap Ranges	Market-Cap Attribution
< $250M	1.31
$250M to $500M	1.29
$500M to $750M	0.67
$750M to $1B	0.13
> $1B	0.54
Total for CAM Small-Cap Portfolio	3.94

ranges based on various fundamental characteristics, such as price-earnings (P/E), ROE, dividend yield, or any other fundamental characteristics that we determine to be appropriate. When dealing with fundamental data, information will not always be available for each and every stock in a given portfolio. Stocks in which you do not have the appropriate fundamental data can be eliminated from the analysis or given a number that is in line with peer averages or industry norms. While we could have selected from a wide variety of fundamental characteristics, we will review only the P/E ratio in this chapter.

The P/E range attribution results (Exhibit 9.8) are interesting because they clearly indicate that all of the portfolio's return came from stocks with P/Es at the higher end of the range of stocks held by the portfolio. I would be curious to see how this analysis would look over a longer time frame. The growth factors that CAM utilizes in its selection process likely play a role in the selection of many of the stocks with higher P/Es. If the long-term statistics confirm these results, we might come to the conclusion that CAM's unique growth criteria provide the bulk of their value added. This would obviously impact how we view them and have a potential asset allocation effect.

Regional/Country–Level Attribution Analysis　　For portfolios with non-U.S. exposure, it is possible to build an absolute attribution analysis by region and/or country. As stated previously, once we calculate the IPA for each stock in a portfolio, we have the ability to build any summary-level attribution that we desire. In the case of regional/country attribution, we would simply classify each stock by region or country (depending on the desired result) and sum the IPAs by those classifications.

Because CAM's portfolio is dedicated to the U.S. small-cap market, we do not need to create this type of analysis. However, since CAM does own an ADR (which is a foreign stock traded on a U.S. exchange), we could create an "ADR" category or a "non-U.S." category. Given that CAM rarely purchases ADRs, I did not create any additional categories. If, on the other hand, CAM

EXHIBIT 9.8　P/E-Level Attribution for CAM Small-Cap Portolio

Price/Earnings Ranges	P/E Attribution
< 10	−0.01
10 to 15	−0.57
15 to 20	3.11
> 20	1.41
Total for CAM Small-Cap Portfolio	3.94

(or some other manager under review) does actively employ foreign stocks in addition to U.S. stocks, it might be a good idea to break out the exposures.

RELATIVE ATTRIBUTION ANALYSIS

The objective of absolute attribution is to dissect a portfolio to better understand where its performance record came from. The objective of relative attribution is to compare the components of the portfolio's return to an appropriate benchmark to better understand where the "excess performance" comes from. Relative attribution starts by determining whether a portfolio added value over its appropriate index and then strives to explain exactly what portfolio decisions (or manager skills) led to the over- or underperformance relative to that benchmark. To that end, relative attribution can be considered an explanatory tool for active management.

Relative attribution can be broken into a number of different components based on the main contributors to a portfolio's total performance; however, I have found that two simple classifications of a manager's value added over/under a benchmark are more than sufficient. The components are asset allocation and stock selection. When dealing with portfolios that contain securities outside the United States, we will need to factor into our analysis the impact on the portfolio due to currency movements. In addition, for portfolios that hedge currency exposure, an additional factor must be added to the relative attribution analysis: currency-hedging effect. This section will explain each component of the relative attribution analysis and provide explicit examples of how they work and, more importantly, how they are interpreted.

Because we have the ability to build a relative attribution analysis that covers sectors, industries, market-cap ranges, and fundamental characteristics, it is easy to create an analysis that can get a bit out of hand. So rather than creating a different section for each classification, I have chosen relative sector analysis as the primary example that I will use throughout this section of the chapter. Just keep in mind that the formulas and calculations are the same regardless of the classification chosen. The only difference is how the stocks are combined into separate categories.

Relative Sector Attribution Analysis

Active management can add value over an index by making investment decisions that differ from the index. The first differentiation can be accomplished through asset allocation. An investment manager can choose to hold an overweight or underweight position in a given sector, thus making an active decision to differ from an index. This decision can turn out to be positive or negative relative to that index. For example, if an investment manager decides to allocate 10% of a portfolio's assets to the technology sector versus a 20% weighting held by the index, the portfolio's relative performance will vary based on the performance of the technology sector as a whole. If the technology sector substantially increases, then the portfolio's relative performance in the technology sector based on the decision to underweight that sector will be negative compared to the benchmark. The opposite holds true as well. If the technology sector were to fall precipitously, then the portfolio manager's decision to underweight that sector would be positive relative to the index.

The second active decision that has an impact on a portfolio's relative performance is stock selection. For example, if a portfolio manager decides to allocate 20% of a portfolio's assets to the technology sector (the same weight as the index), then the only way the manager can add value over the index in that sector would be through favorable stock selection. If the manager selected technology stocks that returned 5 percent versus a 3 percent gain by the index, then the manager would have added value relative to the index.

Formula 9.4 (Allocation Effect)

$$AE_s = [(PSW - ISW) \times (ISR - ITR)]$$

where AE_s = Allocation effect for a given sector.
         PSW = Portfolio sector weight at the beginning of the period.
         ISW = Index sector weight at the beginning of the period.
         ISR = Index's sector return for the period.
         ITR = Index's total return for the period.

Just as with the absolute attribution, beginning-of-period weights are used so we do not overstate the impact of the variable. The first part of the formula (PSW – ISW) is pretty straightforward. It determines whether the portfolio under review is overweight or underweight relative to the index in a given sector. The second part of the formula (ISR – ITR) determines if the sector in question performed better or worse than the total index return. This can best be explained by an example. If a particular sector, let's say the technology sector, gains 5% over a period versus a 10% gain for the index as a whole, it is very easy to conclude that a portfolio with an overweight technology allocation will be negatively impacted relative to the index. Conversely, a portfolio with an overweight technology allocation at a time when the technology sector performs better than the overall index will be positively impacted.

We use index sector returns because we wish to isolate the impact due solely to asset allocation. If we were to use the portfolio's sector return, we would introduce stock selection into the equation, which is properly accounted for in the Selection effect.

Formula 9.5 (Selection Effect)

$$SE_s = [(PSR - ISR) \times PSW]$$

where SE_s = Selection effect for a given sector.
      PSR = Portfolio sector return for the period.
      ISR = Index sector return for the period.
      PSW = Portfolio sector weight at the beginning of the period.

The first part of the formula (PSR − ISR) determines if the portfolio's return for the sector in question was higher or lower than the respective index return for that sector. The out/underperformance is then multiplied by the portfolio's weight for that sector at the beginning of the period (beginning-of-period weight is used to avoid double counting the impact). It is important to note that in the selection effect formula, many people use the ISW (index sector weight) instead of the PSW (portfolio sector weight). Both methods are correct, but when using the ISW as the reference weight, you must also add a third element to the analysis: the interaction effect.

Formula 9.6 (Interaction Effect by Sector)

$$IE_s = [(PSR - ISR) \times (PSW - ISW)]$$

The interaction effect, which is summarized in formula 9.6, is used to estimate the impact that asset allocation *and* stock selection might have on one another. While this formula is valid, I have found that it is easier to incorporate this effect directly into the formula for selection effect (formula 9.5). If you decide to include the interaction impact in your analysis, simply change the reference weight in formula 9.5 from the PSW to the ISW.

Finally, we can derive the value added or subtracted to a portfolio's performance relative to an index for a given sector by simply adding the impacts due to allocation and selection together.

Formula 9.7 (Total Effect by Sector)

$$TE_s = AE_s + SE_s$$

where TE_s = Total effect for a given sector.
      AE_s = Allocation effect for a given sector.
      SE_s = Selection effect for a given sector.

Formula 9.8 (Total Relative Value)

$$TRV_p = \sum TE_{s1} \ldots TE_{sn}$$

where TRV_p = Total value added or subtracted for a portfolio relative to the appropriate index.

TE_{s1} = Total effect for sector 1.

TE_{sn} = Total effect for sector n; where n stands for the final sector. For example, if there were 10 sectors, then n would equal 10.

It is important to note that all the sectors included in the index need to be included in the analysis even if the portfolio under review does not allocate assets to them. A portfolio manager's decision to avoid certain sectors completely is an asset allocation decision. It might prove favorable (if that sector performs worse than the overall index) or unfavorable (if that sector performs better than the overall index). Because the selection impact formula uses the portfolio's sector weights, there could be no selection impact when the portfolio is not allocated to a given sector.

The net result of the relative sector attribution analysis can be found in Exhibit 9.9. The weights used in this analysis are as of the beginning of the

EXHIBIT 9.9 Example of Relative Sector Attribution Analysis

Sector	CAM Weight	SCV Weight	CAM Return	SCV Return	Allocation Effect	Selection Effect	Total Effect
Basic Materials	0.0%	8.1%	n/a	2.05	0.09	0.00	0.09
Commercial Services	1.7%	6.4%	−13.94	2.45	0.03	−0.27	−0.24
Consumer Cyclical	20.8%	14.6%	5.91	4.21	0.07	0.35	0.42
Consumer Noncyclical	2.5%	4.0%	10.98	6.56	−0.05	0.11	0.06
Consumer Services	4.0%	7.2%	21.71	8.45	−0.17	0.53	0.36
Energy	10.4%	4.2%	0.72	1.13	−0.12	−0.04	−0.17
Financials	26.8%	17.3%	2.18	2.76	−0.04	−0.16	−0.19
Health Care	23.0%	6.2%	5.73	4.98	0.31	0.17	0.48
Industrials	2.6%	8.2%	−20.20	−5.32	0.47	−0.39	0.08
Technology	8.4%	14.3%	4.35	5.87	−0.16	−0.13	−0.29
Telecommunications	0.0%	0.5%	n/a	4.43	−0.01	0.00	−0.01
Transportation	0.0%	3.7%	n/a	0.54	0.10	0.00	0.10
Utilities	0.0%	5.3%	n/a	1.14	0.11	0.00	0.11
Total			3.94	3.15	0.62	0.18	0.80

CAM	3.94
SCV	3.15
Difference	0.79

period under review (just as in the absolute attribution analysis). The sector returns for the CAM portfolio and the small-cap value index are a weighted average return of the stocks in each sector. The difference between the 79-basis-point difference and the 80-basis-point difference calculated in the attribution results is due to rounding. Exhibit 9.10 lists examples of how the individual sector returns were calculated for the CAM portfolio.

where $Pweight_{bp}$ = Individual holding's weight in the total portfolio. In the example the sum of the positions in the $Pweight_{bp}$ column equals 22.96% of the total portfolio.

       $Sweight_{bp}$ = Individual holding's weight in its appropriate sector. This weight is calculated in the following way:

$$\frac{Pweight_{bp(individual\ stock)}}{\sum Pweight_{bp(appropriate\ sector)}}$$

Using Acambis ADR as an example, the calculation is:

$$Sweight_{bp(Acambis\ ADR)} = \frac{3.06}{22.96} = 13.33\%$$

          CTR_s = Contribution to return for each individual stock.

EXHIBIT 9.10   Determination of Health Care Sector's Weighted Return

	$Pweight_{bp}$	$Sweight_{bp}$	$Return_{fp}$	CTR_s
Acambis ADR	3.06%	13.33%	−14.9	(1.99)
Cantel Medical	1.82%	7.93%	−0.6	(0.05)
ICU Medical	2.29%	9.96%	−12.7	(1.26)
Interpore Int'l	2.66%	11.60%	21.1	2.45
Nat'l Med. Hlth. Card	1.23%	5.35%	39.9	2.14
Option Care	2.09%	9.10%	4.3	0.39
Orthodontic Centers	0.93%	4.03%	−1.6	(0.07)
Pediatrix Med'l Grp.	1.95%	8.51%	29.2	2.48
Polymedica	0.88%	3.82%	15.6	0.59
Possis Medical	1.05%	4.56%	14.7	0.67
Rehabcare Group	1.45%	6.32%	16.4	1.03
Renal Care Group	2.26%	9.83%	−3.0	(0.30)
U.S. Physical Therapy	1.30%	5.65%	−6.6	(0.37)
Total	22.96%	100.00%		5.73

The weighted return for the sector is simply the sum of the individual CTR_s's.

$$\text{Weighted Sector Return} = \sum CTR_{s1}...CTR_{sn}$$

where CTR_{s1} = Contribution to return for first stock in a given sector.

CTR_{sn} = Contribution to return for the last stock in a given sector.

INTERPRETATION OF RELATIVE ATTRIBUTION RESULTS

The best way to understand the power of this type of analysis is to roll up our sleeves and review the CAM example listed in Exhibit 9.9. In this section, we will review the results of the analysis sector by sector.

Basic Materials

The CAM portfolio did not have any holdings in the basic materials sector, while the index had a weight of 8.1% (remember, we are talking about weights at the beginning of the period). The index's sector return was 2.05%. Because CAM had no holdings in this sector, the selection effect must equal zero (see Exhibit 9.11).

The allocation effect measures whether the decision to over/underweight a sector was positive or negative relative to the overall marketplace. As a result, we use the index returns (for the sector and total index) as a basis of comparison. The index return for the sector was 2.05% versus 3.15% for the entire small-cap value index. The analysis is simple at this point. If the sector performed better than the market (small-cap value index) as a whole, then it would have been positive to overweight it and negative to underweight it. However, in this case the reverse is true—the basic materials sector underperformed the market as a whole, so CAM's decision to underweight this sector was a good one. The allocation effect of CAM's

EXHIBIT 9.11 Basic Materials

Sector	CAM Weight	SCV Weight	CAM Return	SCV Return	Allocation Effect	Selection Effect	Total Effect
Basic Materials	0.0%	8.1%	n/a	2.05	0.09	0.00	0.09
Total			3.94	3.15	0.62	0.18	0.80

zero weight in the sector was 0.09%, which was derived by multiplying the weighting differential by the return differential between the sector and the overall index.

Weighting differential = 0% − 8.1% = −8.1%
Return differential = 2.05% − 3.15% = −1.1%
Allocation effect = −8.1% × −1.1% = 0.09%

As we can see in Exhibit 9.9, the portfolio return was 0.80% better than the index return over the period, with 0.62% and 0.18% coming from allocation and selection, respectively. The 0.09% attributed to CAM's allocation decision in this sector is interpreted as having added 9 basis points to the portfolio's relative outperformance. Another way of thinking about the 9-basis-point contribution is with respect to its percentage contribution to the total value added. The 9 basis points represent 11.3% of the 80-basis-point outperformance. So just over 11% of the portfolio's total outperformance can be attributed to its decision to avoid the basic materials sector.

Commercial Services

In contrast to the basic materials sector, which added value relative to the index, CAM's investment decisions regarding the commercial services sector detracted from relative performance (see Exhibit 9.12). The portfolio was underweight the sector (1.7% versus 6.4%) and because this sector underperformed the overall index, its allocation effect was positive, at 0.03%.

However, CAM's stock selection in this sector was very poor. CAM's only holding in this sector, Catalina Marketing, declined (−13.9%) over the period versus a positive 2.45% return by the stocks held by the index in this sector. As a result, the selection effect was negative. The selection effect is determined by multiplying the return differential between the portfolio

EXHIBIT 9.12 Commercial Services

Sector	CAM Weight	SCV Weight	CAM Return	SCV Return	Allocation Effect	Selection Effect	Total Effect
Commercial Services	1.7%	6.4%	−13.94	2.45	0.03	−0.27	−0.24
Total			3.94	3.15	0.62	0.18	0.80

and the index's sector return by the portfolio's weight at the beginning of the period.

Return differential = −13.94% − 2.45% = −16.39%
Portfolio weight = 1.7%
Selection effect = −16.39 × 1.7% = −0.27%

It is easy to see how one bad stock (if it has a large enough weighting) can negatively impact a portfolio's relative performance.

Now that we have broken out actual examples of the allocation and selection effects and explained how to evaluate and interpret them in detail, we will briefly review the remaining sectors.

Consumer Cyclical

Allocation Effect: CAM's overweight position in a sector that performed better than the overall index contributed 7 basis points to the outperformance (see Exhibit 9.13).

Selection Effect: CAM's stock selection in this sector was better than the index's sector performance and because the sector is a large component of CAM's portfolio, the impact due to selection was fairly sizable, at 35 basis points.

Consumer Noncyclical

Allocation Effect: CAM's underweight position in a sector that performed better than the overall index subtracted 5 basis points from the overall value added (see Exhibit 9.14).

Selection Effect: CAM's stock selection in this sector was significantly higher than the sector return for the index, so the selection effect was a positive 11 basis points.

EXHIBIT 9.13 Consumer Cyclical

Sector	CAM Weight	SCV Weight	CAM Return	SCV Return	Allocation Effect	Selection Effect	Total Effect
Consumer Cyclical	20.8%	14.6%	5.91	4.21	0.07	0.35	0.42
Total			3.94	3.15	0.62	0.18	0.80

EXHIBIT 9.14   Consumer Noncyclical

Sector	CAM Weight	SCV Weight	CAM Return	SCV Return	Allocation Effect	Selection Effect	Total Effect
Consumer Noncyclical	2.5%	4.0%	10.98	6.56	−0.05	0.11	0.06
Total			3.94	3.15	0.62	0.18	0.80

Consumer Services

Allocation Effect: CAM's underweight position in a sector that performed significantly better than the overall index subtracted 17 basis points from the overall value added (see Exhibit 9.15).

Selection Effect: CAM's stock selection in this sector was a great deal higher than the sector return for the index (21.7% versus 8.5%), so the selection effect was a positive 53 basis points. The consumer services selection effect, at 53 basis points, was the single largest factor in the portfolio's relative outperformance.

Energy

Allocation Effect: CAM's overweight position in a sector that performed worse than the overall index subtracted 12 basis points from the overall value added (see Exhibit 9.16).

EXHIBIT 9.15   Consumer Services

Sector	CAM Weight	SCV Weight	CAM Return	SCV Return	Allocation Effect	Selection Effect	Total Effect
Consumer Services	4.0%	7.2%	21.71	8.45	−0.17	0.53	0.36
Total			3.94	3.15	0.62	0.18	0.80

EXHIBIT 9.16   Energy

Sector	CAM Weight	SCV Weight	CAM Return	SCV Return	Allocation Effect	Selection Effect	Total Effect
Energy	10.4%	4.2%	0.72	1.13	−0.12	−0.04	−0.17
Total			3.94	3.15	0.62	0.18	0.80

Selection Effect: CAM's stock selection in this sector was slightly lower than the sector return for the index, so the selection effect was a modest negative, at –4 basis points.

Financials

Allocation Effect: CAM's overweight position in a sector that slightly underperformed the overall index subtracted 4 basis points from the overall value added (see Exhibit 9.17).

Selection Effect: CAM's stock selection in this sector was slightly lower than the sector return for the index, so the selection effect was negative (–16 basis points).

Health Care

Allocation Effect: CAM's overweight position in a sector that performed better than the overall index (4.98% versus 3.15%) added 31 basis points to the overall value added (see Exhibit 9.18).

Selection Effect: CAM's stock selection in this sector was higher than the sector return for the index, so the selection effect was a positive 17 basis points.

EXHIBIT 9.17   Financials

Sector	CAM Weight	SCV Weight	CAM Return	SCV Return	Allocation Effect	Selection Effect	Total Effect
Financials	26.8%	17.3%	2.18	2.76	–0.04	–0.16	–0.19
Total			3.94	3.15	0.62	0.18	0.80

EXHIBIT 9.18   Health Care

Sector	CAM Weight	SCV Weight	CAM Return	SCV Return	Allocation Effect	Selection Effect	Total Effect
Health Care	23.0%	6.2%	5.73	4.98	0.31	0.17	0.48
Total			3.94	3.15	0.62	0.18	0.80

Industrials

Allocation Effect: CAM's underweight position in a sector that performed much worse than the overall index (−5.32% versus 3.15%) added 47 basis points to the overall value added (see Exhibit 9.19). This sector was the worst-performing sector in the index for the period, so the underweight position was favorable.

Selection Effect: While the decision to underweight this sector added considerably to the overall value added, the portfolio's holdings in this sector performed quite poorly (−20.2% versus −5.3%). As a result, stock selection subtracted 37 basis points from the overall value added. The negative selection effect negated most of the value added from the underweight position. The net effect for the sector was a modest 8 basis points.

Information Technology

Allocation Effect: CAM's underweight position in a sector that performed better than the overall index subtracted 16 basis points from the overall value added (see Exhibit 9.20).

Selection Effect: CAM's stock selection in this sector was lower than the sector return for the index, so the selection effect was a negative −13 basis points.

EXHIBIT 9.19 Industrials

Sector	CAM Weight	SCV Weight	CAM Return	SCV Return	Allocation Effect	Selection Effect	Total Effect
Industrials	2.6%	8.2%	−20.20	−5.32	0.47	−0.39	0.08
Total			3.94	3.15	0.62	0.18	0.80

EXHIBIT 9.20 Information Technology

Sector	CAM Weight	SCV Weight	CAM Return	SCV Return	Allocation Effect	Selection Effect	Total Effect
Information Technology	8.4%	14.3%	4.35	5.87	−0.16	−0.13	−0.29
Total			3.94	3.15	0.62	0.18	0.80

Telecommunications/Transportation/Utilities

Because CAM did not have any exposure to any of these sectors, they were combined in Exhibit 9.21 for a simple evaluation.

Allocation Effect: CAM's lack of exposure to telecom was slightly negative (–1 basis point), but the lack of exposure to transportation and utilities added 10 basis points and 11 basis points, respectively.

Selection Effect: CAM's zero weight in these sectors led to the neutral results in the selection category.

HISTORICAL ATTRIBUTION ANALYSIS

While it is useful to calculate relative attribution analysis for specific months, quarters, and even years, the maximum benefit is derived when you are able to watch a trend over a longer period of time. The relative attribution analysis used as an example previously in this chapter represents a three-month period of time (the third quarter of 2003). It is useful information in and of itself, but it would be even more meaningful if it could be linked onto an analysis that extends further back in time.

Our analysis based on CAM's 3Q 2003 portfolio indicated that the overall level of outperformance over the index (80 basis points) was a combination of the positive effects due to allocation (62 basis points) and selection (18 basis points). We can test to see if this relationship holds up when we delve deeper into CAM's previous portfolio weightings and allocations. The examples in Exhibits 9.22, 9.23, and 9.24 illustrate the components of CAM's relative performance over the two-and-a-half-year period ending June 2003.

Over the 30 months illustrated in the historical attribution analysis, the average total monthly value added over the small-cap value index was 21 basis points. Over that period, allocation decisions were positive in 17 out of the 30 months reviewed (Exhibit 9.22). The average contribution

EXHIBIT 9.21 Telecommunications/Transportation/Utilities

Sector	CAM Weight	SCV Weight	CAM Return	SCV Return	Allocation Effect	Selection Effect	Total Effect
Telecommunications	0.0%	0.5%	n/a	4.43	–0.01	0.00	–0.01
Transportation	0.0%	3.7%	n/a	0.54	0.10	0.00	0.10
Utilities	0.0%	5.3%	n/a	1.14	0.11	0.00	0.11
Total			3.94	3.15	0.62	0.18	0.80

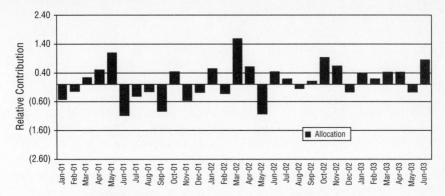

EXHIBIT 9.22 CAM's Historical Allocation Effect

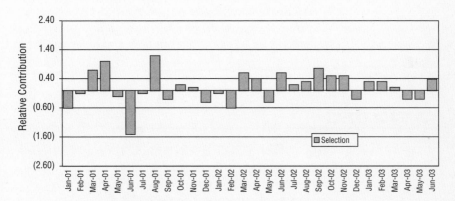

EXHIBIT 9.23 CAM's Historical Selection Effect

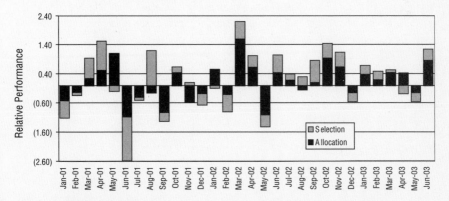

EXHIBIT 9.24 CAM's Historical Combined Attribution Analysis

due to sector allocation was just 11 basis points (out of the 21-basis-point total) or 54% of the total.

Over the 30-month analysis, selection positively impacted relative performance in 17 months out of the 30 (Exhibit 9.23). The average contribution to value added was 10 basis points out of the total average value added of 21 basis points (46%). The results clearly indicate that most of CAM's value added relative to the small-cap value index was balanced between sector allocation and stock selection effects.

The chart in Exhibit 9.24 combines the impact on relative performance due to both allocation and selection. The black part of the bar represents the allocation effect, while the gray part of the bar represents selection effects. This graph provides a quick snapshot of how CAM has performed and how the relative performance was derived.

But this is just one of the many graphs (or tables) that are available to us once we calculate the historical attribution figures. For example, we could create allocation/selection graphs for any of the underlying sectors, industries, market-cap ranges, or fundamental characteristic ranges.

CURRENCY EFFECT

When analyzing portfolios that include stocks from outside of the United States, currency plays a role in performance calculations and evaluation. When purchasing foreign financial instruments, an investor must typically purchase the securities in local currency. For example, the euro must be used when purchasing stocks on the French stock exchange. For a U.S.-based investor, the fluctuation between the U.S. dollar and the currencies to which a portfolio has exposure makes a big difference to the bottom line. For an investor with a U.S.-dollar-denominated asset base, a strong dollar will hurt returns while a weak dollar will help returns (when translated back to the U.S. dollar).

A simple example can explain the impact of currency movements on a U.S.-dollar-denominated portfolio. Let's keep matters simple and highlight a single stock purchase of a U.S.-based investor of a stock traded on the French stock exchange.

At Time of Purchase

Stock price at time of purchase: 15 euros
Exchange rate at time of purchase: 1.25 euros per 1.00 U.S. dollar
Stock price at time of purchase converted to U.S. dollars: $12.00
   (€15 ÷ €1.25)

One Month after Purchase

Stock price one month after purchase: 20 euros
Exchange rate at time of purchase: 1.50 euros per 1.00 U.S. dollar
Stock price at time of purchase converted to U.S. dollars: $13.33

Stock Price Movement during Month

Return stated in euros: (Ending Price – Beginning Price)/Beginning Price
$(20 - 15)/15 = 33.33\%$

Return stated in U.S. dollars: (Ending Price – Beginning Price)/Beginning Price
$(13.33 - 12.00)/12.00 = 11.08\%$

The strength of the U.S. dollar versus the euro over the one-month period (the dollar strengthened by 20%) reduced the return to the U.S.-based investor because at the end of the period he was able to convert 20% fewer euros to U.S. dollars than at the beginning of the period. If the exchange rate had remained the same, the return would have been identical between the two currencies (33.33%).

Now that we have established that currency can play a large role in a portfolio's returns, we can include the currency effect as a component of any relative attribution analysis in which foreign stocks are included. When conducting relative attribution analysis for portfolios that invest in more than one country, it is customary to compare the portfolio to the index on a regional and/or country basis. Sector, industry, market cap, and fundamental characteristics–level attribution can be done for each region or country.

Formula 9.9 (Currency Effect)

$$CE = \left[\left(PCW_{bp(country)} - ICW_{bp(country)} \right) \times \left(ICR_{country} - ITCR \right) \right]$$

where $PCW_{bp(country)}$ = Portfolio country weight at the beginning of the period for a given country.

    $ICW_{bp(country)}$ = Index country weight at the beginning of the period for a given country.

    $ICR_{country}$ = Index currency return for a given country. This is calculated by dividing the change in the spot exchange rates for the period by the beginning exchange rate.

$$ICR_{country} = \frac{\text{Ending Exchange Rate} - \text{Beginning Exchange Rate}}{\text{Beginning Exchange Rate}}$$

ITCR = Index total currency return. This is calculated by calculating the return differential for the total index in U.S. minus local currency terms. An alternative method is to sum the product of each country's index weight by that country's currency return for the period.

Relative Attribution for Portfolios with Non-U.S. Holdings

The method of calculating relative attribution for portfolios that include non-U.S. holdings is virtually the same as identified in formulas 9.4 and 9.5. However, we need to make one change to the formulas referenced. Because we are looking to isolate the effects due to currency fluctuations, we need to change the portfolio and index returns in formulas 9.4 and 9.5 to use local currency returns instead of U.S. dollar returns (or base returns).

Formula 9.10 (Allocation Effect in Multicurrency Portfolios)

$$AE_c = [(PW_c - IW_c) \times (ILR_c - ITR_l)]$$

where AE_c = Allocation effect for a given country.
PW_c = Portfolio country weight at the beginning of the period.
ILR_c = Index local currency return for a given country for the period.
ITR_l = Index's total return stated in local currency terms for the period.

Formula 9.11 (Selection Effect in Multicurrency Portfolios)

$$SE_c = [(PLR_c - ILR_c) \times PW_c]$$

where SE_c = Selection effect for a given country.
PLR_c = Portfolio local currency return for a given country for the period.
ILR_c = Index local currency return for a given country for the period.
PW_c = Portfolio country weight at the beginning of the period.

Multicurrency Relative Attribution Example

To illustrate the minor differences between the single-currency and multicurrency attribution models, we will review a simple two-country example in Exhibits 9.25 and 9.26.

EXHIBIT 9.25 Data for Two-Country Multicurrency Attribution Example

Country	Portfolio Weight	Index Weight	Portfolio Return		Index Return		Allocation Effect	Selection Effect	Currency Effect	Total Effect
			USD	Local	USD	Local				
United States	50.0%	60.0%	5.00	5.00	5.00	5.00	-0.12	0.00	0.04	-0.08
Canada	50.0%	40.0%	4.00	3.00	3.00	2.00	-0.18	0.50	0.06	0.38
Total			4.50	4.00	4.20	3.80	-0.30	0.50	0.10	0.30

EXHIBIT 9.26   Results of Two-Country Multicurrency
Attribution Example

Country	Allocation Effect	Selection Effect	Currency Effect	Total Effect
United States	−0.12	0.00	0.04	−0.08
Canada	−0.18	0.50	0.06	0.38
Total	−0.30	0.50	0.10	0.30

The portfolio in this example is invested in just two countries, the United States and Canada. The portfolio's allocations were evenly split between the two countries at the beginning of the period, while the comparative index had 60% invested in the United States and 40% in Canada. As a result, there will likely be some kind of allocation effect. On a performance basis, the portfolio's U.S. holdings matched the index's U.S. holdings, returning 5% for the period. The portfolio's Canadian holdings, however, performed better than the index's Canadian holdings. As a result, we should expect no selection effect for the U.S. segment and some impact on the Canadian segment based on the portfolio's better performance. Because the U.S. dollar is the reference currency (or base currency), there is no currency return differential for the U.S. segment but there will be a currency effect. Since the Canadian holdings must be converted back to the reference currency (U.S. dollars), currency may play a role in the portfolio's absolute and relative performance.

Summary—United States   *Allocation Effect:* The portfolio's relative underweight position in the United States (50% versus 60% for the index) detracted from performance because the U.S. component performed better than the overall index (5.00% versus 3.80% for the total index) in local currency terms.

Selection Effect: The portfolio's U.S. stocks had the same return as the stocks held by the index; therefore, the selection effect was zero.

Currency Effect: The portfolio was underweight the U.S. market relative to the index. The U.S. dollar's currency return was zero (because the dollar was the reference currency) and the index's total currency return was +0.40%. The resulting currency effect was a positive 4 basis points. The explanation can best be communicated as follows: the portfolio was underweight a currency that had a lower return (which was 0%) than the total currency return of the index (which was +0.40%). So, from a currency perspective, it was a good idea to underweight this currency, hence the resulting positive (4 basis point) contribution to relative performance due to the change in exchange rates.

Summary—Canada *Allocation Effect:* The portfolio was overweight this market, which underperformed the overall index (2.0% versus 3.8%) in local currency terms. As a result, the relative effect was –18 basis points.

Selection Effect: The portfolio experienced better performance in the Canadian segment than did the index, so the selection effect was a positive 50 basis points.

Currency Effect: The U.S. dollar weakened by 1% relative to the Canadian dollar over the period, so returns to U.S.-dollar-based investors would be higher in U.S. dollar terms than in Canadian dollar terms. As a result, the decision to overweight the Canadian market, and hence its currency, was favorable (adding 6 basis points to relative performance).

The proof for this example is:

$$\text{Relative Outperformance} = \text{Portfolio Total Return (USD)}$$
$$- \text{Index Total Return (USD)}$$
$$= 4.50\% - 4.20\% = 0.30\%$$

Attribution Results

Allocation effect:	–0.30%
Selection effect:	0.50%
Currency effect:	0.10%
Total:	0.30%

The portfolio outperformed the index by 30 basis points, and the sum of the attribution effects also equals 30 basis points.

## CHAPTER 10

Style Analysis

Style analysis is generally performed based on the regression of a portfolio's historical performance against a variety of different benchmarks. The combination of benchmarks that best fits the portfolio's historical performance is considered to be the style benchmark by which an analyst can compare performance. Returns-based style analysis is yet another invention of William Sharpe. Once Sharpe developed the returns-based style analysis, he took it one step further and created a method by which we can break a manager's performance into two distinct categories: (1) value added due to asset allocation and (2) value added due to selection. The methodology is simple, yet elegant: Because we have already determined the style benchmark, we simply apply the predetermined weights to the index returns and sum the results. The difference between the portfolio's actual return and the return of the style benchmark is the "style" or asset allocation effect. The residual is the "selection" effect.

RETURNS-BASED STYLE ANALYSIS

Returns-based style analysis regresses a portfolio's historical returns against a variety of benchmarks to determine what the appropriate benchmark mix for a given product should be. In this sense, it is a means of determining an appropriate benchmark. This type of analysis also provides a good way of tracking how faithful a portfolio is to its stated style by comparing its regressed style benchmark over a period of time (often rolling periods).

William Sharpe, in his seminal papers, "Determining a Fund's Effective Asset Mix" (*Investment Management Review*, volume 2, number 6, pages 59–69) and "Asset Allocation: Management Style and Performance Measurement" (*Journal of Portfolio Management*, volume 18, number 2, pages 7–19), laid out a simple, yet elegant method of matching a fund's historical returns to the mix of investment benchmarks that best explains the historical variations in performance. This book will henceforth refer to returns-based style analysis as "Sharpe style analysis" and the derived style indexes as "Sharpe style indexes."

Sharpe's style analysis utilizes quadratic programming techniques to find the combination of benchmarks that determines the lowest squared error term from the regression of the portfolio (fund) under review against a series of benchmarks. While this sounds pretty difficult, this book demonstrates that anyone with Microsoft Excel can create a style analysis template relatively easily. Exhibit 10.1 represents an example of the style worksheet that we discuss in this chapter. Use it as a reference point, but understand that it can easily be altered to meet any user's specific needs.

To calculate the style analysis outlined in the style worksheet, you need the data for portfolio and benchmark returns, as well as Microsoft Excel.

Historical Portfolio/Fund Returns (Column B)

Monthly data is used most often. As stated elsewhere in this book, it is important to have an adequate number of data points when calculating statis-

	A	B	C	D	E	F	G	H	I	J
		Portfolio		Index Returns			Contribution to Performance		Squared Variables	
2	Month	CAM	LCG	LCV	SCG	SCV	Style	Selection	Selection^2	CAM^2
3	Jan-98	−1.23	3.36	−1.23	−1.82	−2.07	−1.95	0.72	0.51	1.51
4	Feb-98	8.34	6.95	7.50	9.87	8.37	9.11	−0.77	0.59	69.56
5	Mar-98	5.67	5.17	5.07	2.65	4.96	3.82	1.85	3.41	32.15
6	Apr-98	1.21	0.84	1.18	0.52	0.65	0.59	0.62	0.39	1.46
7	May-98	−5.21	−2.01	−1.41	−6.25	−4.37	−5.29	0.08	0.01	27.14
8	Jun-98	1.89	7.13	0.76	0.65	−0.05	0.30	1.59	2.54	3.57
9	Jul-98	−8.34	−0.06	−2.17	−6.11	−9.25	−7.70	−0.64	0.41	69.56
10	Aug-98	−19.45	−13.01	−16.08	−20.52	−18.04	−19.26	−0.19	0.04	378.30
11	Sep-98	6.45	6.69	6.08	6.96	5.31	6.12	0.33	0.11	41.60
57	⋮	⋮	⋮	⋮	⋮	⋮	⋮	⋮	⋮	⋮
58										
59										
60	Oct-02	3.45	9.25	8.31	4.34	2.01	3.15	0.30	0.09	11.90
61	Nov-02	6.54	4.85	7.03	5.02	5.40	5.21	1.33	1.76	42.77
62	Dec-02	−3.21	−6.50	−5.20	−4.06	−2.65	−3.34	0.13	0.02	10.30
63	Jan-03	−3.45	−2.50	−2.74	−2.74	−4.13	−3.45	0.00	0.00	11.90
64	Feb-03	−3.21	−0.30	−2.72	−2.71	−3.70	−3.21	0.00	0.00	10.30
65	Mar-03	0.23	2.03	−0.13	1.91	−0.31	0.79	−0.56	0.31	0.05
66	Apr-03	9.17	6.70	9.89	7.15	9.05	8.11	1.06	0.12	84.09
67	May-03	8.76	3.26	7.36	6.76	9.32	8.06	0.70	0.49	76.74
68	Jun-03	4.21	1.82	0.73	2.19	2.97	2.58	1.63	2.65	17.72
69	Average	0.99	—	—	—	—	0.53	0.47	—	—
70	Sum	—	—	—	—	—	—	—	139.46	2,844.73
71										
72										
73	Optimized Weights			Optimization Constraints			RESULTS			
74	LCG	0.00		1. Sum of optimized						
75	LCV	0.00		weights = 1			% Return due to			
76	SCG	0.49		2. Optimized weights			Style	95.1%		
77	SCV	0.51		between 0 and 1			Selection	4.9%		
78	Total	1.00								
79							Average Contribution to Performance			
80							Actual Return	0.99		
81							Style	0.53		
82							Selection	0.47		
83										

EXHIBIT 10.1 Style Analysis Worksheet

tics like the ones in this worksheet. As a general rule, I look for a minimum of three years' worth of monthly data (36 data points).

Historical Benchmark Returns (Columns C through F)

The first rule of thumb when selecting benchmarks for the style analysis is that the benchmarks should each represent a different asset class. Asset class distinctions can be defined by geography, style, market cap, financial instrument, and so on. In his research papers Sharpe identifies about a dozen U.S. and non-U.S. benchmarks that cover equities, bonds, cash, small-cap, and large-cap asset classes—most of the investment options available to a particular portfolio/fund. By including all the asset class alternatives, we can set up a template to analyze just about any portfolio/fund without knowing anything about its objective or mandate.

Because we as investment manager analysts spend a great deal of time and expend a great deal of effort analyzing specific investment managers and their portfolios, we should be able to narrow that list of possible style benchmarks to fit our specific purposes. Using CAM's small-cap value product as an example, we narrowed the list of possible style benchmarks to four: large-cap value, large-cap growth, small-cap value, and small-cap growth. In the CAM example, we could have included additional style benchmarks, but they would either add nothing to the analysis (foreign benchmarks or fixed income benchmarks for example) or possibly skew the results (mid-cap value and mid-cap growth). The latter could possibly skew the results because the mid-cap benchmarks have such a high correlation to the small-cap and large-cap benchmarks used in the analysis. When highly correlated variables are used as independent variables in a regression analysis, we can encounter a statistical problem known as autocorrelation. To avoid this problem, I simply eliminated the mid-cap benchmarks. It is advisable to run a correlation analysis on the variables prior to calculating the style analysis to help avoid potential issues *before* they occur.

Software—Microsoft Excel with the "Solver" Add-In

As discussed in previous chapters, Excel is one of the most powerful tools in the investment manager analyst's toolbox; however, some of the advanced functionality needs to be loaded separately. Solver is one of the advanced programs that must be loaded separately. To load the Solver program, follow these steps:

1. Open Excel and click "Tools" on the toolbar. Down toward the bottom of the list of options is "Add-Ins." Click that option.

2. A new box will open. Put a check mark (click the option) next to "Solver Add-In." Excel will likely ask for the original Microsoft Excel CDs to download the program from, so make sure you have the disks ready. Excel will then download and install the Solver program in a matter of seconds—you are now all set to go.

STYLE ANALYSIS EXPLAINED

Using Exhibit 10.1 as a reference point, this section explains the methodology behind the style analysis worksheet so anyone can re-create the worksheet on their own and revise it to meet their own needs. We look at each formula used and explain in detail the use of the Solver program. Please note that Exhibit 10.1 is a cropped version of the actual style analysis worksheet—the rows of dots in the center of the illustration are meant to convey that a portion of the historical data is hidden from view due to space limitations. This was done to simulate the look and feel of the spreadsheet. The column and row labels were left for easy reference.

In the style worksheet, after the month column the next five columns contain the historical monthly returns for CAM's portfolio and the four benchmarks. The next two columns represent a simplistic attribution analysis based on the monthly results of the style analysis (more on this later). The formulas for the style contribution and selection contribution are shown in formulas 10.1 and 10.2.

Formula 10.1 (Style Contribution)

$$\text{Style Contribution} = [(\text{IR}_{1m} \times \text{OWI}_1) + (\text{IR}_{2m} \times \text{OWI}_2) + \dots + (\text{IR}_{nm} \times \text{OWI}_n)]$$

where IR_{1m} = Return for index 1 for the month.
$\quad \text{OWI}_1$ = Optimized weight for index 1.
$\quad \text{IR}_{2m}$ = Return for index 2 for the month.
$\quad \text{OWI}_2$ = Optimized weight for index 2.
$\quad \text{IR}_{nm}$ = Return for index n (the final index) for the month.
$\quad \text{OWI}_n$ = Optimized weight for index n (the final index).

Example from CAM Style Analysis (Using Cells Referenced from Spreadsheet in Exhibit 10.1)

Cell G3 = Style contribution for the CAM portfolio for the month of January 1998.
Cell G3 = (C3 × B74) + (D3 × B75) + (E3 × B76) + (F3 × B77)

Cell G3 = (3.36 × 0.00) + (–1.23 × 0.00) + (–1.82 × 0.49) + (–2.07 × 0.51)

Cell G3 = –1.95

Formula 10.2 (Selection Contribution)

Selection Contribution = Actual Portfolio Monthly Return
– Style Contribution for Month

Example from CAM Style Analysis (See Exhibit 10.1)

Cell H3 = Selection contribution for the CAM portfolio for the month of January 1998.

Cell H3 = B3 – G3

Cell H3 = –1.23 – (–1.95)

Cell H3 = 0.72

January 1998 Portfolio Attribution for CAM

CAM's actual January return: –1.23

Style (allocation) effect: –1.95

Selection effect: 0.72

Proof: Style effect (–1.95) + Selection effect (0.72) = CAM's actual return (–1.23)

The rightmost two columns represent statistical measures required for the analysis. Each of the monthly calculations in the "Selection^2" column represents the square of the corresponding monthly selection effect. Each of the monthly calculations in the "CAM^2" column represents the square of the corresponding monthly returns for the CAM portfolio. The sum of the values in the latter column is the critical factor in estimating the overall style index and the resulting attribution analysis.

The shaded box titled "Optimized Weights" represents the results of the regression analysis or the actual "best fit" style index. The shaded box titled "Optimization Constraints" is included as a reminder of the constraints to be used when using the Solver program. To perform the analysis, follow these steps:

Step One: Set each of the values in the optimized weights box (cells B74 through B77) equal to zero. You can actually enter any numbers you like in these cells, but they must adhere to the optimization constraints. By setting the values of these cells to zero, we are setting a starting point for the Solver program.

Step Two: Click "Tools" from the menu bar and click "Solver" from the list. Remember that Solver will only be available if you have gone through the "Add-In" process. Once you click on the Solver button, a separate Solver box will pop up on your screen. At this stage the Solver box will look like Exhibit 10.2.

We need to fill in the data for the Solver program as follows (see Exhibit 10.3):

Solver Data Entry	Description
(1) Set Target Cell:	Sum of monthly squared selection numbers
(2) Equal To:	Minimize sum of monthly squared selection numbers
(3) Value of:	Zero
(4) By Changing Cells:	Index optimized weights in optimized weights box
(5) Subject to the Constraints:	Sum of optimized weights >= 1
	Optimized weights > 1

Once the appropriate data is entered, simply click the "Solve" button and Excel will determine the optimized weights at which the sum of the squared selection returns (the error term) is minimized (as close to zero as possible). Please note that Solver has a number of advanced options available to users (click the "Options" button to review). Using default options, the Solver program runs through 100 iterations to minimize the error term.

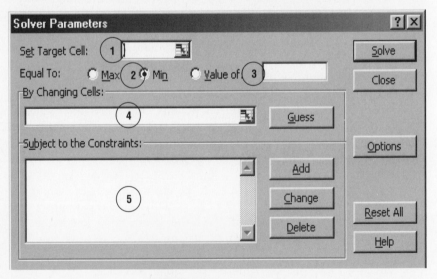

EXHIBIT 10.2   Solver Box

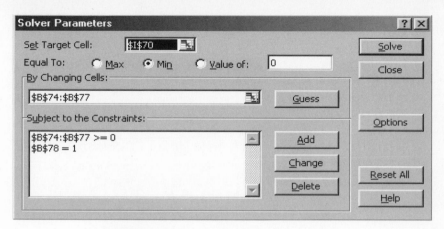

EXHIBIT 10.3 Solver with All Data Entered

The number of iterations can be adjusted based on the analysis being conducted. Solver will ask if you want to change the results based on the latest data or go back to the original values. Click "Keep Solver Solution" and then click "OK."

Solver will automatically enter the new style index weights in cells B74 through B77 and other calculations that are dependent on the optimized weights will update instantaneously.

EVALUATION OF THE STYLE ANALYSIS RESULTS

The results of the Solver optimization state that the best style index is a combination of small-cap growth (49%) and small-cap value (51%). These results mirror our conclusions drawn from the other analytical reports we have generated for the CAM portfolio. Appropriately, the style analysis results indicate that the large-cap growth and large-cap value indexes each have a zero weight. Once again, we have confirmed through diligent historical portfolio analysis that CAM has not strayed from their stated small cap objective. Overall, the results are an affirmation of the work we have already done.

STYLE GRAPH

One interesting method of displaying the results of the Sharpe style analysis is to create what is known in the industry as a style graph. Exhibit 10.4

EXHIBIT 10.4 Style Graph

Style Chart

Data from Sharpe Style Analysis

LCV		0%
LCG		0%
SCV		51%
SCG		49%

	Formula	Results
Lg	LCV + LCG	0%
Sm	SCV + SCG	100%
Val	LCV + SCV	51%
Gro	LCG + SCG	49%
Cap	Lg – Sm	–100%
Style	Val – Gro	2%

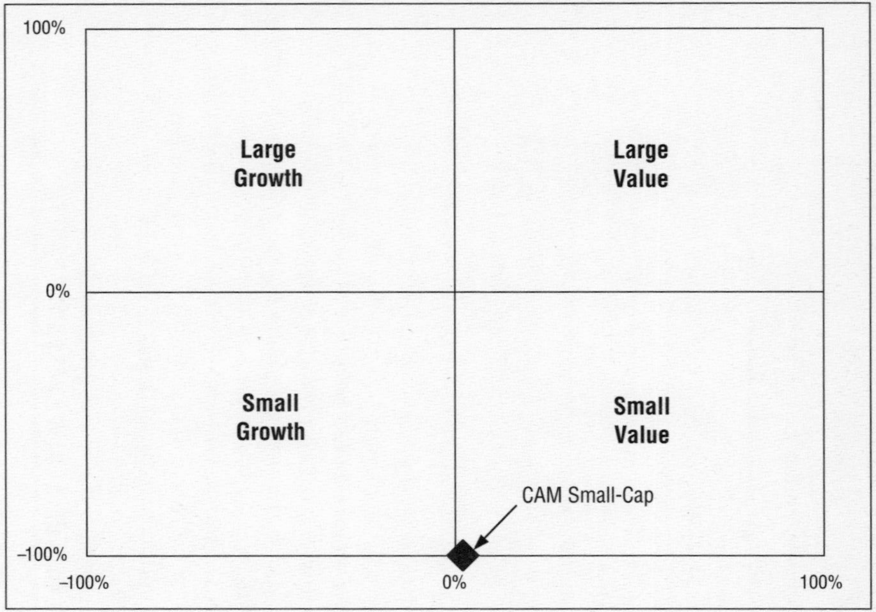

is an example of a style graph that includes the results of the Sharpe style analysis we performed on the CAM portfolio.

The style graph is a way to illustrate the results quickly and make them easily understandable. The graph can be interpreted as follows: The crosshairs in the center of the graph mean that there is a perfectly even split between small/large and value/growth. The four corners represent a perfect score by asset class. For example, a portfolio that lands at the upper left corner of the box would be 100% large-cap growth, whereas a portfolio that lands on the lower right corner of the box would be 100% small-cap value.

The diamond, which represents the score for the CAM portfolio, is slightly in favor of value versus growth and 100% in favor of small-cap versus large-cap. This makes sense because the results of the analysis indicated that 0% of the optimized weights were allocated toward large-cap and the breakout between the remaining small-cap value and small-cap growth allocations was virtually even (with 51% going to small-cap value and 49% going to small-cap growth).

Formulas for determining the x-axis (style) and y-axis (market cap) values are highlighted in the example in Exhibit 10.5.

Exhibit 10.5 is a screen shot from the Excel spreadsheet that I used to calculate the style graph, which is simply an x/y graph. Once we calculate the value for the x-axis and y-axis, we plot the results. The y-axis (which is the vertical axis) is calculated in cell C17, and the x-axis (the horizontal axis) is calculated in cell C18. The formulas for each are stated in cells B17 and B18.

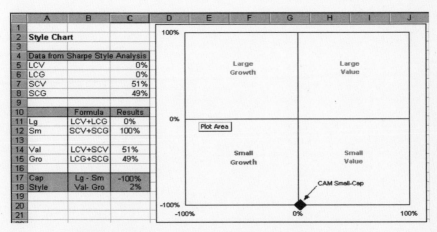

EXHIBIT 10.5 Style Graph Including Data and Formulas

ROLLING STYLE ANALYSIS GRAPH

In Exhibit 10.6 we have created a historical analysis of the CAM small-cap portfolio's style analysis based on rolling three-year results. To create this analysis, calculate the Sharpe style analysis optimized weights for consecutive rolling periods. Using the example in Exhibit 10.6, the black diamond represents the latest three-year style analysis results. The gray diamonds represent the three-year rolling results of the Sharpe style analysis going back in time in three-month increments (three years ended 6/03, three years ended 3/03, three years ended 12/02, etc.).

The rolling results can help us to gain an understanding of how a portfolio has behaved over time. The actual CAM results indicate that the portfolio has been managed consistently over time, as the diamonds are all clustered close together. This graph is a quick and reasonably effective way of assessing what is known as style drift, which measures how closely a portfolio has stayed true to its stated style/cap objectives or how it has drifted over time.

We can also utilize the style graph in another way by including the results of a portfolio's peer group (in whole or in part). Exhibit 10.7 compares CAM's results to the other finalists in our small-cap search.

The results show that all of the finalists have a decided small-cap bias,

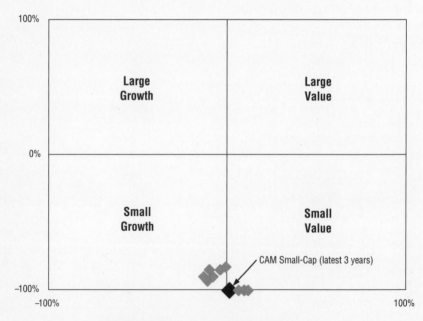

EXHIBIT 10.6 Rolling Style Analysis Graph

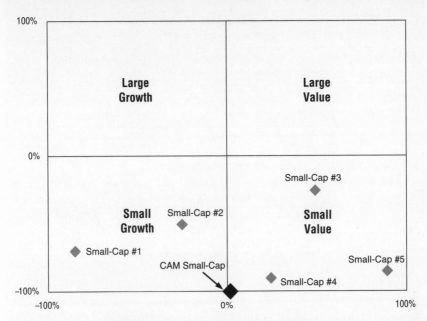

EXHIBIT 10.7 Comparison of Style Results

but they are all over the place with respect to investment style. Small-cap portfolio #1 has a strong growth bias, while small-cap portfolio # 5 has a strong value bias.

ATTRIBUTION ANALYSIS USING STYLE ANALYSIS RESULTS

Now that we have determined the appropriate style index and can confirm its validity based on a variety of other analytical techniques, we can take this style analysis to the next level. We know from Chapter 5 ("Risk Analysis") that the coefficient of determination (R^2) is the statistical measure of the predictive power of the regression results. R^2 is calculated by dividing the sum of the squared error numbers by the sum of the squared total numbers. Our style analysis worksheet automatically calculates each of these terms. Referring to Exhibit 10.1, the sum of the squared error numbers is calculated in cell I70 and the sum of the squared total numbers is calculated in cell J70. The R^2 statistic represents the percentage of the underlying portfolio's return that is due to the style index or, stated another way, the percentage of the underlying portfolio's return that is explained by asset allocation decisions.

EXHIBIT 10.8 Comparison of Historical Attribution Results—
Stated as a Percent of Total Value Added

Effect	Sector Attribution	Sharpe Attribution
Allocation	54%	54%
Selection	46%	46%

Attribution Results Using Sharpe Style Analysis

$$\% \text{ Return Due to Style} = \left(1 - \frac{I70}{J70}\right) = \left(1 - \frac{139.48}{2,844.73}\right) = 95.1\%$$

$$\% \text{ Return Due to Selection} = 1 - \% \text{ Return Due to Style} = 1 - .951 = 4.9\%$$

The results of this analysis, however, are slightly different from the results we achieved in the relative sector attribution model, which calculated
the percentage return due to allocation as contributing 54% and the stock
selection effect as contributing 46% to relative performance. While the attribution based on the Sharpe style analysis is widely used in the industry, I
have never been comfortable with the results. However, we can use the
Sharpe style analysis results in another way.

Again, referring to the data in Exhibit 10.1, we can take the average
return of the underlying portfolio (B69) and compare it to the average contribution to return due to style (G69) and the average contribution to return due to selection (H69). The results are summarized in Exhibit 10.8.
The results of this analysis indicate that style (allocation) accounts for 54
basis points of the average return to the underlying portfolio (99 basis
points), while selection accounts for the remaining 46 basis points. These
numbers are more realistic and in line with the results achieved in the historical relative sector analysis.

We have achieved roughly the same breakout utilizing two completely
different approaches and based on different types of data. Since CAM utilizes bottom-up stock selection, it is apparent that their process leads them
not only to individual stocks that perform well, but to areas of the marketplace that generally perform better than average.

## CHAPTER 11

On-Site Meeting

At this point we have gathered and analyzed a great deal of information. Even if the information thus far looks very attractive and we have met face-to-face with one or more investment professionals elsewhere, it is necessary to make a trip to the manager's offices. This is essential because a visit to the offices will give us access to all of the relevant investment, back-office, legal, and operational professionals that we need to speak with in one neat and clean trip. In addition, there are some things that cannot translate well via a phone interview or an off-site meeting.

Before I make any on-site visit, I gather all of the information that I have amassed on the firm, the product(s) under review, and the appropriate professionals, and combine it with the news I have obtained myself and the analytical reports that I have generated. To be organized, I usually punch and bind the materials or, if the package is too big, put it into a three-ring binder.

Once the information is gathered and neatly arranged, I create a list of general and specific questions that need to be addressed during the on-site visit. I find this is necessary because it is not uncommon to lose track of time during on-site meetings and find that your time is up before you have had a chance to address all of your questions or issues. Another helpful thing to do is to set aside a fair amount of time for the visit. Some on-site visits can be completed in a few hours, but others might take a full day. Given the trend toward firms with multiple (even dozens) of investment products, the on-site process can take a while.

The on-site visit can be broken into several distinct phases:

INTERVIEWS WITH INVESTMENT PROFESSIONALS

By the time we conduct an actual on-site meeting, we have spoken to one or more investment professionals through phone interviews and/or face-to-face meetings (at our offices, at conferences, over lunch/dinner, etc.). During this visit, we need to spend most of our time with the key investment personnel, but also must spend time with all secondary and supporting investment personnel. This includes: analysts, traders, and any other person who might have a role in the management of the product under review.

When I plan an on-site meeting, I often attempt to set it up in such a way that I get time alone with each of the investment personnel (although this is not always possible). I do this because I have found that when I conduct a meeting with two or more people, the flow of the meeting is often skewed toward the person in charge. If I am meeting with a senior portfolio manager and two junior analysts, the senior portfolio manager tends to answer most questions and the junior analysts' answers may be influenced by the presence of their boss (what I refer to as "follow the leader" syndrome). In addition, meetings with several people at once can fall prey to groupthink.

However, meetings with multiple investment personnel can also be very helpful when it comes to gauging how the team works together and how in tune they are with one another. Meetings where one person starts a sentence and another person finishes it tend to tell me that they either (1) are very much on the same page or (2) have their marketing pitch down cold.

When meeting with investment professionals, I like to sit with them in their own personal office space if possible. A person's office space can speak volumes about the type of person he or she is, offer clues as to organizational skills, and even give me an idea of what each person is currently working on. In addition, conducting a meeting in their own space can put people at ease and make a discussion of what they do and how they do it much easier and more effective.

Regardless of where the meetings are held, I always ask to see actual examples of each individual's work. I prefer to sit down with personnel in front of their computers and go through examples of their research. The goal here is to gain a better understanding of what they do and how they do it so that I can form a complete picture of their strengths and weaknesses. Secondly, I am looking to see how their investment-related systems work in practical terms. It is one thing to hear how a system works from a marketer or see a fancy flowchart or diagram in a marketing presentation; it is another thing entirely to see it in action. Not to be too cynical, there have been many occasions where I have found that someone's description of a system or process is very different from the actual system or process. It is not uncommon for a marketer to tell me in the phone interview how they have automated their portfolio allocation system; however, when I visit and look at the system for myself, I discover that the "automated" system is actually very manual and sometimes inefficient.

After conducting interviews with the investment professionals, we should be in a position to answer the following general questions (comments appear in italics):

1. Who is in charge of the day-to-day management of the portfolio?

   It is critically important to be able to distinguish the key decision maker(s) from the other investment professionals. The people in charge are the ones who actually decide what and when to buy and sell securities. While it is important to get to know all the investment professionals, it is more important that we have a very strong understanding of the key decision maker's background, experience, skills, strengths, weaknesses, and workload. It is important to ascertain what other responsibilities the key decision makers have so we can make a judgment regarding their ability to focus on the product under review.

2. How do the different members of the investment team work together?

   While there is no set formula regarding successful teamwork, it is important to understand the team dynamic. A team in which all members clearly know their responsibilities and work together in the best interests of the underlying portfolio is what we are looking for. Compensation plays a role in this area as well. If, for example, a firm has a team of "generalist" analysts who are compensated based on the stock ideas that they bring to the portfolio managers, then it is possible that the analysts will compete against one another instead of working toward a common goal. However, conclusions are made on a case-by-case basis; what might work for one firm might not work for another firm.

3. What are each of the investment professionals' responsibilities?

   This is related to question 1. The difference is that we are looking to get a full rundown on all the investment professionals' responsibilities. When we conduct the portfolio attribution, we can then determine who is adding value to the portfolio and who is not. In addition, this information will prove beneficial in the future is we find out that one or more investment professionals have left the investment firm. You can quickly refer back to your notes and see whether the departures are critical.

4. What areas of specialization (if any) do each of the investment professionals' concentrate on?

   Related to the previous question. The focus here is specifically on investment-related functions.

5. Who is responsible for trading the portfolio?

   This question will help us to determine if the trading and analytical functions are separate. If the function is not separate, it will help us to gain a full picture of job responsibilities. Since trading is such an important function in any investment firm, it is good to know who is responsible for doing it and for understanding whether this function adds to or subtracts from performance.

6. Who is the lead portfolio manager's backup (if any)?

   What if the lead portfolio manager were to go on vacation or decide to leave the firm? Would you still have enough confidence in the team to keep your money with them? These are the questions that we are looking to answer internally. A firm with one lead portfolio manager and no real backup would likely be fired in the event that manager decided to leave the firm. However, a firm that has one or more strong backups will help to ease our worries should one of the lead portfolio managers leave. If the firm has strong backup(s), we need to meet with them and get to know them just as well as the lead portfolio manager.

7. What is the process the firm uses to select buy candidates, and what criteria are used to identify sell candidates?

   This is where we start to get into the actual portfolio management questions. This is a process-oriented question that can lead the discussion directly into specific buy and sell examples.

8. What are some specific examples of stocks that you have purchased and sold?

   Examples help the investment manager analyst form a complete picture of the firm's investment process and the research skills of the team. I typically spend a great deal of time discussing real-life examples of stocks that they have recently traded as well as some older trades.

9. How is the portfolio constructed? Are there constraints on position size, sectors, industries, or fundamental characteristics (P/E, P/B,etc.)?

   This is where the portfolio analysis we have performed comes in handy. By referring to the portfolio analytics report, we can ask targeted questions about specific sector/industry weightings and holdings. The portfolio construction answer should also cover how the investment professionals decide on individual weightings. For example, why does one position represent a 3% weight in the portfolio versus another position that represents only 1% of the portfolio? Who makes those decisions and how are the decisions reached?

10. Who is in charge of the portfolio's asset allocation? What systems do they use to assure that portfolios are allocated properly?

    This question is meant to determine responsibility as well as find out what (if any) systems are in place to do the work. A composite with wide dispersion results might have resulted in poor allocation among the different client portfolios.

11. Who is in charge of conducting portfolio risk analysis?

Internal risk analysis is a critical element in any investment firm's overall process and methodology. When analyzing a given investment firm, we conduct a variety of performance, risk, portfolio, and style analytics to determine the potential rewards and risks of hiring a given investment firm. However, we will never be in a position to monitor and assess risk as well as the actual firm under review. When we hire a firm because we believe that they can deliver x, y, and z, it is reassuring to know that the firm in question has controls in place to assure that we actually get x, y, and z.

12. What systems and other resources are used by the investment staff, and how are they each applied to the product under review?

Computer hardware and software often play an important role in the management of investment portfolios. It is important to get a feel for the third-party systems used by the firm, as well as any internally generated programs or spreadsheets that the firm relies on to effectively research and manage the underlying portfolio. This is often a good point to ask to see how the firm's internal systems work. I always ask to sit with someone at a computer and to have the individual demonstrate how the systems work.

13. Are any of the investment staff working on any other products?

Division of responsibilities is important. I have met with investment professionals who work on as many as three or four different investment products. While each case is different, I tend to be biased toward investment professionals who are mostly dedicated to the product that they are managing for me. This way, I can be assured that on any given day they have my best interests at heart. However, I have hired firms in which the investment professionals are spread out among different products. For example, many large investment firms hire analysts to focus on specific countries or sectors. The analysts conduct research on stocks that fall into their area of specialization. The portfolio managers look at this collective research and then create and maintain their portfolios. In this instance, I would not penalize the analyst because that is the way the firm is set up.

14. How often does the investment staff meet to discuss the portfolio?

This helps to assess organization and to provide additional hints regarding the overall level of teamwork. The answer should cover both formal and informal meetings.

15. Have any investment professionals' roles changed within the firm or with regard to the product in question?

This question is important because it helps us to properly assess a portfolio's historical record. It is also another way to find out if anyone has left the firm or if anyone currently at the firm had contributed to the portfolio in the past but no longer has any portfolio responsibilities specific to the portfolio under review. For example, we might find out that the firm's technology analyst started to cover health care stocks in the last year. Further questioning may uncover that the technology analyst had to take on the health care sector because the health care analyst is no longer with the firm. This might be important information if the health care sector has historically been the largest contributor to the portfolio's total performance.

16. What is the firm's sell discipline?

Anyone can buy a stock; the best investment professionals know when to sell it as well. I refer to sales when a stock is up as well as when a stock is down. The former refers to "locking in gains," while the latter refers to "knowing when enough is enough." When inquiring about a firm's sell discipline, make a point of asking if they have a stop-loss for stocks that decline in price. If so, ask about the parameters and go through specific examples. In addition, ask if they have ever violated the stop-loss parameters. If the firm does not have a stop-loss procedure, ask how they handle stocks that lose value. At what point will they throw in the towel and sell a stock? Another good question to ask is whether they have bought (or would buy) more shares of a stock that has depreciated in price, which is commonly referred to as "doubling down."

17. What level of research is conducted on each stock in the portfolio and under review for possible inclusion in the portfolio?

This is a perfect segue into a discussion of individual stocks. I typically ask to see examples of the stock research that a manager does by asking to review their computer models and hard copy files (if they have them). This is also a good time to discuss with the investment managers any stocks that we have identified as outliers in the portfolio analysis report. The portfolio analysis we perform often identifies several specific stocks that seem to violate one or more of the investment parameters set by the firm.

18. What constraints have been put on the portfolio, and how are they enforced?

This might be fully covered in question 9, but I always ask the question in a more generalized way to see if there are any nonweighting constraints put on the portfolio.

Specific questions to ask each investment professional:

1. What is your investment experience?

    Ask this of each and every investment professional. The answers help us to create a "career track record" for the investment professionals and help build confidence in the people behind the product. If track records from previous firms are mentioned, request the performance and disclosures so you can verify their assertions.

2. Have you changed your style of investing during your career? Or, put another way, how has your style/method of investing evolved over your career?

    Change is not good or bad . . . it is what it is. However, knowing how an investment professional has evolved over the years can help to gain a fuller understanding of that person's current skill level and help shed some additional light on the underlying portfolio's style and historical attribution.

3. What are the best and worst investment decisions you have made for the product under review?

    I find that most investment managers like to talk about their winners. I also ask for examples of stocks that did not work out so well. We can use the portfolio analytics we created previously to identify specific stocks that have experienced declines in price. I usually pick these stocks prior to conducting the on-site meeting so I can do some research on them myself. My goal is to get to know these companies well enough to ask intelligent questions during the on-site meeting and to put myself in a position to know when the investment manager's answer is insufficient. If I didn't take the time to get to know the stocks, how could I assess the manager's answer?

4. How do you personally interact with your fellow investment staff?

    This goes toward the issue of teamwork. By asking each person this question, I get a better idea of how the team works. It is not uncommon for different people to give different stories.

5. Can you go through (in detail) some of the stocks that you have researched that are in the portfolio?

    This is related to question 3, but is more open-ended. The manager can pick any stocks to discuss here (not just defined winners and losers).

6. Can you take me through your personal investment process by picking a stock you are currently researching and bring me up to speed on your progress?

    By "currently researching," I mean stocks that are not currently in the underlying portfolio. Asking about these stocks ensures that I don't get any polished answers. I'm looking to get into the manager's head and see how he or she dissects a stock prior to purchase.

7. Can you give me a demonstration of your firm's technical research and portfolio management capabilities?

   I'm looking for practical, real-life examples of the firm's research and portfolio management systems.

8. Which brokerage firms conduct the bulk of your trades, and what is your average commission?

   When asking this question, make a point of discussing any "soft dollar" arrangements that the firm may have. Soft dollars are accumulated at the brokerage and are based on the commissions paid on all transactions. Many investment firms have arrangements with their brokers whereby the broker uses the soft dollars accumulated in an investment firm's account to pay for research and other items. An obvious conflict may arise regarding the commission rate paid on trades (higher commissions might result in more soft dollars). Since soft dollars are accumulated based on client trades, it is important that the investment firm have the client's best interests at heart. Simply ask for a list (in writing) of all expenses paid for by soft dollars.

9. What are your strengths and weaknesses?

   A general question that often yields surprisingly candid results. As investment manager analysts, we must make our own assessment of each investment professional's strengths and weaknesses, but I have always found the investment professional's own assessments useful. Also ask team members to describe their co-workers' strengths and weaknesses.

10. Can you provide personal references from your previous employment history?

    While reference sources generally speak glowingly about the person in question, this question sets a tone and helps us to be as thorough as possible. Reference, background, and credit checks are not necessary in all cases, but I always ask for references just to see if I can get them. Refusal to provide references often tells me more than speaking to references. Chapter 13 will describe this process in greater detail.

Obviously, there are many questions that will be specific to the individual investment professionals under review. The questions previously listed are general and are meant to stir up additional conversations. However, many of the questions specific to each individual investment professional will come from the print materials that you have collected during the previous stages of the due diligence process combined with any follow-up questions you may have based on previous meetings and/or phone conversations.

INTERVIEWS WITH ACCOUNTING AND OPERATIONS PERSONNEL

Operational risk is something that tends to get very little attention, but it is very important to the relationship an investor has with the investment firm/manager. Operations can be thought of as the foundation, whereas portfolio management can be considered the actual structure that is built on top of the foundation. The structure might be sound and it might look good from afar, but without a strong foundation it will eventually fall down. I tend to include the following areas under operations: marketing, client service, accounting, administration, and business development. Conversations with the chief operating officer, chief executive officer, and chief financial officer help to shed light on all the operational aspects of the firm.

Marketers play a very important role in the growth of investment management firms. It is their role to spread the word and to help put the firm in a position to gain assets. An effective marketing professional or team helps to create a good first impression for the firm and, ultimately, for the investment products under management. Marketers are often given little attention in the due diligence process, but because they play such a vital role in firm growth (and growth in assets is an important element in the overall due diligence process) I have found it very helpful to assess how effective a firm's marketing staff is. The marketing function is especially important when conducting due diligence on young or emerging investment firms. From a business plan perspective, emerging companies need revenue to survive. Often, an emerging company survives due mostly to the principals' own capital. A marketing staff that does not introduce new assets (and the resulting revenues) places stress on the company's viability as an ongoing entity.

Questions to ask the marketing professionals:

1. What is your historical track record raising assets?

   Marketers are a vital component of any investment firm's success. I have met with many wonderful but very small investment firms that can't seem to make it to the next level with respect to assets under management. Often their story is good, but they do not have anyone to tell it. Since an investment professional's compensation often is based in some way on the underlying investment performance in relation to product assets, the ability to raise assets is critical.

2. What areas of the pension market (public, corporate, foundation, endowment, Taft Hartley) are your strengths and weaknesses?

3. What products have you marketed in the past? What is your level of familiarity with the fundamental and technical aspects of the asset classes that relate to those products?

4. What resources do you have at your disposal?

   Resources refers to human, financial, and technical.

5. How are you (and the other professionals at the firm) compensated with respect to assets raised?

   Compensation (for better or worse) is a very good form of motivation.

6. Do you currently charge any other client a lower rate for the product than you have quoted to me?

   Many managers offer lower fees based on the amount of assets they manage for the client. I have no problem with this. However, if the firm charges another client a lower level of fees when we have the same amount of assets managed by the firm, then I have an issue.

Client service professionals and support staff represent another area that tends to get precious little attention prior to hire, but a great deal of attention after hire. When I ask for references, I make a point of asking current and former clients about the level of client service they get (or had gotten) from the firm under review. Client service can be divided into three separate levels: quality, quantity, and timeliness. High-quality client service professionals will be able to answer your questions and concerns in an effective manner and will make the monitoring process an easier and more enjoyable experience. Frequency refers to the number of times you receive communications from the client service staff. This includes things like monthly/quarterly market and product commentary; portfolio reconciliations (including the ability to address issues with custodians for separate accounts); and other communications that relate to the product, your relationship, and the market/economic environment. Timeliness is self-explanatory. High quality and frequency can be completely negated by extreme tardiness or even total lack of response by the client service team.

Questions for client service professionals:

1. Can you tell me your level of familiarity with the asset class in general and the product under review in particular?

   The answer to this question will tell me what I can expect from the firm's client service staff. If, for example, the client service representative has a weak understanding of a given product, then I would not expect them to be able to answer any difficult questions. In this case, I would likely contact the portfolio manager or one of the other investment professionals directly when I have a question.

2. Can you provide me with examples of your client communications, including research reports, commentaries, portfolio accounting/reconciliations, and any other communications you normally send to clients? Please indicate the timing.

When asking for examples of reporting, ask for reports going back
a year or more. These reports serve as a means of getting up to speed
on the product for a time prior to the due diligence period.

3. How many clients do you service?

Or put another way, how quickly will my phone calls get returned? A firm with many clients and a limited client service staff
might not be able to handle the addition of new clients.

4. What resources do you have at your disposal?

This is a standard question that I ask everyone I speak with. It
helps me to get a better handle on overall firm resources. At the end of
the due diligence process, I can review the answers that each of the
professionals gave me to get a better idea of resources at the firm level.
It is also a way of checking the accuracy of each individual's answer.

5. To what extent would you be available to me if I hired your firm?

I want to know (up front) what I can expect from the firm. When
firms make promises to me, I usually include those promises right in
the underlying investment contract. Like the lawyers always say: "Get
it in writing."

6. How many clients do you personally service? If there are other client
service professionals at the firm, ask how clients are distributed among
the staff, and ask if there is a maximum number of client relationships
given to staff.

This is another way of addressing the resources question.

Lastly, a great deal of information about the firm and its future can be
gleaned from conversations with the C-level executives (CEO, COO, and
CFO). However, in many small investment firms, the investment professionals also manage the business affairs of the firm. In midsize to large investment firms, it can be rather difficult to gain access to the C's, and in
some cases meetings with the C's are not all that useful. A good investment
manager analyst will make this assessment on a case-by-case basis. As a
general rule, I would make a point of meeting with one or more of the C's
when analyzing emerging or small investment companies and would place
less weight on these meetings for midsize to large firms.

INTERVIEWS WITH TECHNICAL/SYSTEMS PERSONNEL

Given the fact that the investment business is based in large part on information dissemination, this part of the on-site visit is essential. The computer systems, software, in-house coding, backup systems, off-site storage,
and work flow are critical elements of a firm's overall efficiency and effectiveness. As such, it is a good idea to spend some time with the person or

people who are in charge of ensuring that the technical side of the business flows smoothly.

Questions to ask the technical staff:

1. What systems does the firm use for all elements of the investment process and portfolio management process? Who maintains the systems?

   The answer should cover both external systems and internal systems. If outside parties are responsible for any of the systems or programs used by the firm, find out how the firm can make changes or modifications to those systems or programs. If the investment firm out-sources this function completely, get the details for the person or firm that is responsible for this function and contact them directly.

2. What type of internal network do you maintain?

   We are looking to assess the effectiveness and efficiency of the firm's networking systems.

3. Do you employ any kind of "virtual private network" to employees when they are off-site?

   We are asking here if any firm employees can access the network from home or when they are traveling.

4. What is your system for backing up files?

   The backup function is a major one. It is one of those functions that go largely unnoticed until a computer virus hits and disables the network. Firms with no backup plan or systems can be crippled by the unexpected loss of data files. I require any firm that I hire to provide to me in writing the details of the backup system and procedures, including: who is responsible for the function, what systems are used, with what frequency are files backed up, where the backup files are stored, and how long it would take to reinstall backed-up files.

5. What is your disaster recovery system?

   In the event of a fire, computer virus, theft, or natural disaster what is the procedure? This question is related to the previous one, but it is much more expansive. For example, in the case of a firm whose building burns to the ground, effectively destroying everything, what are the plans to get the firm up and running again? Things to consider: Where are the backup files? How easily and fast can investment professionals access portfolios to effectively continue managing them? Does the firm have alternative office space arrangements? What I look for is a plan of action that is well thought out, clearly delineates responsibilities during a crisis, is widely understood by management, and is written.

6. Who is your backup?

   Computer and systems professionals keep crazy hours. Systems can go down at any time (24/7), and little nitpicky problems always seem to arise during the normal course of business. A good computer/systems staff will keep the work flow steady and when problems do arise, fix them in short order. As a result, good computer/systems staff is essential. Just like we do with the investment team, we want to ask if there is any real backup to the person (people) in charge of this function.

7. What security procedures do you employ?

What does the firm do to protect itself from computer viruses, hackers, and other illegal activities?

8. Do you outsource any of the technical/systems work?

If yes, get the details and call the supplier to verify.

9. How often do you upgrade hardware and software?

Once again, we are attempting to ascertain the firm's effectiveness and efficiency. While it is not imperative that a firm uses the most current versions of all software programs, an upgrade sometimes has an effect. For example, a firm that is using a version of portfolio management software that is outdated might not have the ability to perform some of the analytics based on more recent advancements in the industry or unique advancements created by the specific software company. The status of computer hardware (laptops, desktops, towers, network computers, printers, scanners, etc.) can speak volumes about the firm's level of efficiency and effectiveness. For example, when I sit at a portfolio manager or analyst's desk to review research, I can quickly make an assessment as to the efficiency of the computer systems. During these meetings, I have seen systems that range from the cutting edge of technological progress to old, slow, inefficient setups that actually have a negative impact on a professional's ability to do the job.

INTERVIEWS WITH LEGAL/COMPLIANCE PERSONNEL

This is another area that is often overlooked, but is essential to gaining a full and complete picture of the organization. By spending time with the firm's legal and compliance personnel, we can better understand how thorough and timely the firm is with regard to regulatory issues, policies, and internal governance/compliance. It is entirely possible that these functions are performed by the COO, CFO, CEO, or some combination thereof. As a result, you can often get the answers to legal and compliance questions from them.

Questions to ask legal/compliance professionals:

1. May I have a copy of your firm's compliance procedures?

Firms with little or no compliance procedures are more susceptible to ethical or legal violations than firms that have tightly written procedures that are stringently enforced.

2. How do you track possible employee violations of internal procedures and regulatory requirements?

   This question will help us to get an understanding of what steps a firm takes to identify any possible violations. It is important to know who is in charge of this process and how often it is done.

3. Has your firm been questioned or charged with any regulatory violations since your last Form ADV filing?

   The Form ADV lists any previous regulatory violations, and you should make a point of discussing any violations that the firm may have had in the past. This question will help to bring us up to date regarding regulatory violations, as ADVs are not constantly updated.

ASSESSING THE OFFICE

When conducting your on-site visit, you must also make an assessment of the office space. For example, it is important to discover if the firm has enough space for its current staff and for potential future growth. The physical layout of the office can also provide useful information relating to work flow and professional interaction. At a basic level, a tour of the office space can also give clues about the firm's efficiency, effectiveness, and desire and ability to spend on physical necessities. You should be able to answer the following questions based on your on-site visit:

- Is the firm laid out efficiently?
- Does the firm have enough office space to accommodate future growth?
- Does the office have enough room for hard-copy filing?
- Does the firm keep old files on-site or archive them off-site?
- Where are the network servers located and what, if any, safeguards do they employ?
- What is the physical condition of the office?
- What is the physical condition of the computers in the office?

ON-SITE MEETING MEMO

This memo will be structured just like the initial interview memo, but will have an emphasis on the different people that you meet and your various observations about the office space. Exhibit 11.1 is a sample on-site meeting memo based on the CAM example used throughout the book. I normally break my memos out by job function (investment, operations, etc.), but since CAM is small and the partners wear many hats I elected simply to list the notes from each interview in succession.

EXHIBIT 11.1 CAM On-Site Meeting Memo

To:

From:

Re:

INTERVIEW NOTES

As a follow-up to the previous phone conversation with Mark Innes, I arranged an on-site visit to meet with all the members of the CAM team. The meeting took place at CAM's offices on Monday, November 15, 2003, from approximately 9:00 A.M. to 1:30 P.M. I met with each of the partners as well as the support staff.

Mark Innes

I met with Mark after getting a tour of the office space and being briefly introduced to everyone along the way. The office space is a bit tight and my initial impression was that they would be able to comfortably hire only one or two additional employees before they would have to get more space or move to bigger offices. The reception area is staffed by long-term temporary help. Mark explained that receptionists are hard to find and, once found and hired, very hard to keep. CAM thought it was easier to let the temp agency deal with it all for them. The inner offices and general work area are to the right of the reception desk.

Mark and Jim share a large office, but Andy has his own (albeit a very small one). Tara and the group's administrative assistant, Jenny, work in an open area that has been partitioned into four cubicles—Tara and Jenny use two of them, and the other two are presumably to accommodate future growth. One of the open cubicles houses their shared portfolio management systems (Bloomberg, FactSet, etc.). A back room is used as a kitchen (mini refrigerator, microwave, and pantry). It also houses CAM's network server as well as filing, storage, copying, and binding. The back room is pretty full and the network server is buried in the back. I asked Mark about the office space and the back room, and his response was they are fully staffed and that any additional hires they may make in the future will be administrative in nature. He said that the two open cubicles would allow for this growth. When the tour was done, we settled into the conference room (Jim was on a conference call with a portfolio company in their shared office). I asked Mark about technical support, and he replied that they outsource it to a local computer firm. They do not have the time or expertise to do it in-house. They have a contract with a local firm that comes into their office once a week to perform systems maintenance and to check that all systems are optimized. If they have any computer problems, they simply call their service guy and he is contractually obligated to come to the office within three hours

(Continued)

EXHIBIT 11.1   *(Continued)*

of the call. Since we were already on the topic, I asked about computer backup and disaster recovery. Mark explained that Tara would be better to speak to about this.

After the discussion about the office, we talked about CAM's investment process and about the portfolio. As we spoke, my initial concern about the relationship between Mark and his partners was alleviated. Mark explained how he and his partners complement each other. He stated that while he and Jim do not formally break the stock universe into sector responsibilities, Jim has better skills at researching financials and consumer companies, while Mark has more of an expertise regarding the health care and technology sectors. Mark stated that his sectors played a larger role in the portfolio in the past, but Jim's sectors dominate the portfolio now and have been in the 50% to 70% range for the past year and a half. He stated that they have managed to beat their peers during the "growth push" as well as the current "value environment." He feels that he and Jim complement each other and that together they are a better team than either one of them would be operating on his own. [*Refer to the attached portfolio analysis section for a sector breakout.*]

We spent some time talking about the portfolio's historical positioning, specifically the firm's exposure to growth stocks. [*Refer to the portfolio analysis section for a stock-by-stock review of the portfolio in the 1999–2000 time frame.*] However, I can summarize the findings here. Mark was mostly responsible for the inclusion of the technology and health care names that we had discussed in the phone interview previously. I was concerned that they had taken their growth exposure to an extreme and that, as a result, it would be very difficult to consider CAM a true value investor. Mark highlighted that they did not invest in any of the IPOs or Internet-related companies with no track record and no earnings during that period. We went through the list of names he had e-mailed me following of initial interview and, for the most part, he is correct—the stocks CAM purchased were reasonably established health care and technology names with strong track records. He stated that many of the names they purchased advanced well beyond the values they calculated based on their internal intrinsic value models. In the 1999–2000 period, they did tend to hold on to those kinds of stocks a bit longer than they would normally because sentiment was like a "strong wind at their back." However, during that period, turnover in the portfolio increased from their long-term average of 30% to the 50%–60% range.

Currently, Mark is finding numerous values in the health care sector, specifically in the services and supplies industries (he calls them "the boring areas that put most analysts to sleep"). Mark pointed out that CAM's only biotechnology holding, Acambis ADR, is not in any of the speculative biotech areas; rather, it is in the "unsexy" business of producing smallpox vaccines.

Mark and I spent the final part of the interview talking about the hedge fund. He stated that it was originally created as a method of managing the partners' money. It grew to friends and family and, before long, had become a full-fledged product in and of itself. Many clients, who had lost assets in the market downturn of the past few years, seemed to like the hedge fund's ability to protect against market fluctuations by going short, and as a result assets came to the hedge fund

EXHIBIT 11.1   *(Continued)*

with absolutely no marketing effort at all. Mark informed me that they have closed the small-cap hedge fund to new assets, but may open it to additional assets once they have had a chance to review the situation early next year. He stressed that product capacity is a critical issue at CAM and they want to assure any clients and potential clients that they will close all products long before they reach any hard product capacity issues. I did find out, however, that the long portion of the hedge fund has only a 60% crossover with the long-only small-cap product. This differs from his statement to me on our conference call that the long portion of the hedge fund is essentially the same as the small cap product. When I asked him about this, he stated that in the recent past the crossover had dropped. Mark has been buying more micro-cap positions in the hedge fund because he feels that the one-year lockup on assets and the quarterly liquidity (and 30-day notice period) insulated the hedge fund from a fast flow of assets into and out of the fund. After our conversation had ended, Mark led me to his office to meet with Jim.

I was surprised by his answer, given that he did not mention this during our initial phone conference. I asked about capacity and he responded by stating that the hedge fund would focus more on the micro-cap space than the small-cap space. This alarmed me because it now appears as if Mark's responsibilities would increase and potentially distract him from managing the small-cap value product.

I asked him where the firm's revenues came from and he responded that given the hedge fund's strong performance and its 20% incentive fee, it contributed more to revenue than the small-cap value product (despite the differential in asset size).

Jim Bradshaw

By the time Mark brought me over to speak with Jim, his conference call had concluded. Since Mark was on his way off-site to visit with a local pension client, I took the opportunity to have my conversation with Jim in his office. Because I had not previously met or spoken with Jim, we spent a fair amount of time going over his biography. Jim and Andy met at Victory Asset Management in the mid-1980s. While Andy was in the operations area, Jim started off as an analyst for the firm's equity, fixed income, and balanced products. Both he and Andy stayed with Victory up until the time they left (with Mark) to start CAM. Jim's position and responsibilities progressed over the years at Victory. At the time of his departure, Jim was the senior portfolio manager in charge of all high net worth accounts. Jim stated that both he and Andy left because they felt that the next step in their professional careers should be equity ownership; unfortunately, VAM had made it clear that equity would remain solely with the firm's founder and his family.

We discussed Jim's experience at VAM and I can summarize it as by stating that VAM is a value-oriented shop that emphasizes capital preservation over all things. The equity product and the equity portion of the balanced product

(Continued)

EXHIBIT 11.1 *(Continued)*

success. A typical equity portfolio was spread out over 60 to 80 names for added diversification. Jim mentioned that he was always frustrated by his inability to dip into the mid-cap and small-cap names, so when Andy approached him with the idea of teaming up with Mark to form a small-cap equity firm, he was all for it. I asked if his analytical process or style has changed (1) as a result of looking at small caps versus large caps or (2) as a result of working with Mark. Jim stated that the fundamental process he employs now is almost exactly what he had used while at VAM. The only changes are in the length of historical data (which tends to be a bit shorter) and the accessibility of top company management (which is better). Jim explained that it is actually easier to get in touch with senior members of a company's management team in the micro-/small-cap space than in the large-cap space.

I asked Jim about the product's heavy weighting in the technology and health care sectors back in the 1999–2000 period and was told that both he and Mark took the portfolio to the extreme and that they had learned their lesson from the experience. He stated that CAM had developed several allocation constraints in the years since that period. Specifically, he told me that they would not hold more than 25% in any given sector (except times when the small-cap value index has sectors that exceed the 25% maximum). I found it interesting that Jim and Mark seem to have different ideas regarding portfolio sector exposures. Jim stated that Mark had lobbied for a maximum exposure constraint in the 30% to 35% range, but was voted down by Jim and Andy. In fact, when asked the same question, Mark said maximum sector exposure was 33%.

I spent the rest of the interview discussing individual stocks in the portfolio. While we focused on names in which Jim was the lead analyst, we also went through some of the stocks that Mark had taken the lead on. Jim was a fountain of knowledge on all of the stocks we discussed (both his and Mark's). He took me through the research process by opening the research files he had stored on his laptop. He stated that Tara is a "magician" with the stock databases and with Excel modeling. I found CAM's research to be expansive and organized. In addition, it appears that all four professionals take part in the stock discussions and play a role in the selection of new names and the sale of old ones.

I also asked Jim about the office space and was told that they were discussing the possibility of new office space. He predicted that based on client service needs, they would have to hire one to two people to properly service clients going forward. The new people could fit in the current office space, but it would be tight.

After my interview with Jim had concluded, he walked me over to Andy's office, where I had a brief chat with him.

Andy Wares

Andy essentially reiterated the story that Jim gave me regarding VAM and their reasons for starting CAM. He stated that he had started at VAM as an equity consisted of mostly large-cap, well-established companies with long records of

EXHIBIT 11.1 *(Continued)*

analyst, but quickly realized that his true skill set was more on the operations side of the business. He described his current role at CAM as "all things non-investment-related." He manages the daily affairs of the firm and uses Jenny as his support staff. He told me that Jenny is considered to be an "all-purpose" administrative assistant, meaning that she works for the team in a variety of capacities. However, most of her time is spent with Andy on operational functions. I asked Andy if he had any role in the management of the small-cap portfolio or the hedge fund and he stated that he sits in on the investment discussions, but does not have any formal authority regarding the products. However, Andy stated that he is quite vocal about names that are proposed as buys for the portfolio. I asked him about risk controls and firm compliance, and he stated that he manages these processes. As for portfolio risk management, he works with Tara to produce monthly internally generated portfolio analytics from their FactSet database. The risk analysis consists of position-level reports broken out by sector, industry, market cap, and a variety of market factors they believe are good bellwethers. As for internal compliance, Jim stated that he would e-mail me a copy of their procedures manual and that he would be happy to discuss any questions I had after reviewing it.

Tara Fitzpatrick

Tara and I met in the conference room after my meeting with Andy. I was interested to talk to Tara because it was apparent even in my previous phone call with Mark that she seems to be responsible for a great number of things at the firm. I joked with Tara about this, and she replied that her days seem to just fly by because she is always so busy. However, she stated that when she worked at other firms she had never had a chance to show what she could do. CAM, on the other hand, challenges her to be at her best and teaches her more and more about the business.

I asked about Tara's work experience and she told me that she graduated from Hunter College with a degree in English literature. She had hoped to become a journalist, but it did not pan out. As a result, she spent the past five years moving from one position to another doing everything from secretarial work to being a clerk at a video store. Once she signed on at CAM, her life changed. She never knew much about the stock market, but found out that she enjoyed it greatly. She was initially hired as an administrative assistant to Mark and Jim, but quickly became a junior analyst in charge of all database functions. She has been with CAM since they opened their doors, and in that time her responsibilities have grown geometrically. When asked what she spends most of her time doing, she replied that she is in charge of the stock and research databases and working with the portfolio managers on the day-to-day management of the products. She also stated that she had recently taken the lead research role on three stocks under consideration and that one of those stocks (American Woodmark) had made it

(Continued)

EXHIBIT 11.1   *(Continued)*

into the portfolio. I asked Tara to tell me about the three stocks she had researched and quickly found out that she could spend the rest of the day doing so. Like both Mark and Jim, she was completely on top of her stocks.

I was surprised to hear that Tara's stock research role had progressed that far (based on my conversation with Mark earlier). I was particularly suprised to find out that she did all the work for American Woodmark, which is a current holding. I asked Tara how long she had been doing stock research and she told me it had been about six months (which is in line with what Mark told me). We then spent some time talking about their network, systems, and technical support. I found out that they do have a contract for weekly systems maintenance, but Tara is actively looking to replace that firm due to pricing and (poor) service issues. I asked for a contact at the systems consultant that I could call to verify systems integrity (I will also ask the systems consultant's opinion of CAM).

Conclusion

I am convinced that the professionals at CAM know what they are doing and are capable of excellent stock research. I am, however, concerned that they do not seem to have a firm grasp of portfolio risk and how to control it. This leads me to conclude that the CAM small-cap value portfolio is a bottom-up, "best ideas" portfolio. However, the portfolio is diversified across roughly 50 holdings, with a nonformal position maximum at roughly 4% of the portfolio.

The office is barely sufficient for current needs, and I would expect that CAM will have to expand both space and personnel in the near future. I am also concerned that Mark seems to be at odds with the rest of the team regarding space, personnel, and the portfolio's sector/position constraints. However, after meeting with Andy (and Jim), I am confident that Mark will get the job done efficiently.

Action Plan

- Score CAM using the "manager scoring model."
- Create comparison analysis for all small-cap value finalists.
- Conduct reference checks.
- Review contract.
- Fully review the hedge fund.
- Call the systems consultant.

## CHAPTER 12

Investment Manager Scoring Model

*The best way to make an informed
decision is to be fully informed.*

Investment manager scoring or ranking models have been in existence for years, but I feel that they have been used in a manner that places far too much weight on the final score than is appropriate. A scoring model can best be defined as a series of quantitative measures that, when viewed together, create a single numerical score/rank/grade. The grade generally consists of a number of individual factors (or variables) that are weighted and totaled. The theory is that the higher the score, the better the manager or fund under review. While this makes intuitive sense, biases and structural flaws might render the results meaningless. The following bullet points highlight some of the problems that might impact a scoring model (explicitly or subtly):

■ *Structure.* The model itself may be structurally flawed due to bias (weighting) toward or against certain factors. The structural biases can result from incorrect weighting schemes or unintentional crossover among the factors. For example, structural flaws might include an unintentional bias toward or from investment philosophies that are fundamentally based versus quantitatively oriented. The bias can also be intentional, but its implications must be disseminated and fully understood by anyone using it to score managers or anyone reviewing the scoring results.

■ *Inconsistency.* There may be a lack of consensus about factor scoring and/or lack of consistent application of factor scoring. The inconsistent scoring of factors within the model can be done by one person over

time or, most likely, among different people working at the same organization. A score must mean the same thing to everyone involved in
the scoring and reviewing process or the results will be inconsistently
applied and possibly misinterpreted.

■ *Factor robustness.* The model might not allow for all possible data, so
some kinds of information might be forced into categories where they
do not necessarily fit.

■ *Differentiation.* The final tabulated scores between managers must offer a wide enough range of possible scores so that the analyst can adequately differentiate among good, bad, and average scores. Although
one should never hire an investment manager/product based solely on
the bottom-line score created by this model, the comparison of different managers' scores should offer a strong indication as to which products should be considered the favorites and which should not be
considered at all. Hopefully, after reading this book you will not place
emphasis on any single attribute that a particular investment man-
ager/product might possess. This includes the scoring model results.
The best way to make an informed decision is to be fully informed.

The scoring model highlighted in this chapter is a generic one that I
created to cover any traditional asset class. The investment manager analyst charged with reviewing/scoring managers can simply use the model
as it appears in this chapter (adjusting several factors to accommodate
different asset classes), or tweak the model to better reflect the asset class
under review.

THE MODEL

The model highlighted in this chapter is used to score managers/funds in
traditional asset classes. It has six different generalized areas of focus,
with a total of 30 factors that must each be scored according to strict
criteria. The six sections that are highlighted in this model are listed in
Exhibit 12.1.

It should be clear from Exhibit 12.1 that the model relies very little on
past performance. In fact, the section labeled "Performance-Related
Risk/Reward" places more emphasis on volatility (risk) and consistency of
returns (safety) than it does on the pure performance of the product under
review. Nearly half of the model's weight is represented by the people involved in managing the product and the process that they use to manage it
(45% combined). Another interesting element of the model is that it places
an emphasis on the organization and the operations (back office) of the firm
under review. These elements of the score are often ignored or downgraded

EXHIBIT 12.1   Manager Scoring Model Sections

Section	Model Weight	Number of Factors
Investment Professionals	30%	5
Process	15%	4
Portfolio Risk	15%	5
Performance-Related Risk/Reward	15%	5
Organization	15%	7
Operations	10%	4
Total	100%	30

by many investment manager analysts and others charged with researching investment products. A final point is that the model contains 30 separate and distinct factors that must be completed in order to reach a final score. The number of factors was not set beforehand and filled in later; rather, the number of factors and the questions they ask effectively cover all aspects of any thorough investment manager review. I have found the scoring model to be a good guideline to follow when researching a manager/product and especially when conducting interviews (both in person and via phone). The model, while not perfect, forces me to analyze each manager in a consistent manner and serves as a reminder of all the questions that need to be answered during the course of the entire due diligence analysis.

SCORING METHODOLOGY

The goal in creating any quantitative model is to produce results that are (1) meaningful, (2) understandable, and (3) usable. To make the model meaningful, it has been designed to cover every aspect of the investment manager/product analysis process detailed in this book. Each section has been weighted based on the principles outlined in the previous chapters, with a decided emphasis on the people involved, the process employed, and the underlying risk of the portfolio under review. Risk is a complicated topic, and as a result it is scored in the model in some obvious and some less than obvious ways. Historical volatility is an obvious measure of risk employed by the model, whereas employee ownership/incentives is a less obvious risk. The risk we are measuring when we score ownership/incentives is the risk of the firm losing employees (who may seek better compensation and/or an equity stake), and we are forming a general view regarding overall employee enthusiasm and desire to achieve the best results possible. As you will see in the following sections, many factors can be considered pseudo risk factors.

To make the model's results understandable and usable, I have created a scoring system is very similar to the grading system used when taking a test in school. The model scores products from zero to 100. The best score any manager could ever receive is 100, and the worst is, theoretically, zero. However, I have never had a manager score a perfect hundred or a zero. The resulting scores are meant to be compared when reviewing similar products. In the CAM small-cap value example, we should score CAM and compare the final score (as well as the section scores) to those of other small-cap value managers/products. Based on years of using this scoring model, I generally interpret the final scores according to the table in Exhibit 12.2.

These ranges have generally held true over the years, but they are not perfect. The manager scoring model is not designed as a final decision-making tool. Instead, it should be used as part of a thorough and rigorous due diligence process. In a perfect world, you will have several manager/product options available to you when you are making the decision to hire an investment manager. When several investment options are available, results of the model should not be the reason you hire (or don't hire) a manager/product. The model is best used to help create an institutionalized methodology for the consistent analysis of similar managers. A manager that scores a 77 is not necessarily a better fit in your overall portfolio than a manager that scores a 75. Nor would I definitively state that a manager that scores two points higher than another manager is clearly better. No model can be that precise. Moreover, the selection of any investment manager/product can only be made after fully evaluating the impact it may have on your total portfolio. In other words, how well does the manager/product under review fit with your existing managers? For example, you might conclude that CAM is a great small-cap value manager, but if CAM's product is very similar to that of another manager that manages assets for you, the decision to hire CAM becomes more complicated. In this case, you have several options: (1) fire the existing manager and hire CAM in its place, (2) give some assets to CAM in addition to the existing manager (presumably to diversify manager risk), or (3) do not hire CAM, but place CAM on your "bench." As

EXHIBIT 12.2 Manager Scoring Model Grades

Score	Interpretation
Greater than 80	Exceptional
75 to 80	Excellent
65 to 75	Above average
60 to 65	Average
Less than 60	Poor

discussed previously, the bench represents a group of managers that you would be comfortable hiring should the need arise.

I would, however, feel comfortable stating that a manager/product that scores 10 points higher than another manager/product is of higher quality. I have found the model's results to be more directional than precise. The range of possible scores, while technically zero to 100, is realistically in the 50 to 80 range because managers/products that make it far enough to receive a score have already made it past a number of hurdles and typically represent reasonably attractive candidates for hire. The reason why the scoring model is not completed earlier in the due diligence process is because the information required to complete some of the major sections in the model can only be done after extensive analysis, including an on-site visit.

To score the individual factors, the grades range from zero (worst) to five (best). Exhibit 12.3 details the individual scores and how they can best be interpreted.

Each of the 30 individual factors scored in the model must receive a score based on the table in Exhibit 12.3. The scores and their interpretations are relatively straightforward, but their application will vary from factor to factor. Because this is a general model designed to cover many different asset classes, the individual scores need to be generic at this level. For example, liquidity means something different when analyzing large-cap U.S. equities than it does when analyzing emerging markets, with the former being significantly more liquid than the latter. So when evaluating large-cap products, the score you give to a product must be reflective of the relevant asset class.

To better illustrate how the model works and how to properly score each factor, we will use the CAM small-cap value product as an example and work our way through each factor and each section.

Exhibit 12.4 shows the final results of the model using CAM's small-cap value product as an example. As you can see, the model covers a variety

EXHIBIT 12.3 Individual Factor Grades

Individual Variable Scoring Methodology

Score	Interpretation
5	Excellent
4	Above average
3	Average
2	Below average
1	Poor
0	Horrible/nonexistent

EXHIBIT 12.4   Scoring Model Example

#	Section/Factors	% Breakout Variable	Maximum Points Variable	Manager Score 0 to 5	Scaled Score	%
	Investment Professionals		30.0		24.0	80.0%
1	Direct product experience	20%	6.0	4		
2	Manager/team skill	20%	6.0	4		
3	Portfolio knowledge	20%	6.0	5		
4	Depth (backup)	20%	6.0	4		
5	Research capabilities	20%	6.0	3		
	Process		15		10.5	70.0%
6	Consistent application	25%	3.8	4		
7	Well thought out/ disciplined	25%	3.8	3		
8	Portfolio consistent with process	25%	3.8	4		
9	Portfolio construction/ review process	25%	3.8	3		
	Portfolio Risk		15		9.0	60.0%
10	Diversification	20%	3.0	2		
11	Style drift	20%	3.0	5		
12	Liquidity	20%	3.0	3		
13	Sell discipline	20%	3.0	2		
14	Capacity	20%	3.0	2		
	Performance-Related Risk/Reward		15		12.6	84.0%
15	Performance relative to benchmark	20%	3.0	5		
16	Performance relative to peers	20%	3.0	5		
17	Absolute/relative standard deviation	20%	3.0	3		
18	Drawdown	20%	3.0	3		
19	Consistency	20%	3.0	5		
	Organization		15		10.7	71.4%
20	Turnover	10%	1.5	5		
21	Succession plan	15%	2.3	4		
22	Accommodation of growth	15%	2.3	3		
23	Ownership/incentive	25%	3.8	4		
24	Backup/recovery	15%	2.3	3		
25	Computer systems	10%	1.5	3		
26	Compliance	10%	1.5	3		

EXHIBIT 12.4 *(Continued)*

#	Section/Factors	% Breakout Variable	Maximum Points Variable	Manager Score 0 to 5	Scaled Score	%
	Operations		10		6.5	65.0%
27	Reconciliation/ administration	25%	2.5	3		
28	Reporting	25%	2.5	3		
29	Client service	25%	2.5	3		
30	Quality/quantity of people	25%	2.5	4		
	Manual Adjustment (range +3 to −3)			−1		
	Final Score					72%

Manual Adjustment Note: One point was subtracted because the hedge fund might prove to be a distraction to Mark and because the long-only small cap assets in the hedge fund are not being counted by CAM toward capacity constraints.

of factors, resulting in a score for each individual factor, each section, and the total model. In addition, you can see at the bottom of the model an area where points can be subjectively added or subtracted based on factors not covered in the model. The remainder of this chapter highlights each section and its underlying factors, including factor definitions and guidelines for the actual scores. Using the CAM data from previous chapters, we will further explore each factor through detailed examples that culminate in actual scores for the CAM product as well as the reasoning behind each score.

INVESTMENT PROFESSIONALS

Exhibit 12.5 shows each of the factors scored in the investment professionals section. As stated previously, this section is worth a total of 30 points out of 100 (30%). Each of the five factors is equal weighted (at 20% of the 30-point total), which translates to a six-point maximum score for each. This data is static; the only thing that you need to do as you score a new manager is to give each factor its individual grade, which ranges from zero to five points. However, a deep understanding of each individual factor is required before any grading can take place. The remainder of this chapter will define each factor and, using CAM as the test case, create an actual score based on the research, analysis, and interviews that we have conducted on this firm throughout the book.

EXHIBIT 12.5   Manager Scoring Model—Investment Professionals Section

#	Section/Factors	% Breakout Variable	Maximum Points Variable	Manager Score 0 to 5	Scaled Score	%
	Investment Professionals		30.0		24.0	80.0%
1	Direct product experience	20%	6.0	4		
2	Manager/team skill	20%	6.0	4		
3	Portfolio knowledge	20%	6.0	5		
4	Depth (backup)	20%	6.0	4		
5	Research capabilities	20%	6.0	3		

Before we go into each section and the underlying factors in detail, I will explain what each of the column headings mean. If you refer to Exhibit 12.4, you will see that the model's summary report has seven columns.

Column 1 (#) highlights the number of each specific factor.

Column 2 (Section/Factors) lists the names for each of the six broad sections and each of the 30 factors.

Column 3 (% Breakout Variable) represents each factor's percentage contribution to the score in its respective section.

Column 4 (Maximum Points Variable) lists the maximum number of points allotted to each section and individual factor.

Column 5 (Manager Score 0 to 5) lists the grade we give to each individual factor, from 0 (low) to 5 (high).

Column 6 (Scaled Score). In order to keep the model's maximum total score to 100, we need to scale the individual factors and sections because the sum of all the individual factors when they are unscaled actually exceeds 100 (30 factors with a maximum score of 5 each would result in a possible maximum score of 150. This is done by adding the scores for all the factors in a given section and dividing that figure by the total possible score and then multiplying the result by the maximum points available for the section. For example, the scaled score for the first section (Investment Professionals) was calculated as follows:

$$\text{Scaled Score} = \frac{\sum \text{IFS}}{\text{MFS}} \times \text{MPS} = \frac{20}{30} \times 30 = 24$$

where   IFS = Individual factor scores.
         MFS = Maximum factor score for the section.
         MPS = Maximum points for the section.

Column 7 (%) lists the score for each broad section and the total model based on a scale of 0% to 100%. Using the preceding example, the percentage for the Investment Professionals section would be: 24/30 = 80%.

Factor 1: Direct Product Experience

This factor asks the question: How many years of relevant experience does the person or team managing the product under review have? The critical differentiating word is "relevant." It is important to note that the managers' experience should be comparable to their current responsibilities (a portfolio manager being reviewed today should have experience as a portfolio manager in the same asset class).

Score/Methodology

0 No experience managing a portfolio or in any investment-related capacity.

1 Key decision maker(s) have less than one year of actual portfolio management experience relating specifically to the product under review.

2 Key decision maker(s) have one to two years of actual portfolio management experience relating specifically to the product under review.

3 Key decision maker(s) have three to five years of actual portfolio management experience relating specifically to the product under review.

4. Key decision maker(s) have six to nine years of actual portfolio management experience relating specifically to the product under review.

5 Key investment decision maker(s) have greater than 10 years of actual portfolio management experience relating specifically to the product under review.

It is important to note that when grading a team it is best to grade each member of the team and to weight the final score based on each team member's ultimate level of responsibility for the product under review.

CAM's grade: 4

Reasoning: Mark clearly has more than 10 years of direct portfolio management experience in the small cap asset class, so he received a perfect 5. However, while Jim has more than 10 years' experience as a portfolio manager, he focused mostly on large-cap stocks and conservative fixed income securities. His five years of small cap experience at CAM combined with his strong portfolio management experience at VAM combine to give him a grade of 4. Because I always err toward being more conservative when grading factors and scoring managers overall, I elected to give CAM a final score of 4.

Factor 2: Manager/Team Skill

The first factor simply measures the experience level of the key decision makers; this factor expands the measure to cover all investment professionals who work on the product. We are essentially making critical judgments as to their level of skill. Skill, however, is a combination of subjective and quantitative assessments. The grade in this factor is based on how well the investment professionals can apply their experience and individual skills toward the effective management of the product under review. In addition, the skill of the team as a whole can be greater that the skill set of any individual person. Teams where members complement each other's personal skill sets can receive better marks than teams where some deficiency is present.

Score/Methodology

0 No discernible skill set.
1 Poor skill set; team does not work well together.
2 Below-average skills; team members work as separate entities.
3 Skill set in line with industry peer group. The team has a good working relationship.
4 Above-average skills and teamwork.
5 Highly skillful and competent team that works well together.

CAM's grade: 4
Reasoning: As you can read in the meeting memo notes highlighted in Chapters 8 (initial interview) and 11 (on-site meeting), I came to the conclusion that the key investment professionals, Mark and Jim, are highly skilled and very thorough with regard to stock analysis. I do, however, feel that they are a bit deficient with regard to the use of the firm's stock database as well as modeling stock valuations in spreadsheets. Tara, on the other hand, is at the bottom of a steep learning curve with respect to stock analysis, but has an extremely high level of competence with regard to the stocks database and spreadsheet modeling. Furthermore, I was impressed with her stock analysis skills—she has clearly benefited from working closely with Mark and Jim. This is an example of the blending of complementary skills across the investment team. I do have concerns about Tara's workload, but that is addressed in another factor.

My slight concern that Tara might not become a partner in the firm is alleviated at this time because she has a very generous compensation package and her role in the firm is understood and appreciated by the three partners. In addition, the issue of ownership and incentives are addressed in factor 23.

Factor 3: Portfolio Knowledge

This factor measures the team's knowledge of the portfolio that they manage—both its history and its current structure. High grades are given to managers who know their portfolio holdings very well. Managers' knowledge of their underlying portfolio reflects directly on them as stewards of their clients' assets. The answers to the following questions are helpful when grading this factor: (1) Does the manager have an intimate knowledge of each stock in the portfolio? (2) Can the manager explain the investment thesis behind each purchase and the reasoning behind each sale? (3) Does the manager know how the portfolio is positioned broadly and understand the risk aspects based on portfolio construction? The best forum for determining a manager's overall knowledge of the portfolio is via the interview process.

Score/Methodology

0   Does not seem to know anything about the portfolio. While this grade is rarely given, it does happen from time to time following an initial interview.

1   Knows a few things, but the knowledge seems scripted. People who fall into this category tend to read directly from presentations, but struggle when questions not addressed in the firm's presentation book are asked.

2   Adequate knowledge of the portfolio, but clearly needs to refer to notes and/or pass questions off to someone else. Examples include marketers masquerading as investment professionals; investment professionals who manage a variety of different products and, as a result, are stretched too thin; and investment personnel with little practical experience.

3   Good knowledge of the portfolio, but cannot elaborate on every holding.

4   Strong knowledge regarding portfolio and its holdings.

5   Fountain of knowledge. Can talk forever about any portfolio holding and has complete understanding of how portfolio holdings and structure can impact the portfolio's overall level of risk.

While the key investment professionals will skew the grading of this factor, it is important to gauge the knowledge of all the investment professionals who play active roles in the management of the portfolio (this includes analysts and traders). If a firm divides its analytical responsibilities by country, sector, industry, instrument type, or some other classification, you should not penalize investment professionals for less than perfect (or even no) knowledge of areas outside of their responsibilities. For example, a firm's dedicated technology analyst might not know much about the firm's energy holdings because the analyst specializes exclusively in technology stocks. In this case, you would evaluate the technology analyst in the context of knowledge of the technology universe and technology stocks held in the portfolio. Just be cognizant of the fact that someone or some group of people must be responsible the overall management of a given portfolio.

CAM's grade: 5

Reasoning: In my discussions with Mark, Jim, and Tara, I was highly impressed by their encyclopedic knowledge of every stock that we discussed. After the phone interview and the on-site meetings, we had discussed roughly three-quarters of the stocks that they currently hold as well as a dozen or so names that they had held in the past.

Factor 4: Depth (Backup)

This factor measures the depth of the investment team and their ability to adequately manage the portfolio. It is important to note that depth is a relative term. While it might be easier to simply grade this factor based on the absolute number of investment professionals, it is more effective to overlay the number of investment professionals with an assessment of the team's overall level of efficiency and effectiveness. For example, three highly experienced investment professionals who have worked together as a team for a decade might be more effective than a team of five junior investment professionals who have just started working together. Backup is another important element when scoring this factor. When the lead portfolio manager is out of the office, is there a strong second in command? The question I always ask myself is: What if the lead portfolio manager resigned from the firm today—would I have enough confidence that the remaining team members could manage the portfolio just as effectively? The answers to these questions guide the grading of this factor.

Score/Methodology

0   One-person shop; clearly cannot handle job responsibilities (which includes many non-investment-related functions). No backup. *This firm should not be hired until changes are made.*

1 Single manager (or team) with inconsistent record of effectiveness; no backup or very weak backup. *Automatic redemption of assets following the departure of the lead portfolio manager.*

2 Team or single manager that barely can get the job done; no backup or weak backup. *Automatic redemption of assets following the departure of the lead portfolio manager.*

3 Team can adequately handle portfolio (but will need to expand as assets grow) and selected non-investment-related activities (such as marketing and client service). Weak backup that could effectively stabilize the portfolio following the lead portfolio manager's departure, but who would not make the cut if reviewed on their own. *In this scenario, we would likely pull all or part of our assets if the lead manager left.*

4 Deep team with one strong backup.

5 Deep team with more than one strong backup.

CAM's grade: 4

Reasoning: Because CAM focuses on one asset class (small cap) and because Mark and Jim seem to be very effective portfolio managers and Tara appears to be a talented analyst who is growing (and is being nurtured by the firm's principals), I gave them high scores. However, two issues kept me from giving them a perfect score: (1) Tara seems to have too much on her plate and, in my opinion, CAM will have to hire someone to help her out (or take over her secondary responsibilities so that she can focus on direct stock analysis), and (2) the hedge fund may interfere with the management of the product under review (small cap portfolio). The second concern is targeted toward Mark, as he is chiefly responsible for the hedge fund product. However, given these concerns, the on-site meetings that I had with each of the team members left me confident that they can handle the current portfolio responsibilities. Mark and Jim back each other up well, so CAM receives a score of 4.

Factor 5: Research Capabilities

This is related somewhat to the preceding factor. The difference is that this factor focuses exclusively on the team's research capabilities. It is, in effect, a way to measure how effective the team might be going forward.

Score/Methodology

0 No systems or access to data. Makes decisions based exclusively on outside research. *While outside research is not necessarily as bad thing, it is widely available to all investment managers so there is no real advantage (based on the value added due to proprietary research) to hiring this firm.*

1   Heavy reliance on outside research.
2   Reliance on outside research, but some level of internal research is performed.
3   Average research systems and access to data. Investment team uses both internal and external research.
4   Strong, capable research facilities based on proprietary models and techniques.
5   Top-of-the-line research capabilities. Top-notch research systems, access to data, and time to conduct thorough analysis on all holdings.

CAM's grade: 3

Reasoning: CAM has access to a good deal of information through Bloomberg and FactSet, but the portfolio managers seem to rely very heavily on Tara's ability to transform that data into something that they can use in making their investment decisions. If they did not have such a heavy reliance on Tara, I would give CAM a grade of 4. If CAM hires another quality analyst, I would likely boost the score from a 3 to a 4. The research sheets produced by Tara are also very labor intensive (manual). CAM might also receive a higher score if they were to find a way of automating all or part of the process.

PROCESS

Exhibit 12.6 shows each of the factors scored in the process section. This section of the model is worth 15 points (15%) and is comprised of four equal-weighted factors. This section measures the investment team's

EXHIBIT 12.6   Manager Scoring Model—Process Section

#	Section/Factors	% Breakout Variable	Maximum Points Variable	Manager Score 0 to 5	Scaled Score	%
	Process		15		10.5	70.0%
6	Consistent application	25%	3.8	4		
7	Well thought out/ disciplined	25%	3.8	3		
8	Portfolio consistent with process	25%	3.8	4		
9	Portfolio construction/ review process	25%	3.8	3		

process in absolute terms and grades the consistency with which the team manages the product.

Factor 6: Consistent Application

This factor measures how consistently the team applies the stated process. The theory behind this factor is that a product that is managed in a more consistent manner will have a better chance of repeating past successes than a product that is managed inconsistently. In addition, it is easier to understand and monitor the progress of a product that is managed in a consistent manner.

Score/Methodology

0   No discernible process.
1   Frequent breaks in the application of the process based on the whims of the management team.
2   Process has shifted over time, but management has reasonable explanations.
3   Reasonably consistent and dependable application of the process.
4   Consistent process with occasional modest deviations
5   Strict adherence to process—no exceptions made. Long history of consistent application.

CAM's grade: 4

Reasoning: CAM's management labels their product small-cap value. Our analysis indicates that this is incorrect and that their style is more indicative of GARP due largely to the inclusion of growth factors in their process. This should have no impact on the score for this factor because our analysis tells us that they have consistently applied their GARP process since the firm's inception. In fact, it is fair to say that Mark has been investing in this manner for over a dozen years. They did not receive a perfect score because there seems to be a bit of internal discussion regarding portfolio constraints that date back to the 1999–2000 period. My conversations with the team tell me that there might be some tightening of the process in the near future. In any case, when a process changes, it needs time to be proved out in real life.

Factor 7: Well Thought Out/Disciplined

This factor is interrelated to its predecessor. The difference is that we are making a judgment regarding the soundness of the process. A process can be consistently applied but not well thought out.

Score/Methodology

0   Process does not seem to work very well.
1   Process is lacking in several key areas.
2   Process is lacking in one key area.
3   Process is reasonably effective, but does not differentiate the firm
     from its peer group. *Most managers I grade score a 3.*
4   Process is well thought out and offers a positive point of
     differentiation compared to peers.
5   Process is very well thought out and unique among its peer group.

CAM's grade: 3

Reasoning: CAM does consistently apply their process, but the process itself does not differentiate the product from their many small cap peers. Remember that CAM's process should be compared to GARP managers more than to value managers, despite the label of the fund. Our previous performance, portfolio, attribution, and style analysis strongly support this statement.

Factor 8: Portfolio Consistent with Process

Now that we have determined whether the process is well thought out and consistently applied, we need to measure how all this translates to the final product (the underlying portfolio). The nuance here is that we want to grade how closely correlated the portfolio's characteristics are to the process employed by the manager.

Score/Methodology

0   Portfolio characteristics are diametrically opposed to underlying
     process/methodology employed.
1   Portfolio characteristics consistent with process some of the time.
2   Portfolio characteristics are mostly consistent with process, but
     major inconsistencies pop up from time to time.
3   Portfolio characteristics are generally consistent with process.
4   Portfolio's historical performance and underlying portfolio
     characteristics are very consistent with process.
5   Portfolio and process are perfectly aligned. Portfolio
     characteristics are predictable based on process.

CAM's grade: 4

Reasoning: Based on the extensive analysis we performed on CAM and the interviews that I conducted with the investment team, the portfolio has a strong correlation to the process employed. This relationship has held over the life of the product. However, since CAM is in the process of tightening the portfolio constraints, I held back from giving CAM a perfect score. Like the previous factor, CAM may be eligible for an upgrade, but we will need to examine the changes over a period of time before changing this grade.

Factor 9: Portfolio Construction/Review Process

The portfolio construction and review factor measures the level of portfolio risk controls employed by the manager. This factor is the cumulative assessment of individual issue constraints, sector and industry constraints, geographical constraints, and fundamental constraints.

Score/Methodology

0   No discernible portfolio construction methodology and no review process in place.
1   Inconsistent portfolio construction methodology, inconsistent review process in place.
2   Some level of portfolio construction constraints, no review process in place.
3   Good portfolio construction methodology and adequate means of portfolio review.
4   Portfolio constraints reasonably strict with reasonably consistent and adequate means of review.
5   Portfolio construction process allows for strict constraints across all relevant exposures as well as providing for a thorough and consistent review process.

CAM's grade: 3

Reasoning: Based on the extensive analysis we had performed on CAM and the interviews that I conducted with the investment team, the portfolio construction matches the underlying investment process and methodology. While CAM clearly reviews the portfolio, there seems to be a disagreement with regard to specific portfolio constraints.

PORTFOLIO RISK

Exhibit 12.7 shows each of the factors scored in the portfolio risk section. This section of the model is worth 15 points (15%) and is comprised of five equal-weighted factors. This section measures the investment team's process in absolute terms and grades the consistency with which the team manages the product.

EXHIBIT 12.7 Manager Scoring Model—Portfolio Risk Section

#	Section/Factors	% Breakout Variable	Maximum Points Variable	Manager Score 0 to 5	Scaled Score	%
	Portfolio Risk		15.0		9.0	60.0%
10	Diversification	0.2	3.0	2		
11	Style drift	0.2	3.0	5		
12	Liquidity	0.2	3.0	3		
13	Sell discipline	0.2	3.0	2		
14	Capacity	0.2	3.0	2		

Factor 10: Diversification

A portfolio can be diversified in a number of ways: number of individual positions, sectors, industries, or fundamental characteristics. This factor is meant to grade the portfolio under review based on the underlying asset class. For example, a small cap portfolio should not be considered undiversified because it focuses solely on small caps. However, a portfolio that can invest across the market capitalization spectrum can receive a lower grade if it is highly concentrated in small-cap stocks. In the second example, we are not judging the investment manager's decision to overweight small cap names—we are simply making a statement that concentration in any one area (particularly in smaller names) is generally riskier than a portfolio that is invested broadly across the entire market. When grading this measure, it is important to give slightly more weight to portfolio exposures, but not to forget about historical diversification.

A portfolio that is currently highly diversified should receive a high grade, but that grade should be scaled back if the portfolio had been highly concentrated in the past. It is also important to consider portfolio investments in the same underlying company across the capital structure (equity, warrants, bonds). Lastly, this grade should not be made based on deviations from an index. The purpose of the manager scoring model discussed throughout this chapter is to measure a manager's skill and the overall level of appropriateness of the portfolio—not to see who is a closet indexer. Diversifiers are defined as any measure of diversification directly related to the portfolio under review. Using CAM as an example, the diversifiers are: individual positions, micro-cap, small-cap, sectors, industries, and growth stocks.

Score/Methodology

0   Highly concentrated. Manager does not have portfolio risk measures in place.

1   Concentrated in two of the diversifiers currently. Manager does not have portfolio risk measures in place.
2   Concentrated in two of the diversifiers currently. Manager has some level of portfolio risk controls in place.
3   Concentrated in one of the diversifiers currently or two of the diversifiers in the past. Manager has good portfolio risk measures in place.
4   Currently well diversified, but has been moderately concentrated in the past. Manager has good portfolio risk measures in place.
5   Highly diversified throughout the product's history with strong risk measures in place.

CAM's grade: 2

Reasoning: CAM's current portfolio is concentrated by sector and industry. In addition, the portfolio has been concentrated in the past (individual positions, sector, industry). Lastly, CAM has not formally adopted any portfolio risk measures designed to rein in overall portfolio risk. Based on the on-site meeting, it appears that Jim and Mark need to come to some kind of agreement on this subject.

Factor 11: Style Drift

Style drift to me is a bit different than to most people. When I think of style drift, I refer as much to the underlying process as to the final results (performance). As highlighted in the portfolio style section of this book, we can run a simple regression of the portfolio's historical returns against several style and capitalization benchmarks. The results can give us an indication of how closely the portfolio's returns mirror the individual style/cap benchmarks as well as some combination of them. I firmly believe that any good style analysis will look at the results of the style regression, but will then overlay those results with an evaluation of the process or method employed that produced the returns. Because I believe that fundamental portfolio analysis is a better indicator of investment style, I place much more of an emphasis on it versus the results of a returns-based style regression.

Score/Methodology

0   Manager has no consistent style.
1   Fundamental portfolio analysis indicates that the product has been consistent for periods of time, but those periods were few and far between.

2   Fundamental portfolio analysis indicates that the product is basically consistent right now, but has been inconsistent in the past.

3   Fundamental portfolio analysis indicates that the product has been reasonably consistent over time, and the results of the style regression analysis generally back up that assessment.

4   Fundamental portfolio analysis indicates that the product has been very consistent over time and the results of the style regression analysis strongly back up that assessment.

5   Both the style regression and the fundamental evaluation of the process lead to a very strong conviction that the manager has been highly consistent.

CAM's grade: 5

Reasoning: Again, it is important to understand that we are not scoring CAM based on the name of the fund (which has the term "value" in it). Instead, we are grading the portfolio based on its merits. The detailed analysis that we conducted on the portfolio's performance and portfolio, in combination with the many interviews we conducted, led us to firmly conclude that the CAM portfolio is not managed in the value style, but in the GARP style. Once the style was identified, we simply graded the portfolio based on deviation from the GARP style. Since the management team at CAM has been highly consistent in their approach and the results of the style regression match perfectly (51% value, 49% growth), CAM gets a score of 5.

Factor 12: Liquidity

This is an absolute measure designed to grade the portfolio under review based on the time it would take to fully liquidate the portfolio without having a material negative impact on the prices of the underlying holdings. Like the other factors, this one is meant to be scored relative to similar products. The underlying premise is that the product under review consists of marketable securities. The way to score this factor is to ask the following question: How long would it take to liquidate 95% of the underlying portfolio without a negative impact on pricing? The remaining 5% can accommodate nonmarketable securities or securities that are less liquid.

Score/Methodology

0   More than five days.
1   Less than five days.
2   Less than four days.

3   Less than three days.
4   Less than two days.
5   Less than one day.

CAM's grade: 3

Reasoning: Half of CAM's portfolio is currently invested in micro-cap stocks, which can have lower levels of liquidity. In addition, the results of our liquidity analysis indicate that this portfolio can be liquidated within three to four days without negatively impacting the prices of the underlying stocks. This liquidity analysis tabulates the weighted average daily liquidity for the portfolio of stocks under review and determines how many days it would take to liquidate the portfolio. The portfolio could be liquidated in one day, but it is highly likely that it would experience some negative pricing implications.

Factor 13: Sell Discipline

A good sell discipline can help manage downside risk. A well-thought-out sell discipline makes a statement about the overall level of portfolio risk. However, a well-thought-out sell discipline means nothing if the manager does not follow the rules, so you must make a determination during the course of your manager evaluation whether a sell discipline exists and is actually adhered to.

Score/Methodology

0   No sell discipline at all—sales are made at the whim of management.
1   Sell discipline is inconsistent with stated policy (formal or nonformal).
2   Sell discipline is sometimes inconsistent with stated policy (formal or nonformal).
3   Reasonable sell discipline that is not necessarily formalized, but is adhered to.
4   Well-thought-out sell discipline that is strictly adhered to. Lead portfolio manager makes the sell decision.
5   Well-thought-out sell discipline that is strictly adhered to. Someone other than the lead portfolio manager can force automatic sales once the downside criteria are met.

CAM's grade: 2

Reasoning: Based on our portfolio analysis and the interviews with CAM's investment personnel, we can safely conclude that CAM had clearly violated their unwritten policy in the past. In addition, it seems that Mark and Jim are not quite in agreement on the issue of individual stock weight limits.

Factor 14: Capacity

Capacity refers to the size of the product under review relative to the optimal level of assets the manager can manage. A product that is closed shy of that optimal level actually receives a top score. This factor is not designed to grade based on whether the product in question is still open to new investment because it is assumed that by the time you get to this stage of the due diligence process, you would have already determined that it is a viable candidate for hire (which includes its status as open). If the product closes after we hire the firm and has ample room for growth, this score can be adjusted upward. This factor also takes into account a firm that has closed the underlying portfolio in the past and reopened it once capacity was no longer an issue. Firms that close and subsequently reopen a product can do so for the following reasons: (1) to take a breather following fast asset growth (this is a good thing); (2) assets have reached their internal optimal level (can be a good thing if they have left room to grow or a bad thing if they are managing assets at capacity); or (3) assets have exceeded capacity (a bad thing). As a result, we need to grade each product based on its own unique set of circumstances. For the grading, optimal capacity assumes that there will be room for the product to grow.

Score/Methodology

0   Product is open and is well beyond optimal capacity.
1   Product is open and has assets that are greater than 90% of the optimal capacity.
2   Product is open and has assets that are between 70% and 90% of the optimal capacity.
3   Product is open and has assets that are between 50% and 70% of the optimal capacity.
4   Product is open and has assets that are between 20% and 50% of the optimal capacity.
5   Product is open and has assets that are less than 20% of the optimal capacity.

CAM's grade: 2
Reasoning: CAM is currently managing assets that represent roughly 75% of its stated optimal capacity ($450M in assets out of $600M). The long-only portion of the hedge fund represents roughly another $50M.

EXHIBIT 12.8 Manager Scoring Model—Performance-Related Risk/
Reward Section

#	Section/Factors	% Breakout Variable	Maximum Points Variable	Manager Score 0 to 5	Scaled Score	%
	Performance-Related Risk/Reward		15.0		12.6	84.0%
15	Performance relative to benchmark	0.2	3.0	5		
16	Performance relative to peers	0.2	3.0	5		
17	Absolute/relative standard deviation	0.2	3.0	3		
18	Drawdown	0.2	3.0	3		
19	Consistency	0.2	3.0	5		

PERFORMANCE-RELATED RISK/REWARD

Exhibit 12.8 shows each of the factors scored in the performance-related risk/return section. This section of the model is worth 15 points (15%) and is comprised of five equal-weighted factors. The first two factors refer to the reward aspects of the historical performance, whereas the final three factors relate to risk (volatility, risk of loss, and consistency).

Factor 15: Performance Relative to Benchmark

For actively managed products, it is always useful to compare the performance (net of all fees) of the product under review to the appropriate benchmark. While it can be difficult at times to select a specific benchmark to match each and every portfolio that you might measure, generally most products have a reasonably good benchmark that can be used for comparative purposes. Refer to Chapter 4 for a list of generally accepted benchmarks for U.S. and non-U.S.-based products. When arriving at a grade for historical performance relative to the stated benchmark, I generally look at performance over several time periods (one year, three years, five years, and since inception). For products with short track records, I review the actual performance record for whatever time frame is available, score them based on that record, then penalize products in the following way:

■ Track record less than three years (subtract one point). *As a result, the maximum score is 4.*

■ Track record less than two years (subtract two points). *As a result, the maximum score is 3.*

■ Track record less than one year (subtract three points). *As a result, the maximum score is 2.*

The portfolios return and the benchmark's return should be compared on an absolute basis. For example, if the portfolio has a 10% return and the index has a 5% return, the differential is 5% (10% − 5%).

Score/Methodology

0   Historical performance relative to appropriate benchmark is more than 5% below the benchmark over the same time frame.

1   Historical performance relative to appropriate benchmark is between 3% and 5% below the benchmark over the same time frame.

2   Historical performance relative to appropriate benchmark is between 1% and 3% below the benchmark over the same time frame.

3   Historical performance relative to appropriate benchmark is roughly equivalent (may be a little above or below) over the same time frame.

4   Historical performance relative to appropriate benchmark is between 1% and 5% above the benchmark over the same time frame.

5   Historical performance relative to appropriate benchmark is more than 5% above the benchmark over the same time frame.

CAM's grade: 5

Reasoning: CAM's historical performance is far in excess of all the small-cap benchmarks regardless of style orientation.

Factor 16: Performance Relative to Peers

This factor is graded just like factor 15 (including the penalties assessed for short track records).

Score/Methodology

0   Historical performance relative to peers is more than 5% below the peer group over the same time frame.

1   Historical performance relative to peers is between 3% and 5% below the peer group over the same time frame.

2   Historical performance relative to peers is between 1% and 3% below the peer group over the same time frame.

3   Historical performance relative to peers is roughly equivalent (may be a little above or below) over the same time frame.
4   Historical performance relative to peers is between 1% and 5% above the peer group over the same time frame.
5   Historical performance relative to peers is more than 5% above the peer group over the same time frame.

CAM's grade: 5
Reasoning: CAM's historical performance is far in excess of its peer group.

Factor 17: Absolute/Relative Standard Deviation

This factor measures the portfolio's historical level of volatility. The grade is based on both absolute as well as relative terms (compared to appropriate benchmark and peer group averages).

Score/Methodology

0   Historical standard deviation is more than 15% above that of the benchmark/peer group.
1   Historical standard deviation is 10% to 15% above that of the benchmark/peer group.
2   Historical standard deviation is 5% to 10% above that of the benchmark/peer group.
3   Historical standard deviation roughly equal to that of the benchmark/peer group (+/– 5%).
4   Historical standard deviation is 5% to 10% below that of the benchmark/peer group.
5   Historical standard deviation is more than 10% below that of the benchmark/peer group.

Note: When scoring this factor, keep in mind that the percentages used are not absolute. For example, if a product has historical standard deviation of 10% compared to 15% for the benchmark, the differential is not –5% (10% – 15%). We are actually looking to assess the relative percentage differential, so the difference is calculated as follows:

Differential = (Product Standard Deviation – Index Standard Deviation) ÷ Product Standard Deviation
= (10% – 15%) ÷ 10%
= –5% ÷ 10% = –50%

In this example, the standard deviation of the product under review was 50% lower than the index, so it would receive a score of zero.

CAM's grade: 3

Reasoning: By all measures, CAM's historical track record is roughly in line with benchmarks and peer group.

Factor 18: Drawdown

This factor measures the maximum peak-to-valley drawdown of the portfolio compared to the appropriate benchmarks and peer group. The reasoning behind this factor is that volatility (as measured by standard deviation in the preceding factor) can add risk, but downside volatility can be worse. I measure this by comparing the largest consecutive peak-to-valley drawdown (consecutive months of negative performance) of the portfolio to the appropriate indexes and the peer group. A product that experiences greater drawdown based on number of consecutive period drawdowns and magnitude of the drawdowns is inherently more risky than a product that does not. Rather than measuring the absolute drawdowns, I compare the drawdown figures to the appropriate benchmark and peer group so I do not penalize a product for negative performance when the market was negative as well. For example, the fact that a product has a peak-to-valley drawdown over a defined period of –10% simply tells us that the product lost 10%. However, if the appropriate benchmark had a –15% drawdown over the same period and the peer group had a –14% drawdown over the same time period, we can conclude that the product under review should receive a higher grade (as it lost only 10%). If a product does not have any drawdown over the period measured, it automatically receives a perfect grade (5). For products with short track records, I review the actual performance record for whatever time frame is available, score them based on that record, then penalize products in the following way:

■ Track record less than three years (subtract one point).
■ Track record less than two years (subtract two points).
■ Track record less than one year (subtract three points).

Score/Methodology

0   The number of negative months is significantly higher than the index and the peak-to-valley loss is greater than 7% worse than the index.

1   The number of negative months is significantly higher than the index and the peak-to-valley loss is 5% to 7% worse than the index.

2   The number of negative months is slightly higher than the index and the peak-to-valley loss is 2% to 5% worse than the index.

3   The number of negative months is roughly equal to the index and the peak-to-valley loss is within a 2% range better or worse than the index.

4   The number of negative months is slightly lower than the index and the peak-to-valley loss is 2% to 5% better than the index.

5   The number of negative months is significantly lower than the index and the peak-to-valley loss is more than 5% better than the index.

CAM's grade: 3

Reasoning: CAM's drawdowns are roughly in line with the small cap benchmarks and the peer group.

Factor 19: Consistency

I generally use two statistics to measure performance consistency: (1) the information ratio, which is a measure of consistency versus the appropriate index, and (2) the percentile ranking relative to peers (over multiple time periods), which measures a product's consistency relative to the peer group. To calculate the percentile consistency number, take a simple average of the quarterly or calendar year percentile rankings rather than looking just at the percentile ranking for the entire period. The reasoning behind this factor is intuitive. If given the choice between two products that have the same historical performance over a defined period of time, but one product takes extreme swings between very good and very bad performance while the other product performs in an even, consistent manner, which one would you choose? I would choose the product with the even returns over the product with the scattered returns. When scoring this factor, you can deduct up to two points if one of the consistency measures is in line with a particular grade but the other one is not.

Score/Methodology

0   Percentile ranking less than 30. Based on the information ratio and peer group performance.

1   Percentile ranking from 30 to 40. Based on the information ratio and peer group performance.

2   Percentile ranking from 40 to 50. Based on the information ratio and peer group performance.

3   Percentile ranking from 50 to 60. Based on the information ratio and peer group performance.

4   Percentile ranking from 60 to 70. Based on the information ratio and peer group performance.

5   Percentile ranking greater than 70. Based on the information ratio and peer group performance.

CAM's grade: 5

Reasoning: CAM has consistently performed in excess of the 70th percentile on a quarterly and calendar year basis. In addition, CAM's information ratio is far in excess of the peer group's score (0.33 for CAM versus 0.21 for the peer group).

ORGANIZATION

Exhibit 12.9 shows each of the factors scored in the organization section. This section of the model is worth 15 points (15%) and is comprised of seven factors. This is the only section in which the individual factors are not equally weighted. The factor with the biggest weight in this section, ownership/incentive, receives a 25% weighting, which translates to a maximum contribution to the overall model's score of 3.8 (see Exhibit 12.4).

Factor 20: Turnover

This factor refers to turnover of any professional employed by the firm, including both investment- and non-investment-related positions. Non-investment-related employees include marketing, client service, administrative, and legal. The grade is subjective and must take into consideration the

EXHIBIT 12.9   Manager Scoring Model—Organization Section

#	Section/Factors	% Breakout Variable	Maximum Points Variable	Manager Score 0 to 5	Scaled Score	%
	Organization		15		10.7	71.4%
20	Turnover	10%	1.5	5		
21	Succession plan	15%	2.3	4		
22	Accommodation of growth	15%	2.3	3		
23	Ownership/incentive	25%	3.8	4		
24	Backup/recovery	15%	2.3	3		
25	Computer systems	10%	1.5	3		
26	Compliance	10%	1.5	3		

reason(s) for any employee's departure. For example, if an employee leaves to become a stay-at-home mom/dad, the firm being reviewed should not be penalized. However, an employee's departure based on compensation issues is another thing entirely. A "key employee" is defined as an individual that has a tangible impact on the firm with respect to specific responsibilities and functions. For example, a key employee would be an analyst who contributes ideas to the portfolio.

Score/Methodology

0   Loss of more than two key employees.

1   Loss of two key employees.

2   Loss of one key employee in past year.

3   Loss of one key employee in past two years.

4   Very low turnover—loss of one key employee in past three years; any other employee departures were due principally to reasons beyond the firm's control.

5   Never lost an employee.

When deciding on a score, please keep in mind that the loss of one key professional might mean more to a small firm with a handful of employees than to a large firm with hundreds of employees. Score each firm based on its unique circumstances.

CAM's grade: 5

Reasoning: CAM has never lost an employee.

Factor 21: Succession Plan

This factor relates to how effectively an investment firm has prepared for the growth of the organization by investing in human capital. Human capital includes quality of personnel, time with firm, level of training, and so on. A firm with a well-thought-out and clearly delineated succession plan puts its investors in a better position as time goes on. Also, in the case of an emergency (when key investment personnel are incapacitated temporarily or permanently) a firm with a strong succession plan will likely be in a better position to handle the crisis.

Score/Methodology

0   One-person shop or a larger firm with no plan or thoughts with regard to succession. Should an emergency take place, the firm will not be in a position to properly handle client assets. *In a scenario like this, you would be better off taking your portfolio from the firm "in-kind" (which means that you would take*

possession of the actual portfolio holdings) and either transfer the portfolio holdings to the manager you have selected as a replacement or liquidate the assets yourself.

1   No formal plan, and should an emergency take place, the firm's ability to protect client assets is questionable.

2   No formal plan, and should an emergency take place, the firm would be able to protect client assets during liquidation procedures.

3   The firm may or may not have a formal plan, but the firm has invested wisely in human capital, and should an emergency take place the firm will be in a position to protect client assets for a period of time.

4   The firm may or may not have a formal plan, but the firm has invested wisely in human capital, and should an emergency take place the firm will be in a position to continue managing the portfolio without any major negative impact or to protect client assets.

5   Well-thought-out succession plan that will allow the firm to not only protect client assets in case of an emergency, but also continue with operation with no distraction.

CAM's grade: 4

Reasoning: The firm has two key portfolio managers. In the case of an emergency, there is no question that CAM will be in a position to protect client interests. I do, however, question if the product would be as attractive should Jim or Mark leave the firm. If either Jim or Mark left, I would redeem either all or part of my assets with CAM (assuming that I end up hiring CAM in the first place).

Factor 22: Accommodation of Growth

Growth can be measured in a number of ways: additional employees, new assets, and/or new clients. This factor was designed to measure how well a firm can cope with the operations today as well as how well it can cope with operations assuming some defined growth curve. A firm that adequately matches its current needs and resources but does not factor in future growth may experience growing pains. However, a firm that currently matches its needs and resources but plans to add strategically to resources may be in a better position to handle growth and, hence, experience fewer distractions. Resources can be defined as human resources, systems, office space, storage, or anything else required to run the operation smoothly.

Score/Methodology

0   Current needs vastly exceed current resources, and the firm has
    no defined plans to stay ahead of the growth curve.
1   Current needs moderately exceed current resources, and the firm
    has no defined plans to stay ahead of the growth curve.
2   Current needs moderately exceed current resources, but the firm
    has defined plans to stay ahead of the growth curve.
3   Current resources roughly match current needs.
4   Current resources roughly match current needs, and the firm has
    defined plans to stay ahead of the growth curve.
5   Current resources exceed current needs, and the firm has defined
    plans to stay ahead of the growth curve.

CAM's grade: 3

Reasoning: CAM's needs are currently being met by their resources,
but the dependence on Tara is stretching the human resource too thin. In
addition, CAM's offices seem inadequate for their needs. Given their asset
level and the fees generated from the long-only product and the hedge
fund, CAM should be in a position to lock in more ample office space and
add a minimum of two additional people to the team (another analyst and
an in-house technical professional).

Factor 23: Ownership/Incentive

This factor measures how incentivized the firm's professionals are. Ownership is an obvious means of providing incentive. It stands to reason that a
person will work harder when the results of the labor have a direct impact
on their livelihood. However, equity ownership is not the only way to create motivation. Many firms employ shadow stock or tracking stock, which
is not actual ownership in the underlying company, but ownership of the
revenues based on the contractual figures. But employees do not have to be
owners (actual or through the use of shadow stock) to be incentivized. A
generous compensation package that consists of a base and bonus can provide ample motivation. Lastly, motivation can also be fostered in nonfinan-
cial ways. An employee who is being mentored may be incentivized; an
employee who is allowed to work a flexible schedule to accommodate family needs may be incentivized; and an employee who is being put through
school by the firm may be incentivized. Compensation is a relative measure, as the same job function may receive a higher or lower compensation
package based on geography. Note that it should not be a given that equity
ownership is required to incentivize people. For example, investment professionals who are equity owners and nearing the end of their careers

might not have the same incentive as young, aggressive analysts looking to gain equity ownership.

Score/Methodology

0   Very few (if any) incentives. Flight risk is great.

1   Compensation is far below other investment management firms in the asset class and geographical area. No key investment professional has an equity stake in the company.

2   Compensation is moderately below other investment management firms in the asset class and geographical area. No key investment professional has an equity stake in the company.

3   Compensation is roughly on a par with other investment management firms in the asset class and geographical area. At least one key investment professional has an equity stake in the company.

4   Compensation is generally higher than at other investment management firms in the asset class and geographical area. At least two key investment professionals have equity stakes in the company.

5   Compensation is generally higher than at other investment management firms in the asset class and geographical area. All investment professionals either have an equity stake in the company or are on the path to getting an equity stake.

CAM's grade: 4

Reasoning: The two key investment professionals, Jim and Mark, are partners (along with the COO, Andy). Despite the fact that Tara does not have an equity stake, she seems happy at work because she is being given a chance to learn from highly experienced investment professionals and because she genuinely enjoys what she is doing (after spending several years searching for the right position).

Factor 24: Backup/Recovery

An investment company's ability to recover information in the case of an emergency (such as a building fire, a computer virus, theft, etc.) is a critical safety criterion. An investment company that cannot retrieve all data in case of an emergency might negatively impact client assets in a number of ways. In addition, the timing and depth of the recovery are essential. A firm that can continue with normal daily operations in minutes following some disaster is in a better position to manage client assets than a firm that takes a week to recover clients' portfolio holdings. Frequency (daily backup preferred) and time to full recovery (less than an hour is best) are essential elements in grading this factor.

Score/Methodology

0   No backup/recovery plans in effect.

1   Less than full daily backup (weekly, monthly, periodic) with files kept on-site. It would take more than a full day to recover in an emergency.

2   Full daily backup with files kept off-site. It would take more than a full day to recover in an emergency.

3   Full daily backup with files kept off-site. It would take a full day to recover in an emergency.

4   Full daily backup with files kept off-site. It would take an hour or more (but less than a full day) to recover in an emergency.

5   Full daily backup with files kept off-site. Would take less than one hour to recover in an emergency.

CAM's grade: 3

Reasoning: CAM's backup system is very good and the system is backed up daily; however, since the computer systems function is out-sourced (and because no one internally seemed to know or understand the recovery process), it is likely that the recovery would take a full day to complete. I could have given CAM a grade of 4 on this measure because the outsource company is top rate and because CAM signed up for the pre-mium service, but anytime external personnel are required the time to com-pletion tends to widen. In addition, CAM appears to be shopping for a new systems consultant. Should any event take place during the transition, it may slow the recovery time temporarily.

Factor 25: Computer Systems

This factor is completely different from the previous one (backup/recovery) in that it refers to the general condition of systems in combination with the overall level of the computer systems efficiency. For example, two firms with identical systems can receive different scores if one of the firms uses the systems more efficiently. When conducting an on-site visit, take a tour of the office space and make note of the age and wear of the systems. When sitting with investment professionals in their offices (or at their desks), ask for a tour of their internal systems.

Score/Methodology

0   Computer systems are grossly inadequate for the firm's needs.

1   Computer systems are less than adequate for the firm's needs and may be interfering with the firm's overall efficiency and/or the efficiency of the investment staff. Firm needs to upgrade hardware/software now.

2   Computer systems are moderately less than adequate for the
     firm's needs. Firm may need to upgrade hardware/software in the
     near future.
3   Computer systems are adequate for the firm's needs. Most firms
     receive this grade unless the computer systems/software adds
     value (higher grade) or detracts value (lower grade) from firm's
     ability to operate efficiently.
4   Computer systems are more than adequate for the firm's needs.
5   Computer systems are excellent and can be considered a value
     added to the firm and even the investment process.

CAM's grade: 3

Reasoning: CAM's computer systems are relatively up to date. My
walk through the office indicated that the computers were relatively new
(purchased in the last two years). When I sat with Jim and Tara, I noticed
that the latest versions of software packages were loaded and they did not
seem to be in need of any new software.

Factor 26: Compliance

This factor refers to a firm's stated policies regarding prohibited transactions as well as the firm's record of meeting all federal and state compliance
requirements. With regard to prohibited transactions, it is important to
measure not just the stated policy but how diligently a firm monitors and
enforces it.

Score/Methodology

0   No discernible internal compliance policy; regulatory compliance
     neglected.
1   Loose and informal internal compliance policy; regulatory
     compliance frequently neglected.
2   Either inadequate compliance policies or inadequate regulatory
     compliance.
3   Formal compliance procedures (either written or verbal) are
     properly communicated to all employees. Periodic checks for
     compliance. Federal/state compliance is given a high priority.
4   Formal, written compliance procedures are properly
     communicated to all employees. Frequent checks for compliance.
     Federal/state compliance is given a high priority.
5   Formal, written compliance procedures for prohibited internal
     transactions are rigorously monitored and enforced by separate
     legal/compliance personnel. Client portfolios are given clear
     preference over employee transactions. Federal/state compliance is
     given a high priority.

CAM's grade: 3

Reasoning: CAM's compliance procedures are written out and are in line with industry standards. The firm requires all employees to submit brokerage account reports to Andy at the end of each quarter.

OPERATIONS

Exhibit 12.10 shows each of the factors scored in the operations section. This section of the model is worth 15 points (15%) and is comprised of four equally weighted factors. Operations are often overlooked when evaluating investment management firms because the focus is usually exclusively on the investment product and team under review. However, a good investment product that is backed by poor operations can quickly become a problem. I have heard from many investment firms' operations personnel that they are surprised that I am interested in talking to them. I always ask how often other due diligence analysts speak to them and often find out that I am the first person (or one of just a handful) to formally request time with back-office staff.

Factor 27: Reconciliation/Administration

This factor refers to the accuracy and timeliness of the portfolio accounting function. Whether investing in a separate account or some pool of assets (limited partnership, commingled trust), it is essential that the portfolio accounting function accurately reconcile the portfolio on a timely basis. While it is difficult to make an assessment of this function prior to actually hiring a firm, it is possible to form a reasonable opinion based on strategic questioning and through the reference checks. When I contact references provided to me by the firm, I generally spend a good portion of my time on

EXHIBIT 12.10 Manager Scoring Model—Operations Section

#	Section/Factors	% Breakout Variable	Maximum Points Variable	Manager Score 0 to 5	Scaled Score	%
	Operations		10		6.5	65.0%
27	Reconciliation/ administration	25%	2.5	3		
28	Reporting	25%	2.5	3		
29	Client service	25%	2.5	3		
30	Quality/quantity of people	25%	2.5	4		

the phone with them discussing operational and organizational issues. I prefer to address most of the investment-related questions myself during the analytical phase of the due diligence process. I don't need the references to tell me how wonderful the portfolio is (I do my own portfolio analysis) or how superb the performance is (I likewise run a series of performance-related statistics as well). I find it more useful to ask for information that I generally can't get in the due diligence process.

Score/Methodology

0   Unacceptable.
1   Scattered.
2   Below average.
3   Generally accurate and timely.
4   Above average.
5   Among the best in the business and always getting better.

CAM's grade: 3
Reasoning: CAM gets a grade of 3 based on the conversations I had with the references given to me by Andy. In addition, the bulk of the reconciliation work is done by Tara and it is clear that Tara has a very full plate.

Factor 28: Reporting

Reporting refers to any written or verbal dissemination of information given by the investment firm to its clients. The scope, frequency, and timeliness are all taken into consideration when determining this grade.

Score/Methodology

0   No formal reporting. Often difficult to track down manager for discussion.
1   Monthly/quarterly performance data provided, but not on a timely basis. No additional data provided.
2   Monthly/quarterly performance data provided on a timely basis. No additional data provided.
3   Reports that are average and timely. "Average" can be defined as brief, summary-level information provided in addition to performance data.
4   Reports that are above average and timely. "Above average" can be defined as commentary in addition to summary statistics.
5   Detailed reports provided monthly (and possibly quarterly) and on a timely basis. Manager (or client service professional) is generally available for phone discussion or meeting.

CAM's grade: 3

Reasoning: On request, CAM provided me with copies of monthly client reports for the past 12 months. The reports offer basic performance reporting versus the benchmark, top 10 holdings, and a pie chart of the product's sector breakout. Client references indicated that Mark and Jim are usually pretty easy to get on the phone for a quick update. CAM's reporting is in line with industry norms.

Factor 29: Client Service

There is a maxim in the investment business that good client service can go unnoticed when underlying performance is favorable, but helps to save client relationships (for a time) when performance flies south for the winter. Client service means more than occasional calls and office visits; it means that every question I have and any issue that might pop up gets resolved quickly and efficiently. As with the other factors in this section, I often ask questions about the level of client service when talking to clients referred to me by the investment firm being reviewed.

Score/Methodology

0   Client service is virtually nonexistent.

1   Client service staff falls short of meeting the basic needs of the firm's investor base. The firm has no plans to hire new staff or move people internally to improve the service.

2   Client service staff falls short of meeting the basic needs of the firm's investor base. The firm will be hiring new staff or moving staff internally in the near future to address the issue.

3   Client service staff meets the basic needs of the firm's investor base.

4   Client service staff exceeds the basic needs of the firm's investor base.

5   Client service staff is among the best in the industry.

CAM's grade: 3

Reasoning: Based on the conversations I had with several of the clients referred to us by CAM, I concluded that the firm provides an average level of client service. All the clients I spoke with stated that Tara was always available for questions and that the three partners were generally available (with a slight lag between initial contact and callback). CAM also hired Jenny recently and Andy stated that they would likely hire an additional person in the next six months.

Factor 30: Quality/Quantity of People

This factor basically draws on the grades assessed in the previous three factors and measures the quality and quantity of the operational staff. Quality does not necessarily refer to pedigree. It should be viewed as a measure of effectiveness and efficiency. After going through the entire due diligence process with an investment firm, it is usually pretty easy to determine if the firm is appropriately staffed. The meetings with operational staff are critical in grading this factor. In addition, it is usually apparent when a firm has either lower-quality staff, too few support staff, or a combination of the two. Examples of things that can help to grade this factor include: a firm that consistently sends inaccurate information in response to direct questions or a firm that sends information to me long after it is due (or promised to be delivered). Quality of operations staff can also be graded based on the number of times a person says, "I'll have to get back to you." Quality personnel know the answers to most (if not all) questions that a potential investor will likely ask. When grading this factor, take into account the entire operations function, which includes accounting, administration, trading, client service, marketing, and operations.

Score/Methodology

0   Vastly below average.
1   Staff is below-average quality; quantity does not meet needs.
2   Staff is average quality; quantity does not meet needs.
3   Staff is above-average quality; quantity meets needs.
4   Staff is high quality; quantity meets needs.
5   Staff is high quality; quantity exceeds needs; plans to hire
    additional staff to stay ahead of growth.

CAM's grade: 4
Reasoning: The three partners (Mark, Jim, and Andy) are very good in their respective roles. Tara, the analyst/assistant is also top quality. However, while the current team can adequately meet current needs, Tara appears to be stretched thin!

MANUAL ADJUSTMENT

This section was added to the model to help address any issues or concerns that are not fully addressed in the 30 factors being scored (see Exhibit 12.11). The person scoring a manager can add or subtract up to three points to or from the total score. I infrequently find it necessary to enter a

EXHIBIT 12.11   Manager Scoring Model—Manual Adjustment Section

#	Section/Factors	% Breakout Variable	Maximum Points Variable	Manager Score 0 to 5	Scaled Score	%
	Manual Adjustment (range +3 to –3)			–1		

Manual Adjustment Note: One point was subtracted because the hedge fund might prove to be a distraction to Mark and because the long-only small cap assets in the hedge fund are not being counted by CAM toward capacity constraints.

score in this space, but decided to deduct a point from CAM's score for the reasons listed in the notes section.

MODEL INTERPRETATION

We can refer to the summary table in Exhibit 12.12 to begin our interpretation of the model's results.

Based on its final score of 72, we can state that CAM scores in the upper range of the "above average" category (see Exhibit 12.2). In addition, we can make assessments based on any single section total or any combination. The summary statistics in Exhibit 12.12 show that CAM scored very well in investment professionalism (80%) and performance (84%), but scored low in portfolio risk (60%).

The beauty of the model is in its simplicity. To better understand what is driving the section scores, simply look at the factors that make up that particular section. For example, the portfolio risk section's score of 60% is

EXHIBIT 12.12   Summary Statistics

Section	CAM Asset Management
Investment Professionals	80%
Process	70%
Portfolio Risk	60%
Performance-Related Risk/Reward	84%
Organization	71%
Operations	65%
Average	72%

far lower than the scores CAM received in any of the other sections. The reasons for the lower score are:

■ The score for factor 10, diversification, was 2 (which is at the low end of the scoring range) based on the sector and industry concentrations that CAM's product has exhibited in the past as well as its current sector and industry concentrations.
■ Factor 13, sell discipline, also received a score of 2, which was based on the fact that the portfolio had violated its unwritten position constraints in the past and that Mark and Jim do not seem to agree on maximum position weights.

The model forces the investment manager analyst to score each and every factor, effectively putting all products reviewed on a level playing field. A quick glance at the summary table will highlight an investment firm's strengths, and weaknesses. A further look at the 30 underlying factors will give a comprehensive picture of a given firm's capabilities, strengths, and weaknesses, while providing a tangible means of evaluating and comparing both quantitative and qualitative data.

The table in Exhibit 12.13 is a summary for CAM's small-cap value product compared to summaries of the four other small-cap value managers that were identified in our search. Note that one of the managers we had initially identified (refer to Chapter 2, Exhibit 2.8), Kiuley Capital, has been eliminated. By lining the summary scores up against one another, we can see how each of the contenders stacks up against the peer group. We can see that the scores are reasonably tight, but that CAM, Zenith, and Revco have better scores than Alders and Eagle. We can also create a summary table for the five managers that list all 30 fac-

EXHIBIT 12.13 Manager Scoring Model—Summary Comparison

Section	CAM	Zenith	Revco	Alders	Eagle
Investment Professionals	80%	72%	80%	70%	65%
Process	70%	73%	75%	65%	65%
Portfolio Risk	60%	68%	70%	72%	70%
Performance-Related Risk/Reward	84%	67%	75%	65%	70%
Organization	71%	70%	65%	60%	60%
Operations	65%	65%	65%	60%	60%
Average	72%	70%	73%	66%	65%

EXHIBIT 12.14 Manager Scoring Model with Notes

#	Section/Factors	% Breakout Variable	Maximum Points Variable	Manager Score 0 to 5	Scaled Score	%	Notes
	Investment Professionals		30.0		24.0	80.0%	
1	Direct product experience	20%	6.0	4			Mark (5), Jim (4), Tara (0)
2	Manager/team skill	20%	6.0	4			Strong, skillful team
3	Portfolio knowledge	20%	6.0	5			Encyclopedic knowedge of portfolio/positions
4	Depth (backup)	20%	6.0	4			Mark/Jim can back each other up
5	Research capabilities	20%	6.0	3			Average/above average; need automation
	Process		15		10.5	70.0%	
6	Consistent application	25%	3.8	4			Despite "value" label, style is consistently GARP
7	Well thought out/disciplined	25%	3.8	3			
8	Portfolio consistent with process	25%	3.8	4			Portfolio holdings/characteristics consistent
9	Portfolio construction/review process	25%	3.8	3			Mark/Jim need to agree on constraints
	Portfolio Risk		15		9.0	60.0%	
10	Diversification	20%	3.0	2			Currently 70% in three sectors; concentration in past
11	Style drift	20%	3.0	5			None, pretty consistent GARP style
12	Liquidity	20%	3.0	3			50% in micro-cap stocks, which are less liquid
13	Sell discipline	20%	3.0	2			Related to #9; need to formalize this
14	Capacity	20%	3.0	3			Nearing capacity, but have left room for growth
	Performance-Related Risk/Reward		15		12.6	84.0%	
15	Performance relative to benchmark	20%	3.0	5			Excellent
16	Performance relative to peers	20%	3.0	5			Excellent

(Continued)

EXHIBIT 12.14 (Continued)

#	Section/Factors	% Breakout Variable	Maximum Points Variable	Manager Score 0 to 5	Scaled Score	%	Notes
17	Absolute/relative standard deviation	20%	3.0	3			Standard deviation in line with small-cap benchmarks/peers
18	Drawdown	20%	3.0	3			Consistent with small-cap market movements
19	Consistency	20%	3.0	5			Information ratio/percentile peer ranking typically high
	Organization		**15**		**10.7**	**71.4%**	
20	Turnover	10%	1.5	5			Never lost an employee
21	Succession plan	15%	2.3	4			Mark/Jim good backup, but problems if one leaves
22	Accommodate growth	15%	2.3	3			Can accommodate one or two people, but no more
23	Ownership/incentive	25%	3.8	4			Three key people are partners; Tara is incentivized
24	Backup/recovery	15%	2.3	3			Decent system/setup, but outsourced
25	Computer systems	10%	1.5	3			Hardware/software reasonably up to date
26	Compliance	10%	1.5	3			Fully compliant, internal checks periodic
	Operations		**10**		**6.5**	**65.0%**	
27	Reconciliation/administration	25%	2.5	3			Tara is busy, but seems to get job done
28	Reporting	25%	2.5	3			Standard reporting, Jim/Mark available
29	Client service	25%	2.5	3			
30	Quality/quantity of people	25%	2.5	4			Need to hire an additional person
	Manual Adjustment (range +3 to −3)			**−1**			Distraction due to hedge fund, capacity issues
	Final Score (Average %)					**72%**	

Manual Adjustment Note: One point was subtracted because the hedge fund might prove to be a distraction to Mark and because the long-only small cap assets in the hedge fund are not being counted by CAM toward capacity constraints.

tors alongside one another to facilitate a more detailed evaluation and comparison.

Lastly, in order to keep all the facts and figures gleaned from our evaluation of a given investment manager, I typically add brief notes right next to each of the individual factors' scores in the scoring model worksheet. An example of the model, complete with notes, appears in Exhibit 12.14.

## CHAPTER 13

Background Checks and Contracts

Now that we have identified one or more candidates for hire, we need to conduct a thorough check to ensure that the information we have received is factual. This is our last chance to find a reason not to hire someone or some firm. There are some pretty simple things that you can do to check into people's past, and there are some more time-consuming (and sometimes expensive) methods.

One of the easiest things you can do is to check a list of references provided by the investment manager, analyst, trader, or any other key investment professional under review.

REFERENCE CHECKS

Reference checks are often overlooked by investment manager analysts because they are thought of as always being upbeat and positive. After all, who is going to list someone as a reference if they don't know ahead of time that they are going to receive a glowing reference? The answer is sometimes surprising. Some people assume that I will not actually call the references that they provide, so they include the names of individuals who will not give a glowing review and, in some cases, the names of people who don't really seem to know the person being reviewed.

In addition, even when the reference check is with someone who clearly likes the person under review, it is often possible to glean some small bit of information that you did not find on your own.

I divide reference checks into three categories:

1. *Personal references.* These references are typically friends and/or former co-workers who have some personal connection with the person under review.

2. *Employer references.* I typically ask the person or people under review for names of former supervisors or, in the case of people who were in charge at their last job, for names of people who worked for them.
3. *Client references.* This is generally one of the most useful reference checks for me because I tend to focus on questions that are not typical.

When asking for references, I focus more on previous employer and client references, but will ask for (and check) personal references as well. I will not hire anyone who is not willing to share references with me. In fact, while I generally wait until the end of the due diligence process to check references, I will ask for references earlier in the process if I do not buy into what I am being told. If, for example, an investment manager tells me that he was responsible for all buy and sell decisions at a former place of employment, I may ask for the names of people whom I can call for verification if I have information to the contrary or if something he told me does not seem to ring true.

The following section highlights some generic questions to ask during a reference check. I will refer to the person whose references we are checking as the "referencee." Each question is followed by some commentary in italics.

Questions for personal references:

1. How long have you known the referencee?

   This question should be asked of all references provided to you. It helps to establish a basis for the questions and answers that follow.
2. What is your relationship to the referencee?

   This seems like an innocent question, but it is not. I want to find out if the reference has any relationship with the referencee that will negate the effectiveness or appropriateness of the interview. For example, if the reference has a business relationship with the referencee, I need to know this information so I know how much I can/will trust the answers.
3. Can you tell me about yourself?

   I don't want a resume, but it is often nice to know whom I am speaking with. If the person has investment industry experience, I may ask more investment-related questions than if the person does not have industry experience.
4. Do you have (or have you had) any financial or business arrangements with the referencee currently (or in the past year)?

   Question 2 gives the reference the opportunity to offer this information. If the information is not offered in response to question 2, I bluntly ask if there is or has been any financial or business relationship now or in the past.

5. Are you related in any way to the referencee?

   Often, a referencee will include on a reference list people who are related but have different last names (a brother-in-law, for example). I ask this question just to make sure that I know exactly whom I am speaking to.

6. Would you hire the referencee to manage money for you personally? Why or why not?

   This is a good question because after they say "yes" (and they almost always do), I ask why. Some of the answers that come in response to the latter part of the question are very telling. At a minimum, the answer to the "why" part of the question tells you immediately how well the reference is acquainted with the referencee's investment expertise.

7. What is one negative thing about the referencee?

   Half of the people I ask this question of reply that they can't think of any negative things to say or tell me that they are not comfortable answering this question. If someone is uncomfortable answering any question, I apologize and move along. The other half sometimes surprise me with their answers.

Questions for former co-workers (many of the questions are the same, so I comment only on the new questions):

1. How long have you known the referencee?
2. What is your relationship to the referencee?
3. Can you tell me about yourself?
4. Do you have (or have you had) any financial or business arrangements with the referencee currently (or in the past year)?
5. Are you related in any way to the referencee?
6. How long had you worked for/with the referencee?

   Typically addressed in the earlier questions, but meant as a follow-up if the previous answers were not complete.

7. What was/were the referencee's job function/responsibilities while you worked together?

   With this question, we start to verify what the referencee has told us about his/her positions at previous firms. The answer to this question can cause the questioning to veer into many different directions.

8. Why did the referencee leave the firm where you had worked together?

   Most of the time, the answers jibe with what the referencee has told me, but sometimes I can get some additional insight from former co-workers.

9. What were/are the referencee's strengths and weaknesses?

   This is a typical question. I like to ask it because it gives me the ability move the questioning into different areas.

10. Would you hire the referencee to manage assets for you or your firm? Why?

    The yes/no part of the question is pretty straightforward, but the "why" part can sometimes yield additional nuggets of information.

11. Tell me one negative thing about the referencee.

Questions for former and current clients:

1. How long have you known the referencee?
2. What is your relationship to the referencee?
3. Can you tell me about yourself?
4. Do you have (or have you had) any financial or business arrangements with the referencee currently (or in the past year)?
5. Are you related in any way to the referencee?
6. What are your expectations of the referencee? Has the referencee performed up to your expectations?

   It's nice to know how other people see the referencee and the product under review. Clients can often provide some good commentary because they have already done their research and, presumably, have a strong knowledge of the firm, its people, and the underlying investment product.

7. What is your opinion of the referencee's portfolio management capabilities?

   This is related to question 6, but it hones in specifically on portfolio management.

8. What is your opinion of the referencee's investment team or staff?

   This is related to question 6, but it hones in specifically on the people behind the product. The question is directed not just toward the referencee, but the entire investment staff.

9. What is your opinion of the referencee's risk management skills?

   This is related to question 6, but it hones in specifically on risk issues.

10. How timely is the referencee's firm in providing reporting, fund reconciliations, NAVs, and so on?

    This question asks how effective the referencee's firm is with respect to operational and client service functions. Remember that I sit with some of the operational staff to understand what level of support the investment team receives internally, but also to gauge what level of service I might receive as a client. Now I get to check their answers by asking an actual client about the operational/back-office capabilities.

11. How did you find out about the referencee?

   I'm always interested in how people are connected. It is possible that the reference and the referencee do not have any personal or financial relationships, but they are connected somehow through a third party.

12. Who are some of the other investment managers that you currently use?

   This question does two things: (1) gives me some potential new leads and (2) tells me what kind of investor the reference is.

BACKGROUND CHECKS

Background checks are designed to verify details about an investment professional's life and covers a wide variety of areas, including: education, employment, legal, and financial. As a result, they tend to be time-consuming and expensive. Most firms elect to outsource this function to firms that specialize in conducting background checks. Good background checks can cost between $1,000 and $3,000 depending on the depth of background check required.

While a full-blown background check is a valuable tool, it is not always necessary when conducting our analysis. I will often spot-check an investment professional's background by picking one or two items and obtaining verification. For example, I might elect to verify an individual's graduate degree or status as a CFA. I typically request a full background check when I am dealing with a younger or smaller firm or when I do not have any personal connection to any of the investment professionals managing the product under review.

A good background check will look into and verify the following:

■ *Educational history*—verbal/written verification of all the educational institutions as well as any awards, certifications, or recognized achievements listed by the referencee in his/her resume or biography.

■ *Employment history*—verbal/written verification of the referencee's places of employment as well as verification of the time frames and, if possible, job responsibilities.

■ *Legal status*—written verification of the referencee's current status regarding lawsuits in the United States (and abroad, if appropriate).

■ *Certifications/designations/licenses*—verbal/written verification that the referencee has all of the certifications, designations, and licenses listed on the resume or highlighted in the ADV form and biography.

An example would be a simple check to see that an individual who claims to be a CPA or CFA has achieved that designation.
■ *Regulatory violations/censures*—SEC or exchange violations or censures.

It is important to conduct reference checks whenever you conduct a background check because many organizations will provide only a bare minimum of information to someone conducting a background check. This is because organizations wish to avoid lawsuits from former employees who might claim that false or misleading information prevented them from landing jobs. Many employers are hesitant to state facts because a former employee can still sue, forcing the employer to spend time (and money) defending their actions in court.

CREDIT CHECKS

To obtain a credit check on an individual, you will need a signed release form giving you permission to receive a copy of the credit report. The cost of a credit report is relatively low (typically less than $50).

I do not generally ask for a credit check, but I have done so when the situation warrants it. For example, if I am contemplating hiring a small (or young) investment firm with a low level of assets under management, I want to be assured that the firm has ample capital to stay in business until the assets rise to an appropriate level.

INVESTMENT CONTRACTS

There are two main types of investment contracts that you will need to be aware of: (1) separate (managed) account contracts and (2) fund or limited partnership contracts. The following sections highlight what to look for in an investment contract.

Guidelines for Separate Accounts

The submanager guidelines (SMG) section is typically included in the investment manager's contract as an addendum. However, because they represent the actual reason for hiring and subsequently maintaining the relationship with the investment manager (or in some cases, the firing of the investment manager), I believe they represent the most important component of the overall investment manager contract. Due to its importance and propensity for being misinterpreted, the SMG should be as complete as possible. Investment manager analysts spend a great deal of time conducting searches and, as a result, are often unable to recall many aspects of the search and each of the individual finalists off the top of their heads. In some cases this leads the analyst to construct SMG that are not highly detailed and may cause issues in the future.

For example, have a look at the following "investment criteria" section of an SMG:

> *The Investment Manager is responsible for creating and maintaining a portfolio of U.S. large capitalization stocks. In order to maintain adequate diversification, the portfolio managed by the Investment Manager must contain a minimum of 40 stocks at all times. For comparative purposes, the benchmark is the Standard & Poor's 500 Index. The Investment Manager is expected to outperform the Index by a minimum of 200 basis points. Failure to outperform the Index by 200 basis points will result in the Investment Manager's termination.*

This paragraph seems to clearly state the investment manager's portfolio responsibilities and indicates five criteria:

1. U.S. stock focus.
2. Large cap orientation.
3. Comparison to S&P 500 index.
4. Performance expected to exceed S&P 500 index by 200 basis points.
5. Minimum of 40 stocks.

While I do believe that brevity is a wonderful character trait, it has no place in an SMG. As you will see in the sample SMG included in this chapter, it is possible to be very detailed while keeping the overall length quite manageable. Several potential problems are contained in the preceding passage:

1. How are "large cap" stocks defined? Everyone seems to have their own definition of the breakpoints between small-/mid-/large-cap stocks. You may feel that a stock is large-cap once it crosses the $10 billion threshold, while the investment manager may feel that $5 billion is more appropriate.
2. What happens if the investment manager purchases a "large cap" stock, but due to price depreciation it falls into the mid- or small-cap range?
3. Are ADRs viewed as "U.S." stocks? If so, are there any limitations on the weight that they can reach in the portfolio?

4. Are stocks defined as shares of common stock or can the investment manager invest in other equity securities (preferred stock or convertible shares)?
5. How much cash can the manager hold (if any) at any given time?
6. What is the performance evaluation period? It is stated that the investment manager must outperform the S&P 500 index by a minimum of 200 basis points, but over what time frame—monthly, quarterly, or annually?
7. What method of performance calculation will be employed? Will cash flows into and out of the portfolio be time weighted or will the portfolio's performance be completed daily and chain-linked? Who is responsible for calculating the performance, and what is the procedure for any disagreements with regard to the performance calculation? What is the frequency and time frame in which performance will be calculated?
8. The guidelines state that the investment manager must hold a minimum of 40 stocks at any given time. Is there a maximum number of stocks that the manager can hold?
9. Concentration: What is the maximum weight the manager can hold in any single stock? Is there a limitation on the weight of the portfolio's top 10 holdings?
10. Weightings: Are there any maximum or minimum requirements with regard to sector or industry weights either in absolute terms or relative to the index?

The 10 points listed are just a start. I could probably list several dozen potential issues if I elected to do so. Any term that can be open to interpretation should be written in such a way that there is no question of its meaning. The advice I always give people with regard to the SMG is to write it in such a way that an independent third party could read it and have no questions. In fact I make a point of showing any guidelines that I write to someone else at the firm who did not work on this particular search with me. This way, they do not review the document with any preconceived notions.

The SMG will set the tone for the investment manager as well as the investment manager analyst before and during the search process, in addition to serving as a template for all monitoring activity that will follow once the manager is officially hired. A well-written SMG will: (1) state exactly what the firm has been hired to manage, (2) define the asset class and all permissible financial instruments the manager can invest in, (3) define asset allocation ranges, and (4) state any investment restrictions.

Sample Investment Manager Contract

The sample SMG that follows is for an investment management firm that is being hired to manage a diversified U.S. small-cap value portfolio. The Market Leaders Fund is hiring CAM Asset Management to run an active small-cap value portfolio, but has placed several restrictions based on fundamental characteristics, market capitalization, and investment style.

INVESTMENT MANAGER POLICY AND GUIDELINES FROM THE U.S. EQUITY MARKET LEADERS FUND TO CAM ASSET MANAGEMENT

This is a statement of investment-related guidelines which the U.S. Equity Market Leaders Fund ("the Fund") directs CAM Asset Management ("the Manager") to follow in managing the Fund's Investment Account ("the Account") assets. The Fund and Manager agree that these guidelines are incorporated into the Investment Management Agreement ("the Agreement") between them and executed as of [insert date]. The Manager shall consider these guidelines when investing the Fund's assets and shall adhere to these guidelines unless and until it provides the Fund written advance notice to the contrary and receives written approval from individual(s) authorized to do so by the Fund.

A. Investment Strategy: The Manager is responsible for a portfolio of domestic small-cap equities with a value-oriented style. Small-cap stocks are defined as those companies having a market cap less than $1 billion at the time of purchase and less than $2 billion at the time of sale. Stocks held in this portfolio that grow to a market capitalization of greater than $2 billion must be sold within 60 days of reaching that threshold unless the market capitalizations of stocks in question subsequently fall back below $2 billion during that period. The Manager may not hold at any time more than 10% of the overall portfolio's weight in stocks with market capitalizations below $500 million (defined as micro-cap stocks) regardless of whether they were purchased at that level or fell to that level due to price declines. Value is defined by the fundamental characteristics of the Frank Russell 2000 small-cap value index (FR2000SCVI). The portfolio's overall fundamental characteristics with regard to P/E, P/B, P/S, and P/CF must not exceed a 10% premium to the fundamental characteristics of the FR2000SCVI. The index statistics will be monitored on a monthly basis and will come from the index data published by the Frank Russell Company on their company web site.

Comments: In the investment strategy section, it is critical to precisely define what the investment manager is being hired to do. While this might seem straightforward, problems often arise because terms were not defined and limitations were not set. In this example I have defined the asset class, outlier limits, comparative benchmark, and the methodology for determining if the manager is complying with the mandate (from both a capitalization and a style perspective). It is important to discuss this section directly with the portfolio manager or a representative of the investment team to avoid potential misunderstandings later on. I rarely put fundamental restraints in a contract. I included in this sample contract to illustrate one method of insuring style conformity. After reading the preceeding chapters, it should be clear that CAM's GARP style would not fit in with the fundamental constraints listed in this contract.

B. Return Objective and Risk Tolerance:

    a. Return Objective: Return is defined as portfolio performance net of management fees. Minimum of 200 basis points above the Russell 2000 small-cap value index on an annual basis.

    b. Risk Tolerance: Risk is defined as annualized standard deviation. May not exceed a premium of 10% above the standard deviation of the Russell 2000 small-cap value index over the same time period.

Comments: Brief and to the point. It is essential that these guidelines be clearly understood by the investment manager.

C. Cash and Equivalents: The portfolio must be invested at all times, which is defined as being a minimum of 95% invested in small-cap equity holdings. To accommodate multiday transaction settlements, this rule will be considered in violation if the portfolio is less than 95% invested for five full consecutive business days. Any cash held in the portfolio will be automatically swept into a money market fund by the custodian on a daily basis and will be available to the Manager for any transactions requested within a one-day period. Interest earned on this cash will be accounted for by the Fund's custodian and treated as income in all portfolio performance calculations.

Comments: Cash might or might not be an issue at your organization; regardless, it is important to specify any limits you might have or any policies you want the Manager to adhere to.

D. Permissible Investments: The Manager may invest in public equity securities traded on the New York Stock Exchange, Nasdaq, Nasdaq small company exchange, or American Stock Exchange. Convertible securities will be treated as equities and are therefore permissible. Ownership of foreign companies trading on U.S. exchanges, such as ADRs, is allowed but may not exceed more than 10% of the portfolio at any time.

Comments: The SMG should leave nothing open to interpretation. This section coincides with the investment strategy section and takes it a step further. This section could easily be included directly in the investment strategy section, but I have found that the document reads better when it is broken into different components.

E. Diversification: The Manager is responsible for the following diversification guidelines:

a. Economic Sector: Using the Frank Russell small-cap value index as a proxy, the Manager may not hold at any time more than 2× the index weight in any sector with an index weighting over 10% or 3× the index weight in any sector with an index weighting under 10%. The Manager may choose, at their discretion, not to hold securities in a given sector. The Manager may not, however, exceed 40% on an absolute basis of the total portfolio in any sector at any time.

b. Industry: Using the Frank Russell small-cap value index as a proxy, the Manager may not hold at any time more than 2× the index weight in any industry with an index weighting over 10% or 3× the index weight in any industry with an index weighting under 10%. The Manager may choose, at their discretion, not to hold securities in a given industry.

c. Number of Equity Holdings in Portfolio: The maximum exposure to any single company must not exceed 8% of the overall portfolio (including cash and equivalents). In addition, the Manager may not hold fewer than 30 securities in the portfolio at any time.

Comments: This section naturally depends on any diversification requirements your organization may place on a specific mandate. In this example, I have included language that ensures diversification by sector, industry, and number of stocks. Note that each requirement is defined in easy-to-understand terms. The investment manager must read and understand this section so the firm can fully comply with your specific investment mandate.

F. Portfolio/Performance Evaluation:

a. Methodology: The portfolio will be measured on a total return basis, which includes changes in market value as well as any income received. Contributions to or redemptions from the portfolio will be time weighted and calculated by chain-linking daily returns, which is generally accepted as being the most precise method available.

b. Frequency: The portfolio's characteristics and performance will be reviewed on a quarterly basis within three weeks of each quarter's end and will require a telephone interview for a minimum of one hour at an agreed-upon date and time. On an annual basis, the Manager will be required to visit our offices for a face-to-face meeting no later than 30 days after year-end. The management of the Manager will also make themselves available for at least one on-site visit whereby we will conduct a formal review of the portfolio as well as the Manager as a business entity. The evaluation will be based on the following:

1. Adherence to value investment style, which has been defined previously.

2. Value added over the Russell 2000 small-cap value index, net of any management fees. The Manager is expected to exceed the index by a minimum of 200 basis points on an annual basis. Once the portfolio builds a three-year track record, it will also be measured on a four-quarter rolling basis against the benchmark.

3. Performance relative to peer group. The peer group is defined by the total universe of U.S. small-cap value equity the Managers currently included in the peer universes provided by the Frank Russell Company. The Manager is expected to perform in the top quartile of this universe. Two successive quarters of performance below that threshold will place the Manager on warning and will warrant a face-to-face review. A third consecutive quarter of underperformance will likely result in either a complete or a partial redemption of assets. Four consecutive quarters of underperformance will result in termination.

Comments: Try to be as specific as possible in this section because it will be an area that you frequently and consistently discuss with the investment manager. Failure by the manager to meet the minimum standards set in this section will likely lead to termination.

G. Prohibited Transactions:

a. Short sales, margin purchases, or borrowing.

b. Private placements or restricted securities, including those under rule 144A.

c. Futures or options.

d. Warrants or other options except when acquired as part of a security purchased for the portfolio.

e. Commodities.

f. Direct purchases of real estate.

g. Foreign securities, with the exception of ADRs (which, as specified previously, may not collectively exceed 10% of the overall portfolio weight).

Comments: Make this section as complete as possible. You can also state here that specific investments may be allowed pending written permission from you or some member of your organization. For example, you might state that 144A securities may be purchased on an exception basis only after written approval and within a stated portfolio maximum weight.

H. Reporting Requirements:

a. The Manager shall maintain records of all activity in the Account and shall provide the Fund and the administrator with monthly transaction statements and portfolio holdings in the Fund's Account within seven (7) days after the end of the month. The information provided shall include realized and unrealized gains/losses, dividend and interest income earned, and any capital additions or withdrawals for the prior month.

b. The Manager shall on a monthly basis reconcile its record of Account activity with the Fund's custodian.

c. The Manager shall notify the client and its administrator of any unreconciled items.

d. The Manager shall prepare a brief written commentary on a monthly basis and a more detailed commentary on a quarterly basis.

Comments: Most organizations require that investment managers reconcile their accounts with the organization's custodian or with a member of the firm itself. With respect to written reports, it is important to state what is expected of the manager before being hired. The delivery date should be specified as well.

I. Proxy Voting: The Manager, not the Fund, is responsible for voting proxies. The Manager shall take such action, and tender any advice, with respect to the voting of proxies regarding portfolio securities as are solely in the interest of the Fund.

J. General Issues:

a. The accounting, settlement, and performance measurement currency is the United States dollar.

b. The Manager shall notify the Fund of any material changes in the philosophy, style, or management of the portfolio within one month of the change(s). Should any investment personnel leave the firm, cease to work on the portfolio for the Fund, or in any way experience a change in their job descriptions, the Manager shall notify the Fund within five business days verbally and within fifteen business days in writing.

c. For the purposes of these guidelines, the Manager submits that the following personnel are responsible for the management and operations of the portfolio for the Fund:

1. Investment Personnel:

i. Mark Innes: Principal/Co-Portfolio Manager—Shares responsibility for all buy and sell decisions with Jim Bradshaw. Covers technology and health care sectors.

    ii. James Bradshaw: Principal/Co-Portfolio Manager—Shares responsibility for financial and consumer sectors with Mark Innes.

    iii. Tara Fitzpatrick: Junior analyst—Responsible for database management, financial modeling, some selected stock research.

    iv. Etc.

2. Operational Personnel:

    i. Andrew Wares: Principal/COO—Manages firm's operational business and performs client service.

    ii. Jenny Kramer: Operational assistant—Responsible for providing support to Andrew and Tara.

    iii. Etc.

Comments: This is where I usually include any items that do not fit in the other sections, so the list usually changes from contract to contract. However, I always insist on including a section on the underlying investment personnel. This helps me to properly assess the investment manager if the firm experiences any investment professional turnover. I have found that when faced with questions about professional turnover, many investment managers downplay the significance of the investment professionals who have departed. If a section that states who is on the investment team and their responsibilities is included in the contract (which is signed by the manager), many of these issues can be avoided. I always ask for this information during the interview stage and include the results in the written meeting memos that I prepare, but have found that their inclusion in the contract eliminates potential disagreements later on.

    The SMG should be prepared by the investment manager analyst of the firm that is hiring the manager because the analyst has a better idea of what the analyst firm expects from the relationship. Once the SMG is written, it should be reviewed by the investment manager or some other investment professional who works on the product in question, not just the manager's legal department. Often, the investment professionals turn the contract over to their legal departments and let them deal with the details. This can lead to problems. Legal departments do a great job of checking for legal inaccuracies and finding issues that may lead to potential liability, but are often not equipped to uncover any subtle investment-related issues that the document may contain. I usually spend half an hour discussing the SMG line by line with the investment manager so that potential problems can be avoided.

Fund or Limited Partnership Agreements

A fund or limited partnership (LP) agreement is similar in scope to the separate (managed) account contract in most ways. The big exception is that a fund or LP agreement is mostly nonnegotiable. The whole idea behind the fund concept is that every investor in the fund is treated exactly the same. The investors' assets are pooled together in the fund entity and managed as a pool of assets. Each fund client owns a portion (share) of the fund, so the clients all share in the fund's expenses as well as the profits in relation to their ownership shares.

CHAPTER **14**

Fixed Income Manager Analysis

BEFORE THE ANALYSIS

In the first three chapters, we took a general look at how to formulate a plan of attack when conducting a search for an investment manager in any asset class. The process employed was pretty straightforward:

1. Define the search.
2. Find the most appropriate investment products.
3. Request information for review and analysis.

To make the explanation of this process more meaningful, I created a fictitious search and took you through each of the three steps. In step one, we stated that we were looking for a small-cap value manager. In step two, we conducted a search for appropriate investment products based on third party databases, internal databases, news sources, and industry networking. In the final step, we reduced the list of potential firms (which started at well over 10,000) to a much more manageable number (five). Once we identified the five candidates, we contacted them and requested some basic information about each firm, in general, and its small-cap value product, in particular.

EQUITY MANAGER ANALYSIS

We then selected one of the five candidates (CAM Asset Management) as our test case and performed a complete due diligence workup on CAM and its small-cap value product. The entire analysis started with Chapter 4 and concluded with the preceding chapter (13). Along the way, we analyzed performance, risk, style, attribution of returns, and the current/historical portfolio holdings. We also reviewed all of the firm's documentation, including its internal marketing presentation, our questionnaire, the Form

ADV, and a variety of news stories gathered from various sources. In addition to performing our analysis, we conducted two meetings with the investment professionals at CAM, which included a telephone conference and a more detailed on-site visit. Afterward, we checked references and conducted a background check of the firm's principals.

When all was said and done, we came to the conclusion that CAM is a quality investment firm and its small cap product, while not managed according to strict "value" criteria, is a good product.

FIXED INCOME MANAGER ANALYSIS

While there are a great many differences between equity and fixed income, the process that we use to analyze equity and fixed income managers is quite similar. Conceptually, there is no difference. The only difference is in the underlying characteristics of the financial instruments under review. For example, the performance calculations discussed in Chapter 4 with respect to equity portfolios are exactly the same for fixed income. The Sharpe ratio is also the same regardless of asset class distinctions.

Because much of the analysis and many of the calculations and analytical tools are the same across asset classes, I have greatly truncated the fixed income portion of this book. Rather than simply repeating all of the information we have already covered in detail, I have elected to highlight only the areas in which there is a clear analytical distinction between equity manager and fixed income manager analysis.

The remainder of this chapter will follow in the same order as the equity manager analysis section (see Exhibit 14.1 for an outline). I have

EXHIBIT 14.1 Outline of Fixed Income Manager Analysis Process

1 Performance Analysis
2 Risk Analysis
3 Portfolio Analysis
4 Information Gathering
5 Initial Interview
6 Attribution Analysis
7 Style Analysis
8 On-site Visit
9 Manager Scorecard
10 Reference/Background Checks

started each section with a brief discussion of the similarities and differences between the equity and fixed income manager analysis.

PERFORMANCE ANALYSIS

As the table in Exhibit 14.2 illustrates, the performance calculations are the same for equity and fixed income portfolios. It is important to note that, at this point, we are just looking at the overall product's returns, not the underlying securities. One obvious difference between equity performance analysis and the fixed income performance analysis is that the indexes used will be different. Because we are always looking to make apples-to-apples comparisons, we will use specialized fixed income benchmarks and will create peer group comparisons based on the underlying fixed income instruments used (in addition to geography, duration, maturity, etc.).

RISK ANALYSIS

The returns-based risk analysis that we perform on fixed income portfolio is the same as we perform on equity portfolios (see Exhibit 14.3).

EXHIBIT 14.2 Comparison of Investment Manager Analysis Process by Asset Class—Performance

	Analysis/Technique	Equity	Fixed Income
Performance Analysis	Dollar weighted returns	✖	✖
	Chain-linked returns	✖	✖
	Cumulative returns	✖	✖
	Annualized returns	✖	✖
	Calendar year returns	✖	✖
	Time weighted returns	✖	✖
	Performance relative to index	✖	✖
	Performance relative to peers	✖	✖
	Up market/down market analysis	✖	✖
	Composite analysis	✖	✖

EXHIBIT 14.3   Comparison of Investment Manager Analysis Process by Asset
Class—Risk Analysis

	Analysis/Technique	Equity	Fixed Income
Risk Analysis	Return histogram	✖	✖
	Standard deviation	✖	✖
	Risk/return graph	✖	✖
	Sharpe ratio	✖	✖
	M^2 ratio	✖	✖
	Information ratio	✖	✖
	Treynor ratio	✖	✖
	Jensen ratio	✖	✖
	Downside deviation	✖	✖
	Sortino ratio	✖	✖
	Correlation matrix	✖	✖
	Covariance	✖	✖
	R^2	✖	✖
	VaR	✖	✖

PORTFOLIO ANALYSIS

This is where the differences inherent in the underlying financial instruments start to create differences in the analytics. When we analyze a fixed income manager, we want to review the underlying portfolio holdings and make assessments based on individual positions, as well as specific groupings. In that respect, there is no difference between equity and fixed income manager analysis. However, equities and fixed income securities have different investment characteristics and, as a result, need to be analyzed in different ways.

As the table in Exhibit 14.4 illustrates, the real differences between equity and fixed income manager analysis occur at the "characteristics" level. Like equities, we should analyze fixed income portfolios based on a geographical, sector, and industry basis. Unlike equities, we are not concerned with things like P/E, P/B, and ROE. Those are mainly equity characteristics. When we review a fixed income portfolio and look to analyze it based on discrete fundamental characteristic ranges, we need to focus on things like maturity, duration, and quality.

■ *Maturity.* The maturity of a bond is the amount of time left until it matures. For example, assuming today's date is January 1, 2004, a bond with a maturity date of December 31, 2005, would have a maturity of

EXHIBIT 14.4 Comparison of Investment Manager Analysis Process by Asset Class—Portfolio Analysis

	Analysis/Technique	Equity	Fixed Income
Portfolio Analysis	Sector weights	✖	✖
	Industry weights	✖	✖
	Regional/country weights	✖	✖
	Market cap range weights	✖	✖
	Fundamental characteristics range weights	✖	✖
	P/E	✖	—
	P/B	✖	—
	Earnings growth	✖	—
	Yield	✖	✖
	Duration	—	✖
	Maturity	—	✖
	Quality	—	✖
	Position weights/constraints	✖	✖
	Concentration	✖	✖

two years (all of 2004 and all of 2005). Maturity is an important statistic because bond prices swing more violently with interest rates the longer the maturity of the bond is. Knowing the relationship between maturities and coupons (the bonds' interest rates) is critical is making an assessment of an individual bond position and, as a result, of entire bond portfolios.

■ *Duration.* Duration picks up where maturity leaves off. Formally, duration is the weighted average of the times that interest payments and the final return of principal are received. The weights are the amounts of the payments discounted by the yield-to-maturity of the bond. Duration, in effect, represents a means of allowing bonds of different maturities and different coupon rates to be compared directly (apples-to-apples). The most practical way to think of duration is as follows: The percentage change in the price of a bond is its duration multiplied by the change in interest rates. For example, if a bond has duration of 10 years and intermediate-term interest rates fall from 8% to 6%, the bond's price will rise by approximately 20% (remember that bond prices have an inverse relationship with interest rates—a decline in rates translates to a gain in bond prices). The higher a bond's duration, the greater its interest rate risk.

Example Details

Duration:	10 years
Interest rate change:	8% − 6% = 2%
Bond's price change:	10 × 2% = 20%

It should be noted that any bond with a nonzero coupon would have a duration figure less than its actual maturity, whereas a zero-coupon bond's duration and maturity will be the same.

■ *Quality.* Credit quality ratings refer to the ability of the issuer to make payments of interest and principal on loan securities such as bonds or notes. The credit quality of an issuer could be thought of as the probability that the issuer will default. Credit quality is measured by rating agencies such as Standard & Poor's and Moody's. Credit ratings can broadly be classified as: (1) investment grade (highest quality); (2) non–investment grade (mid-to-low quality, commonly referred to as "high yield" debt); and (3) speculative (securities of firms that have defaulted on their debt, commonly referred to as "distressed" debt).

A good working knowledge of the three bond measures defined can aid the investment manager analyst in the evaluation of fixed income managers, but the body of knowledge needed to properly assess fixed income managers and put their track records and investment processes in perspective is far more expansive. As the previous section states, this book is not a tutorial on the assets classes reviewed within. Instead, it is assumed that the reader has the basic knowledge to understand the securities discussed. In this section, we are discussing bonds, so I make the assumption that you, the reader, already possess a basic understanding of fixed income instruments.

While the underlying fundamental characteristics may be different, the formulas, methods and analytical techniques remain the same. When analyzing a fixed income portfolio, we look to see if the portfolio is concentrated in any broad categories, such as investment type (U.S. Treasuries, corporate bonds, investment-grade bonds, non-investment-grade bonds, etc.). When looking at a portfolio's duration, it is important to assess the underlying risk based on our initial risk assumptions and, if appropriate, compared to some benchmark. For example, a fixed income portfolio with a significantly higher exposure to zero-coupon bonds than its peers or relevant benchmarks should be viewed as potentially carrying with it heightened interest rate risk. Contrast that portfolio example with a portfolio of high-grade corporate and Treasury bonds with maturities on a par with the first example. Assuming no derivatives are being used to hedge out interest rate risk, the second portfolio would likely exhibit less interest rate risk than the first example. Should interest rates spike up, the first portfolio would likely be hit harder than the first.

INFORMATION GATHERING

As shown in Exhibit 14.5, the approach for equity manager analysis is the same as with fixed income manager analysis. When conducting fixed income analysis, we will gather all of the publicly available data for a firm, the product under review, and the people in charge of the portfolio. We will supplement that info with documents provided to us by the investment firm. Lastly, we will interview the investment professionals charged with portfolio management a minimum of two times, including a detailed on-site visit.

The information that we gather in this stage will be used in all facets of the analytical process. In fact, it is fair to say that the information-gathering stage is not a stage at all because we are gathering information throughout the due diligence process. Regardless of whether we elect to hire (or not to hire) a manager, we would still be on the lookout for any information that could impact our decision to allocate (or not to allocate) assets to a given manager.

FIXED INCOME QUESTIONNAIRE

The investment questionnaire that is highlighted in Chapter 7 is a generic one that can be sent to just about any kind of investment firm with just the simple alteration of replacing the fourth section, which asks for specific equity portfolio data; in this chapter, we substitute the following "fixed income" section. The same methodology is employed when we look at hedge funds in Chapter 15.

EXHIBIT 14.5 Comparison of Investment Manager Analysis Process by Asset Class—Information Gathering

	Analysis/Technique	Equity	Fixed Income
Information Gathering	Marketing presentations	✖	✖
	Portfolio commentary	✖	✖
	Market commentary	✖	✖
	Questionnaire	✖	✖
	Form ADV	✖	✖
	Internet-based news search	✖	✖

SECTION FOUR: PRODUCT INFORMATION (FIXED INCOME)

Clients/Assets

1. Provide the following data for the firm and product-specific assets (in millions). Insert additional rows if you have more than four products. Include the status of each product (open to new clients/assets or closed).

	Open/Closed	12/03	12/02	12/01	12/00	12/99
Product #1						
Product #2						
Product #3						
Product #4						
Total firm assets						

2. Please list any products that your firm has completely liquidated or merged with existing products. Include the reasons why the product was liquidated and/or merged with another product.
3. Complete the following client-related information:

	12/03	12/02	12/01	12/00	12/99
Total Firm					
# Clients					
# Clients gained (year)					
# Clients lost (year)					
Assets					
Assets gained (year)					
Assets lost (year)					
% Firm assets with top five clients					
Product-Specific					
# Clients					
# Clients gained (year)					
# Clients lost (year)					
Assets					
Assets gained (year)					
Assets lost (year)					
% Firm assets with top five clients					

Performance Data

4. Provide monthly historical performance figures (net of all fees) in the following table. Add rows to the table if the track record goes back further than five years.

	Jan	Feb	Mar	Apr	May	Jun	Jul	Aug	Sep	Oct	Nov	Dec
2003												
2002												
2001												
2000												
1999												

5. Is the performance history submitted AIMR compliant? If yes, has this performance history been certified by an independent auditor? Please provide a copy of the audit results. If no, please explain.
6. Please describe the data and methodology used to calculate the performance record stated in the previous question.

Description	Y/N	Explanation
Composite of separate accounts		
Equal weighted		
Size weighted		
Record linked from prior affiliation		
Representative account		
Commingled/mutual fund		
Simulated performance		

7. Please provide a copy of the full performance disclosures for the product under review. The disclosure should include the following for each year-end:

   a. Number of accounts included in the composite.
   b. Assets of those accounts.
   c. Number of accounts managed in a similar style, but not included in the composite.
   d. Assets of those accounts.
   e. Reasons why those accounts were not included in the composite.
   f. Number of accounts added to/subtracted from the composite in each year.

8. Please state the most appropriate benchmark for the product under review and include its performance history for the same time period listed previously for the product.

	Jan	Feb	Mar	Apr	May	Jun	Jul	Aug	Sep	Oct	Nov	Dec
2003												
2002												
2001												
2000												
1999												

9. Please provide performance attribution in the following format:

Year	Product Return	Index Return	+/−	Reasons for Out/Underperformance (please be as thorough as possible)
2003				
2002				
2001				

10. Do you utilize any internal or third party performance and/or attribution software/systems? If yes, please provide a list of the systems used and their purposes. In addition, please include with this questionnaire a sample of the attribution report for the latest month or quarter end.
11. What is the product's capacity? At what point would you close to new clients? At what point would you close to new assets from existing clients?

Portfolio Data

12. Please provide a representative portfolio for each of the last four quarter-end dates. The portfolios should be provided in Microsoft Excel format and should include the following information: security identifier, number of shares held, and each security's name. Include the following information regarding the selected representative account:

   a. Type of account.
   b. Account's inception date.
   c. Account size.
   d. Monthly historical performance for the account (to determine how closely it tracks the composite).

13. Provide the following sector data for the portfolio in percentage of total assets:

Sector	12/03	12/02	12/01	12/00	12/99
Cash and Equivalents					
U.S. Treasury/Agency					
U.S. Corporate—Investment Grade					
U.S. Corporate—Non-Inv Grade					
U.S. Corporate—Not Rated					
U.S. Corporate—Convertibles					
U.S. Corporate—Common Stock					
$ Denominated Non-U.S. Govt/Agency					
$ Denominated Non-U.S. Corporate					
Non-U.S. Dollar Bonds					
Emerging Markets Debt					
MBS/ABS/CMO					
Other					

14. Provide the following allocation data for the portfolio's corporate bond component in percentage of total assets (please use the sector descriptions provided in the table):

Sector	12/03	12/02	12/01	12/00	12/99
Basic Materials					
Commercial Services					
Consumer Cyclicals					
Consumer Noncyclicals					
Consumer Services					
Energy					
Financial Services					
Health Care					
Industrials					
Technology					
Telecommunications					
Transportation					
Utilities					

15. Provide the following summary data for the portfolio in percentage of total assets:

	12/03	12/02	12/01	12/00	12/99
Fundamental Characteristics					
Average Quality					
Yield to Maturity					
Modified Duration					
Average Maturity					
% Maturity < 3 years					
% Maturity 3–5 years					
% Maturity 5–10 years					
% Maturity > 10 years					

Dedicated Product Investment Professionals

16. Include the names of all investment professionals (portfolio managers, analysts, traders, etc.) who work directly on the product under review.

Name	Product Responsibility	Years Working at Firm	Years Working on Product	Other Products Individual Works On	Other Responsibilities

17. Provide the names of all investment professionals who have worked on the product and have resigned, been terminated, or transferred/rotated to another department within the past five years. Provide a brief explanation for each departure. List any replacements for these vacancies.

Employee Name/Title	Resignation/ Termination/ Rotation	Reason(s)	Name of Replacement

18. Describe the structure of the investment management team. Include the following information:
    a. Name(s) of key decision maker(s). Be specific—identify the individual(s) who actually make(s) buy and sell decisions.
    b. Lead portfolio manager.
    c. Portfolio manager's backup.

Investment Philosophy and Process

19. Define your investment philosophy.
20. Define your investment style.
21. Describe your investment process/philosophy with respect to the following factors. Please include any other factors you believe are an important part of your process or value added.
    a. Duration management.
    b. Yield curve positioning.
    c. Security selection.
    d. Sector rotation.
    e. Credit quality management.
    f. Leverage.
    g. Currency management.
    h. Other.

22. Please indicate how you would rank the following factors in terms of their importance to the ongoing management of the product. In addition, please describe how you expect each factor to impact the overall portfolio return going forward.
    a. Duration management.
    b. Yield curve positioning.
    c. Security selection.
    d. Sector rotation.
    e. Credit quality management.
    f. Leverage.
    g. Currency management.
    h. Other.

23. Describe in detail the investment process employed by the investment team in the management of the product. Include a description of how individual research and ideas make it (or don't make it) into the portfolio.
24. Buy/sell discipline. Please include any minimum and/or maximum portfolio constraints with respect to:
    a. Geography.
    b. Credit quality.

    c. Liquidity.
    d. Duration.
    e. Maturity.

25. Do you have stop-loss procedures in place? If yes, describe the details. If no, explain your methodology regarding bonds that drop significantly in price. Please list the three largest percentage losers currently in the portfolio and explain the investment thesis for each.

26. Do you set price targets for all purchases? If yes, do you ever hold a bond beyond the initial price target? Explain.

27. Describe your portfolio construction procedures. Include detail on each of the following:

    a. What types of securities are considered for purchase?
    b. What is the universe of possible investments?
    c. Do you have a minimum number of holdings?
    d. What were the fewest and most holdings ever held in the portfolio? Indicate the appropriate dates.
    e. How are individual position weights determined?
    f. What is the maximum position size at cost and at market value for any individual position? Have you ever violated this constraint?
    g. List any portfolio constraints regarding geography, sector, industry, market cap, maturity, duration, and liquidity.

28. What is the minimum size a bond issue has to be for consideration for investment?

29. What, if any, bond issue size or size range do you prefer to invest in? Why?

30. What is your investment edge? What differentiates you from your competition? Include a list of the firms/products that you consider to be your biggest competitors.

31. Is there a sector or industry in which you believe your firm has a particular edge? If yes, please elaborate.

32. Describe your objectives, policies, and practices regarding the use of derivatives. Describe any restrictions and/or portfolio constraints you place on the use of derivatives.

33. In addition to the new issues market, how are new investment ideas generated?

34. What percentage of the portfolio is from the new market versus the secondary market?

35. How do you monitor the credit quality of the holdings in the portfolio? Do you make bets based on anticipated upgrades and/or downgrades?

36. Do you actively monitor the product's adherence to its stated investment style? If yes, please explain how this process is performed and with what frequency.

Risk Controls

37. Describe how you evaluate and monitor liquidity risk. Comment on how you would handle a "liquidity event."
38. Do you actively monitor and track the portfolio's duration, or is it a residual to the asset allocation and portfolio construction processes?
39. Describe your risk controls regarding credit quality, callability, interest rate volatility, and default losses.
40. If you invest in non-U.S.-dollar-denominated bonds, do you actively manage currency risk? If yes, please explain the process and methodology. Include any guidelines and/or restrictions you may have. If no, explain the impact that currency fluctuations have played on the product's historical track record.
41. Are cash and cash equivalents used as a means of risk control? If so, please elaborate.
42. Who is responsible for the product's risk management?
43. With what frequency are risk management reports created and evaluated by the appropriate personnel?
44. What (if any) systems do you have in place to help manage risk?
45. Do you employ any third parties to conduct regular or periodic risk analysis or generate risk reports? If yes, please provide a list of the firms' names and their specific functions.
46. What is the 1-day, 10-day, and 30-day VaR for the current portfolio?
47. Do you perform scenario analysis or stress testing of the portfolio? If yes, provide an example based on the most recent results. If no, please explain why not.
48. Do you manage the product based on specific benchmark tracking statistics? If so, please describe the benchmark and the acceptable benchmark tracking error ranges. How is the tracking error measured and monitored?

Fees/Minimum

49. What is the product's fee schedule?
50. Do you currently offer the same product to any entity based on a reduced fee scale? If yes, explain.
51. Has the fee schedule changed in the past three years?
52. What is the product's minimum account size?

Now that we have deleted the equity section of the questionnaire and replaced it with the preceding fixed income section, we can send it to any fixed income manager we may review. The remaining aspects of the investment manager analysis process closely resemble the equity manager process, with a few exceptions.

INTERVIEWING PROCESS

The interviewing process outlined previously with respect to equity manager analysis is the same conceptually in fixed income manager analysis (see Exhibit 14.6). We have to speak to one or more of the investment professionals before we make a decision to move ahead in the due diligence process. We also need to meet with the manager and/or analyst face-to-face and conduct a detailed on-site visit. The questions are mostly the same, with the only real difference coming from the differences in the underlying financial instruments.

ATTRIBUTION/STYLE ANALYSIS

As with the other steps in the due diligence process, the concept behind attribution and style analysis is basically the same in both equity and fixed income (see Exhibit 14.7). When conducting attribution analysis, we are simply trying to ascertain what the investment management team's skill set is by looking back on what has worked and what has not worked for the portfolio. Absolute attribution is a simple way of determining how a product's return is broken down. The absolute attribution results can tell us how much of a portfolio's return is due to investment type, sector, quality, maturity, and yield.

The relative attribution analysis will do the same thing as the absolute attribution analysis, but will focus on the portfolio's relative out/underperformance relative to some stated benchmark. Relative attribution can be thought of as a means of assessing a portfolio's value added over a benchmark or explaining the reasons why a portfolio has underperformed the benchmark.

The style analysis is a means of statistically determining or verifying a given portfolio's style. The style analysis can also help to select which benchmark or combination of benchmarks is best suited to the portfolio for comparative purposes.

Using the Sharpe style analysis that we defined and explained in detail

EXHIBIT 14.6 Comparison of Investment Manager Analysis Process by Asset Class—Initial Interview/On-Site Visit

	Analysis/Technique	Equity	Fixed Income
Initial interview		✖	✖
On-site visit		✖	✖

EXHIBIT 14.7 Comparison of Investment Manager Analysis Process by Asset Class—Attribution and Style Analysis

	Analysis/Technique	Equity	Fixed Income
Attribution Analysis	Absolute attribution	✖	✖
	• Sector	✖	✖
	• Industry	✖	✖
	• Geography	✖	✖
	• Market cap	✖	✖
	• Fundamental characteristics	✖	✖
	P/E	✖	—
	P/B	✖	—
	Earnings growth	✖	—
	Yield	✖	✖
	Duration	—	✖
	Maturity	—	✖
	Quality	—	✖
	Relative attribution	✖	✖
	• Sector	✖	✖
	• Industry	✖	✖
	• Geography	✖	✖
	• Market cap	✖	✖
	• Fundamental characteristics	✖	✖
	P/E	✖	—
	P/B	✖	—
	Earnings growth	✖	—
	Yield	✖	✖
	Duration	—	✖
	Maturity	—	✖
	Quality	—	✖
Style Analysis	Sharpe style optimization	✖	✖
	Sharpe style attribution	✖	✖

in Chapter 10, we can use the historical returns from a bond fund to see how the calculations apply to fixed income portfolios. The style worksheet highlighted in Exhibit 14.8 shows how the Sharpe style analysis regression works for a fixed income portfolio.

The fixed income portfolio has a track record that begins in January 1999 and has an investment objective of purchasing sovereign debt from G-10 countries. As a result, we would intuitively expect that the results of the style regression point toward a global bond benchmark.

As you can see from the optimized weights in the shaded box at the bottom of the return data, the Sharpe style regression optimized this

	A	B	C	D	E	F	G	H	I	J
1		Manager		Index Returns				Contribution to Performance		Squared Variables
2	Month	Portfolio	LB Agg	3moTbill	ML HY	SSB Wld	Style	Selection	Selection²	CAM²
3	Jan-99	−0.82	6.11	2.02	−1.36	−0.92	−0.69	−0.13	0.02	0.67
4	Feb-99	0.21	−3.92	−2.15	−9.83	−3.21	−3.81	4.01	16.10	0.04
5	Mar-99	4.96	4.84	3.03	2.88	0.25	0.78	4.17	17.43	24.59
6	Apr-99	3.35	−0.19	8.62	4.58	−0.04	1.25	2.10	4.40	11.20
7	May-99	−5.33	−2.92	−1.77	0.88	−1.68	−1.42	−3.91	15.31	28.44
8	Jun-99	1.01	7.16	3.84	5.32	−1.75	−0.49	1.50	2.24	1.01
9	Jul-99	−2.59	−3.16	−3.08	−0.24	2.45	1.65	−4.24	18.01	6.71
10	⋮	⋮	⋮	⋮	⋮	⋮	⋮	⋮	⋮	⋮
51	⋮	⋮	⋮	⋮	⋮	⋮	⋮	⋮	⋮	⋮
52	⋮	⋮	⋮	⋮	⋮	⋮	⋮	⋮	⋮	⋮
53	Mar-03	1.91	2.03	−0.13	1.91	0.31	0.44	1.47	2.16	3.63
54	Apr-03	4.32	6.70	9.89	7.15	1.20	2.63	1.69	2.84	18.63
55	May-03	5.10	3.26	7.36	6.76	4.34	4.87	0.23	0.05	26.05
56	Jun-03	−0.13	1.82	0.73	2.19	−1.62	−1.00	0.87	0.76	0.02
57	Average	0.86	−0.39	0.01	0.46	0.41	0.38	0.49	—	—
58	Sum	—	—	—	—	—	—	—	381.12	402.09
59										
60	Optimized Weights			Optimization Constraints						
61	LB Agg	0.00		1. Sum of optimized				RESULTS		
62	3moTbill	0.09		weights = 1						
63	ML HY	0.10		2. Optimized weights				% Return due to:		
64	SSB Wld	0.80		between 0 and 1				Style	5.2%	
65	Total	1.00						Selection	94.8%	
66										
67	Legend:							Average Contribution to Performance		
68	LB Agg = Lehman Aggregate Bond Index							Actual Return	0.86	
69	3moTbill - 3-month Treasury bill							Style	0.38	
70	ML HY = Merrill Lynch High Yield Bond Index							Selection	0.49	
71	SSB Wld = Salomon World Bond Index (USD)									
72										

EXHIBIT 14.8   Sample Style Analysis

portfolio's style index as 80% Salomon World Bond Index, 10% Merrill Lynch High Yield Index, and 9% three-month Treasury bills. The total adds to 99% due to rounding. Just like we have seen in the equity version of the Sharpe style analysis, the results are very close to the portfolio's underlying objectives.

Once we verified that the portfolio was best described by the Salomon World Bond Index, we could take the analysis to the next level by focusing the benchmarks (independent variables) on the individual country-level returns that comprise the Salomon World Bond Index. The goal would be to make an assessment of which regional and country-specific returns best fit the portfolio's historical return stream. This can help us to better evaluate the manager's asset allocation and prepare us for any conversations we may have with the investment firm regarding historical performance and allocations.

INVESTMENT MANAGER SCORING MODEL

Exhibit 14.9 lists the sections that make up the investment manager scoring model. The model was designed to be "most things to most people." In other words, its design can easily accommodate evaluations of investment products across a wide array of asset classes. If you read through the de-

EXHIBIT 14.9 Comparison of Investment Manager Analysis Process by Asset Class—Manager Scorecard

	Analysis/Technique	Equity	Fixed Income
Manager Scorecard	Six broad categories	✖	✖
	• Investment Professionals	✖	✖
	• Process	✖	✖
	• Portfolio Risk	✖	✖
	• Performance-Related Risk/Reward	✖	✖
	• Organization	✖	✖
	• Operations	✖	✖
	Thirty individual factors	✖	✖

scriptions of each of the 30 variables, you will quickly see that they were written in a relatively generic manner. The same can be said of the definitions for the six scoring gradations (from zero through 5) that can be placed on any given factor. However, the beauty of the model lies in its flexibility. Exhibit 14.10 is a summary of the model's weights according to the six broad sections.

Each section's weight is fixed regardless of the asset class of the product under review. The model makes the assumption that the investment staff is just as important in the management of an equity product as the investment staff managing a fixed income product. Even quantitatively oriented products are scored in the same manner. Despite the fact that quantitatively based products tend to have a heavy reliance on mathematical models and computer systems, the models and systems did not invent themselves—people did. As such, the people in charge of quantitative products are still integral to their future success (or failure).

EXHIBIT 14.10 Manager Scoring Model Summary

Section	Model Weight	Number of Factors
Investment Professionals	30%	5
Process	15%	4
Portfolio Risk	15%	5
Performance-Related Risk/Reward	15%	5
Organization	15%	7
Operations	10%	4
Total	100%	30

The interpretation of product scores remains constant from one asset class to another (see Exhibit 14.11). A product that scores higher than 80 should generally be considered exceptional regardless of the underlying asset class. The model is flexible because the individual factors and their underlying grade definitions are automatically transferable from equity manager analysis to fixed income manager analysis. To illustrate this point, I have selected one factor from each section.

Investment Professionals

Factor 1: Direct Product Experience   This factor asks the question: How many years of relevant experience does the person or team managing the product in question have? The critical differentiating word is "relevant."

Score/Methodology

0   No experience managing a portfolio or in any investment-related capacity.

1   Key decision maker(s) have less than one year of actual portfolio management experience relating specifically to the product under review.

2   Key decision maker(s) have one to two years of actual portfolio management experience relating specifically to the product under review.

3   Key decision maker(s) have three to five years of actual portfolio management experience relating specifically to the product under review.

4   Key decision maker(s) have six to nine years of actual portfolio management experience relating specifically to the product under review.

5   Key investment decision maker(s) have greater than 10 years of actual portfolio management experience relating specifically to the product under review.

EXHIBIT 14.11   Overall Model Scoring

Score	Interpretation
Greater than 80	Exceptional
75 to 80	Excellent
65 to 75	Above average
60 to 65	Average
Less than 60	Poor

Commentary A quick read through factor 1's description sets the tone. This factor is asking the reviewer to make an assessment of the person or team's level of experience based on background(s) managing or conducting research/analysis for the asset class in which the product under review is focused. The grades, which range from 0 (worst) to 5 (best) allow the reviewer to clearly draw a line in the sand with respect to that experience. The grades are based simply on the number of years that the person or team managed similar assets. If we are talking about a team, we basically take a weighted average of the individual team members' experience. The weighting factor in this case would be importance within the team structure. For a example, the lead portfolio manager would receive a higher weight than a junior analyst.

Process

Factor 6: Consistent Application This factor measures how consistently the team applies the stated process. The theory behind this factor is that a product that is managed in a more consistent manner will have a better chance of repeating past successes than a product that is managed inconsistently. In addition, it is easier to understand and monitor the progress of a product that is managed in a consistent manner.

Score/Methodology

0 No discernible process.
1 Frequent breaks in the application of the process based on the whims of the management team.
2 Process has shifted over time, but management has reasonable explanations.
3 Reasonably consistent and dependable application of the process.
4 Consistent process with occasional deviations.
5 Strict adherence to process—no exceptions made. Long history of consistent application.

Commentary As with the previous example, the language allows for an evaluation regardless of the product under review. Naturally, when making the determination of process consistency, the reviewer must assess the product under review based on the fundamentals and characteristics of the underlying asset class. When reviewing an equity manager, the reviewer must look for the consistent application based on equity characteristics, including market cap, P/E, ROE, earnings growth, and so on. When reviewing a fixed income manager, the language remains the same, but the underlying characteristics change to things such as credit quality, duration, and yield.

Portfolio Risk

Factor 10: Diversification   A portfolio can be diversified in a number of ways: number of individual positions, sectors, industries, or fundamental characteristics. This factor is meant to grade the portfolio under review based on the underlying asset class. For example, a bond portfolio should not be considered undiversified because it focuses solely on high yield issues. However, a portfolio that is mandated to invest exclusively in high yield debt can receive a lower grade if it is highly concentrated in a single sector or industry. When grading this measure, it is important to give slightly more weight to current portfolio exposures, but not to forget about historical diversification.

A portfolio that is currently highly diversified should receive a high grade, but that grade should be scaled back if the portfolio has been highly concentrated in the past. It is also important to consider portfolio investments in the same underlying company across the capital structure (equity, warrants, bonds). Lastly, this grade should not be made based on deviations from an index. The purpose of the manager scoring model is to measure a manager's skill and the overall level of appropriateness of the portfolio—not to see who is a closet indexer. Diversifiers are defined as any measure of diversification directly related to the portfolio under review. The broader a product's investment mandate, the more diversifiers. While the opposite is true for products with narrow investment mandates, that does not mean that there are not enough diversifiers to make clear distinctions for comparative purposes.

Score/Methodology

0   Highly concentrated. Manager does not have portfolio risk measures in place.

1   Concentrated in two of the diversifiers. Manager does not have portfolio risk measures in place.

2   Concentrated in two of the diversifiers. Manager has some level of portfolio risk controls in place.

3   Concentrated in one of the diversifiers. Manager has good portfolio risk measures in place.

4   Reasonable level of diversification across all possible diversifiers. Manager has good portfolio risk measures in place.

5   Highly diversified with strong risk measures in place.

Commentary   The definition of this variable is pretty straightforward. We are looking to make an assessment of a product's overall level of diversification based not just on current statistics, but also on the product's historical allocations. When looking at equity products, we focus on one set of diversifiers; when looking at fixed income, we focus on a different set of diversifiers.

Performance-Related Risk/Reward

Factor 15: Performance Relative to Benchmark For actively managed products, it is always useful to compare the performance (net of all fees) of the product under review to the appropriate benchmark. While it can be difficult at times to select a specific benchmark to match each and every portfolio that you might measure, generally most products have a reasonably good benchmark that can be used for comparative purposes. When arriving at a grade for historical performance relative to the stated benchmark, I generally look at performance over several time periods (one year, three years, five years, since inception). For products with short track records, I review the actual performance record for whatever time frame is available, score them based on that record, then penalize products in the following way:

■ Track record less than three years (subtract one point). *As a result, the maximum score is 4.*
■ Track record less than two years (subtract two points). *As a result, the maximum score is 3.*
■ Track record less than one year (subtract three points). *As a result, the maximum score is 2.*

Score/Methodology
0   Historical performance relative to appropriate benchmark is more than 5% below the benchmark.
1   Historical performance relative to appropriate benchmark is between 3% and 5% below the benchmark.
2   Historical performance relative to appropriate benchmark is between 1% and 3% below the benchmark.
3   Historical performance relative to appropriate benchmark is roughly equivalent (may be a little above or below).
4   Historical performance relative to appropriate benchmark is between 1% and 5% above the benchmark.
5   Historical performance relative to appropriate benchmark is more than 5% above the benchmark.

Commentary Performance analysis is asset class agnostic as long as the product's performance is put into proper perspective. Performance evaluations should be made against benchmarks that are representative of the product's asset class and style. We would use a high yield benchmark to evaluate the performance of a high yield product; we would use a global index to evaluate the performance of a global bond product; and so on.

Organization

Factor 20: Turnover   This factor refers to turnover of non-investment-related employees, not portfolio turnover. Non-investment-related employees include marketing, client service, administrative, and legal. The grade is subjective and must take into consideration the reasons for the employees' departures. For example, if an employee leaves to become a stay-at-home mom/dad, the firm being reviewed should not be penalized. However, an employee's departure based on compensation issues is another thing entirely.

Score/Methodology

0   Loss of more than two key employees.
1   Loss of two key employees.
2   Loss of one key employee in past year.
3   Loss of one key employee in past two years.
4   Very low turnover—loss of one key employee in past three years; any other employee departures were due principally to reasons beyond the firm's control.
5   Never lost an employee.

Operations

Factor 27: Reconciliation/Administration   This factor refers to the accuracy and timeliness of the portfolio accounting function. Whether investing in a separate account or some pool of assets (limited partnership, commingled trust), it is essential that the portfolio accounting function accurately reconcile the portfolio on a timely basis. While it is difficult to make an assessment of this function prior to actually hiring a firm, it is possible to form a reasonable opinion based on strategic questioning and through the reference checks. When I contact references provided to me by the firm, I generally spend the bulk of my time on the phone with them discussing operational and organizational issues. I prefer to address most of the investment-related questions myself during the analytical phase of the due diligence process. I don't need the references to tell me how wonderful the portfolio is (I do my own portfolio analysis) or how superb the performance is (I likewise run a series of performance-related statistics as well). I find it more useful to ask for information that I generally can't get in the due diligence process.

Score/Methodology

0   Unacceptable.
1   Scattered.
2   Below average.
3   Generally accurate and timely.
4   Above average.
5   Among the best in the business and always getting better.

Commentary   The examples from the organization and operations sections are obviously relevant to any firm under review because they are concerned with organizational and back-office functions.

REFERENCES AND BACKGROUND CHECKS

Before hiring any investment firm or investment manager, you should make a point of conducting some base level of reference and background checks. Ask the investment professionals who manage the product to furnish at least two references. I generally like to speak to a current/former client and to a former business associate. When talking to references, bear in mind that they will likely paint a pretty rosy picture of the performer whose references you are checking (that's why you were given their names in the first place). Don't be embarrassed to ask any of the questions that I outlined in Chapter 13. I have found out plenty from calling these handpicked references over the years.

Chapter 13 also outlines the process for checking into a person's background. I personally do not conduct complete background checks on anyone. I hire professional investigative firms to do this for me. But I do conduct spot checks when I do not feel a complete check is needed. A spot check can be a simple verification of an individual's educational background, a check of employment history, or a verification of any professional certifications or designations listed in a biography.

PART

Three

Alternative Investment Manager Analysis

## CHAPTER 15

Hedge Fund Manager Analysis

Hedge funds were initially invented to address the issue of portfolio risk. However, in the wake of several spectacular hedge fund failures (such as Long-Term Capital Management), the term *hedge fund* has become perceived as synonymous with excessive risk Because of these high-profile blowups and the fact that most hedge funds shun the spotlight, mainstream news regarding hedge funds has been a bit skewed toward the negative side. Nothing could be further than the truth.

A hedge fund can best be defined as a commingled or pooled investment vehicle that is privately organized and managed by professional investment managers. Hedge funds are different from mutual funds because they are available only to wealthy individuals (who meet strict criteria) and institutional managers. However, the biggest difference between hedge funds and mutual funds is that hedge funds are able to sell securities short and employ leverage to amplify potential returns. In addition, hedge funds often use derivatives to adjust portfolio and/or position risk levels. U.S. hedge funds are exempt from SEC reporting requirements, as well as from regulatory restrictions concerning leverage or trading strategies.

The preceding definition is not very specific—by design. Hedge funds, in general, can cover dozens of broad strategic categories and can appear anywhere on the risk/return curve depending on the underlying strategy, style, and investment objectives. As a result, hedge funds can be different things to different people. To some, hedge funds represent "return diversifiers," and to others they may represent "return enhancers." The former can be used to help minimize risk, while the latter can be used to generate excess returns.

Regardless of how hedge funds are defined, they tend to exhibit a number of similar traits:

■ Hedge funds tend to have a focus on absolute returns instead of relative returns.
■ Hedge fund managers have a broader range of financial instruments available to them for investment.

- Hedge funds have significantly fewer investment constraints, and can employ derivatives, short selling, leverage, and so on.
- Hedge funds typically provide less transparency than traditionally managed investment products.
- Hedge funds typically have low correlation with traditional asset classes, such as long-only equity and fixed income.
- Hedge funds have a base plus incentive fee structure whereas traditional investment products tend to charge a base fee only.
- Hedge fund managers tend to have ownership in the investment firm and have a large portion of their own capital invested in their funds.

The long and short (pun intended) is that hedge funds are designed to perform well in both up and down market environments. This focus on "absolute" performance is quite different from traditionally managed investment products. Traditional long-only investment products are often managed to perform well relative to some stated benchmark. As a result, traditional investment products are often thought to have performed well when they outperform their stated benchmark—even when their returns are negative. For example, a traditional long-only equity product would likely be considered to have performed well if it declined 10% when its benchmark declined 12% (a 2% relative performance advantage). Hedge funds do not generally rely on benchmark comparisons. In fact, most hedge funds could not care less about benchmarks. They focus on what they do best and hedge to ensure that returns are positive—regardless of the market environment.

As a result, is might be fair to say that hedge funds represent a purer application of an investment manager's skills. For example, a traditional equity manager might not like a particular stock, but might be forced to hold it in client accounts because it is a large component in the comparative index. In this instance, the decision not to hold the stock could negatively impact that manager's ability to outperform the index for a given period of time. Hedge fund managers, in contrast, have no index constraints and are essentially free to invest in the manner they see fit (staying within their stated investment objectives and guidelines, of course).

Hedge funds can also benefit in poor market environments by establishing short positions or carrying a net short exposure for the entire portfolio. "Net short" means that when the value of the long and short positions are added together (long positions are positive, while short positions are negative) the sum is negative. In this instance, the underlying hedge fund might be in a good position if the market falls.

The table in Exhibit 15.1 highlights the performance of the Credit Suisse First Boston (CSFB)/Tremont Hedge Fund Index and its component strategies against the S&P 500 index and the MSCI World index.

EXHIBIT 15.1 Historical Hedge Fund Performance

Credit Suisse First Boston/Tremont Index
Data through December 31, 2003

| | | Cumulative | | | Since Inception (1/94) | | Sharpe |
	1 Year	3 Years	5 Years	Cumulative	Cumulative	Annualized	Ratio
Hedge Fund Index	**15.4**	**24.2**	**60.7**		**186.9**	**11.1**	**0.8**
Hedge Fund Strategies							
Equity Long/Short	17.3	11.2	67.1		214.9	12.2	0.7
Dedicated Short	−32.6	−23.2	−23.8		−27.6	−3.2	−0.4
Equity Market Neutral	7.1	25.7	66.7		175.2	10.7	0.2
Convertible Arbitrage	12.9	34.6	96.2		171.2	10.5	1.3
Global Macro	18.0	60.2	89.3		286.2	14.5	0.9
Fixed Income Arbitrage	8.0	23.4	47.0		93.1	6.8	0.7
Emerging Markets	28.8	46.3	100.2		98.6	7.1	0.2
Event Driven	20.0	34.0	75.7		194.3	11.4	1.2
Risk Arbitrage	9.0	11.2	44.4		124.5	8.4	1.0
Distressed	25.1	49.1	85.7		251.5	13.4	1.3
Multistrategy Event Driven	17.2	26.7	74.3		166.5	10.3	1.0
S&P 500 Index	28.7	−11.7	−2.8		185.6	11.1	0.4
MSCI World Index	33.8	−10.2	−1.9		107.7	7.6	0.2

The returns show that for the three and five years ended December 2003, the long-only equity benchmarks had negative performance. The broad hedge fund index, in contrast, had positive performance over all the time periods shown.

Over the past 10 years, the S&P 500 index experienced three calendar-year declines: −9.1% in 2000, −11.9% in 2001, and −22.1% in 2002. The MSCI World Index also experienced negative returns in those three years: −12.9% in 2000, −16.5% in 2001, and −19.5% in 2002. The CSFB/Tremont Hedge Fund Index, though, turned in positive performance in that three-year period: 4.9% in 2000, 4.4% in 2001, and 3.0% in 2002. While not shown in Exhibit 15.1, the only times the Hedge Fund Index declined were in 1994 (−4.4%) and 1998 (−0.4%). These figures make a simplistic case for the inclusion of hedge fund strategies in a total portfolio because of the diversification they provide when paired with traditional asset classes.

Over the 10-year period beginning in January 1994 and ending in December 2003, the CSFB/Tremont Hedge Fund Index exhibited a low level of correlation compared to the standard equity benchmarks (see Exhibit 15.2).

With the exception of the Nasdaq, the Hedge Fund Index had 10-year correlation statistics below 0.50. These statistics are just for the broad Hedge Fund Index versus the major equity benchmarks, as many of the different strategies that make up the Hedge Fund Index have much lower (or negative) correlations when compared to traditional equity benchmarks.

Exhibit 15.1 also provides data regarding Sharpe ratios for the broad Hedge Fund Index, its subcategories, and the traditional equity benchmarks. Looking at the column on the far right, it should be immediately noticed that the broad Hedge Fund Index's 0.80 Sharpe ratio is

EXHIBIT 15.2 CSFB/Tremont Hedge Fund Index—Correlation Table

Correlation Table Jan 1994 to Dec 2003	
	CSFB/Tremont Hedge Fund Index
Dow	0.40
MSCI World	0.47
MSCI EAFE	0.41
S&P 500	0.47
Nasdaq	0.53

twice that of the S&P 500 and four times that of the MSCI World. In fact, several of the individual hedge fund strategies listed in the table have Sharpe ratios far greater than that of the overall Hedge Fund Index itself. The convertible arbitrage and distressed strategies had 10-year Sharpe ratios of 1.3, followed closely by several other strategies that had Sharpe ratios above 1.0.

HEDGE FUND HISTORY

While the concept of hedging investment risk has been around for quite some time, the actual term *hedge fund* is of more recent origin. Alfred Winslow Jones, who is considered the grandfather of the hedge fund industry, coined the term in 1949. Jones, a reporter for *Fortune* magazine, wrote an article stating that investors could achieve better, more stable returns by incorporating hedging techniques alongside traditional buy and sell strategies.

Jones created the first hedge fund general partnership in 1949 and a few years later converted it to a limited partnership. The initial fund started with $100,000 in capital, $40,000 of which was Jones'. Jones also added a 20% incentive (performance) fee based on the profits he was able to generate for the limited partners. Jones managed his hedge fund in virtual anonymity from its inception to 1966, when *Fortune* magazine published an article titled "The Jones that Nobody Can Keep Up With." The article pointed out some startling statistics. For example, Jones' fund had outperformed the best-performing mutual fund by more than 85% (net of fees) over the five years from 1962 to 1966.

The *Fortune* article caused a bit of frenzy as investors sought to invest in this new fund structure and professional money managers started their own hedge funds to take advantage of the favorable fee schedule. As a result, nearly 200 hedge funds came into existence between 1966 and 1968. The only problem was that many of the new funds that called themselves hedge funds were not hedge funds at all. Many of them did not sell short (or hedge) their portfolios and had taken on leverage to amplify returns. While this may work in good equity markets (markets that are rising), it can be disastrous when the market turns bearish—which is exactly what happened in the 1969–1970 and 1973–1974 periods. As a result, a great many hedge funds went out of business and new hedge funds had a hard time raising money so soon after the recent bloodletting. Things had gotten so bad in the hedge fund industry that by the mid-1980s fewer than 100 hedge funds were up and running.

The next twist in the hedge fund saga came in the late 1980s and early 1990s, when the successful exploits of hedge fund legends such as George

Soros, Julian Robertson, Michael Steinhardt, and Leon Cooperman piqued investors' imaginations, starting a slow and steady migration of assets back into hedge fund strategies. Hedge funds in the 1990s took the Jones model of hedge fund investing and created a variety of offshoots, which included currencies, futures, options, and so on. The equity long/short model was no longer the only game in town, as hedge fund strategies were expanded to include strategies such as global macro, fixed income arbitrage, and merger arbitrage, among others. As the hedge fund industry began to grow once again, it was being funded largely by high-net-worth individuals, instead of the professionally managed institutional pension plans and funds.

HEDGE FUND STRATEGY EVOLUTION

The hedge fund market's structure in the early 1990s was very different from the way it is structured today. The majority of the hedge funds available for investment were what are known as "global macro" funds. These global macro funds often have extremely broad mandates that can shift a fund's focus from Asian currencies one month to European bonds the next. We will define each of the hedge fund strategies later in the chapter and list the questions that you should ask each type of hedge fund manager when conducting due diligence.

As seen in Exhibit 15.3, the pie that represents 1990 clearly indicates that the hedge fund universe was dominated by global macro funds (71%). This was followed by equity long/short funds (16%) and risk arbitrage (4%). These three strategies made up more than 90% of the universe back then; the remainder of the strategies made up the difference.

However, the tide shifted from pure alpha-driven global macro funds in the early 1990s toward more risk-conscious strategies aimed at adding an additional layer of diversification to investors' total portfolios. Global macro strategies fell from 71% in 1990 to just 15% in 2001.

HEDGE FUND STRATEGIES

In order to perform due diligence on a specific hedge fund, it is critical that the investment manager analyst have a thorough understanding of the underlying strategy or strategies that the hedge fund manager employs in the management of the fund under review. Because hedge funds cover such a wide array of investment strategies, techniques, and financial instruments, due diligence can be significantly more complicated and involved. This section of the chapter will define each of the major hedge fund strategies, explain how they work, and offer specific examples for further emphasis.

1990

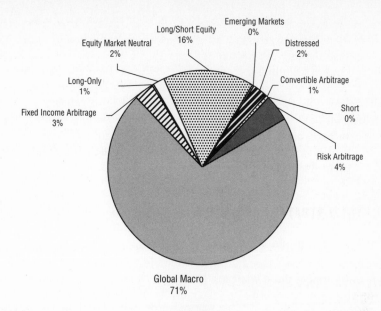

2001

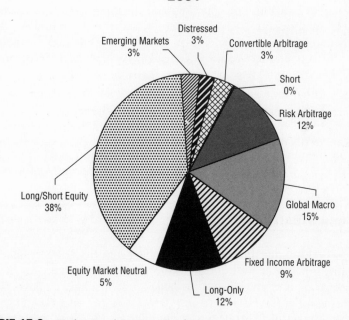

EXHIBIT 15.3 Hedge Fund Strategy Evolution
Source: Undiscovered Managers: Alternative Investments and the Semi-Affluent Investor, Chapter 2: "Absolute Return Strategies."

Once we have finished defining each of the strategies, the next section of this chapter will list a series of specific questions that can be addressed to hedge fund managers during the due diligence process. Exhibit 15.4 highlights each of the major hedge fund strategies and places them within defined risk categories.

Based on a simplistic form of risk, standard deviation, the major hedge fund strategies fall into one of the three risk categories. Lower-risk strategies are represented by strategies that had annualized 10-year standard deviations less than 5%. Of the four strategies that fall into this risk category, equity market neutral had the lowest annualized standard deviation, at 3.1%. The higher-risk strategies are represented by strategies that had annualized 10-year standard deviations in excess of 10%. Of the four strategies that fall into this category, emerging markets exhibited the highest standard deviation, at 23.8%. The middle level is represented by strategies that fall in between the other two (5% to 10%).

Equity Long/Short Strategy

As the name implies, equity long/short funds have the ability to purchase stocks long and/or sell stocks short. A hedge fund manager can look to add alpha (generate gains) on both the long and short positions (double alpha) or can hedge a position's market exposure by shorting a position that has a high correlation to it or is in the same industry/sector. An example of double alpha would be when a portfolio manager buys shares of IBM because in the belief that it will rise in price and sells shares of GE because he feels it is overvalued and will likely fall in price. The two trades are done independently of one another and each was made to generate gains for the fund. An example of a hedged position (paired trade) would be if the same portfolio manager bought shares in IBM based on the belief that it was undervalued and would rise in price, but rather than selling GE short, sold Cisco short because the two stocks (IBM and Cisco) are highly correlated. The paired

Risk*		
Lower		**Higher**
Standard Deviation < 5%	*Standard Deviation from 5% to 10%*	*Standard Deviation > 10%*
Convertible Arbitrage	Distressed	Equity Long/Short
Fixed Income Arbitrage	Multistrategy Event Driven	Dedicated Long and Short
Equity Market Neutral		Global Macro
Risk Arbitrage		Emerging Markets

EXHIBIT 15.4 Hedge Fund Strategy Risk Categories
*Risk is defined as variability of returns (standard deviation).

trade attempts to nullify the impact of market moves (systematic risk) by buying and simultaneously selling two stocks that move in the same direction when the market/sector moves up or down. The resulting gain or loss is then due exclusively to the investment manager's stock selection skill.

Equity long/short managers are typically thought of as taking directional bets on the market based on the fund's net exposure.

$$\text{Net Exposure} = \frac{\text{Longs} - \text{Shorts}}{\text{Fund Capital}}$$

For example, a hedge fund with $100 million in long positions and $50 million in short positions is said to be 50% net long. This means that the fund will likely benefit when the market moves up and may take a hit when the market moves down. For a hedge fund with a net short exposure, it would be the opposite. Generally, when the market moves up, hedge funds that pair trades will typically lag the performance of their long-only peers; and when the market moves down, they tend to fall less than long-only funds (and sometimes even rise in value). The funds that look to pair their trades in an attempt to hedge out market risk generally fall under the "relative value" heading. Hedge funds that look to add alpha on both the long and short side can be viewed as more opportunistic than seeking relative value because their shorts, in theory, can make money in an up market environment and their longs can make money in a down market environment. However, there is no guarantee that this will actually happen, so these opportunistic funds are thought to carry more risk than equity long/short funds that attempt to hedge out market risk. The graph in Exhibit 15.5 illustrates this point nicely. In the 1995 to 1999 bull market, the

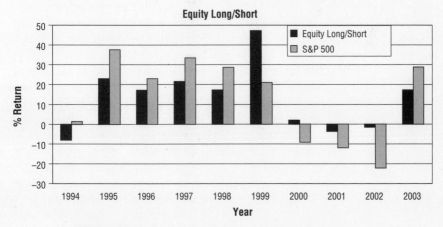

EXHIBIT 15.5 Equity Long/Short—Calendar Year Returns
Source: CSFB Tremont.

S&P 500 index rose significantly each year. With the exception of 1999, the equity long/short funds lagged each calendar year. However, when the market turned negative in the 2000 to 2002 period, the equity long/short funds fell significantly less than the long-only index. In fact, the equity long/short funds actually gained 2.1% versus a −9.1% loss for the S&P 500 in 2000. In 2003, the up market pattern returned, with the S&P performing very well and, thus, outperforming the long/short group

Equity long/short funds typically borrow money (taking on leverage) to amplify returns. A fund's gross exposure indicates how much leverage the fund has taken on.

$$\text{Gross Exposure} = \frac{\text{Longs} + \text{Shorts}}{\text{Fund Capital}}$$

If a hedge fund has $100 million in long positions and another $50 million in short positions with contributed fund capital of $100 million, the fund is said to have gross exposure of 150% or 1.5×.

In this strategy, a gross exposure of 200% (2.0×) and above is generally thought to be high compared to the universe of peer funds. The higher the leverage, the more risk that the fund and its investors assume.

Convertible Arbitrage Strategy

A convertible bond is a bond that can be converted to a specific number of shares of the underlying company's stock. A convertible bond arbitrageur will typically purchase a position in a convertible bond (long position) and sell short a specific number of shares in the stock of the underlying company. Because convertible bonds exhibit characteristics of both equity and bonds, their valuation must properly reflect both types of securities. When the equity market is falling, convertible bonds tend to fall less than the equity shares in its underlying company stock (see Exhibit 15.6). However, when the equity market is rising, they tend to follow the movement of the underlying company stock more closely. In other words, convertible bonds generally enjoy much of the upside in the movement of the underlying company stock, but protect (hedge) against a good portion of the downside. It is this relationship that hedge fund managers attempt to exploit when constructing convertible bond portfolios or individual trades.

To properly analyze investment managers that employ convertible bond strategies, it is important to understand some of the techniques used to value convertible positions. As stated previously, a convertible bond is a hybrid between equity and fixed income instruments. The fixed income component of a convertible bond's valuation is referred to as its

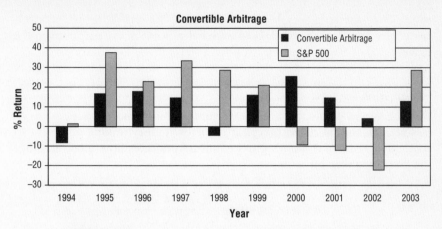

EXHIBIT 15.6 Convertible Arbitrage—Calendar Year Return
Source: CSFB Tremont.

"investment value." The investment value can be considered the lowest value for a given convertible bond if the value of the underlying company stock were to fall to zero. Exceptions to this rule are referred to as "busted convertibles," which represent the bonds of a company that has experienced a downgrade in quality ratings due to some form of fundamental deterioration.

Changes in interest rates also have an impact on convertible bonds just as they do for standard corporate and/or Treasury bonds. An increase in interest rates will have a negative impact on the price of existing convertible bonds, and a decrease in rates will have a positive impact.

A convertible bond that has a market value in excess of its investment value is said to be trading at a premium. A large premium results from a high valuation of the underlying company stock. When the underlying stock is rising, the convertible bond generally mimics the rise in the stock's price. When the underlying stock is falling, the convertible bond tends to mimic the decrease in price, but starts to act more like the bond as its total value approaches that of its investment value (the bond component's valuation).

The conversion price is the price an investor receives to convert the bonds to equity, and the conversion ratio is calculated by taking the par value of the bond as a percentage of its stated conversion price. Since we have already defined how to calculate the value of the bond component, we can calculate the value of the equity component by multiplying the conversion ratio by the current market price of the underlying company's common stock.

If we take the difference between the current price of a convertible bond and its conversion value and divide the result by the conversion value, we will have calculated what is known as the "conversion premium."

$$\text{Conversion Premium} = \frac{\text{Bond's Current Price} - \text{Bond's Conversion Value}}{\text{Bond's Conversion Value}}$$

The conversion premium can essentially be thought of as the value of the option to convert the bond to common stock.

A convertible bond manager can create three types of hedges when constructing convertible bond portfolios or individual positions:

1. *Neutral hedge.* A neutral hedge is called a "delta" neutral hedge. Delta is a statistical calculation that measures how the price of a convertible bond will react to changes in the price of the underlying stock.
2. *Bullish hedge.* This is a long-biased hedge that is achieved by selling short fewer shares than would be necessary to engage in a neutral hedge. A bullish hedge allows the fund to take advantage of the increase in the bond's price that follows the increase in the price of the underlying stock. However, by doing so, the fund is exposed to more potential downside because the hedge will not fully offset any downward price moves.
3. *Bearish hedge.* This is the opposite of a bullish hedge. The fund manager effectively shorts more of the common stock than is needed to be neutral. A convertible hedge fund manager might enact a bearish hedge when he believes that the price of the underlying stock will decline.

Hedge ratios are important to get right when setting up the initial trades, but they also need to be dynamically adjusted to reflect changes in the price of the underlying financial instruments. A perfectly neutral hedge on Monday might become less perfect as prices change throughout a given week. As a result, fund managers often have to sell additional shares short or cover some of the existing short positions depending on price shifts.

Convertible bond managers can also employ leverage to amplify portfolio/position returns. However, higher levels of leverage can add additional risk to the underlying portfolio. Just as with equity long/short funds, it is important to evaluate the amount of leverage that a convertible bond manager takes in comparison to other convertible bond funds.

Fixed Income Arbitrage Strategy

Fixed income arbitrage involves the simultaneous purchase of a bond that is considered to be undervalued and the shorting of a similar type of bond that is considered to be overvalued. Unlike equity long/short, where the valuation spread can be quite wide, the spread in fixed income arbitrage trades is often based on a few basis points. As a result, leverage is often employed to amplify the modest spreads to something more meaningful (see Exhibit 15.7).

One of the key characteristics of fixed income arbitrage strategies is that the offsetting trades need to be made with investments that are similar. This is done so that when rates rise or fall, the impact of the rate change on the long position will effectively be neutralized by the change on the short position. The only thing that remains is the valuation spread that was initially identified. When the two positions converge on their predetermined fair prices, the positions are unwound and the profit is locked in. Fixed income arbitrageurs do not normally take directional bets; instead they rely on their ability to properly identify bonds that are cheap and bonds that are expensive.

Fixed income arbitrage managers generally rely on advanced computer models to identify pricing disparities and to create paired trades that effectively neutralize the impact of exogenous factors.

Some of the most prevalent types of trades performed by fixed income arbitrage managers include:

- *Basis trades*—simultaneous purchase of bonds and the sale of futures contracts on those bonds.
- *Asset swaps*—the purchase of a bond and the simultaneous swapping of that bond's fixed-rate cash flows for another bond's floating-rate cash flows.

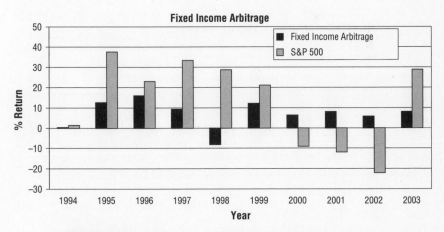

EXHIBIT 15.7 Fixed Income Arbitrage—Calendar Year Returns
Source: CSFB Tremont.

- *Yield curve arbitrage*—simultaneous purchase and short sale of bonds that are positioned at different points on the yield curve.
- *Relative value trades*—trades that are designed to take advantage of pricing differentials between bonds in different sectors and/or points on the yield curve.

Equity Market Neutral Strategy

In its simplest form, equity market neutral funds hold a large number of long and short positions in the equity market with roughly an equal dollar amount of both longs and shorts. The result is referred to as a dollar neutral portfolio. By holding a large number of securities and matching the dollar exposure of the long and short positions, the equity market neutral manager attempts to negate any systematic (market) effects on the portfolio. The resulting portfolio will rise in value if the return of the long positions is greater than the return of the short positions. Because market effects are hedged out, these funds can theoretically achieve consistent returns in both positive and negative market environments (see Exhibit 15.8).

Many equity market neutral funds extend the definition of neutrality to include a wide variety of factors, including:

- *Beta neutral.* A fund that is beta neutral should be effectively insensitive to changes in the overall stock market or to a specific index, such as the S&P 500.
- *Style neutral.* A fund that is style neutral should be indifferent to style-specific factors and/or cycles by being long one style (value for example) and short an equal amount in the offsetting style (such as growth).

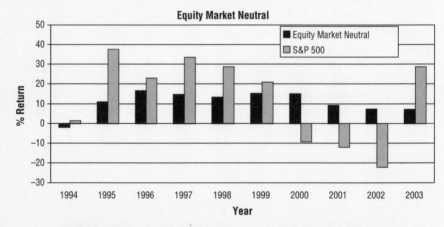

EXHIBIT 15.8 Equity Market Neutral—Calendar Year Returns
Source: CSFB Tremont.

■ *Sector neutral.* A fund that is sector neutral will simultaneously purchase a specified dollar amount within each sector and offset the sector exposure by shorting an equal amount in each sector.

■ *Market capitalization.* A fund that is market cap neutral will be impervious to large- and small-cap cycles.

Equity market neutral managers tend to rely on fairly sophisticated computer models to identify longs and shorts and to effectively hedge out any of the relevant factor exposures based on historical relationships.

Global Macro Strategy

Global macro hedge funds focus on macroeconomic opportunities across multiple markets and financial instruments. Managers in this strategy do not make bets in individual stocks based on fundamental research; rather, they make bets on entire countries, markets, currencies, and so on. Some of the factors that global macro managers focus on include changes in government policy, interest rates, currencies, inflation, stock and bond market volatility, and labor issues. As a result, decisions made by fund managers in this strategy are considered to be made from the top down.

Global macro managers look to find an imbalance or disparity between a specific market's or financial instrument's perceived value and its actual value. However, these types of imbalances occur irregularly and infrequently, so the managers often elect to utilize a variety of other strategies while waiting for the next big directional bet.

Because this strategy relies on large directional bets and can often involve a fair degree of leverage, these funds tend to be more volatile than most other hedge fund strategies (see Exhibit 15.9). Of all the hedge fund strategies listed at the beginning of the chapter, only emerging markets and dedicated short strategies had a higher level of standard deviation over the past 10 years.

Global macro funds can be among the hardest funds in which to conduct due diligence because of the infrequency and the variability of the directional bets that the fund manager or team makes over time. For example, a global macro fund might make three of four large bets in any given year. Those three or four bets might all be in different countries, asset classes, or financial instruments. To illustrate this point, let's look at the following conceptual trades for a global macro fund manager in a given year:

■ *February:* Made a large bet on the Japanese yen versus the U.S. dollar based on a bet that the Japanese government would buy yen in the immediate future to prop up its value.

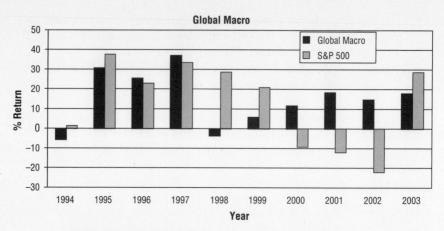

EXHIBIT 15.9 Global Macro—Calendar Year Returns
Source: CSFB Tremont.

- *June:* Made a large bet on the price of crude oil based on internal projections that Russia would be dumping excess oil in the marketplace in late summer and early fall season to help fund a variety of political initiatives.
- *September:* Made large bet on the debt of several Eastern European nations based on the premise that they were spectacularly undervalued and would experience a pop based on a variety of economic projections.

Because each of these trades (bets) is so different from the others, it is very difficult to make any kind of assessment of the manager's consistent ability to identify and act on various market inefficiencies. Unlike each of the other strategies discussed thus far, global macro managers often do not have a single systematic approach that we can evaluate. Many managers in this strategy rely on several (and sometimes dozens of) different economic and financial models to determine if imbalances exist across a wide variety of markets and financial instruments.

Risk (Merger) Arbitrage Strategy

Risk or merger arbitrage funds specialize in mergers and acquisitions, hence the name "merger" arbitrage. A general formula indicative of this type of strategy is to buy a long position in the stock of a company that is being acquired and sell short stock in the company that is the acquirer. The reasoning behind the trade is that the stock of the company being acquired typically trades at a discount until the actual merger takes place. The discount is usually in place to account for any unforeseen event risk that would break the deal before it is completed (see Exhibit 15.10).

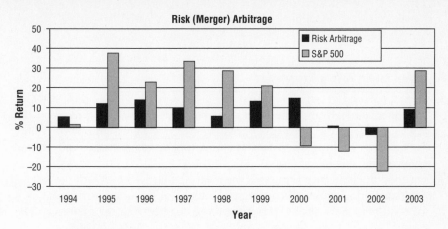

EXHIBIT 15.10 Risk Arbitrage—Calendar Year Returns
Source: CSFB Tremont.

When a proposed merger falls apart, though, it is likely that the price of the stock of the company being acquired will fall, and in some cases the fall can be quite dramatic. Portfolio managers that specialize in this type of arbitrage estimate the annualized return they can achieve from the spread between the current price of the stock of the company being acquired and its stated price upon completion of the merger. Once this is done, they estimate the probability that the merger will actually take place and make an assessment as to whether the estimated return (spread) is worth the risk (probability that the deal will break).

When an announced merger deal is likely to be successfully completed, the merger arbitrage manager will buy shares in the target company (the one being acquired) and simultaneously short shares of the acquiring company in the same ratio as called for by the merger agreement. For example, if under the terms of the merger shareholders of the target, Company A, are entitled to 1.5 shares of the acquirer, Company B, for each share they own, the manager would short 1,500 shares of Company B for every 1,000 shares of Company A that the manager purchases. This is done to hedge against a decline in the value of the acquiring company's securities before the acquisition is complete. The end effect is a neutral bias with regard to market exposure. The gain in share price of the long position is offset by the loss from the corresponding short position, and vice versa. The only time that a merger arbitrage manager does not short shares of the acquirer is when the merger is structured as an all-cash deal.

True risk arbitrage managers will deal only with mergers that have officially been announced as opposed to guessing which companies might become takeover candidates at some point in time. Hedge fund managers that trade based on rumors versus announced mergers are said to be conducting "rumortrage."

HEDGE FUND DUE DILIGENCE

While hedge funds are inherently different from traditional products, the process of performing investment manager analysis is essentially the same. We are still looking to assess the investment team's skill and decide whether they will be successful in the future. One of the critical elements of any good due diligence process is the meeting that we have with the investment staff. How can we be expected to make an accurate assessment of a portfolio manager's skill without speaking directly with the manager? The answer is that we would not be able to.

One of the big issues regarding hedge fund investment is the issue of transparency. Unlike traditional investment products, many hedge funds do not provide their investors with the underlying positions in the hedge funds. This makes it very difficult to perform the type of in-depth analysis outlined in previous chapters. The challenge is to find a level of transparency that can accommodate our due diligence process. The hedge funds that do not provide any tangible level of transparency are automatically kicked out of the due diligence process. Now that I have raised the issue of transparency, let me state that I can typically obtain a sufficient level of data from most of the hedge funds that I speak with. One of the ways around the issues surrounding transparency is to request information that is lagged. In other words, ask for fund snapshots or data for points in time or periods of time that would not have any impact on the fund manager's current positions or portfolio. I find that most of the arguments that hedge fund managers raise regarding transparency are no longer valid when the data I request is from three, six, or a dozen months ago.

Thus far in this chapter, we have defined the broad hedge fund industry, charted its history and progress, and explained how many of the major hedge fund strategies work. The remainder of this chapter will take that information and transform it into various steps in the due diligence process, starting with hedge fund manager interviews, hedge fund questionnaires, and hedge fund scoring model.

HEDGE FUND MANAGER INTERVIEW

When conducting interviews with hedge fund managers via phone conferences or face-to-face meetings, there are a number of generic questions that will apply regardless of the strategy under review. In addition, there are numerous questions that are strategy specific. The following sections list the generic questions first and follow them up with strategy-specific questions. The investment manager analyst should be able to answer most or all of the questions before making a decision to hire a given hedge fund.

Organization and Fund Structure

Is your firm a registered investment adviser?

Are you registered or certified by any organization?

What are the fund's minimum initial and follow-on contribution amounts?

What are the base fee and the incentive fee for the fund and how frequently are they paid?

What is the fund's current level of assets (contributed capital, not including leverage)?

Have you set any soft and/or hard close amounts?

Is there any lockup period?

What is the fund's liquidity?

What is the notice period for contributions and redemptions?

Have you changed auditors/prime brokers/administrators at any time in the firm or fund's history?

Describe your firm's usage of soft dollars.

What kind of liquidity do you offer to clients?

What kind of reporting do you provide to clients?

What kind of transparency do you provide to clients?

How available are investment professionals for phone conversations and/or face-to-face meetings?

Who are the primary decision makers?

Who backs up the primary decision makers?

What risk controls do you have in place?

Equity Long/Short

What is your current gross exposure? How has the exposure changed over time?

What is your current net exposure? How has the exposure changed over time?

What is your average and maximum position size?

Do you allow any concentrations by sector, industry, market cap, style, and so on?

Do you attempt to generate alpha on both longs and shorts, or do you pair transactions to hedge out market risk?

How long would it take you to liquidate your portfolio if you needed to?

What is your sell discipline? Do you have a stop-loss procedure in place?

Do you perform stress testing on your portfolio?

Do you perform VaR analysis on your portfolio? If yes, what are the results? If no, what risk measures do you employ?

Convertible Arbitrage

What is your average level of leverage that you employ? What is the current level of leverage?

What is your average and maximum position size?

Do you allow any concentrations by sector, industry, market cap, or style?

Do you always seek to create a neutral hedge, or do you make bearish and/or bullish hedges?

What is the fund's current premium exposure?

What is the fund's credit quality?

Do you focus on volatility or capital structure trades?

Do you participate in busted convertibles?

How often do you review and adjust your hedge ratio?

What is your exposure to interest rate and stock market risk?

How did you perform during the unfavorable convertible bond markets in 1994 and the third quarter of 1998?

Fixed Income Arbitrage

How much leverage does the fund employ?

Do you make directional trades or attempt to completely neutralize market effects?

Do you target a specific VaR figure or range?

What are the current 1-day, 10-day, and 30-day VaR statistics?

What is the fund's turnover ratio?

What are the fund's average quality, maturity, and duration?

Do you purchase any securities in which you mark to market?

What measures have you taken to combat the effects of a market disaster like the one that occurred in the latter half of 1998?

Do you invest in illiquid debt instruments?

Do you invest in emerging markets debt?

Do you hedge currency exposure?

How did you perform during the unfavorable bond markets in 1994 and the third quarter of 1998?

Equity Market Neutral

What is your current gross exposure?

What is your current net exposure?

What is your beta-adjusted exposure?

What is your average and maximum position size?

What factors do you attempt to neutralize (market, sector, industry, capitalization, style, etc.)?

Do you employ derivatives to hedge out market risk?

What systems do you employ to create and maintain factor neutrality?

How dramatically do you adjust the portfolio to maintain factor neutrality?

Has the portfolio ever exhibited unexpected correlation to the market? Why?

Global Macro

What markets and financial instruments do you target?

What amount of leverage do you typically employ?

What is the typical size of a macro bet as a percentage of total assets?

How many models do you employ to find your macro bets?

For each of the past five years, explain which bets had the greatest impact on calendar year performance.

Discuss three investment ideas you made in recent years that did not work and explain your thesis and the reasons why they didn't work.

What market or financial instruments do you avoid?

Risk (Merger) Arbitrage

What is your current gross exposure?

What is your current net exposure?

Do you invest in deals outside of the United States? If so, how do you perform the legal/regulatory due diligence?

Do you use outside consultants for legal opinions on sector/country-specific issues? If so, may I contact them?

What is your average and maximum position size?

What is the current size of your investable universe?

Do you invest in hostile takeover deals?

How many deals have you invested in that fell apart?

How long does it take you to properly analyze a proposed deal before you make an investment?

Commodity Trading Advisers (CTAs)/Managed Futures

What percentage of your fund is systematic versus discretionary?

Do you accept notional money? If yes, what is the minimum funding level?

What is your margin-to-equity ratio?

What sectors do you trade?

What trading approaches do you follow (technical, fundamental, trend following, contrarian, breakout, multisystem)?

How do your trading models adapt to changing market conditions?

Do you take purely directional bets, or are you taking advantages of market nuances?

How does 24-hour (or close to 24-hour) trading affect your trading approach?

How automated are your execution and clearing platforms? How are out-trades or incorrect fills detected?

Do you use the same models/systems for each market, or is each market traded using different models/systems?

In addition to the many questions listed in previous chapters, this list of questions will help investment manager analysts to conduct informed meetings with a variety of different hedge fund strategies.

HEDGE FUND QUESTIONNAIRE

Chapter 7, "Information Gathering," outlined a general-purpose investment manager questionnaire that can be used for most asset classes. It consists of four sections, the first three of which remain the same for hedge funds. The questionnaire was designed so that the only section that needs to be adjusted from asset class to asset class is the final section, which asks for information on the specific product under review.

Section One: Organization

This section asks about the firm's structure, ownership, offices, auditors, regulatory issues, insurance, and so on.

Section Two: Firmwide Professional Staff

This section asks a variety of questions about all of the professional staff employed by the firm, including people who work directly on the product under review as well as other professionals who work on other products.

Section Three: Operations

This section covers topics such as reporting, client service, administration, custody, investment compliance, backup systems, and disaster recovery.

Section Four: Product Information

While the first three sections remain the same for all asset classes, the fourth and final section can be cut and pasted depending on the asset class. The section that follows represents the fourth (product-specific) section of the hedge fund questionnaire.

SECTION FOUR: PRODUCT INFORMATION

Clients/Assets

1. Provide the following data for the firm and product-specific assets (in millions). Insert additional rows if you have more than four products. Include the status of each product (open to new clients/assets or closed).

	Open/Closed	12/03	12/02	12/01	12/00	12/99
Product #1						
Product #2						
Product #3						
Product #4						
Total firm assets						

2. Please list any products that your firm has completely liquidated or merged with existing products. Include the reasons why the product was liquidated and/or merged with another product.

3. Complete the following client-related information:

	12/03	12/02	12/01	12/00	12/99
Total Firm					
# Clients					
# Clients gained (year)					
# Clients lost (year)					
Assets					
Assets gained (year)					
Assets lost (year)					
% Firm assets with top five clients					
Product-Specific					
# Clients					
# Clients gained (year)					
# Clients lost (year)					
Assets					
Assets gained (year)					
Assets lost (year)					
% Firm assets with top five clients					

Performance Data

4. Provide monthly historical performance figures (net of all fees) in the following table. Add rows to the table if the track record goes back further than five years.

	Jan	Feb	Mar	Apr	May	Jun	Jul	Aug	Sep	Oct	Nov	Dec
2003												
2002												
2001												
2000												
1999												

5. Has the fund's performance been certified by an independent auditor? If yes, please provide a copy of the audit results. If no, please explain.
6. Please state the most appropriate benchmark for the product under review

and include its performance history for the same time period listed previously for the product.

	Jan	Feb	Mar	Apr	May	Jun	Jul	Aug	Sep	Oct	Nov	Dec
2003												
2002												
2001												
2000												
1999												

7. Please provide performance attribution in the following format:

Year	Product Return	Index Return	+/–	Reasons for Out/Underperformance (please be as thorough as possible)
2003				
2002				
2001				

8. Do you utilize any internal or third party performance and/or attribution software/systems? If yes, please provide a list of the systems used and their purposes. In addition, please include with this questionnaire a sample of the attribution report for the latest month or quarter end.
9. What is the product's capacity? At what point would you close to new clients? At what point would you close to new assets from existing clients?
10. What databases does your firm report to?

Portfolio Data

11. Describe the maximum and average position size for longs, shorts, hedged (paired) positions, and unhedged positions.
12. Describe the maximum and average level of leverage used to manage the fund. Please include all "hidden" leverage such as derivatives.
13. Please provide the following data for the fund for each of the last four quarter-end dates. The portfolios should be provided in Microsoft Excel format and should include the following information: security identifier (ticker), number of shares held, and each security's name.

14. Please provide the following data regarding instrument types:

	Invest (Y/N)	Average Long (%)	Average Short (%)
Listed equities			
FX futures			
FX forwards			
Single equity options			
Single equity warrants			
OTC options			
OTC warrants			
Equity index futures			
Naked equity options			
Regulation S securities			
Regulation D securities			
Contingent claims			
Mortgage-backed securities			
Structured securities			
Hot issues			
Convertible securities			
Debt obligations			
Unlisted equities			
Real estate			
Physical commodities			
Mandatory convertibles			
Credit default swaps			
Asset swaps			
Interest rate swaps			
Corporate bonds			
U.S. government bonds			
Closed-end funds			
Open-end mutual funds			
Bank debt			
American depositary receipts (ADRs)			
Global depositary receipts (GDRs)			
Other (Describe and add rows if needed)			

15. Provide the following geographical allocation data for the product in percentage of total assets:

Country	12/03	12/02	12/01	12/00	12/99
North America					
United States					
Canada					
Europe					
Austria					
Belgium					
Denmark					
Finland					
France					
Germany					
Ireland					
Italy					
Netherlands					
Norway					
Spain					
Sweden					
Switzerland					
United Kingdom					
Other					
Pacific Basin					
Australia					
New Zealand					
Hong Kong					
Japan					
Other					
Cash and Equivalents					

16. Provide the following sector allocation data for the portfolio in percentage of total assets (please use the sector descriptions provided in the table):

Sector	12/03	12/02	12/01	12/00	12/99
Basic Materials					
Commercial Services					
Consumer Cyclicals					
Consumer Noncyclicals					
Consumer Services					
Energy					
Financial Services					
Health Care					
Industrials					
Technology					
Telecommunications					
Transportation					
Utilities					

17. Provide industry allocation data for the portfolio in percentage of total assets for the top 20 industries:

12/03			12/02			12/02		
#	Industry	Weight	#	Industry	Weight	#	Industry	Weight
1			1			1		
2			2			2		
3			3			3		
4			4			4		
5			5			5		
6			6			6		
7			7			7		
8			8			8		
9			9			9		
10			10			10		
11			11			11		

12/03			12/02			12/02		
#	Industry	Weight	#	Industry	Weight	#	Industry	Weight
12			12			12		
13			13			13		
14			14			14		
15			15			15		
16			16			16		
17			17			17		
18			18			18		
19			19			19		
20			20			20		

18. Provide the following summary data for the portfolio in percentage of total assets:

	12/03	12/02	12/01	12/00	12/99
Fundamental Characteristics					
P/E (historical—last 12 months)					
P/E (forward 12 months)					
Earnings growth (1 year)					
Earnings growth (3 years)					
ROE					
Dividend yield					
Portfolio turnover					
Market Capitalization					
Weighted market cap					
Average market cap					
% market cap < $100M					
% market cap from $100M to $500M					
% market cap from $500M to $1B					
% market cap from $1B to $2B					
% market cap from $2B to $3B					
% market cap from $3B to $5B					
% market cap from $5B to $10B					
% market cap > $10B					

19. Provide the following sector data for the portfolio's fixed income positions in percentage of total assets:

Sector	12/03	12/02	12/01	12/00	12/99
Cash and equivalents					
U.S. Treasury/agency					
AAA rated					
AA rated					
A rated					
BBB rated					
BB rated					
B rated					
CCC rated					
In default					
Not rated					
U.S. corporate—common stock					
$ Denominated non-U.S. govt/agency					
$ Denominated non-U.S. corporate					
Non-U.S. dollar bonds					
Emerging markets debt					
MBS/ABS/CMO					
Other					

20. Provide the following summary data for the portfolio in percentage of total assets:

	12/03	12/02	12/01	12/00	12/99
Fundamental Characteristics					
Average quality					
Yield to maturity					
Modified duration					
Average maturity					
% Maturity < 3 years					
% Maturity 3–5 years					
% Maturity 5–10 years					
% Maturity > 10 years					

21. Please answer each of the following questions pertaining to currency hedging:

    a. Do you hedge currency exposure?
    b. Do you always hedge currency exposure? If no, please explain under what conditions you would not hedge currency exposure. Include the most recent example that applies to the fund.
    c. If you answered yes to either 21.a or 21.b, please describe what financial instruments you use and the process that you employ.
    d. Are there any markets that you will not hedge?
    e. Do you ever seek returns through currency positions or use currency positions for any purpose other than to reduce net currency exposure?

22. What is the average turnover of investments? What was the fund's turnover in each of the past five calendar years?
23. What is the average number of open positions currently?
24. What is the average number of transactions (tickers) per day?

Dedicated Product Investment Professionals

25. Include the names of all investment professionals (portfolio managers, analysts, traders, etc.) who work directly on the product under review.

Name	Product Responsibility	Years Working at Firm	Years Working on Product	Other Products Individual Works On	Other Responsibilities

26. Provide the names of all investment professionals who have worked on the product and have resigned, been terminated, or transferred/rotated to another department within the past five years. Provide a brief explanation for each departure. List any replacements for these vacancies.

Employee Name/Title	Resignation/ Termination/ Rotation	Reason(s)	Name of Replacement

27. Describe the structure of the investment management team. Include the following information:

   a. Name(s) of key decision maker(s). Be specific—identify the individual(s) who actually make(s) buy and sell decisions.
   b. Lead portfolio manager.
   c. Portfolio manager's backup.

28. Do any of the firm's principals and/or key investment professionals have any of their personal assets invested in the fund? Please specify how much each investment professional has invested in the fund currently.
29. Have any key investment professionals ever redeemed assets from the fund? If so, please explain why.
30. Are any of the firm's principals and/or key investment professionals not currently invested in the fund?
31. Do you include noncompete clauses in employee contracts? If so, who has signed and how long is the term of the noncompete?

Investment Philosophy and Process

32. Please list any and all strategies that the fund is currently and has previously invested in (e.g., long/short, convertible arbitrage, fixed income arbitrage, merger arbitrage).
33. Define your investment philosophy.
34. Define your investment style.
35. Describe in detail the investment process employed by the investment team in the management of the product. Include a description of how individual research and ideas make it (or don't make it) into the portfolio.
36. Buy/sell discipline:

   a. Market-cap restrictions.
   b. Geographical restrictions.
   c. Percent ownership of underlying companies.
   d. Fundamental characteristics.
   e. Liquidity constraints.

37. Do you have stop-loss procedures in place? If yes, describe the details. If no, explain your methodology regarding stocks that drop significantly in price. Please list the three largest percentage losers currently in the portfolio and explain the investment thesis for each.
38. Do you set price targets for all purchases? If yes, do you ever hold a security beyond the initial price target? Explain.

39. Describe your portfolio construction procedures. Include detail on each of the following:

    a. What types of securities are considered for purchase?
    b. What is the universe of possible investments?
    c. Do you have a minimum number of holdings?
    d. What were the fewest and most holdings ever held in the portfolio? Indicate the appropriate dates.
    e. How are individual position weights determined?
    f. What is the maximum position size at cost and at market value for any individual position? Have you ever violated this constraint?
    g. List any portfolio constraints regarding geography, sector, industry, market cap, and liquidity.

40. What is your investment edge? What differentiates you from your competition? Include a list of the firms/products that you consider to be your biggest competitors.

41. Is there a sector or industry in which you believe your firm has a particular edge? If yes, please elaborate.

42. What is the fund's investment universe?

43. What is the fund's target rate of return and volatility?

Risk Controls

44. Describe your firm's risk management controls and procedures.

45. What risk factors do you measure, and what is the frequency?

46. Who is responsible for the product's risk management?

47. With what frequency are risk management reports created and evaluated by the appropriate personnel?

48. What (if any) systems do you have in place to help manage risk?

49. Do you employ any third parties to conduct regular or periodic risk analysis or generate risk reports? If yes, please provide a list of the firms' names and their specific functions.

50. What is the 1-day, 10-day, and 30-day VaR for the current portfolio?

51. Do you perform scenario analysis or stress testing of the portfolio? If yes, provide the most recent results. If no, please explain why not.

Fees/Minimum

52. What is the fund's management fee? Has it changed since the fund's inception? If yes, explain.

53. What is the fund's performance fee?
54. What is the frequency with which you collect management and performance fees?
55. Is there a hurdle rate?
56. Is there a high-water mark?
57. Are there any lockups? If yes, please explain.
58. Are there any fees for early redemptions?
59. What is the notice period for subscriptions and redemptions?
60. How frequently do you accept subscriptions and redemptions?
61. How are the fund's fees calculated and charged in terms of equalization structure?

Fund Capacity

62. What is the fund's target capacity?
63. What is the maximum capacity that the fund could handle and still maintain its edge?
64. Have you ever closed the fund in the past? If yes, state when and what the fund's assets were each time the fund closed.
65. Do you plan on having a soft close at some predetermined asset level? If yes, please explain.
66. Do you have any limitations set with respect to asset growth on a monthly or quarterly basis?

HEDGE FUND SCORING MODEL

The scoring model used for hedge funds is very similar to the equity manager scoring model discussed in detail in Chapter 12. However, because hedge funds are different in some important ways, we will have to make a few adjustments to the equity manager scoring model.

Before we delve into the actual changes to the model, we should review the model itself. The scoring model was designed to help the investment manager analyst to process all of the data collected during the due diligence process. Because we can easily become inundated with paperwork and loads of useless statistics and facts, the model serves as a means of focusing only on the information we will need to make the hire/fire decision. In addition, it has the added benefit of putting all funds reviewed on a level playing field. We will answer the same exact questions regardless of who the investment manager is and what the underlying strategy might be. By doing this, we reduce the possibility of hiring our favorite managers and, thus, we increase our chances of hiring the best or right managers/funds.

When grading each individual factor, we are forced to keep the range of grades from 0 (worst) to 5 (best). Each of the model's factors must be scored before we can review the final score. Exhibit 15.11 illustrates how to interpret the individual grades.

The grades and the interpretations listed in this exhibit are generalizations. Each of the factors in the scoring model has detailed criteria behind it. We will not repeat each and every factor and the underlying grades in this chapter; instead we will highlight only those factors that have changes or have been added.

When all of the factors have been graded, the model scales the scores so that the maximum score that can be attained is 100. Exhibit 15.12 provides a brief explanation of how to interpret an individual hedge fund's final score.

As explained in Chapter 12, the scores were designed to look like the scores we would receive when taking a test, with zero being the theoretical worst score and 100 being the theoretical best score. I use the term "theoretical" because in practice no hedge fund will ever score either zero or 100. After years of working with this model, I have found that the ranges listed in Exhibit 15.12 generally hold true. However, it is important to mention that the final scores are not meant to force hire/fire decisions. No quantitatively derived scoring model can be that precise. Instead, the scores were designed to be a support mechanism for investment manager analysts when they make hire/fire decisions. A hedge fund that receives a score of 75 is not necessarily better than a hedge fund that scores a 74. On the other hand, a fund that scores a 75 would likely be viewed as better than a fund that receives a 65.

EXHIBIT 15.11 Individual Factor Grades

Individual Variable Scoring Methodology

Score	Interpretation
5	Excellent
4	Above average
3	Average
2	Below average
1	Poor
0	Horrible/nonexistent

EXHIBIT 15.12 Final Score Summary

Score	Interpretation
Greater than 80	Exceptional
75 to 80	Excellent
65 to 75	Above average
60 to 65	Average
Less than 60	Poor

The manager scoring model highlighted in Chapter 12 consists of 30 individual factors spread out across six broad categories. The model we use when evaluating hedge funds is also broken into six broad categories, but we have adjusted two of the factors and added two new ones as well. Lastly, the category weights are slightly adjusted to better fit with the hedge fund asset class. Exhibit 15.13 shows the details for the broad categories in the model and compares them to the data from the equity/fixed income manager model. Each of the changes and adjustments will be highlighted and discussed in detail.

The highlighted portions of the table represent changes or adjustments. While the six broad categories have remained the same, we have made adjustments to the category weights and to the number of factors. In the hedge fund scoring model, we have increased the weight given to

EXHIBIT 15.13 Hedge Fund Scoring Model—Category Data

Section	Equity/Bond Manager Model Weight	Hedge Fund Model Weight	Equity/Bond Manager Number of Factors	Hedge Fund Number of Factors
Investment Professionals	30%	30%	5	5
Process	15%	15%	4	4
Portfolio Risk	15%	20%	5	7
Performance-Related Risk/ Reward	15%	15%	5	5
Organization	15%	10%	7	7
Operations	10%	10%	4	4
Total	100%	100%	30	32

"Portfolio Risk" to 20 percent from 15 percent to accommodate two additional factors. The additional weight given to the "Portfolio Risk" category was taken from the "Organization" category. In addition to the two new factors, two of the existing factors were modified. The net result is that the hedge fund scoring model has a total of 32 factors versus 30 for the equity/fixed income model.

Just as we did in the fixed income section in Chapter 14, we will discuss only the factors that are different as well as the newly added factors. Exhibit 15.14 shows the full hedge fund scoring model and highlights the factors and weights that have changed.

ALTERATIONS TO THE MODEL

Factor 1: Direct Hedge Fund Experience

In the equity/fixed income manager scoring model the first factor focuses on a given product's investment team and their individual and overall level of experience managing a portfolio similar to the one under review. This subtle, but important, change in the hedge fund model is that we are grading the investment team on the level of experience managing a *hedge fund* in a manner similar to the fund under review. The distinction might seem minor, but it is not. A hedge fund is very different from a long-only product. Many high-quality long-only managers are not able to make the switch from being effective long-only managers to being effective hedge fund managers. A stellar long-only track record does not tell us anything about a manager's skill set on the short side of the book. In addition, since most hedge funds enjoy a great deal of freedom when making investment selections, some long-only portfolio managers find the wide choice a bit overwhelming.

The grades listed refer only to direct hedge fund management experience. For example, an investment team with no hedge fund experience would receive a zero. Because many very talented and, ultimately, successful long-only managers make the transition to hedge funds easily, I incorporated a "fudge factor" in the grading. When grading this factor, you can subjectively add up to two points if you have a very strong conviction that a given portfolio manager or team will have no problem making the transition from long-only to hedge fund format.

Again, the focus of this variable is not just hedge fund experience, but relevant hedge fund experience. This means that the manager or team must have previous direct experience managing a hedge fund in the same asset class, strategy, and style. For example, a portfolio manager or team that has five years' experience managing a fixed income arbitrage

EXHIBIT 15.14 Hedge Fund Manager Scoring Model

#	Section/Factors	% Breakout Variable	Maximum Points Variable	Manager Score 0 to 5	Scaled Score	%
	Investment Professionals		30.0			
1	Direct **hedge fund** experience	20%	6.0			
2	Manager/team skill	20%	6.0			
3	Portfolio knowledge	20%	6.0			
4	Depth (backup)	20%	6.0			
5	Research capabilities	20%	6.0			
	Process		15			
6	Consistent application	25%	3.8			
7	Well thought out/ disciplined	25%	3.8			
8	Portfolio consistent with process	25%				
9	Portfolio construction/ review process	25%	3.8			
	Portfolio Risk		20			
10	Diversification	14%	2.9			
11	Style/**strategy** drift	14%	2.9			
12	Liquidity	14%	2.9			
13	**Leverage**	14%	2.9			
14	Sell discipline	14%	2.9			
15	Capacity	14%	2.9			
16	**Transparency**	14%	2.9			
	Performance-Related Risk/Reward		15			
17	Performance relative to benchmark	20%	3.0			
18	Performance relative to peers	20%	3.0			
19	Absolute/relative standard deviation	20%	3.0			
20	Drawdown	20%	3.0			
21	Consistency	20%	3.0			
	Organization		10			
22	Turnover	10%	1.0			
23	Succession plan	15%	1.5			
24	Accommodation of growth	15%	1.5			
25	Ownership/incentive	25%	2.5			

EXHIBIT 15.14 *(Continued)*

#	Section/Factors	% Breakout Variable	Maximum Points Variable	Manager Score 0 to 5	Scaled Score	%
26	Backup/recovery	15%	1.5			
27	Computer systems	10%	1.0			
28	Compliance	10%	1.0			
	Operations		10			
29	Reconciliation/ administration	25%	2.5			
30	Reporting	25%	2.5			
31	Client service	25%	2.5			
32	Quality/quantity of people	25%	2.5			
	Manual Adjustment (range +3 to −3)					
	Final Score (Average %)					

fund would receive a score of zero if they were starting up a new equity long/short fund.

Score/Methodology

0   No experience managing a hedge fund or in any investment-related capacity.

1   Key decision maker(s) have less than one year of actual hedge fund experience relating specifically to the strategy under review.

2   Key decision maker(s) have one to two years of actual hedge fund experience relating specifically to the strategy under review.

3   Key decision maker(s) have three years of actual hedge fund experience relating specifically to the strategy under review.

4   Key investment decision maker(s) have four to five years of actual hedge fund experience relating specifically to the strategy under review.

5   Key investment decision maker(s) have more than five years of actual hedge fund experience relating specifically to the strategy under review.

It is important to note that when grading a team, it is best to grade each member of the team and to weight the final score based on each team member's ultimate level of responsibility for the product under review.

Factor 11: Style/Strategy Drift

This factor was altered to include the term "strategy." When we evaluate traditional equity and fixed income products it is normal for a given product to focus on a single strategy, such as value, growth, low duration bonds, high yield bonds, and so on. As stated previously, hedge funds often enjoy a great deal of freedom when making investments, so it is not uncommon to review a hedge fund whose objective is to gain positive absolute returns across more than one investment strategy. In fact, an entire category of hedge funds is called "multistrategy" to accommodate these types of funds. However, most funds focus on a single strategy and, as such, should be evaluated consistently based on that strategy and compared to other hedge funds in that strategy.

Strategy drift, therefore, represents a deviation from a hedge fund's stated investment objective or strategy. For example, a fixed income arbitrage fund might incorporate high yield and/or distressed bonds in the fund when those strategies are performing well. This could be a good thing or it could be a bad thing. However, if we buy into a fund expecting one thing and all of a sudden we get something else, we might find ourselves in a bit of trouble. If an investment team wants to begin incorporating a new strategy into the existing strategy, I would treat the new strategy almost like a new fund. As such, I would insist on reviewing the portfolio manager's or team's qualifications and abilities in this new strategy.

The "style" component of the factor remains the same. For example, if we buy into an equity long/short fund with a deep value style, I would be unhappy if the fund switched to a growth style or started to incorporate growth elements into its established deep value style. When I hire an investment management firm based a specific skill set (value, growth, etc.), I do so because I believe that those investment professionals are the best at what they do. A great value manager might be only an average growth manager. Moreover, my experiences indicate that portfolio managers and analysts with deep style convictions find it almost impossible to switch styles. Deep value managers are often puzzled by growth and momentum managers and vice versa.

Score/Methodology

0   Fund has no consistent style. Fund deviates from its stated strategy.
1   Fund's style and strategy have been consistent over the past year.
2   Fund's style and strategy have been consistent over the past two years.

3 Fund's style and strategy have been consistent over the past three years.

4 Fund's style and strategy have been consistent over the past four years.

5 Fund's style and strategy have been consistent over the past five or more years.

Points to consider when grading this factor:

■ Funds that are truly multistrategy should be graded based on the two or more strategies that they are allowed to invest in. For example, a hedge fund that can go long and short equities as well as buy distressed debt should not be penalized simply because it encompasses more than one strategy (equity long/short and distressed). It should be evaluated based on that set of strategy criteria. If the fund in our example were to start actively trading currencies to produce added alpha (in violation of its investment guidelines), we would then penalize that fund.

■ Funds that start off with a specific strategy focus and later switch or add an additional strategy should not automatically be penalized. If, for example, a hedge fund were to hire a team of professionals to manage a new strategy, we should consider their qualifications and make our assessment based on that information. If the new team meets the criteria spelled out in this book and summarized in this model, then we might conclude that the addition of a new strategy is a good thing and grade this factor appropriately.

■ This factor's grades might be seen an unfairly penalizing hedge funds with shorter track records. This is true, but, in my opinion, it is more than fair. How can we determine an informed grade if we do not have any history to evaluate? The answer is that we cannot. Because this model was designed to make a generalized assessment not just of a given hedge fund's attractiveness, but also of its potential risks, the penalty for short track records is appropriate and quite fair.

Factor 13: Leverage

Leverage can best be defined as borrowed money that a hedge fund employs to increase buying power and gain more exposure to an investment. The goal is to increase a fund's overall invested assets in hopes that the returns on its positions will exceed the borrowing costs. Leverage is generally measured by a product's gross exposure, which is defined as the absolute value of all long and short positions.

Leverage or borrowing can amplify a fund's returns, but you need to remember that this is true only when the market or specific investments increase in price. When they decrease in price, losses are amplifed. Leverage can prove to be disastrous when used incorrectly or when there is a global market shock.

This is one of the trickiest factors to grade because the amount of leverage that a fund assumes can be dependent on the strategy in which it focuses. For example, a debt-to-equity ratio of 3.0× would be considered very high for an equity long/short fund, but might be considered very low for a fixed income arbitrage fund. As a result, it is important when grading a hedge fund to do so relative to its appropriate peer group.

Score/Methodology

0 The fund's leverage is consistently 25% to 50% higher than the peer group average.
1 The fund's leverage is consistently 10% to 25% higher than the peer group average.
2 The fund's leverage is consistently within a range of +/–10% higher/lower than the peer group average.
3 The fund's leverage is consistently 10% to 25% lower than the peer group average.
4 The fund's leverage is consistently 25% to 50% lower than the peer group average.
5 The fund's leverage is consistently 50% lower than the peer group average.

Points to consider when grading this factor:

■ A fund that had a higher level of leverage compared to the appropriate peer group in the past but has lessened the leverage recently can subjectively be bumped up by one grade.
■ A fund that frequently changes the amount of leverage it employs can subjectively be bumped up or down by one grade.

Factor 16: Transparency

Transparency refers to the degree to which a hedge fund firm will allow its investors to "look through" the underlying fund, hence the term *transparency*. In practice, it simply refers to how much information about a given hedge fund its portfolio manager(s) will allow investors to have access to. This issue does not generally arise when dealing with traditional long-only asset classes and products, as the overwhelming majority of these managers tend to provide any data that is requested of them.

Hedge funds, on the other hand, run the gamut. Some hedge funds provide full access to position-level data, while other funds simply state their monthly returns and some summary statistics, such as gross/net exposure, top five long holdings, and so on.

Hedge fund transparency is a major issue in the industry at this time. To summarize both sides of the debate:

- *More transparency.* Investors, led by institutions, consulting firms, and fund of funds managers, generally believe that hedge funds should provide more fund data to existing investors so that they can properly analyze the fund's unique risk characteristics and potential rewards. In addition, the lack of transparency makes the decision to hire or not to hire a given hedge fund more difficult because the decision is being made without all the facts and information available.

- *Less transparency.* Hedge fund managers believe that the total dissemination of position-level data could actually be harmful to the fund itself. As an example, the issue of a "short squeeze" is often cited. A short squeeze may occur when short sellers start to feel pressure from a rise in the price of the underlying stock, as they incur losses as the stock continues to rise. For example, if a stock rises by 20% in a given day, those with short positions may be forced to liquidate to cover their positions by purchasing the stock. If enough short sellers buy back the stock, the price can be pushed even higher, thus causing more losses to short sellers who have not wholly or partially covered their short positions. Short squeezes can result in dramatic share price increases in relatively short periods of time. In addition, a small percentage of hedge fund managers also feel that due to the volume or complexity of their trades and positions, most investors wouldn't know what to actually do with the data if they were given it.

My personal viewpoint on the subject falls more in line with the "more transparency" camp. As I have stated throughout this book, the only way we as investors can make an informed hire/fire decision regarding an investment manager/fund is to actually be informed. I automatically eliminate from consideration any hedge fund that refuses to provide data regarding the underlying positions, exposures, risks, and so on. While I do not always need to see daily position-level data, I do require that the hedge fund manager provide a minimum level of data to make an informed decision. The data that I typically require a hedge fund to provide is listed in the hedge fund questionnaire earlier in this chapter.

Score/Methodology

0   No transparency. Monthly returns only. No meetings.

1   Hedge fund provides only a few summary-level statistics. The portfolio management team is not willing to discuss the portfolio in any more detail via phone conference or a face-to-face meeting.

2   Hedge fund provides selected summary statistics, including top positions on a monthly/quarterly basis. The portfolio management team is reluctant to discuss the portfolio in more detail via phone conference or a face-to-face meeting.

3   Hedge fund provides detailed summary statistics, including top positions on a weekly/monthly basis. The portfolio management team is willing to discuss the portfolio in greater detail via phone conference or a face-to-face meeting a few times per year.

4   Full position-level transparency available monthly/quarterly. The portfolio management team is willing to discuss the portfolio in great detail via phone conference or a face-to-face meeting monthly/quarterly.

5   Full position-level transparency available daily. The portfolio management team is willing to discuss the portfolio in great detail via phone conference or a face-to-face meeting anytime.

This factor can impact a hedge fund's total score by 2.9%, which can be significant given the scoring interpretations outlined in Exhibit 15.12. A hedge fund that is viewed as a strong candidate for hire but does not provide any underlying portfolio data to investors would receive a zero grade. When that hedge fund is compared to another hedge fund that is also considered to be a strong candidate for hire (and does provide ample transparency), its poor grade in this factor may impact the hiring decision.

Index